From Imperial Splendour
to Internment

From Imperial Splendour *to* Internment

The German Navy *in the* First World War

NICOLAS WOLZ

Translated by Geoffrey Brooks

Seaforth
PUBLISHING

Copyright © 2013 Deutscher Taschenbuch Verlag GmbH & Co. KG
English translation © Seaforth Publishing 2015

First published in Great Britain in 2015 by
Seaforth Publishing,
Pen & Sword Books Ltd,
47 Church Street,
Barnsley S70 2AS

First published in Germany in 2013 under the title
Und wir Verrosten im Hafen, by Deutscher Taschenbuch Verlag

British Library Cataloguing in Publication Data
A catalogue record for this book is available from the British Library

ISBN 978 1 84832 228 8

The publisher would like to thank Gary Staff for the use
of photographs from his collection.

Typeset and designed by M.A.T.S., Leigh-on-Sea, Essex
Printed and bound in Great Britain by CPI Group (UK) Ltd, Croydon, CR0 4YY

Contents

Photographic plate section between pages 44–45

Foreword

ONCE A YEAR, SHORTLY BEFORE CHRISTMAS, the few remaining survivors of the pocket battleship *Admiral Graf Spee* assemble at the graveside of their former commander, Kapitän zur See Hans Langsdorff, in the German cemetery at Buenos Aires. Together they reminisce about what happened more than seventy years previously, on 17 December 1939, when Langsdorff gave his men the order to scuttle the ship, seriously damaged in the battle of the River Plate fought against three enemy cruisers. The commander did not wish to engage a superior enemy force believed to be waiting outside the port of Montevideo, which would have resulted in the sinking of his ship and certain death for a large part of the thousand officers and men serving aboard her. Because this decision to give up without a fight breached the naval code of honour, which expected an 'heroic death', two days later Langsdorff shot himself dead in a hotel room in Buenos Aires.

After the scuttling of the ship, the officers and crew took refuge in Argentina, and in the months subsequently some of the ship's officers managed to make their way home to Germany. One of these men was Korvettenkapitän Paul Ascher, no 1 gunnery officer. In May 1941 Ascher, who had meanwhile been appointed admiral staff officer to the fleet staff, sailed aboard the battleship *Bismarck* on Operation *Rheinübung*. What had been planned as a commerce-raiding sortie against British merchant shipping ended in disaster. Overwhelmed by a superior British force, the *Bismarck* went down on 27 May 1941 with more than 2200 of her ship's company. Her commandant, Kapitän zur See Ernst Lindemann, refused throughout to strike his flag and thus end the cruel slaughter. Only 115 German sailors lived to tell the tale. Paul Ascher was not amongst them.

The sinking of the *Bismarck* and the scuttling of the *Admiral Graf Spee* are perhaps the two most prominent chapters occurring in the volumes of German naval history and tactical command of the Second World War. The conditions for these two events were created, however, by an earlier war. Langsdorff and Lindemann both began their naval careers in the Imperial German Navy and their future decisions – the capitulation of one as much as the refusal to capitulate of the other – were the result of experiences which they had undergone as naval officers in the Great War.

However, this was not at all self-evident. At the beginning of the twentieth century, Germany was a terrestrial power lacking a naval capacity of any note. It was not until the desire arose for a role of equal status in the circle of world and colonial powers that Kaiser Wilhelm II's passion for warships, and Alfred von Tirpitz's skill at organisation, resulted within a few years in the building of a fleet of powerful battleships intended to bring their major rival, Great Britain, to heel. But this was a miscalculation. Instead of becoming a willing treaty partner, the British became Germany's bitter enemy when war broke out in August 1914.

Another hope was also to remain unfulfilled: instead of giving the German fleet the opportunity, by means of a great naval battle, to demonstrate to the German nation the reason why this great fleet had been built, the Royal Navy adopted a strategy of restraint and limited its activities to a distant blockade of the North Sea. This was something against which the Imperial Navy was relatively powerless, and so it waited, planned, trained and exercised, now and again made a foray into enemy coastal waters, and continued to hope that one day the yearned-for test of strength would at last arrive: proof not only of its unconditional loyalty to the Supreme Commander Wilhelm II, but also of a fearless will to act. Hitler found both these qualities useful later when he called upon his ships to 'fight to the last shell' – the *Bismarck* was by no means the only vessel to comply.

Between 1939 and 1945 the Kriegsmarine feared nothing more than a repeat of its inglorious First World War role on the sidelines. Yet Langsdorff's refusal to permit his men to die a pointless death – the only such case of this kind in the surface fleets in either of the world wars – cannot be understood without knowing the First World War background. On 8 December 1914, Vizeadmiral Maximilian Graf von Spee found himself in a similar fatal trap to that of Langsdorff, and handled it in a manner diametrically opposed. The admiral, whose name Langsdorff's ship was later to bear, accepted battle against a superior British force, even though he knew that he had no prospect of success. In doing so, to a certain extent Spee founded the German naval tradition of 'going down with battle flags flying', which Langsdorff rejected twenty-five years later but then found that he had no honourable option but to shoot himself.

If the fate of Langsdorff and that of the *Bismarck* are much more familiar today than that of Graf Spee and the Imperial Navy, it is mainly because the Second World War is closer to us in time. Hitler, the Holocaust and almost 60 million dead block our retrospective view of that 'originating catastrophe' of the twentieth century, into which the states of Europe, in the words of the historian Christopher Clark, staggered 'like sleepwalkers'. The other reason is that the years 1914 to 1918 are basically remembered in the European collective mind for terrestrial and trench warfare. To this day we recall the First World War primarily from photographs of infantry trenches and deserts of barbed wire. These scenes represent countless hopeless assaults on enemy trenches which could not be taken, as much as for Verdun and the Somme, and for battles in which a hundred thousand horrific deaths was a price worth paying in order to win a couple of yards of muddy ploughed land.

On the other hand the few 'pure' naval engagements, principally the battle of Jutland on 31 May 1916, have tended to make less impression on the consciousness of later generations. Even in the enormous output of literature about the First World War ever since, the war at sea has a subordinate role, and in many accounts it is never mentioned at all. As the subject of study, the strategic and technical aspects stand principally in the foreground: the British concentrate almost exclusively on monographs about Jutland. Until now, there has not been an overall perspective of the Imperial Navy at war, dealing with the military and political aspects alongside the social, the psychological and the everyday.

The question of how the officers and men experienced 'their' war – and not only during the few hours in which their ships were in action, but also in the long months waiting for the next engagement – is an extremely dramatic one. On either side of the North Sea, the inconspicuous role of the fleets *during* the war stood in sharp contrast to the political, military and also social significance which had been ascribed to them *before* the war. Above all, the German fleet, which had been built with such high hopes, never fulfilled its expectations. Isolated by the distant British blockade, it lay practically useless at anchor in Wilhelmshaven and Kiel, and its few operational sorties, no matter how heroic they might appear to their contemporaries, changed nothing. When the war came to its conclusion, the Imperial Navy had become just one more flashpoint for revolution, demonstrating clearly just how the old order of the Kaiser Reich, best represented by the navy, had come through it. 'Seldom,' wrote the historian Michael Salewski, 'has an organisation of such proud eminence fallen so far'.[1]

Yet the Royal Navy, victorious at the end, was also beset by difficulty. Great Britain had expected that the fleet, which had ruled the waves unchallenged since Nelson's victory over the French at Trafalgar in 1805, would give these German upstarts their just deserts at the earliest opportunity. Instead, all the fleet did was hold them in check at a safe distance – effective, but not at all what was expected of a glorious tradition. British sailors, like their German counterparts, had to be satisfied with doing their duty almost as if it were peacetime. Instead of using enemy warships for target practice it was a more than bitter experience to be just bystanders in a war which was supposed to end for the Royal Navy with a repeat of Trafalgar.

How did the naval men of both sides handle this passive role? What sense could they make of this war without a visible opponent? How did they judge their own contribution in comparison to what men of the army endured on the continental battlefields? How could the inactivity of the battleships be reconciled with the elitist view the officers took of themselves? What spawned the desire to fight without question? And when the time came, why were many more prepared to sacrifice their lives for a lost cause rather than simply give in? And finally, what kept a sailor going day in, day out, when his ship was always in harbour?

The answers to these questions can only be found to a limited extent in the official files, archives, service correspondence and memoranda. Much more revealing are the notes made by the participants themselves, their diaries and letters, written during the war. They provide an immediate impression of the prevailing circumstances and events of the time and give us a fascinating insight into the sailor's world of experience and thinking. We see what they saw, experienced, felt and thought: we can observe how they lived, interpreted and handled the war.

Until now such personal documents have been consulted only rarely for maritime historiography. Compared to the total of 13 million soldiers recruited into the German army between 1914 and 1918, the Imperial Navy, with its personnel strength of around 80,000 men, was a minor force. Accordingly, the number of potential letter writers and diarists in its ranks was not large. But just as in the Royal Navy they existed, and their notes are to be found spread across Germany and Great Britain in

archives and museums, in associations and unions, in naval comrades'
societies and in private collections of memorabilia. I collected and
evaluated them for the first time for my dissertation at Tübingen
University.[2] Now they serve as the foundations for this book, aimed at
a much broader readership and which neither seeks to bring in its wake
the academic debate with all its ramifications, nor explore exhaustively
the strategic and operational details of the naval policy of the time. Its
primary aim is to provide the general reader with a personal experience
of the past, by allowing those involved at the time to speak. I have
therefore largely dispensed with footnotes where the quote is not
verbatim.

Naval ranks have been maintained in the original language with a key
in the text. By far the majority of notes quoted are by officers. The view
from the lower deck is depicted principally in the diary of German naval
rating Richard Stumpf, published at the end of the 1920s. The extent
and style of diaries and letters vary: some writers preferred to set down
their experiences and thoughts in relatively terse, sober form while
others put pen to paper on almost every one of the 1500 days of the
war. Especially notable examples of such torrential outpourings are the
diaries of Kapitänleutnant Bogislav von Selchow on the German side,
and Sub Lieutenant Oswald Frewen on the British side. Both of them
preserved notes not only of the war years, but practically their whole
lives in richly decorated volumes complete with notes, sketches,
photographs, newspaper cuttings and poems. The Frewen diaries, bound
post-war in thick leather, fill a large part of the library in the Frewen
country house, Sussex, where Oswald Frewen's great-nephew Jonathan
guards this treasure.

Outstanding amongst the letter writers is Konteradmiral Adolf von
Trotha, who had around four hundred correspondents during the war.
For our purposes, the most interesting are the letters to his wife in which
he expressed himself openly, similar to the diary writers, and without
reservations of a political or service nature.

Trotha's literary trove is kept today at the Lower Saxony State Archive
at Bückeburg. I would like to thank the workers there for their readiness
to help and their active support, and also those at the BA/MA archive at
Freiburg/Breisgau, the military-historical education centre of the
Mürwik Naval Academy at Flensburg, the Association of Naval Officers
at Bonn and the Scientific Institute for Navigation and Naval History at
Hamburg. To the British side my gratitude goes to the archivists of the

Royal Naval Museum at Portsmouth, the National Maritime Museum at Greenwich, the Imperial War Museum and the Public Records Office in London (now The National Archives at Kew), the Churchill Archives Centre at Cambridge and the Liddle Collection at Leeds University.

The German Federal Navy allowed me valuable insight into the everyday life of its modern naval forces, whether it be at the Mürwik Naval Academy, aboard a frigate, a minesweeper, a submarine, or the sail training ship *Gorch Fock*, on which I spent two weeks in the North Atlantic. I thank Deutscher Taschenbuch Verlag and its chief editor Dr Andrea Wörle for our exceptionally fruitful and pleasant co-operation. For their advice and support I am indebted to the historians Dieter Langewiesche (Tübingen), Michael Epkenhans (Potsdam), N A M Rodger (Oxford) and the late Michael Salewski (Kiel, d2010). The greatest thanks, however, I owe to my family without whom this book would probably never have been written.

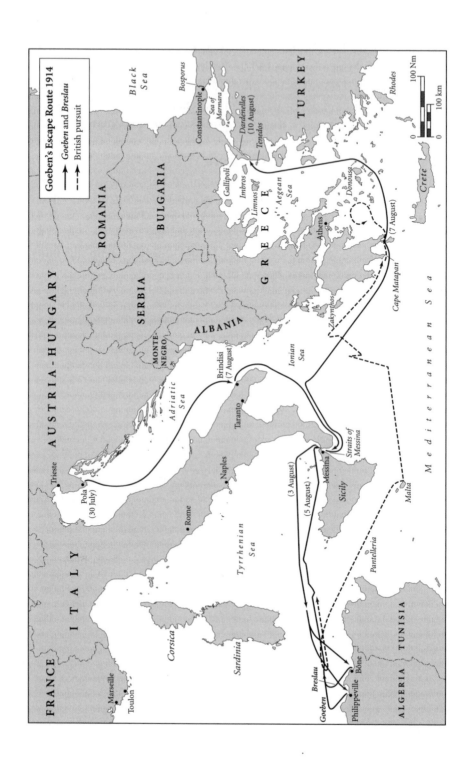

Goeben's Escape Route 1914
→ *Goeben and Breslau*
--→ British pursuit

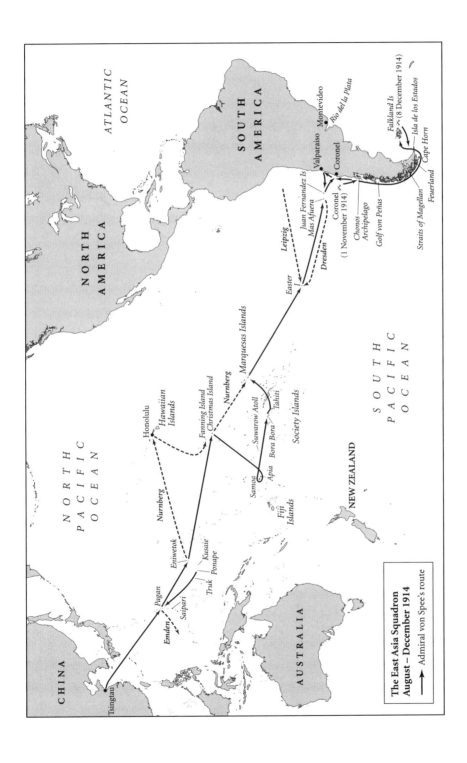

The East Asia Squadron
August – December 1914

→ Admiral von Spee's route

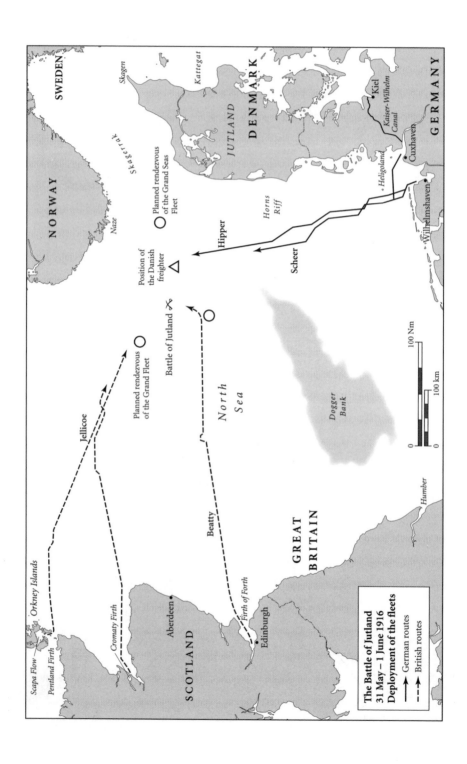

The Battle of Jutland
31 May – 1 June 1916
Deployment of the fleets

→ German routes

⇢ British routes

Prologue

ONE OF THE INCOMPARABLY beautiful days of that balmy summer of 1914 was Tuesday, 28 July. The sun shone down from a cloudless sky over the glittering blue Adriatic Sea. Exactly a month previously at Sarajevo, Serbian nationalists had gunned down the heir to the Austro-Hungarian throne, Archduke Franz Ferdinand and his wife, and plunged Europe into the most serious political crisis of the developing century. On that day news came that Austria–Hungary had declared war on Serbia.

The German battlecruiser SMS *Goeben* lay in the harbour at Pola amongst allied Austrian warships. She displaced 25,000 tons, her crew numbered around 1100 men and she was armed with ten 28cm (11in) guns, making her one of the largest and most modern warships of the time. And also one of the fastest: twenty-four coal-fired boilers deep within the hull provided enough pressure to drive two powerful Parsons turbines and give the steel colossus a top speed of 28 knots. *Goeben* and the small cruiser *Breslau* made up the Mediterranean squadron. They were the only German warships in the entire Mediterranean.

The small but prestigious pair were commanded by Konteradmiral Wilhelm Souchon. Outwardly he was a rather inconspicuous man – in the opinion of a US diplomat he looked more like a parson than an admiral[1] – yet Souchon, born at Leipzig in 1864, had survived a number of ticklish situations in his naval career of over thirty years and was considered an extremely experienced and competent officer.

Following the assassination at Sarajevo, he had taken the *Goeben* to Pola in order to await further developments and meanwhile have his ship's engines overhauled. Now that the Austrians had gone on the offensive against Serbia and the tense atmosphere on the continent was continuing to build up, he had to make an important decision.

Souchon knew that here in the Adriatic he was sitting in a trap should war break out. Even with Austrian support, there was not the slightest prospect that *Goeben* and *Breslau* would be able to do anything against the oppressive superiority of the British and French fleets in this sea region. Maybe, with a bit of luck, he might sink a few troop transports bringing soldiers of the French colonial army to France from Algeria. He decided therefore to leave the Adriatic with his two ships as quickly as possible, go round Sicily and lie in wait off the North African coast.

On 29 July 1914 *Goeben* weighed anchor, left Pola and headed first for Brindisi. From there she steamed to Sicily where *Breslau* was waiting. On the way Souchon learned from the naval staff in Berlin of the chain reaction of declarations of war and mobilisation orders which the Austrian notification to Serbia had unleashed. The treaties which the European powers had signed between themselves in bygone years and decades now divided the continent into allies and enemies. There had been a defensive treaty in existence between Germany and Austria–Hungary since 1879, the *Zweibund*, initially secret, but later admitted to. The German Reich now aligned unconditionally behind its *Zweibund* partner Austria–Hungary and declared war on Russia on 1 August 1914, because Russia had mobilised its army to protect Serbia.

The British and French sided with the Russians under the military treaty known as the 'Triple Entente', signed in 1907 to oppose the *Zweibund*, but still not all the hands had been dealt.

Italy, actually a treaty partner with Germany and Austria in the *Zweibund*, making it into the *Dreibund*, declared its neutrality on the day that *Goeben* reached Sicily and moored alongside the *Breslau* at Messina. On Sunday, 2 August 1914, the Italian authorities refused to coal the battle-cruiser. Souchon was only able to continue his voyage by requisitioning the coal stocks of German merchant vessels lying in the harbour. That evening he wrote to his wife: 'I am in good heart and am glad to have beneath my feet the most powerful and fastest ship.'[2]

The next day, when the German formation left Sicily and steered for the coast of North Africa, he learned that Germany had declared war on France. He thought that his ships were on the right course, but within sight of his goal, Souchon received orders from Berlin: '*Goeben* and *Breslau* proceed immediately to Constantinople'. The reason: Germany and the Ottoman empire had just concluded a treaty to oppose Russia, although this treaty was only of a defensive nature. In order to induce the Turks to enter the war actively on the German side, Berlin needed a military presence in the Bosphorus. Souchon, who had other ideas, ignored the order and continued to his intended destination.

At the Algerian coast, *Goeben* and *Breslau* bombarded the ports of Philippeville and Bône, from where the troop transports sailed for France. Even if the shelling did not inflict too much damage, Souchon was satisfied. He had fulfilled his first mission. He was unaware initially what damage his guns had done; what mattered most to him was to have the chance to fire his guns, to announce: 'The Germans are here, and they are dangerous.' Now he could head back to Messina to re-coal for the 1200-mile (2000km) voyage to Constantinople. The two cruisers turned away and steered east.

They had not put many sea miles behind them when the silhouettes of two British warships suddenly appeared on the horizon. These were HMS *Indomitable* and HMS *Indefatigable*, two modern RN battlecruisers, of similar build to *Goeben*, but fitted with eight 12in (30.5cm) guns. If it came to a fight, the two German ships would be outgunned and have little chance against this far superior enemy force. All ready to fire, the two ships of each side glided past each other at a few thousand yards' distance. It was the morning of 4 August 1914, but Germany and Great Britain were not yet at war.

This encounter at sea was pure chance. After Souchon's two ships had left the Adriatic unnoticed, the British senior commander in the Mediterranean, Admiral Sir Archibald Berkeley Milne, and his deputy, Rear Admiral Ernest Troubridge, puzzled over what plan of action the Germans were likely to be following. Of the pact with Turkey they had no knowledge. Additionally, at the Mediterranean Fleet HQ in Malta they were constantly receiving from London reports and orders which were to some extent contradictory in nature. Since 1911, Winston Churchill had been First Lord of the Admiralty and was accordingly political commander-in-chief of the Royal Navy. He insisted that Milne and Troubridge must locate the two German ships at all costs. What was supposed to happen next remained open at first. *Indomitable* and *Indefatigable* had received the task of monitoring the Straits of Gibraltar should the German ships attempt to escape into the Atlantic, and now they had them broadside to broadside.

Scarcely had the British battlecruisers passed the German units than they turned and put themselves on Souchon's heels. Souchon could not be certain from one moment to the next whether war had been declared between Britain and Germany and feared that the British battlecruisers might open fire on him at any second. He gave orders to shake off the pursuers. Far below in the engine rooms of the *Goeben* and *Breslau* the stokers shovelled coal into the furnaces, literally to the point of exhaustion, to bring their ships up to maximum speed. Slowly the distance widened. The Germans were still within range of the British heavy guns, but the latter remained silent.

What Souchon did not know was that the Cabinet in London had just served on the German government an ultimatum which expired at midnight. Until then, as Churchill signalled, no round must be fired. The British ultimatum required a guarantee that Belgian neutrality would be respected. The Germans could not and would not give this, for the entire strategy of the imperial general staff in the event of war with France – the notorious 'Schlieffen Plan', named after Generalfeldmarschall Alfred von Schlieffen – was based on going round the strong French fortifications in the north of the country and heading for Paris instead of crossing Luxembourg and Belgium.

As the hours passed, gradually the German ships were lost to the sight of the British, although for a while the light cruiser *Dublin*, which had arrived meanwhile, kept contact, losing it at dusk. Towards ten that evening the *Dublin* was ordered to abandon the chase. Two hours later the British ultimatum expired at the stroke of midnight on 4 August 1914: Great Britain and Germany were now officially at war.

Next morning Souchon's two ships reached Medina unscathed, and the Italians allowed him to coal. The exhausted crews had little time to recover. According to the Hague Convention, the warships of belligerent nations were only allowed to remain for twenty-four hours in a neutral port, or be interned. Souchon took the view that now war had been declared, the British would not let him escape a second time. He intended to make a run for it, even if it might mean the loss of his ships. The naval staff gave him licence to act as he saw fit. He wrote later to his wife: 'Disarm in neutral ports, thank God German naval officers would never do so, and one hopes they never will.'[3] Before *Goeben* and *Breslau* weighed anchor on the afternoon of 6 August, Souchon had drafted his will and had it taken ashore.

Upon leaving Italian territorial waters, bearing southeast with guns at readiness, the German ships picked up a tail, the light cruiser HMS *Gloucester*. Not until later did Souchon discover that a serious tactical error on the part of the British had saved him. Admiral Milne thought that Souchon would make another attempt to attack the French troop transports and stationed all his ships, bar the *Gloucester*, west of Sicily, far from Souchon's actual route. When it finally dawned on the British that Souchon was pursuing some other objective, the distance between them was too great.

Only Rear Admiral Troubridge was in a position to intercept. Waiting south of Corfu with four old armoured cruisers, his purpose was to block Souchon's return route into Pola. Each of his four cruisers was individually weaker than the *Goeben*, but together they had considerable firepower. In order to use this advantage, however, Troubridge had to bring his ships within range of the quarry, and his guns had a shorter reach than those of the *Goeben*. Nevertheless, he decided to chance it, and set off in pursuit.

During the night, however, Troubridge had second thoughts. After a conference with his officers, the risk now seemed to him too great of being shot to a wreck by the German guns without being able to reply. Moreover, he had orders not to gamble his ships against a superior enemy. Whether *Goeben* and *Breslau* amounted to a superior enemy for Troubridge's force was something to be mulled over much later.

For Troubridge at least the matter was clear. With a heavy heart and, so it is said, tears in his eyes, the admiral, whose great-grandfather had been at the side of Nelson at Cape St Vincent in 1797 when a Spanish fleet almost twice the size of the British force had been defeated, gave the order to break off the hunt. Only the small *Gloucester* kept going.

Souchon, who knew nothing of all this and assumed that the entire British Mediterranean Fleet was approaching from his rear, exhorted his men to give everything they had to help get clear of their pursuers. This time he got so much steam up that some of the boilers were damaged. Several *Goeben* stokers received fatal scalds. The admiral also ordered that if as a result of battle his ships 'were so badly damaged as not to be able to continue, they were to be scuttled in order to prevent their falling into enemy hands at all cost.'[4]

It never came to that. On the evening of 7 August 1914 *Goeben* and *Breslau* reached the Aegean Sea, never having been in any danger, and set course for the Dardanelles. *Gloucester* now turned away and left the field to the Mediterranean Fleet, steaming up at a leisurely pace. Admiral Milne, who had already guessed wrong once about Souchon's intentions, was convinced that the German ships were in a trap in the Aegean, and he took his time coming for them. Not until he reached the coast of Asia Minor on the late afternoon of 10 August and found it deserted did he realise that Souchon had given him the slip for the second time.

In fact, only a few hours before, the Turks had given Souchon permission to enter the Dardanelles. The two ships passed through the narrows connecting the Aegean with the Sea of Marmara, about forty miles (65 km) long and watched over by powerful forts, and came finally to the domes, towers and minarets of Constantinople. They had arrived at their destination, and now dropped anchor.

A little later, the two ships passed from German into Turkish ownership under the new alliance, and were commissioned into the Turkish navy as

Sultan Yawuz Selim and *Midilli*. The ensign of the Ottoman empire now flew at their mastheads and the German crews wore the fez. Konteradmiral Souchon was appointed commander of the Turkish fleet and at the end of October 1914 bombarded the Russian Black Sea ports, bringing forth declarations of war from the Entente partners Russia, France and Britain against Constantinople. Thus he played his part in bringing the initially hesitant Turks into the war on the side of Germany and Austria–Hungary. During the next three years he dedicated himself successfully to blocking the Turkish Narrows and thus the sea route to Russia.[5] All attempts by the Entente to conquer the Dardanelles and the Bosphorus from the sea failed, as did a major British-led offensive at Gallipoli in the summer of 1915.

For his spectacular flight to Turkish waters Souchon was awarded the Iron Cross, first class, by Kaiser Wilhelm II. On the other hand, the unfortunate British commanders Milne and Troubridge were obliged to explain to a naval board of inquiry how they had let the German ships escape. While Milne's conduct was declared blameless, Troubridge was court-martialled. It was alleged that as the only available British naval commander present, he had had the opportunity of offering Souchon battle, and not done so. His defence was that he was only following orders not to engage a superior enemy force. The court accepted this argument and acquitted him, but his reputation within the Royal Navy was ruined, and he was never given another command.

Since the Battle of Trafalgar in 1805, Nelson's strict dictum held sway: 'No commander can do much wrong by putting his ship alongside an enemy.'[6] No matter if he gets himself sunk doing so. This unwritten law, which does not know the expression 'superior enemy force', wounded Troubridge, even though he had acted correctly. Instead of rejoicing that by reason of the admiral's reservations, ships and lives had been spared which would otherwise in all probability have been sacrificed to no good purpose, the Royal Navy suffered for years under this 'lamentable blow to British naval prestige'.[7]

Above all, this blow was especially painful for the British because it had been inflicted on the Royal Navy, the most powerful navy afloat, with a centuries-old glorious past, by a nation which just a few years before had not even had its own fleet. It was only under the new, young Kaiser Wilhelm II that the German 'land rats' had begun building warships and dreamed of becoming a naval power. Were they now about to make this dream reality?

I

'We desperately need a strong Fleet!'
The German Dream of Naval Power

ON THE EARLY MORNING OF 23 June 1914 the silhouettes of four mighty warships appeared through the swathes of grey mist drifting over Kieler Förde. At the stern of each of the steel giants fluttered a great white ensign, the naval flag of Great Britain. Under the curious gaze of numerous onlookers, the four ships – *King George V, Ajax, Audacious* and *Centurion* – entered Kiel harbour one after another. They made up the 2nd Battleship Squadron under the command of Vice Admiral Sir George Warrender. The three light cruisers, *Southampton, Birmingham* and *Nottingham*, commanded by Commodore William E Goodenough, formed their escort. Kiel awaited these representatives of the world's greatest naval power, for this was Kiel Week, and the visit by the British squadron would lend the festivities a special glamour.

The German hosts were eager to make the stay of the British officers and men as pleasant as possible. They organised balls, parties and sports events: the married British officers were invited into the homes of married German officers. Vice Admiral Warrender frequented the highest circles. He met not only Prince Heinrich of Prussia, the Kaiser's younger brother, and since 1909 Inspector-General of the Navy, but also the Commander-in-Chief of the German Fleet Admiral Friedrich von Ingenohl; the Secretary of State at the Reich Navy Office and Constructor-General of the Fleet Grossadmiral Alfred von Tirpitz, and finally, aboard the Imperial Yacht *Hohenzollern*, Kaiser Wilhelm II himself. In conversations, speeches and toasts, the good comradeship and community feeling existing between the British and German navies was referred to repeatedly.

On 28 June, when news came of the assassination of the heir to the Austrian throne at Sarajevo, a dark shadow was cast over Kiel Week, but the mood amongst the seafarers remained friendly. Two days later the British squadron weighed anchor and headed for home. On the German ships the flag signal *'Glückliche Reise'* was hoisted. The British replied by radio: 'Friends in the past and friends for ever!'[1]. Five weeks later the

First World War began. The most astonishing thing about the Kiel reunion was not the fact that the men of two different countries swore eternal friendship with each other, but that within a blink of the eye they were transformed into deadly enemies.

In October 1914 a 76-year-old man in South Germany asked the authorities if it was true, as he had been told, that a great war had broken out. He lived the life of a recluse in the depths of the forest, without post or newspapers, and had first learned of the upheaval in Europe when a tourist happened to mention it.[2] And if one imagines that this man went to Kiel Week, it would have been almost incredible to him that the Kaiser Reich of 1914 had a navy to keep pace with that of the British. For while Great Britain had the greatest and strongest navy in the world, which had ruled the waves unchallenged since Nelson's legendary victory at Trafalgar more than a century before, Germany had hardly ever given a thought to its naval forces for decades. An exception was the *Reichsflotte*, brought to life by the Frankfurt National Assembly in the year of the 1848 revolution. When the revolution collapsed, the fate of this 'fleet' was sealed, and the ships, which had been conceived as a symbol of German unity, met a sad end under the auctioneer's hammer.

The Germans had good reasons for their backwardness in naval affairs. The German Reich founded in 1871 was, like Prussia before it, a classical continental power with thousands of miles of frontier which needed to be protected against France in the west and Russia in the east. In contrast, the coastline was comparatively short and easy to defend, even without a strong navy. Thus for many years almost the entire military budget went to the army, for it was the army which, in three wars (against Denmark, Austria–Hungary and France), had battled for the unity of the Reich. In none of these wars had the navy particularly made its mark, and the contribution of those sailors who had taken part in the land campaign against France was not even recognised as war service. Nothing illustrates better the insignificance of the naval forces than the fact that until 1888, supreme command of the Kaiserliche Marine, as it had been called officially since 1871, lay in the hands of army officers, namely Generals Albrecht von Stosch and Leo von Caprivi.

All the same, a small fleet did exist, brought from Prussia into the Reich. Prince Adalbert, a nephew of the Prussian King Friedrich Wilhelm III, had built it up. It was principally his responsibility to protect the coast and maritime trade. More extensive ideas, such as a challenge to the maritime hegemony of Great Britain, did not interest him. On the contrary – he consciously sought inspiration and practical support from the sea power he admired. For several decades the British helped in naval development. British firms not only supplied ships, machinery and guns to Germany, but also charts and nautical instruments. 'We were, so to speak, like a creeper around the British navy,' Admiral Tirpitz wrote later about this era. 'We preferred to get things from Britain. If a piece of machinery worked reliably and without breakdowns, if a cable or a chain didn't break, then it was definitely not a domestic piece but made in British workshops, a rope with the famous red thread of the British Navy.'[3]

Up until 1865 the Royal Navy trained whole series of German officers, many of whom later had influential positions in the Imperial Navy. Finally, the British also provided the small German fleet, which had no overseas bases of its own, with logistical support, and so enabled German warships to operate beyond the North Sea and Baltic for the first time. In a nutshell, Britain was and remained 'for half a century the master smoothing the way for his German apprentice on the seas with willing help'.[4]

The British could allow themselves this generosity because German ships were for a long time of a size the British need not bother about from a strategic viewpoint, scarcely more than the harmless playthings of a rich land fascinated by technology. At that time the real danger to the Royal Navy came from Russia and France, both of which countries had been modernising their fleets since the 1880s. It was with these two nations in mind that the 'two-power standard' was laid down in the Naval Defence Act 1889. This stipulated that the Royal Navy always had to be as strong as the next two most powerful navies together: Britain was prepared to make a major effort to maintain the disparity. Only in this way, it was believed, could Britain remain independent of treaty partners, keep open its foreign policy options and preserve a balance of forces in Europe. This was the famous policy of 'splendid isolation', soon to come to an end.

Two men played a decisive role in this: Kaiser Wilhelm II and Konteradmiral Alfred Tirpitz, nominated by him as State Secretary of the Reich Naval Office. Wilhelm II had acceded to the throne in 1888 at the age of twenty-nine on the sudden death of his father, Kaiser Friedrich III. His aim was to found a new era and elevate Germany to be a world power. In his opinion, and also in the view of many of his contemporaries, the Reich had been held in check, and under the leadership of Otto von Bismarck had pursued a policy with a continental orientation. Meanwhile, other great powers had carved up the world between themselves, acquiring one colony after another. This must come to an end if Germany was to preserve its status alongside other great powers. In October 1897 Bernhard von Bülow, appointed Secretary of State for the Foreign Office, formulated the new 'world policy': 'We do not want to put anybody in the shadows, but we also want our place in the sun.'[5]

It was not that such a change of direction in German foreign policy was aimed primarily at Great Britain, the leading world colonial power, and it was not so much 'that from now on Germany tried to force its way, impetuous and demanding, into the ranks of the imperialist States', or the bustling rhetoric of German politicians which turned the Reich into Britain's bitter rival in the years to come.[6] Much more threatening from the British point of view was the military means by which the Kaiser was planning the rise of Germany to a world power: the building of a powerful battle fleet. That, and nothing else, was the 'passbook into the great game'.[7]

The naval enthusiast monarch, who as a boy had stood at the side of his grandmother Queen Victoria in raptures at the annual naval reviews and as Kaiser had a special liking for his admiral's uniform, had thought at first that he should have a fleet of fast cruisers. In comparison to conventional battleships they had weaker armour and guns of smaller calibre, but by virtue of their speed and great range could be deployed anywhere in the world and show the German flag even in the most remote corners of Africa and Asia.

The man whom Wilhelm II had chosen to build this fleet for him had other plans, however. Konteradmiral Tirpitz was forty-eight years of age in June 1897 when he was called to head the Reich Navy Office. He had spent thirty-two of those years in the navy, finally as commander of the Imperial Cruiser Division in East Asia. In the course of this long career, the man with the rounded head and shaggy grey beard had developed his own concept of German naval power, and also quite flagrantly the authority to carry it through. He succeeded in convincing the Kaiser that the new German fleet should not consist of cruisers, but heavy, powerful, seagoing battleships or 'ships of the line' as the Germans called them, with thick armour and large-calibre guns – exactly as the American naval theoretician, Alfred Thayer Mahan, had postulated in his exceedingly influential book, *The Influence of Sea Power upon History*.

Soon after, Wilhelm II became Tirpitz's convert and proclaimed publicly, 'We desperately need a strong German fleet!'[8]

The lesser range and speed of these ships was not important because, in Tirpitz's view, for Germany 'the most dangerous enemy at sea is Britain. She is also the rival against whom we must have most urgently a certain measure of naval power as a political power factor ... our fleet must accordingly be so equipped as to be able to perform at its best between Heligoland and the Thames.' He came to the conclusion that: 'The military situation against Britain demands as many battleships as possible.'[9] According to his train of thought, if Germany had a fleet with which it could threaten Britain *militarily*, then it should also be possible to impress her *politically* with German claims to be a world power. Only a fleet deserving of respect could put Germany, the land power, into a position of being enough of a threat to the naval power Great Britain to persuade the British to come to an arrangement and grant political concessions. Rapprochement through deterrence – that was the basic concept which has gone down in history as the 'Tirpitz Plan'.

The Tirpitz Plan, however, contrary to all appearances, did not have a continuing offensive *military* intention of aiming to undermine British naval supremacy and with it the British position in the European equilibrium, even if this has always been assumed. In 1894 Tirpitz himself saw *strategic* offensive as being the 'natural intended purpose of a fleet'.[10] Constructing a powerful fleet was intended much more as a political lever. The 'strengthening of our political power and significance as seen by Britain' was, as Tirpitz explained in 1897, 'the basic purpose of the fleet-building plan.'[11] What the military objectives of the fleet might be remained relatively uncertain: in general, its role would be simply to protect the German coast against a British attack.

How large would the German fleet need to be for its very existence to be seen by the British as threatening? To answer this question Tirpitz developed his famed 'risk theory', which stated that the fleet must be at least strong enough so that by attacking it the 'most powerful naval opponent [by this he meant Britain] would risk placing her own power base in question.'[12] In order to complete this prediction, by Tirpitz's reckoning the German fleet would have to be not less in size than two-thirds that of the Royal Navy.

His plan envisaged turning out over a period of twenty years an average of three capital ships (ie battleships or armoured cruisers) each year, thus sixty capital ships and the requirement in smaller units (small cruisers, torpedo boats, later U-boats). That was the figure which Tirpitz assumed – he could not know – the British would not be able to exceed by more than half as much again. After twenty years in service, moreover, every ship would be replaced automatically by a new construction, so that the fleet would, in practice, be indefinitely self-renewing. His contemporaries called this *Äternat*, a term probably derived from the English word 'eternise'.

Proposing such a system was one thing. To make it reality was something else. The Tirpitz Plan, as its creators were aware, would be enormously expensive, and without the consent of the Reichstag, which in the German system of parliamentary monarchy controlled the domestic budget, not a single ship would ever be launched. The conservative Prussian farmers saw their traditional position of precedence threatened by the 'ghastly fleet'.[13] Worse, the priority of the SPD (*Sozialdemokratische Partei Deutschlands*) deputies, with barely a third of the seats at the end of the nineteenth century, was social reform. How could they be persuaded to vote initially for a 'powerful seagoing fleet', especially since it was Tirpitz's aim in the long term to deprive parliament of its jurisdiction in the allocation of naval funds?[14] Tirpitz resolved the problem by not going all the way at once. Instead, he proceeded in several stages, intentionally making it more difficult for parliamentarians to see what he was up to. The first naval bill, which Tirpitz presented to the Reichstag only a few months after he took office at the end of 1897, was comparatively moderate. He set the strength of the future German fleet at nineteen battleships (each renewed after twenty-five years), twelve armoured cruisers (each renewed after twenty years), and thirty small cruisers.

Official acceptance of the transition to capital-shipbuilding and the period involved was more important for Tirpitz at this point, than the planned total number of ships. The bill, declared by the Kaiser to be a 'national affair', was passed on 28 March 1898 by the votes of the middle-class and conservative parties: the farmers received protective subsidies as compensation. The SPD and some liberals voted against.

Two years later all the modesty had fallen away. The second naval act, passed on 12 June 1900, doubled the aimed-for inventory of battleships to thirty-eight. Although parliament voted through only two of the next eight armoured cruisers requested and eight small cruisers, the acceptance of the bill was a triumph for Tirpitz and, according to his biographer Patrick Kelly, 'the high point of his career'.[15] The same day the overjoyed Kaiser elevated him to the nobility. For the first time and from now on, the navy had priority over the army in the allocation of funds. In order to achieve his full aims and maintain the fleet at the highest technological level, Tirpitz completed the two naval acts over the next few years by means of amendments in 1906, 1908 and 1912.

During this period Tirpitz made his mark on German politics in a way which reminded many of Bismarck, and it was not always for the best, but was made possible by the continuing support of the Kaiser. The latter prided himself on being the originator of Tirpitz's successes and provided him with a power base which enabled Tirpitz repeatedly to force through his plans against the growing resistance of the Reich political leadership. Tirpitz himself also left no avenue unexplored to win over the public, whose significance as a political force he had recognised early on. For that purpose he started up a broad-based, very professionally managed, public-relations campaign. 'Everywhere in Germany, mass meetings were organised in support of building a fleet, leading figures from politics and business received invitations to fleet reviews, officers worked for the goodwill of Reichstag deputies, popular newspapers and books glorified naval history, naval uniforms came into mode, especially for children, and above all university professors supported the fleet programme in their academic activities'.[16] In parallel with all this, in 1898 at Tirpitz's instigation the *Deutscher Flottenverein* (German fleet association) was founded. Only two years later this association had almost 250,000 members, by 1914 1.1 million.

It was of great benefit to the workers at the Reich Navy Office that in scarcely any other European major power did the public have the same feel for the military as existed in the German Kaiser Reich. The army officer corps had the 'highest standing in the state', and in a world in which a small second lieutenant might be seen as a 'young god', many citizens aspired to have their share of the prestige which wearing 'the Kaiser's mantle' conferred.[17] In the ubiquitous associations of military veterans, memory of the wars for unification and the founding of the Reich were not only kept alive but also 'military and nationalistic thinking for its own sake'.[18] The navy profited from this particular social attitude.

In addition, Tirpitz drew to his side influential 'nationalist' interest groups such as the German Colonial Company and the All-German Federation, which had dreamed for years of a German *Weltreich*, or worldwide empire. Even the powerful Central Federation of German

Industrialists 'found no objections to the Tirpitz Plan', since it promised German heavy industry firm orders for years into the future

The outcome of all this was that at the beginning of the twentieth century press and public opinion in Germany showed as great an interest in the navy as was the case in Great Britain. The Royal Navy traditionally enjoyed great prestige as the 'senior service' for its role as protector of the British Empire. Ship namings and launchings were staged, particularly in the Reich, as 'significant imperial theatre', attracting hundreds of thousands of spectators. Millions of Britons attended the great naval review at Spithead on the occasion of the diamond jubilee of Queen Victoria's accession.[19] On both sides of the North Sea people were fascinated by such exhibitions of maritime power. Modern warships, with their great hulls of armoured steel and massive gun turrets, symbolised the superior state of industry, science and technology almost unlike anything else in the two leading industrial nations of the world. For the Germans, much more than for the British, they fulfilled an important function as symbols of a national identity reaching far beyond the national borders.

Tirpitz's great concern after the passing of the two naval acts was that Britain – as one hundred years previously against the Danish Navy – might make a preventive strike against the fleet under construction. It was therefore of major importance not to draw attention to the fleet, to pursue a cautious policy towards Great Britain and keep the international situation as relaxed as possible until the 'danger period' had passed and a satisfactory defence could be mounted.

Bernhard von Bülow, who in October 1900 rose from Secretary of State at the Foreign Office to Reich Chancellor, struggled to find ways to please everybody, but even he could not prevent the navy falling ever more under the baleful eye of the British, and as a consequence the political premise of the Tirpitz Plan soon tottered.

Great Britain, which was to have been forced by the fleet under construction to acknowledge Germany as an equal partner in the world, reacted quite differently to the expectations of Wilhelm II and Tirpitz. For one thing, the British gave no thought to binding themselves closer to the challenger.

As it became clear that the era of 'splendid isolation' was approaching its end, the British decided to sit at the negotiating table with their old rivals France and Russia, and not with Germany. In 1904 London and Paris concluded the Entente Cordiale, expanded three years later into the

Triple Entente by including Russia. The Germans, who perceived this development as 'encirclement' by the other great powers, remained the only reliable ally of their old *Zweibund* partner Austria–Hungary. (Italy expanded the *Zweibund* into the *Dreibund*, but the Italians proved fickle partners and, as we know, declared their neutrality when war broke out).

Worse, and this was more difficult for Tirpitz to bear, the British government was determined to maintain the supremacy of the Royal Navy at any price. The man entrusted with this task was 63-year-old Admiral Sir John Fisher, former commander of the British Mediterranean Fleet. No other personality made his mark so deeply in the Royal Navy of the nineteenth and twentieth centuries as John 'Jacky' Fisher, and nobody else divided it so deeply either. While some revered him as the genial reformer and strategist, others thought his ideas too radical.

In 1904 Fisher was appointed First Sea Lord, which made him responsible for operational control of the Royal Navy. Only the First Lord of the Admiralty, a civilian and member of the House of Lords, was above him. Fisher immediately embarked on a rigorous programme of reform which, at a stroke, raised the Royal Navy's ability to fight in the North Sea. He sent a large number of old cruisers, sloops and gunboats to the breakers and gradually had the battleships at overseas stations transferred back to home waters.

Fisher's most significant military and historical achievement, however, was to virtually revolutionise warship construction. In 1906, under his decisive influence, HMS *Dreadnought* was completed. This was a new type of capital ship, displacing 17,900 tons, with a speed of 21 knots, armour almost a foot thick, and ten (instead of the usual four) guns of the largest calibre, 12in (30.5cm), making *Dreadnought* far superior to any other warship in the world.

At a stroke, large sections of the fleets of all other sea powers were rendered practically worthless. At the same time, Fisher had turned numerous British warships into scrap metal, for which he came in for heavy criticism from his opponents. From then on the technological development over the next few years advanced so frenziedly that by the outbreak of war in 1914 the *Dreadnought* herself was obsolescent. Launched in October 1912, HMS *Iron Duke*, flagship of the British fleet, displaced 30,000 tons, was 623ft (190m) in length and 90ft (27m) in the beam, could make 22 knots and was armed with ten 13.5in (34.3cm) guns.

The term 'dreadnought' quickly became the synonym for all modern capital ships (all older types were called henceforth pre-dreadnoughts) and embraced battleships and also battlecruisers. The latter replaced large (or heavy) cruisers, also known as armoured cruisers. The first of the new, more efficient type of capital ship entered service in parallel with HMS *Dreadnought* in 1908. This was the battlecruiser HMS *Invincible*, 60–100ft (20–30m) longer and a few metres beamier than battleships. Their armour was thinner and their armament weaker, but was compensated for by higher speed and greater range. The maritime arsenal was completed by light cruisers, which were basically battle-cruiser in concept but on a smaller scale, equipped with medium armament; the destroyers, small, very manoeuvrable, fast ships able to discharge their torpedoes from below the waterline and representing a serious danger to enemy capital ships; and, finally, submarines.

Most surface warships of the time had coal-fired steam turbines. This required an enormous outlay: every ship had to carry several thousand tons of coal and hundreds of stokers shovelled it under often barely tolerable conditions in the dark and stiflingly hot boiler rooms. For this reason the British were very keen on oil-firing, but in the First World War only a small number of their warships were so fitted.

For Tirpitz, Fisher's '*Dreadnought* leap' was a challenge on which he had not reckoned, and so there was nothing he could do but accept it. Only if the German Imperial Navy had ships of the new type would it have a chance of keeping up with the Royal Navy, but it meant that the already immense naval estimates for warship building would have to rise to heights which excited accusations of a swindle. The building costs for the ships themselves would now be 100 per cent greater (a modern dreadnought battleship would cost around 45 million marks), but to accommodate these new giants the shipyards, harbours, dock installations and the Kaiser Wilhelm Canal linking the North Sea and Baltic would all have to be enlarged. In the years 1905 to 1914 the naval estimates doubled and this inflation was a major cause of the armaments expenditure of the Reich rising to almost 90 per cent of the total domestic budget.[20]

Another critical point was personnel. The bigger the ships became, the more men were needed to man them. About 1100 men crewed a battleship, even more a battlecruiser. Whereas the Imperial Navy could draw on conscripted men, who were obliged to serve for three years, the Royal Naval pool was only volunteers who signed up for twelve years. Not until 1916, halfway through the war, did Great Britain introduce conscription.

The problem of personnel was seen most clearly in the recruitment of officer material. Seaman branch officers in the ranks from sub lieutenant/leutnant to admiral headed the maritime hierarchy. They were entrusted with the ships and responsible for men and materials. They represented the nation wherever in the world the ships made their appearance. For that reason both the German and British navies attended to the matter of their selection with special care. In either country one could only be a naval officer with the 'right' background. Especially welcome were the offspring of the nobility and officers, but with rising demand recourse was had more frequently to applicants from the higher ranks of civil servants, and the middle classes.

By way of example, when the later Grossadmiral Karl Dönitz entered the Imperial Navy on 1 April 1910, he was one of 203 young men born between 1890 and 1892 who now formed 'Crew 1910'. They all came from the bourgeoisie: 'their fathers were officers, high school teachers, physicians or academics from other disciplines, rarely from the nobility, but never employees from the lower orders and certainly not the working class'.[21]

Their training, the cost of which exceeded by several hundred per cent the average yearly earnings of an industrial worker, had to be paid for by the cadets out of their own pockets. This also ensured that no 'undesirable elements' crept into the elite circle of naval officers. Other officers, such as marine engineer officers responsible for the highly complex machinery of modern capital ships were subordinate to the seaman branch officers, who looked down upon them as 'second-class officers',

Table 1: Rank Equivalents of Seaman Branch Officers

Imperial German Navy	Royal Navy[22]
Grossadmiral	Admiral of the Fleet
Admiral	Admiral
Vizeadmiral	Vice Admiral
Konteradmiral	Rear Admiral
Kapitän zur See	Captain
Fregattenkapitän	Commander
Korvettenkapitän	Lieutenant Commander
Kapitänleutnant	Lieutenant (senior grade)
Oberleutnant zur See	Lieutenant (junior grade)
Leutnant zur See	Sub Lieutenant
Seekadett/Fähnrich zur See	Naval Cadet/Midshipman

For German naval officers the Tirpitz Plan was a grandiose gift, bestowing as it did on the navy, so long in the shadow of the successful land forces, a breathtaking valuation of their political and military significance. The fleet was for the Germans, 'under the spell of prestige' (Klaus Hildebrand), the key to 'world policy', and the officers in their navy blue uniforms with gold rings and insignia, the Kaiser's crown on the lower sleeves, were the men entrusted by Wilhelm II with the fulfilment of this illustrious mission. Additionally, all naval personnel swore a personal oath of loyalty to the Kaiser, who by virtue of the Reich Constitution of 1871 was overall supreme commander of the army and navy.

Wilhelm II made no attempt to conceal the special place he had in his heart for his 'boys in navy blue'. On the occasion of the opening of the new naval academy at Flensburg-Mürwik in November 1910 he said:

> I do not need to emphasise how close to my heart is the seaman branch officer corps whose uniform I wear. I recognise it from my earliest youth. I have learned to treasure it for its splendid work commanding my ships at home and abroad and in the development of the navy as a whole. I love the calling which you, my young comrades, have chosen for yourselves, and I enjoy with you all the fine and proud things which this calling offers you, namely positions of responsibility at such an early age.[23]

The historian Holger Herwig rightly called the seaman branch officers the 'Kaiser's elite corps', for in the social rankings of the Kaiser Reich they occupied one of the top places, comparable with the Garde du Corps officers of the Prussian army. On his decision to become a naval officer, the young Karl Dönitz followed the path 'into higher, if not the highest social circles which had not been so open quite so obviously to his father.'[24]

Officers rewarded 'their' Kaiser by adopting a decidedly monarchic-conservative, anti-liberal habit of mind, in sharp contrast to their bourgeois/academic upbringing. Social democracy stood on a par with revolution: the SPD had the reputation of being a 'fatherland-less' party, which threatened the system and had to be resisted with all means available. 'Even the slightest suspicion of a social-democrat inclination could finish a naval officer's career or tarnish it.'[25]

Unlike the authoritarian system of the Kaiser Reich, where the military stood fairly aloof from the influence of the Reichstag, in the parliamentary democracy of Great Britain there was not the slightest doubt about the Royal Navy, despite its name, being subordinate to Parliament. There were even 'inspections' of the British fleet by representatives of both Houses of Parliament but not attended by the monarch – in the Germany of Wilhelm II such a thing would have been unthinkable. On the other hand, that did not alter the fact that Royal Navy officers, most of whom came from the conservative ruling class and thus belonged *eo ipso* to the ruling class of the British Empire, were considered politically and socially to be a similar elite to their German counterparts. 'Many British naval officers were fine mariners, brave and imaginative commanders, but as a whole they were a small, reactionary, class-conscious social group withdrawn into themselves.'[26]

A particular characteristic of the German, and also the British, naval officer was a special code of honour at the heart of which were concepts such as loyalty, devotion to duty and fighting spirit, including readiness to sacrifice one's life for king and country. 'It is the first duty of the soldier to uphold the unbreakable oath of loyalty sworn to the Kaiser and to maintain the honour of the flag and colours pure and untarnished' – so read the Imperial Navy's *Articles of War*, a maritime statute book.[27] Some of the sources feeding this archaic concept of honour were heroic epics from antiquity and knightly sagas from the Middle Ages or the *Nibelungenlied*. For German officers, even into the twentieth century, it was usual for them to protect their honour in a duel, provided that the party giving 'offence' had his own honour code and was capable of 'giving satisfaction'. If this was a worker, recourse was always had to a court. During the war 'honour' formed one of the major keynotes for the conduct and decision-making of naval officers – with, to some extent, catastrophic consequences.

Shortage of personnel, lack of finance, British determination: these were just a few of the problems which the '*Dreadnought* leap' had caused the German shipbuilders. Some sober observers even took the view that there were too many problems to be ultimately successful, but Tirpitz refused to accept this, even though he did perceive it. Instead, he held doggedly to his plans and thus led Germany into a ruinous armaments race with Great Britain, which soured the relationship between the two countries, and contributed in no small way to the division of Europe into two opposing treaty-blocs.

In the first of three amendments to the navy acts, passed in May 1906 by the Reichstag, Tirpitz ensured that henceforth Germany would also build all her capital ships based on the design of the *Dreadnought*. For new vessels the amendment only foresaw the six armoured cruisers which parliament had not approved in 1900.

The second amendment, passed in March 1908, was aimed primarily at preventing the deputies putting a stop to the Tirpitz Plan on the grounds of its spiralling costs, and the increasing political isolation of the Reich. In addition the idea was to implement the *Äternat* as soon as possible, the automatic and permanent self-renewal of the fleet. The amendment therefore reduced the life of the battleships, which had been set at twenty-five years in the first navy act, to twenty years. Furthermore, in the next four years 1908 to 1911 inclusive, four capital ships were to be built per year instead of three as previously stipulated. From 1912 the rate of construction would sink to two ships per year and not rise again to three until 1917. All the same, Tirpitz was now planning, if possible, to reduce the five-year period of lesser building activity.

The raising of the tempo of capital-shipbuilding in Germany caused great concern in Great Britain. Shortly after the amendment was passed, the authorities in London made their first attempt to come to an understanding with the Reich on the fleet question. The unyielding attitude of Wilhelm II frustrated this approach: the Kaiser, influenced by Tirpitz, was not prepared to accept cuts in the German shipbuilding programme.

Asquith, the Liberal prime minister in power since 1906 on a manifesto aiming to reduce defence spending in favour of social reforms, now had no choice but to raise drastically the Royal Navy estimates. Between 1909 and 1913 no less than twenty-four battleships and battlecruisers were ordered, double the number in the preceding four years. In 1909 alone, eight ships were ordered after a rumour that Tirpitz was intending to accelerate the German shipbuilding programme caused virtual panic amongst the British public.

Now the German government turned to the British for a way out of the situation they themselves had engineered. Bülow, who as Reich Chancellor had gone along with the Tirpitz Plan, had meanwhile recognised that Germany could not maintain this costly and risky naval armaments programme ad infinitum. He received support from the German ambassador in London, Count Paul Wolff Metternich, who pointed out persistently in his reports that it was only the fleet which stood in the way of a better relationship with Great Britain. 'Nothing and nobody will dissuade the British from the belief that a constantly growing powerful fleet facing its coasts does not amount to a danger, the greatest to which they could be exposed,' the ambassador warned the Chancellor in 1908.[28]

Wilhelm II, who also read Metternich's reports, added marginal observations such as 'don't talk rot', 'rubbish' and 'coward'. Once he wrote: 'I think the best thing would be if Metternich finally shut up.'[29] The Kaiser would only sign a naval agreement with Britain of the kind Bülow had in mind if it contained as one of its conditions Tirpitz's proposal for a ratio of strength between the two fleets of 3:4, favouring the British. This was completely unacceptable for the British, and the negotiations broke down.

All subsequent attempts, initiated by one side or the other in the following years, to come to an agreement came to nothing. The British thought that the Germans continued to want too many concessions in return for cutting back on their shipbuilding programme, while Britain was not prepared to accept an unfavourable strength ratio or – another German request – a promise of neutrality should war break out in Europe. The British thought that a guarantee of this kind might not only endanger their partnerships with France and Russia, but pave the way for German hegemony in Europe.

A last attempt to find a solution was made at the beginning of 1912 by Theobald von Bethmann Hollweg, who had succeeded Bülow as Reich Chancellor in 1909. Tirpitz, irritated by the two ships per year tempo, had just put forward another amendment for three new battleships and a resumption of three ships per year. Bethmann Hollweg did everything he could to stop the amendment. In his view it would have disastrous effects on the Anglo-German relationship.

The chancellor succeeded in diverting a proportion of the money earmarked for the navy into the army budget, but with regard to the extra ships Tirpitz would not budge. He was only prepared to hold back on the three-ship tempo until 1917 for a quid pro quo. Against this background, any agreement with Great Britain was practically out of the question. After the visit to Berlin of the British Minister for War, Richard Haldane, had achieved nothing, on 22 May 1912 the last fleet amendment of the Kaiser Reich was finally passed, and with it the aim of the Tirpitz Plan – a self-renewing fleet of sixty capital ships – was at least theoretically achieved.

The British reply was not long in coming. Since October 1911 the First Lord of the Admiralty had been Winston Churchill. As he saw it, for a land power such as Germany a battle fleet was 'more of a luxury', certainly not a necessity as for Great Britain.[30] After the failure of the Haldane mission and the passing of the Tirpitz amendment, Churchill was determined to make it unmistakably clear to the Germans, once and for all, that the Royal Navy would reply to any threat to British naval supremacy by corresponding countermeasures. For that reason he had a large part of the British Mediterranean Fleet brought back to the North Sea, which at a stroke radically increased British fighting strength locally. He also declared the 'two-power standard' doctrine to be no longer in effect. From then on, according to Churchill, Britain would only build her warships with one nation in mind – against Germany.

Churchill considered a 60 per cent superiority over the German fleet to be sufficient, but let it be known, however, that two British ships would be laid down for any German new building over and above the known programme. The naval estimates, which Churchill forced through in the winter of 1913 against all domestic political resistance, was the equivalent of a billion marks, double the German investment.

That was the end of the Tirpitz Plan. If the Germans still wanted to have a fleet which could endanger Britain, they would have to be in a position to exceed the inexhaustible financing ability of the British Empire. That was out of the question. The army budget passed alongside the fleet amendment in 1912 had left no doubt that from now on it was the army which stood at the forefront of political and military attention. The two Balkan wars in 1912/1913, which resulted in a marked deterioration in the Russo-German relationship, increased this tendency. In June 1913 the Reichstag passed a fresh army budget, the biggest there had ever been.

This put paid to any more ideas of further strengthening the fleet. Additionally, as the Reich Navy Office calculated, because of steeply rising building costs there was barely enough money for the new ships already approved. Even Tirpitz had to finally admit with resignation, 'We can no longer build the ships we envisaged.'[31] Only the outbreak of war relieved the State Secretary of the need to admit his miscalculation publicly. Tirpitz was fully aware that the 'High Seas Fleet', as it was now called officially, was too weak in 1914 to spike the guns of the Royal Navy fatally (see Table 2): the outbreak of war was therefore anything but convenient for him.

Table 2: Strength Ratios in August 1914[32]

	Imperial Navy	Royal Navy
Battleships in commission	15	22
Battleships under construction	5	13
Battlecruisers in commission	5	9
Battlecruisers under construction	3	1
Pre-dreadnought battleships	22	40
Older armoured cruisers	7	40
Small/light cruisers	16	20
Torpedo boats/destroyers	205	330
U-boats/submarines	31	73

With regard to his foreign policy plans, Tirpitz was also destroyed. In the end his risk theory had proved itself to be 'pure fantasy' (Hobson). The British had accepted the challenge of the German fleet and clearly made their own choices. Instead of a desirable treaty partner, Germany had become an isolated power. The building up of the fleet had driven a great wedge between Great Britain and the Kaiser Reich, and ensured that in 1914 Britain would align with her former rivals France and Russia. With the British declaration of war, the last hope that the British would adopt neutrality out of respect for the German fleet evaporated.

Now there remained only one question to be cleared up: would the steel colossi, with which Germany had attempted in vain to score points through diplomacy, at least achieve in the military field what was hoped of them? One could only guess, for it was the first time that Germany the land power had taken to the water. The young Kapitänleutnant Ernst von Weizsäcker wrote later of what had confronted him and his comrades, 'The navy had no fighting tradition. In its short history it had only a few feats of daring behind it in foreign waters and against unequal opponents. How we would fare against the British, the leading sea power – that was what we were now going to find out.'[33]

2

'And if they don't come, then we shall fetch them'
The War Begins

KONTERADMIRAL FRANZ HIPPER, born in 1863 at Weilheim, Upper Bavaria, was the son of an iron and colonial wares dealer and had entered the Imperial Navy in 1881, thus being a contemporary of Wilhelm Souchon. Both made a glittering career for themselves. Unlike almost every other high-ranking naval officer who had served aboard ship and at the naval staff, however, Hipper could say with pride that he had never 'worked in an office or with a higher state authority'.[1] Neither had he gone through naval academy. When war broke out he had spent twenty-five of his thirty-three service years aboard ship.

In 1913 Hipper attained the peak of a career 'totally untypical for a senior officer' when he took command of the naval reconnaissance forces of the High Seas Fleet.[2] Thus he became lord and master of the modern battlecruisers and small cruisers of the Imperial Navy, whose tactical function as 'advance guard' of the battleship squadrons pre-destined him to have an important role in every operation involving the fleet. The personal attributes which qualified him for this elevated position were once described by his erstwhile senior officer Admiral Felix von Bendemann: 'Outstandingly competent officer with great aptitude, energetic, lively, quick to make a decision and of clear vision. Also did well in his last post. Good horseman, passionate hunter. Suitable for promotion.'[3]

At the beginning of July 1914, about the same time as his friend Souchon decided to take the *Goeben* from the Mediterranean to the Austrian naval base at Pola in the Adriatic, Hipper's ships were cruising off the Norwegian coast. After the assassinations at Sarajevo they had gone there with other fleet units for the annual Imperial Navy summer manoeuvres. While ambassadors made their calls to ministries and palaces in the European capitals, exchanged diplomatic notes and attended crisis conferences, the German warships held their routine navigation and gunnery exercises in the idyllic landscape of the Norwegian fjords. The whole idea of 'business as usual' was to keep the political temperature down following the murder, perpetrated by Serb terrorists, of the heir to the Austro-Hungarian throne and his consort. In order to maintain the appearances of normality, Kaiser Wilhelm II had accompanied the fleet in those northern waters aboard the Royal Yacht *Hohenzollern*.

The facade was continued only until the fleet received news that Austria had served an ultimatum on Serbia. On 26 July 1914, Fleet Commander Admiral Friedrich von Ingenohl summoned all ship commanders to the flagship *Friedrich der Grosse* and informed them that in view of the threat of war the voyage was to be terminated and the ships returned to German ports forthwith. A few hours later the German war fleet weighed anchor and headed south. 'Towards what destiny?' Hipper asked.[4]

It was still not certain that it would really come to war and if so, what the British response would be. Would Britain declare war alongside her Entente partners France and Russia or, not for the first time in her history, leave the continent to its problems and attempt to remain neutral for as long as possible? For the navy that was the decisive question. The Tirpitz fleet had been built to challenge Britain, and if need be it would be used against Britain.

On the orders of the Kaiser, the ships returning from Norway steamed into the Baltic first, in case Russia became the principal enemy at sea. A short time later the first reports came through of the preparations the Royal Navy was making for war. Therefore, on 31 July the newest and most powerful ships of I and III Squadrons made the sixty-mile (100km) long voyage through the Kaiser Wilhelm Canal from Kiel to Wilhelms-haven. Since 1912 the town on the Jade had been the main naval base of the High Seas Fleet, and the departure point in the event of a naval war against Great Britain.

Hipper also went there with his battlecruisers. His first priority was to secure the inner German Bight against intrusion by enemy warships and submarines. For that purpose he had been given command of all light naval forces such as torpedo boats, minesweepers, U-boats and aircraft. Even before news came from Berlin that Germany had declared war on Russia, and he had received at Wilhelmshaven official notifi-cation of mobilisation, Hipper had sent a number of torpedo boats and armed fishing steamers to keep watch for suspicious vessels between the islands of Baltrum and Amrum. To support them, in the Outer Jade and the Elbe, a force consisting of several capital ships of the High Seas Fleet waited with steam up for the order to sail.

Hipper ordered all ships to action stations. Guns were kept ready to fire, sentries increased, nets stretched along the ships' sides. In 1807 the British had made a pre-emptive strike, destroying the Danish fleet lying peacefully at anchor at Copenhagen, in order to prevent its falling into Napoleon's hands. There was no reason to doubt that they were capable of doing the same again. That night all lights on the North Sea coast were extinguished; all coastal navigation lights and lightships withdrawn and all light-buoys removed.

While Hipper was organising the security of the German Bight with I and III Squadrons, the other units of the High Seas Fleet took up their positions in the North Sea. II Squadron, composed of pre-dreadnought battleships commanded by Vizeadmiral Reinhard Scheer, anchored in the Elbe estuary between Cuxhaven and Brunsbüttel. A small cruiser and a torpedo-boat flotilla protected the Ems estuary, while ships were also posted at the estuaries of the Jade and Weser. U-boats of the High Seas Fleet were stationed at Heligoland, on the Ems, in the Borkum roads and at Emden. Other operational bases were established later in the occupied Belgian coastal towns of Zeebrugge, Bruges and Ostend. In the Mediterranean, German U-boats began commerce warfare, operating from the Austro-Hungarian bases at Cattaro and Pola on the eastern coasts of the Adriatic, and at the outbreak of war supported Souchon's two-ship Mediterranean squadron, integrated into the Turkish navy in the defence of the Dardanelles, and in operations against Russian units in the Black Sea.

Prince Heinrich von Preussen had command of mainly older ships in the Baltic. Because the Russian fleet had clearly been weakened since its defeat in the war against Japan (1904/05) and, at the request of the German government, the Danes had blocked off the Belt to prevent ingress into the Baltic by enemy naval forces, the naval staff was of the opinion that no great naval presence was necessary to secure Kiel Bay. Additionally, should the need arise, reinforcements could be sent through the Kaiser Wilhelm Canal from the North Sea to Kiel.

On the other hand, the situation might become difficult for all those German warships in foreign waters. If war broke out with Britain, in all probability any return to home ports would be blocked off. Besides Konteradmiral Souchon's Mediterranean division, the main concern was for the East Asia squadron commanded by Vizeadmiral Graf von Spee, based in the German colony of Tsingtau on the coast of China, and the small cruisers *Königsberg*, *Dresden* and *Karlsruhe* elsewhere. It was anticipated that in the event of war all these ships should attempt to remain at sea for as long as possible and engage in commerce warfare. It was clear to all, however, that remote from Germany and without a network of overseas bases (only Tsingtau was equipped to service modern warships) this would be an undertaking with very limited prospects of success.

After all preparations had been completed, the ships of the High Seas Fleet lay at instant readiness off Wilhelmshaven awaiting orders. On 2 August the foreign office informed fleet command that after the incursion of German troops into the Grand Duchy of Luxemburg, an attack by the British was much more likely. At that, Hipper sent more ships out into the North Sea as a precaution. One day later Germany declared war on France.

The strategy of the German general staff envisaged avoiding the powerful French fortifications from Verdun to Belfort in the east and attacking the French army at the rear from the north instead. This meant that German troops had to pass across Belgian soil, the neutrality of which had been guaranteed internationally since 1839. One of the guarantors was Great Britain. When the German army crossed into Belgium on the early morning of 4 August, the British government issued an ultimatum to Germany, requiring that Belgian neutrality be respected. The ultimatum expired at midnight the same day. The British government had waited in vain for contact from Berlin and broke off diplomatic relations with Germany. Now the navy was sure: there was war with Great Britain and the Royal Navy.

The tension which had built up in the foregoing hours and days amongst officers and men alike was now discharged in boundless jubilation and general euphoria. Not only Hipper wrote of 'great enthusiasm'.[5] Aboard Hipper's flagship, the battlecruiser *Seydlitz*, 28-year-old Oberleutnant Heinrich Stenzler told his mother: 'The excitement of those days was very great, our departure from the roads an imposing celebration. All the river banks were filled with crowds of people. Our band played "Wacht am Rhein". Everybody sang along. And then followed cries of "Hurrah! Hurrah!" which never ended.'[6]

For Kapitänleutnant Hermann Graf von Schweinitz, just thirty-one years of age, the news of war against Britain was 'almost a relief'. In his diary he wrote: 'The feeling was too depressing that the navy should stand aside and look on inactive while the army struck on two fronts. Now we are also getting involved.'[7] On the Bosphorus, Konteradmiral

Souchon kicked his heels in frustration at having to experience it all from afar: 'I envy all back home for the impressions of this great moment. Yet we are here in the best and most confident frame of mind and pleased that finally the German Reich has taken up the sword ... after eating humble pie these last decades.'[8]

These positive reactions were by no means isolated cases. Even if there was no communal 'August experience', a great wave of enthusiasm, the like of which had never been seen before, swept everybody in Germany, rich or poor, educated or uneducated, town or country dweller, into the war. Nevertheless, no one could have remained unaffected by the atmosphere at this extraordinary moment. Most Germans embraced 'a spontaneous and overpowering feeling of national unity and one-ness'.[9] The conviction that the Kaiser Reich had been forced into war through no fault of its own and had now to defend itself against a 'world of enemies' united the country across all social levels and political beliefs. This was the 'spirit of 1914', much criticised later. Above all, amongst the less privileged it awoke the expectation that both the burden of war and the possible rewards from it would be shared out justly.

For many young men, particularly from the bourgeoisie, belief in the necessity for the war and the yearning for a great adventure were motivation enough to gamble their lives on the battlefield. They may have felt like Ernst Jünger, who in his controversial memoir *In Stahl-gewittern*, described thus the mood amongst soldiers at the outbreak of war: 'We set out in a sea of flowers, a drunken feeling of roses and blood. The war called us, the great, the strong, the solemn. It seemed to us manly, a joyous shooting match between riflemen on flower-strewn, blood-soaked meadows. "There is no finer death in the world ..." Ah, no staying at home, count me in!'[10]

The 1914 generation of Germans had only a very limited idea of what war really was, especially in its modern, highly technical form. The last military armed conflict, the Franco-Prussian war of 1870/71, was more than forty years previous and, as soon became obvious, was in no way comparable to what awaited the troops on the fighting fronts in Flanders and France.

In the navy it was the officers particularly who ached to prove themselves in a fleet engagement, preferably in a major naval battle. In the long years of peace prior to 1914, those whose 'trade was war' (per Wilhelm Souchon in a letter to his wife)[11] had played out many times hypothetically the situation in which they now actually found themselves. In countless manoeuvres and exercises, with scientific precision they had prepared themselves and their ships for the day when the game would become reality. They had studied the history of naval warfare so intently that now they dreamed of emulating the great heroes of the past (the fact that as a rule these were British was unimportant). And they had sworn a sacred oath to the Kaiser, who by virtue of the constitution was personally the Commander-in-Chief of the Imperial Navy, 'to maintain the honour of the flag and standard, pure and without tarnish'. Now they would have to keep this promise.

That this would possibly mean the loss of one's own life frightened almost no one. So it was that Hermann von Schweinitz, who at the outbreak of war was at a military centre ashore, longingly confided to his diary:

> I really trust that I am present there then. Quite naturally the thought of losing my life there comes to me. I have behind me a good life. Though I have had much joy and recognise how good life has been to me, I know it only from the sunny side. I doubt that it can get any better. But the success of our struggle, I would like to live through that. Something like Nelson at Trafalgar in a small way.[12]

Later he added, 'How I would love to be aboard ship! Obviously, only on a ship at the fighting front, not on one lying in reserve.'[13] After long months of hoping in vain, when at last in April 1915 he was posted aboard the small cruiser SMS *Rostock*, he was beside himself with joy: 'My hour has come! ... I am inwardly exultant, God be thanked, now everything can go well'.[14]

In the German fleet it was expected that the Royal Navy would attack immediately the war began. 'And if they don't come, we shall fetch them,' wrote Richard Stumpf, a 22-year-old pewterer from Nuremberg who had volunteered for the navy in 1912 and experienced the war as a rating aboard the battleship SMS *Helgoland*.[15] The idea that the British could do no other than go on the offensive had been basic to Tirpitz's fleet concept, though in the last few years before the war there had been pointers enough that the contrary might be the case. The strategic planning of the German naval staff in 1914 was based on the theory that in the event of war the British would blockade the German North Sea coast in order to cut off German seaborne commerce and bottle up German warships in the Heligoland Bight. The operational orders for the

North Sea on 30 July 1914 therefore planned that the enemy ships enforcing the close blockade would be reduced by U-boat attacks and mining until such time as a battle 'under favourable circumstances' provided a realistic possibility of success.

Like a naval Schlieffen Plan, the German admirals conceived the ideal 'decisive battle' to be fought near Heligoland and for many years it had been the centrepiece of all their operational thinking and practical fleet training.[16] Already in 1891 Tirpitz had designated the battle as the 'final aim' towards which everything, 'the official channels, the yearly set tasks of the fleet, the training of the battleship companies from the first day onwards ... had to be directed.'[17]

For their part the British were not planning on leaving their home bases for a close blockade of the German coast. In the strategic calculations of the Royal Navy, the possible losses incurred in such a procedure far outweighed the expected gains. As long as the Imperial Navy did not threaten the trade routes in the Atlantic directly (which was practically out of the question), or attack the British coast, it presented no great danger to Great Britain, or at least not so much as to make it worthwhile for the Royal Navy to risk its valuable ships.

By 1912, therefore, the Admiralty in London had abandoned the idea of a close blockade. Instead, it had been decided to make use of the favourable geographical position of the British Isles and all they now proposed to do was block off the Channel and the North Sea passage between Scotland and Norway. This strategy would meet the most important goals of the Royal Navy, to protect British coasts and commercial shipping whilst cutting off the German sea route to and from the Atlantic. This measure would largely halt imports into Germany, while Britain and her allies would have access to the industrial production of the United States and the resources of the British Empire.

The Imperial Navy was practically powerless against this plan. The dilemma which this strategy caused was described by the British historian David Stevenson thus: 'In order to reach the open sea, the Germans had two unenviable options. Either they could brave the Straits of Dover and 200 nautical miles of English Channel, which would be quickly secured by minefields and destroyers, or go around Scotland – a voyage of 1100 nautical miles – in order to reach the Atlantic shipping routes. In this case they had the Grand Fleet between themselves and their Fleet bases.'[18]

The only reason why the British had not settled for the solution of the distant blockade from the outset was the centuries-old Royal Navy tradition which always had an offensive strategy as its priority. Once the war had begun, it was 'common sense' to the British public that at sea the result would follow one or possibly several naval battles. When these ended, equally obviously, the German fleet would have been annihilated. The decision of the Admiralty in London to follow instead a strategy of 'safety first', in which such a scenario was not a definite aim, would become an issue both for naval personnel as well as for the public.

At the beginning of August 1914, instead of heading across the North Sea for the German coast with everything available, the British preferred to divide their forces between the most important strategic locations for a distant blockade. The blocking of the English Channel was undertaken by the Channel Fleet, consisting mainly of pre-dreadnoughts stationed at Portland on the south coast. These would be supported by the strong Harwich Force of light cruisers and modern destroyers which operated between East Anglia and the Dutch coast under the command of Commodore Reginald Tyrwhitt. Also stationed at Harwich were the British submarines commanded by Commodore Roger Keyes. The defence of the English east coast was undertaken by several patrol flotillas, amongst them the 6th Patrol Flotilla, the so-called Dover Patrol, which kept watch on the sea lanes into the Straits of Dover.

Much more difficult and demanding in terms of forces than the security of local waters was the blockading of the second, northern exit from the North Sea. This task was handled by 10th Cruiser Squadron, known in British naval history as the Northern Patrol. Under scarcely tolerable external conditions, particularly in winter, they controlled day in, day out, all merchant vessels attempting to pass through the 200-mile wide strait between Scotland and Norway. Freighters carrying specified goods important for the German war effort ('contraband') were not allowed to proceed, but put under the command of a British boarding party and taken into Scapa Flow.

There, in a barren natural harbour amidst the Orkney Islands off the north coast of Scotland, was the lair where most of the Grand Fleet lay. Its nucleus was twenty modern battleships and four battlecruisers. A thousand years before, the Vikings had used Scapa Flow as a base and now, as in the Second World War, the storm-tossed bay was seen as the ideal departure point for British warships: from there they could sail in case of need to assist the Northern Patrol and make sorties to the southern North Sea. The only disadvantage was that in the opening months of the war the anchorage had no protection against U-boats, so that the ships of the Grand Fleet had to remain mostly at sea. Later, the various entrances into Scapa were protected by booms, nets, mines and old freighters scuttled in the channel.

On the day before war with Germany broke out, Admiral Sir John Jellicoe had been appointed Commander-in-Chief of the Grand Fleet, replacing Admiral Sir George Callaghan, whom Churchill considered too old and weak to head the British fleet in war. The 54-year-old Jellicoe had proved his outstanding professional qualifications for the post on numerous stations (latterly as Second Sea Lord of the Admiralty), and enjoyed great respect from officers and men alike. The British historian Correlli Barnett wrote about him: 'His brain was a well-arranged registry for details: his personality was reflected in his slim, dapper exterior, the tight mouth and the watchful quiet eyes looking out over the jutting nose. He was cool, controlled and always courteous. His reserve was the expression of great self confidence.'[19]

According to a famous saying of Winston Churchill, Jellicoe was the only man on either side of the North Sea who could lose the war in an afternoon. The British Navy minister was not far wrong. If Germany lost her fleet, she still had the strongest army in all Europe. If Britain lost the Grand Fleet, the island was left more or less vulnerable to invasion. In everything he did, Jellicoe was aware of his extraordinary responsibility, and not least for this reason he declined repeatedly to be lured into risky operations with the fleet.

Nobody suffered more from this reservation than the larger-than-life commander of the battlecruiser fleet, Vice Admiral Sir David Beatty. Twelve years younger than Jellicoe, charismatic and offhand, Beatty embodied the dashing daredevil archetype who loves adventure and for whom no price is too high to win honour and fame. In contrast to Jellicoe, Beatty was a controversial figure in naval circles. His meteoric rise – he was the youngest British admiral since Nelson – aroused envy and annoyance; his financial independence – through marriage to the divorced daughter of an American millionaire – provided him with a luxurious lifestyle, but also alienated him from his comrades. All the same, many considered Beatty to be the right man to command the fastest and most tactically flexible ships of the Royal Navy. In order to deploy the battlecruisers more effectively, they were separated out of the Grand Fleet at the end of 1914 and transferred to the Firth of Forth on the Scottish coast near where Edinburgh stands.

Numerous other units scattered about the globe, mostly older ships lacking fighting punch, completed the British naval forces. As a whole, it was the greatest fleet of warships there had ever been. And they were waiting to be let loose on their enemy. While the Imperial Navy dreamed of showing its erstwhile teacher that it had for a long time been its equal, it was important for the Royal Navy to have the German upstart, which so dearly wanted to be a great sea power, kept within bounds once and for all. For more than a hundred years Britain had ruled the waves unchallenged, and still wanted to keep it that way.

Like their German counterparts, British naval personnel had watched tensely as in the first days of August on the continent one state after another had declared war on its neighbour, while only London seemed to hesitate. The greatest concern of the officers was that Britain would if possible stay out of the war. 'I do not see how Britain can possibly refuse to assist France now that Germany has plunged in this way,' wrote 33-year-old Commander Lennon Goldsmith, commander of a destroyer in the Harwich Force, in a letter to his father, 'and there is little doubt in my mind that an Englishman will never be safe from scorn on the Continent if we do hold aloof in an inglorious neutrality.'[20]

News of the outbreak of war was greeted equally as joyously as on the other side of the North Sea. Vice Admiral Beatty told his wife that never before had he known 'such a magnificent and cheerful spirit'.[21] A young officer confided to his diary, 'Everyone's ambition is to be in the action,' and added later, 'Well, we are looking forward very keenly to a jolly good scrap in the near future and I hope we are in the thick of it.'[22] Characteristically, the British side reckoned on a German attack within forty-eight hours of the declaration of war. That the German fleet would hold back and to a certain extent voluntarily abandon the field to the Royal Navy was seen at first in Britain as improbable, just as in the same way the Germans considered it unlikely that the British would opt for an extensive defensive strategy. 'The real tone of high expectation was that at any moment the enemy might come out and the long anticipated fight might take place,'[23] wrote an officer on board the battlecruiser *Lion*, Beatty's flagship.

No Imperial Navy ship appeared, however. The anticipated naval battle awaited by both sides never took place. The only encounter in the first days of the war was the sinking of the former HAPAG-steamer *Königin Luise* on 5 August. Disguised as a British packet, her mission was minelaying off the British coast. She was noticed by a fishing vessel which requested assistance by radio. A destroyer flotilla from the Harwich Force was ordered up, led by the light cruiser *Amphion*, which opened fire on the German ship immediately. She sank after several medium-calibre hits. Seventy-five of the 130-man crew were rescued and locked in the forecastle of the British cruiser, the logic being: 'If we go up on a mine, they might as well go first.'[24] And that was exactly what happened. *Amphion* ploughed into one of the mines laid shortly before by *Königin Luise* and the cruiser sank within fifteen minutes. Of the cruiser's crew, 132 men were lost; only one of the German prisoners survived. These were the first German naval casualties of the war and the first ships of either side to be lost in the Anglo-German naval conflict.

There now ensued a quiet period. In the weeks following, the Royal Navy concentrated on getting the troops of the British Expeditionary Force over the English Channel to France. The Imperial Navy looked on helplessly as almost 100,000 men of the British army crossed safely to the French coast between 9 and 22 August 1914. They then made a decisive contribution at the battle of the Marne in halting the advance of the German armies in France. Now they had to pay the price for the navy and army failing to make combined operational plans. Moreover, Supreme Army Command (OHL) under Generaloberst Helmuth von Moltke had considered it quite unnecessary to prevent the British army from crossing the Channel. The German army never doubted that they would defeat the British – help from the navy was not needed. After the debacle at the Marne, Moltke had a nervous breakdown and was replaced by General Erich von Falkenhayn.

The inactivity of the fleet began to be a problem for naval officers fairly early on. Kapitänleutnant Rudolph Firle, born in 1881 in Bonn and fourteen years in the navy, summed up the morale of those men at Wilhelmshaven awaiting their 'baptism of fire': 'It is getting really tedious. Everyone had imagined that once war broke out there would be Hurrah! attack and then the end of it ... we have had no sign of the enemy, it is hard to keep up people's spirits.'[25] Firle was all the happier when at the end of August he was transferred to the newly formed Special Command Imperial Navy Turkey on the Bosphorus, where he was given command of a torpedo-boat half-flotilla (six boats) under Konteradmiral Souchon.

The small cruiser *Rostock* was also a miserable vessel to be aboard. Kapitänleutnant Reinhold Knobloch, aged thirty-one and the cruiser's gunnery officer, had looked forward to exercising his skill early on against a British opponent. After barely two weeks of war the reality was far from what he had imagined: 'Morale is low, because this was not how war was supposed to have been. Slackness, taking it easy. Humdrum existence, same old workaday routine ... nothing going on ... On board general inattention and boredom, the army is envied.'[26]

Gradually, it began to dawn on naval people that the British were not going to do them the favour of venturing close to the German coast. As Konteradmiral Hipper had discovered, 'the British definitely do not intend to come to the German Bight, and want to avoid battle altogether so long as we do not go to their shores.'[27] The influence of Tirpitz's all-dominating battle-fleet concept was now clearly seen to have led to a 'fundamental miscalculation of British naval strategy' (Werner Rahn).

The consequence was a string of tedious arguments about how the fleet could be used most effectively, given the changed situation. It proved disastrous that German naval command was not a single unit, but split down into a number of command centres. While the significance of the once supremely powerful Reich Navy Office grew steadily less during the war (in March 1916 Tirpitz, unnerved, handed in his resignation) the influence of the naval staff, responsible for strategic planning, increased commensurately. The operational control of the fleet, however, lay in the hands of the fleet commands, whose overlord was the Fleet Commander-in-Chief. Finally, there was also the Imperial Navy Cabinet, responsible for naval personnel matters and the carrying out of the Kaiser's orders.

The monarch wanted to have his say, not least because he had little influence on army command. Under the constitution, the Kaiser was Commander-in-Chief of the armed forces, but Wilhelm II recognised only too well what efforts army high command made to keep him out of all important decision-making. 'If anybody in Germany imagines that I lead the army, they are very much mistaken,' he wrote in a letter to Prince Max of Baden. 'I drink tea, chop wood and take long walks, and then I find out from time to time that this or that has been done just as suits the gentlemen. The only one of them who is a bit kinder to me is the head of the field railway section who tells me everything he is doing and proposing to do.'[28]

Wilhelm saw the navy as his own creation, however, and here he was less easy to force out. His capabilities as a fleet commander were, to say the least, very limited. He neither succeeding in developing a decisive overall plan for deploying the fleet against the Royal Navy, nor gave his admirals a free hand for operations in the North Sea. Instead, he wavered constantly on all questions of strategy and tactics. Only on one thing did he stand firm: Wilhelm II was fundamentally against any risky use of 'his' ships.

In his 'Statement of Will of the All-Highest' of 6 October 1914, he declared that the fleet must in no case be put at risk, but be kept as it stood, in order to bring political pressure on Britain in the event of peace negotiations. As regards the performance of the fleet so far, he expressed himself as 'highly satisfied' but warned: 'His Majesty the Kaiser expects from officers and men that he will not be prejudiced by the present inactivity and that His Majesty can count on the fleet when the All-Highest himself considers that the time for action has arrived.'[29]

Officers and men now found themselves in a new and totally unexpected situation: waiting instead of fighting. For many this was harder to bear than risking one's life in battle. That British naval personnel on the other side of the North Sea might be thinking and feeling the same did not help to mitigate the abrupt disappointment which the Kaiser's standstill order brought about. Even Admiral Hipper, to whom it was obvious that an attack on the Grand Fleet was hazardous, had difficulty in accommodating to the changed situation and was puzzled as to how to handle it. On the one hand he believed: 'Were we now ... to risk battle, we might not only be unsuccessful, the High Seas Fleet could be wiped out at a single stroke, the best thing the British could hope for. Therefore, whether we liked it or not, we had to be patient.'[30] On the other hand, shortly afterwards he suddenly wanted to take the offensive and launch a strike against the Northern Patrol. 'It would be a very audacious undertaking and under certain circumstances might be a flop or lead to the loss of the armoured cruisers, but I have the feeling something ought to happen ... In any case, in the long run this lying around doing nothing leads to slackness, and saps the men's enthusiasm to fight, which is undoubtedly present at a high level.'[31]

The fleet had to do something, but nothing must happen to it – that was the dilemma which throughout the whole war kept Hipper and the German naval command in particular, but also the Royal Navy, hidebound. The history of the naval war seen in this light is also a history of the always desperate attempts to escape this predicament in one way or another. In August 1914 there was still hope that sooner or later the mighty dreadnoughts would have the chance to prove why they had been built. At least for Hipper, Beatty and their two battlecruiser fleets, there were six eventful months to come.

3

'But the flag still flew ...'
Fighting and Dying in the Name of Honour

AFTER THE HIGH TENSION of the early days had died down, aboard the battleships idling peacefully at anchor at Wilhelmshaven one might almost have been forgiven for forgetting that there was a war on. Yet the narrow divide between life and death became evident on 21 August 1914 when the small cruisers *Rostock* and *Strassburg* were sent out with a torpedo-boat flotilla to attack British fishing vessels on the Dogger Bank. This submerged sandbank is in a large area of shallow water in the North Sea, northwest of the German Bight. The operation almost came to grief when a British submarine fired off two torpedoes at *Rostock*, both missing their target. Kapitänleutnant Reinhold Knobloch, *Rostock*'s gunnery officer, had just come up to the bridge to make a report to the commander when a periscope suddenly emerged to starboard.

> At the same moment a surge of water appeared ahead of the submarine and two tracks of bubbles raced towards us. The commander ordered, 'Hard to port,' and 'Full ahead,' at once, and that saved us. The torpedo tracks were then seen on the port side and had therefore passed close under the bow. I gave permission to shoot and nine rounds were fired at irregular intervals at the submarine without hitting it. The gun crews were too surprised by the sudden appearance of the submarine.

The attack by this submarine, as Knobloch wrote later, 'was a healthy lesson to us all, now we saw that the enemy really existed.'[1]

A few days later the enemy showed himself again and this time the Germans did not escape so lightly. On the early morning of 28 August 1914 a British force of submarines and destroyers led by the light cruisers *Fearless* and *Arethusa* headed through thick mist for the Heligoland Bight. Their purpose was to attack the German torpedo boats which kept watch there around the clock. Possibly, so the British calculated, other, larger ships of the Imperial Fleet might come to the assistance of their hard-pressed brethren and provide the lurking submarines with a rewarding target.

Although Commodore Reginald Tyrwhitt, Commander-in-Chief of the Harwich Force, and Commodore Roger Keyes, Commander-in-Chief of the British Submarine Fleet, had carefully planned the operation, its execution was poorly co-ordinated and might almost have resulted in an embarrassing failure. For example, the Admiralty in London had neglected to inform the Commander-in-Chief Grand Fleet of the impending action. When Admiral Jellicoe finally found out about it, he offered to bring out his ships in support of Tyrwhitt and Keyes. The Admiralty told him that it was not necessary, but he could if he wished send a few battlecruisers.

Jellicoe immediately ordered Vice Admiral Beatty to take the battlecruisers *Lion*, *Queen Mary* and *Princess Royal* to the southern North Sea accompanied by a squadron of light cruisers under the command of Commodore William Goodenough (who with three such cruisers had been a guest of the Germans at Kiel Week not two months before). Tyrwhitt and Keyes knew nothing of this. Therefore Goodenough's unannounced presence in the area caused great confusion amongst the British, who assumed at first that his cruisers were German. One of Keyes's submarines even fired a torpedo at Goodenough's light cruiser *Southampton*, but missed by a hair's breadth.

The men aboard the German torpedo boats, taken completely by surprise, had no idea that much stronger British forces were in their vicinity when at 0700 hrs they reported to Wilhelmshaven the approach of enemy destroyers. German naval command responded at first by sending the small cruisers *Stettin* and *Frauenlob* to the Heligoland Bight in support of the torpedo boats. During the course of the morning they were followed by the small cruisers *Cöln*, *Ariadne*, *Strassburg* and *Mainz* which, being unversed in tactics, did not sail as a closed formation but individually, one after another, as they got steam up. Hipper's mighty battlecruisers were unable to sail due to low tide in the Jade and had to wait for the flood around midday.

Meanwhile, for several hours British and German ships skirmished, the action being broken off when one or other ship disappeared into the thick mists. The British succeeded in sinking the torpedo boat *V-187* while the Germans scored several hits on Tyrwhitt's flagship *Arethusa*. Nothing else was achieved, for as visibility deteriorated it became difficult for the two sides to maintain a general view of what was happening in the complicated confusion of cruisers, destroyers, torpedo boats and submarines. The American naval historian Paul Halpern, who went over the charts of the battle, considered that they were perhaps the most difficult to read of the entire war.[2]

The battle would probably have ended inconclusively and without great losses if Vice Admiral Beatty had not decided to go for a victory with his battlecruisers. He held off initially, for fear of U-boat attack so close to the German coast, or being mined, but in the end his almost legendary fighting spirit got the better of him and thus the fate of the German small cruisers was sealed. Within forty minutes Beatty's flagship *Lion* unleashed her 13.5in main armament, reducing the *Ariadne* to a wreck, sinking the *Cöln* and shooting *Mainz* into a sinking condition with several hundred hits. An officer survivor of the latter described the last minutes on board:

All we could do was put out the fires and help the wounded. People came to me and asked if they should jump overboard. I refused permission and they obeyed ... A British destroyer came alongside to get our people off ... 'Come on board!' an officer on the destroyer shouted to me. I merely shook my head. I wanted to remain on the *Mainz* until the end. She was settling ever deeper. The destroyer turned away. They had taken off eighty of our seriously wounded. I gave the order: 'Prepare lifejackets and rolled hammocks!' Oberleutnant zur See Tirpitz (son of the Secretary of State) was on the bridge trying to estimate the depth with a plumbline. The paymaster urged him to leave the ship. Tirpitz took no notice. The *Mainz* was now a dead ship. Anyone else still aboard and alive, apart from ourselves, was hopelessly mutilated and unconscious. The faces were yellow, coloured by the shell gases. It was all very solemn, however. Around us a ring of ships waited in total silence. All the ships' boats maintained a respectful distance in order to avoid being sucked into the vortex when she went down. The *Mainz* was capsizing. Below me I heard a sound of rushing water. At that I ran to the starboard side and jumped into the sea. It was difficult to swim with my one uninjured arm. Despite that I turned round to watch the end of the *Mainz*. She went down by the bows. I drifted amongst wreckage, vats, baskets and rolled hammocks. The last boat still within distance picked up boatswain's mate Mayrhofer, whom I had bound fast to a hammock because I could not manage to support him, Oberleutnant zur See von Tirpitz, who had swum to us after the ship went down ... we were brought aboard the *Liverpool* and given a very friendly welcome in the wardroom. The international warship directory *Jane's Fighting Ships* lay open on the table – SMS *Mainz* was struck out.[3]

When Hipper finally arrived with the battlecruisers, the British had long since headed back to Harwich and Scapa Flow. The day's balance: the Germans had lost three small cruisers and a torpedo boat, three other cruisers had received minor to serious damage; 712 naval personnel were dead, more than five hundred wounded. The British had saved 336 and kept these as prisoners of war. The British had thirty-five dead and forty wounded; none of their ships had been lost.

Three days after the battle a German torpedo boat fished out of the sea a stoker from the *Cöln*, Adolf Neumann, who by some miracle had survived seventy-two hours in those cold North Sea waters. He described how, drifting with other survivors, he had watched his ship go down. Gradually his companions lost their strength, and one after another sank into the depths. 'Leutnant von Forell was said to have taken his leave of another officer with a handshake.'[4]

In Great Britain the battle was celebrated as a great Royal Navy victory. 'We've Gone to Heligoland and Back! Please God, We'll Go Again!' read the *Daily Express* headline. David Beatty was the man of the hour and honoured as a hero. He was satisfied personally with his performance: 'It was good work to be able to do it within twenty miles of their main base, Heligoland, and with the whole of the High Seas Fleet listening to the boom of our guns.'[5] Beatty was indignant that he failed to receive any official recognition for his achievement. Other officers involved in the action thought it was less of a great victory than a narrow escape from catastrophe. Roger Keyes wrote to William Goodenough, 'I think an absurd fuss was made over that small affair.'[6]

In Germany reactions were less friendly. The navy had suffered a serious defeat, of that there could be no doubt. Was it not over-defensive? 'Public opinion is beginning to get sick and tired of the fleet waiting patiently,' Hipper concluded despondently, a few days after the battle. 'In Wilhelmshaven especially, angry voices are heard in connection with our losses of 28th. It makes one despair.'[7] It made little difference that naval seafarers were also sufferers under the passive strategy which had been decreed for the fleet. 'It is we who are the most ashamed for not having put to sea,' Kapitänleutnant Ernst von Weizsäcker wrote to his mother. He only hoped, he added, 'that later on naval officers will be seen as honourable men.'[8]

Weizsäcker, born in 1882, was the son of Karl von Weizsäcker, later prime minister of the kingdom of Württemberg, and his wife Paula. He was attached as admiral staff officer aboard III Battleship Squadron when war broke out. Previously he had served at the Imperial Naval Cabinet in Berlin. He was convinced that the taverns of the naval ports would soon refuse to serve naval officers 'if the newspapers did not report the sinking of a British warship soon'.[9] It did not come to that, which may have been a good thing from Weizsäcker's point of view, but the situation was not saved by the 'big ships' of the High Seas Fleet.

As it was, the few successes which the Imperial Navy could claim in the initial phase of the war were almost exclusively U-boat sinkings. The first British warship to be sunk by a U-boat was the old cruiser *Pathfinder* on 5 September 1914. Less than three weeks later Kapitänleutnant Otto Weddigen, 32-year-old son of a Westphalian linen manufacturer, carried out perhaps the most spectacular blow of the whole war. On the early morning of 22 September in the Hoofden, the sea area in the southern North Sea between Holland and England, his boat *U-9* sighted three warships steaming leisurely in parallel columns. They were the obsolete armoured cruisers *Aboukir*, *Hogue* and *Cressy*.

At first Weddigen thought the three ships, part of the Harwich Force, were the advance guard of a larger formation. As soon as he was sure that no other ships were following, he gave the order to attack. The first torpedo struck the *Aboukir*, which sank at once. While the other two ships attempted to pick up the survivors, Weddigen attacked these as well: two torpedoes at the *Hogue*, three at the *Cressy*. Both these ships sank within a few minutes. This meant that a single U-boat with a 28-man crew had sunk three cruisers of 36,000 tons total displacement in less than an hour. Dutch and British vessels picked up 837 survivors: 1500 British sailors lost their lives.

Back at Wilhelmshaven, Weddigen was decorated with the Iron Cross, first and second class, by Kaiser Wilhelm II; the crew each received the Iron Cross, second class. An iron cross was even painted on the conning tower of *U-9*. A few weeks later, off the Scottish coast, *U-9* sank the British cruiser *Hawke* with the loss of five hundred lives and Otto Weddigen became the first naval officer ever to be awarded the highest Prussian decoration *Pour le Mérite*. All Germany celebrated, the U-boat commander became a hero of the people; his popularity was, 'measured by today's yardstick, scarcely imaginable.'[10]

In the eyes of his officer comrades this honour was well earned, for Weddigen's successes had, as Kapitänleutnant Schweinitz confirmed, 'raised the prestige of the navy within the people, just at the time when the army was stagnating in the west.' He very much regretted the death toll ('I am sorry for it'), 'but ultimately this is war and they were warships.'[11] Weizsäcker also rejoiced and wrote, 'Today one is glad once more to be a naval officer.'[12] Anyone who was keeping score of wins and losses, such as the third gunnery officer of the battleship SMS *Helgoland*, thirty-year-old Kapitänleutnant Walter Zaeschmar, would now calculate, 'The sinking of those three armoured cruisers avenged the loss of the *Cöln* and *Mainz* on 28 August.'[13]

Weddigen's bold stroke showed as clearly as possible the offensive potential of the U-boat, which until then had rather been looked upon as a useful accessory to the dreadnought fleet. Nobody had ever imagined that such a small boat (*U-9* was 57m (187ft) long and 6m (20ft) in the beam, could dive to 50m (164ft) and navigate submerged at 8 knots) would be capable of inflicting such damage. As we shall see, because of Weddigen, in the future course of the war the Germans would not hold back from an increasingly ruthless use of this under-estimated weapon.

For the Royal Navy, on the other hand, submarines on the whole did not have the same strategic significance as for the Imperial Navy bottled up in the German Bight. That may be a reason why many British officers maintained their traditional disdain for these, in their eyes, cowardly and perfidious weapons: 'Anyone, of any nationality, who serves in a submarine is not playing the game'.[14] Geoffrey Harper, a twenty-year-old midshipman, went on to note in his diary, 'I always had a feeling against submarines and nothing would induce me to go in for them because I always thought they were not exactly the Navy, and now I have become quite certain ... It is rotten and underhand and like stabbing a man in the back.'[15] It therefore gave Harper special satisfaction when in March 1915 his own ship, the *Dreadnought*, rammed and sank *U-29*, commanded by Kapitänleutnant Otto Weddigen. He and all hands aboard *U-29* lost their lives.

Harper was fair enough to admit that his criticism of submarines extended to the British fleet, whose submariners were naturally as 'rotten and underhand' as the Germans. Perhaps he also felt the same when the submarine *E-9* under Commander Max Horton sank the German cruiser *Hela* about six nautical miles southwest of Heligoland on 13 September 1914, and three weeks later the torpedo boat *S-116* off the Ems estuary.

But U-boats were not the only new weapons introduced on a large scale during the war. Aircraft, airships and, above all, mines played an increasingly important role when it was necessary to inflict death and destruction on the enemy. The Hague Convention only allowed the laying of mines for *offensive* purposes (not to defend one's own coasts) inside the enemy's three-mile zone of territorial waters. Neither the Germans nor the British held to this in the First World War. The Imperial Navy alone laid a total of 43,000 mines, 25,000 of them in the North Sea. Commodore Tyrwhitt, Commander-in-Chief of the Harwich Force, possibly underestimated German thoroughness in this respect when he observed in August 1914, 'It will be months before the North Sea is safe for yachting.'[16]

Nevertheless, it was also a tiresome business for German ships to find a mine-free channel through the ever larger minefields. Whoever served aboard a minesweeper could not complain of a lack of strenuous and highly dangerous work. The major success credited to a mine in the first half-year of the war was the sinking of the battleship HMS *Audacious* off the Northern Irish coast on 27 October 1914. The minefield had been laid by the Germans only shortly before. The ship's company was rescued in a reckless action by the ocean liner *Olympic*, sister ship to the *Titanic*.

The Germans also invested great hopes in their airships. In the course of the war Zeppelins, flown as a rule by naval officers, made fifty sorties against English cities and bombed London. German propaganda made the most of it and the officer corps read the reports avidly. Thus Wilhelm Souchon to his wife, for example: 'The attacks by our naval airships against the English east coast are a pure joy.'[17] The Zeppelin attacks were in no way comparable to the air raids of the Second World War. The airships of the Kaiser's time were extremely cumbersome dirigibles, difficult to steer in any conditions of wind or heavy weather. The bombs they carried were small and caused comparatively little damage. However, they gave a bitter foretaste of what would come later.

Far more unsettling for Great Britain than the threat from the air was the danger inherent in the Imperial Navy warships scattered far and wide around the globe. After the Mediterranean division under Konteradmiral Souchon evaded its British pursuers, the Royal Navy saw it as essential

to avoid another such setback. That meant taking out the most dangerous enemy grouping beyond home waters before it inflicted a
comparable coup: the German East Asia squadron.

The base for this unit of modern large and small cruisers was Tsingtau
(Qingdao) on the east coast of China, the town being the capital of the
German protectorate of Kiautschou. It provided military support to
German commercial activities in the East Asian and South Pacific region
and protected local German property-owners, particularly in the Pacific
islands of the Marianas, the Carolinas and Samoa. Since 1912 the
squadron had been commanded by Vizeadmiral Maximilian Graf von
Spee, one of the most prominent officers in the Imperial Navy, born in
Copenhagen in 1861, the son of a Danish mother and a father from the
old Prussian nobility.

Spee was cruising with his ships near the Carolinas, well out into the
Pacific, when news of the outbreak of war reached him. Since in his
opinion Tsingtau would soon fall to the enemy, he decided not to return
there, but instead took his squadron, consisting at that time of the
armoured cruisers *Scharnhorst* and *Gneisenau* (11,616 tons displacement, eight 8.26in guns main armament, 22.5 knots) and the small
cruisers *Emden* and *Nürnberg*, across the Pacific to the west coast of
South America. Here there were neutral ports where his ships could re-
coal. The regular supply of coal was the prerequisite for the successful
fulfilment of his mission, the pursuit of enemy merchant shipping.

Spee already sensed that his time was short. He wrote to an acquain-
tance, 'You must not forget that I am quite homeless. I cannot return to
Germany. We have no safe haven in any other place on Earth: I just
have to keep roaming the seas of the world inflicting as much chaos as
I can until we run out of ammunition or an enemy with superior
armament finds me.'[18] The admiral was determined, however, to defy
fate for as long as possible. At first it went well. After various inter-
mediate stops – amongst other adventures, Spee's ships bombarded
Tahiti's capital Papeete and re-coaled at Easter Island from German
colliers ordered there for the purpose – the East Asia squadron reached
the coast of Chile at the end of October 1914, unseen after a voyage of
12,000 nautical miles.

On the way, the small cruisers *Leipzig* and *Dresden* had joined the
squadron. In a counter-move, Spee had released the *Emden* for
commerce warfare in the Indian Ocean, where she bombarded Madras
and Penang, sank a Russian cruiser, a French destroyer and sixteen

British merchant ships before being brought to battle by the cruiser HMAS *Sydney* on 9 November 1914 near the Cocos Keeling islands, where she ran aground. Some of the crew, led by First Officer Hellmuth von Mücke, succeeded in reaching Sumatra, by commandeering the schooner *Ayesha*. From there they made their way to Constantinople, and finally returned to Germany. The rest were made prisoners of war, including the commander of the *Emden*, Fregattenkapitän Karl von Müller. Because of his naval exploits and chivalry at sea, Müller was highly respected by the enemy and as a visible sign of this respect was allowed to carry his dagger in captivity.

The Admiralty in London knew where Spee's East Asia squadron was headed. They now ordered Rear Admiral Sir Christopher Cradock to take the old armoured cruisers HMS *Good Hope* (14,100 tons displacement, two 9.2in guns, main armament, 23 knots) and HMS *Monmouth* (9,800 tons displacement, fourteen 6in guns main armament, 23.5 knots), the light cruiser *Glasgow* and the auxiliary *Otranto*, an armed merchant ship, to the southwest Pacific to track down and destroy the German squadron. Cradock knew that his ships, manned predominantly by reservists, were too weak to take out Spee's squadron, which was renowned for its prowess in gunnery. Repeatedly he requested the Admiralty for reinforcements, but to no avail. Cradock continued in the hunt for the superior enemy force and found it on the late afternoon of 1 November 1914. What happened next in the waters close to the Chilean town of Coronel was in the words of Winston Churchill, 'the saddest naval battle of the war. Of the officers and men of both squadrons who, far from home, faced each other there in the heavy seas, nine out of ten present were condemned to die. On that evening, it was the turn of the Royal Navy men.'[19]

The battle was short and violent and ended with the total destruction of the two armoured cruisers. At about four minutes past seven that evening, the sun had just set when the Germans opened fire at Cradock's squadron from a range of around 12,000yds (11km). The British ships were sharply silhouetted against the bright western horizon, while Spee's cruisers were difficult to pick out against the dusk and mountains to the east. Despite the heavy sea, *Scharnhorst* landed the first hit on the *Good Hope* after a few minutes. A total of twelve 8.26in guns fired off a broadside at the British ships every twenty seconds, while the one remaining 9.2in gun and the lesser 6in guns on the other side managed only one salvo per minute. Within an hour it was all over.

The glowing *Good Hope* was first to go down. *Monmouth* followed her a little later, after *Nürnberg* approached the unmanoeuvrable British cruiser and overwhelmed her with a deadly hail of shells from point-blank range. 'It was terrible to keep firing at those poor boys, unable to defend themselves,' said Leutnant Otto von Spee, son of the admiral and serving aboard *Nürnberg*, after the battle. 'But their flag was still flying. We ceased fire for a few minutes to allow them to strike it, but it remained at the masthead. Therefore we made another approach and *Monmouth* capsized under our shelling. The ship sank with her flag still flying.'[20]

More than 1600 British naval personnel lost their lives in the bitter waters of the Pacific, amongst them Rear Admiral Cradock. From the two armoured cruisers there were no survivors. The German squadron suffered no losses. The *Glasgow* escaped at the last moment before the Germans could concentrate their fire on her; *Otranto* had been dismissed before the battle began.

The battle of Coronel is remarkable for several reasons. First, it was a brilliant victory by Graf von Spee, who inflicted on the British their first naval defeat for over one hundred years. It had been dreamed of in the Imperial Navy, and the glee was correspondingly great. But the battle actually changed the strategic situation as little as any other naval battle of the First World War, including Jutland. The British had lost two old armoured cruisers, but remained the world's strongest naval power. Kapitänleutnant Ernst von Weizsäcker hit the nail on the head when he remarked that Coronel was 'valuable for our self-confidence and upset the British.'[21] No more nor less.

More significant than the military result of the battle was the fact that at Coronel a tradition was re-established which had prevailed in the age of sail: to go down with the flag still flying. In every battle there is a point at which it makes no military sense to keep fighting and, as Carl von Clausewitz, the famed Prussian war theorist, observed, 'to do so is a foolishness born of despair and therefore cannot be approved of from any way of looking at it.'[22] This point was reached by Cradock at Coronel. Unlike the *Mainz* in the battle off Heligoland, the British admiral had no expectation that other ships might arrive in time to help him. The idea that he had to prevent the enemy squadron possibly getting through to the British coast also played no role. Therefore Cradock preferred to die, and take all his men with him, rather than capitulate his worthless wrecks. 'I will take care that I do not suffer the fate of poor Troubridge,' he wrote to an officer friend shortly before the battle – a reference to the unfortunate admiral who had let Konteradmiral Souchon commanding *Goeben* and *Breslau* escape in the Mediterranean without a fight and accordingly ruined his reputation for ever.[23] Certainly, Cradock would also have known the case of the Russian Admiral Nikolai Nebogatov. In 1905 at the battle of Tsushima against the Japanese fleet, upon recognising that his force was hopelessly inferior, he struck his flag. For this he was court-martialled and sentenced to die by firing squad: the sentence was commuted by the tsar to ten years' fortress arrest. Explaining his decision, Nebogatov said, 'I am not a soft-hearted person and would have sacrificed thousands of lives if it had served Russia's purposes ... All the men under me were prepared to sacrifice their lives ... But I had no right, under the circumstances in which we then found ourselves ... to write off 2000 young men uselessly. The law allows lives to be spared if all means of resistance are exhausted ... Therefore I decided on capitulation.'[24] A Japanese officer was of the opinion that to have tackled the greatly superior Japanese fleet would have been as senseless an act for the Russian ships 'as sweeping the sea with a broom.'[25]

The trial of Nebogatow aroused great interest in naval circles, and nearly all officers rejected the course taken by the Russian admiral. 'Nebogatov's capitulation had the effect of a deterrent, not as a model for responsible leadership in defeat.'[26] And so at Coronel, Sir Cristopher Cradock preferred the example of Nelson who, mortally wounded at Trafalgar, asked the commander of his flagship HMS *Victory*: 'I hope, Hardy, that none of our ships struck their flag?' and was told, 'No, my Lord, that would never happen.'[27]

Within the Royal Navy there was no question that Cradock had done the right thing. 'Poor old Kit Cradock has gone, at Coronel, poor old chap. He had a glorious death,' Vice Admiral Beatty stated with regret and admiration.[28] By his sacrificial death Cradock had brought about his apotheosis from loser of a battle to immortal hero and this was demonstrated in 1916 when at York Minster a memorial plaque was unveiled to the battle of Coronel. At the solemn ceremony, Arthur Balfour, former Conservative prime minister and since 1915, Churchill's successor in the office of the First Lord of the Admiralty, declared Cradock's conduct to have been an heroic act:

We shall never know what moved Admiral Cradock at that moment when he realised that he faced an enemy who outgunned and outranged him and success was impossible. He must have known that his hopes had been dashed for ever, that his plan had failed. His body rests in the eternal sea – half the globe separates him from us. Admiral Cradock and his brave comrades may not rest on home soil. But they have fame as their reward. We certainly have the right to declare that they have found an immortal place in the great history of our naval heroes.[29]

The inscription on the plaque reads:

> God forbid that it should happen,
> That I ever flee before the enemy;
> And when our time comes, let us die as men,
> For our brothers,
> And never let us tarnish our honour.[30]

Rear Admiral Cradock's deed was not an exception: rather, it provided the blueprint for everyone whose ships found themselves in a similar situation during the war. And the Germans, in so many things the intelligent scholars of the Royal Navy, were determined to follow their tutors in this example. Graf Spee and the East Asia squadron were the first.

For Spee, it was clear that by defeating Cradock he had given the German navy the greatest triumph of its short history, but at the same time he had signed his own death warrant. When his ships ran into Valparaiso after the battle to re-coal, the admiral received many wishes of good luck from the local German community. Spee thanked somebody who handed him a bouquet of lilies with the words, 'They will look lovely on my grave.'[31]

Spee knew that the British were honour-bound to hunt him down. His situation did not lack alternatives. In a signal, Berlin had given him freedom of manoeuvre, so that it was up to him whether he remained at sea with his ships and risked being brought to battle, or decided to intern his squadron in a neutral port. The latter was equally as unattractive as the option had been a few months before for Konteradmiral Souchon's Mediterranean division. Instead, Spee decided to round Cape Horn, proceed through the Atlantic and then chance forcing the blockade into the North Sea. Beforehand, however, even though he had fired off half his stock of ammunition, he wanted to attack Port Stanley, the British naval base on the Falkland Islands.[32]

This decision proved fatal. As von Spee had anticipated, after Coronel the British had immediately despatched the battlecruisers *Invincible* and *Inflexible* under the command of Rear Admiral Sir Doveton Sturdee to South America. Additionally, all available British naval vessels in South American waters were grouped up into one large squadron, including HMS *Glasgow*, which had escaped at Coronel. The British Admiralty was not leaving anything to chance, but who could have predicted that this force would call in at Port Stanley at that very moment when the German cruisers were arriving on the morning of 8 December 1914?

Sturdee could hardly believe his luck, and before the first rounds were fired he already knew that he had won the battle. In this respect, a naval battle was similar to a mathematical equation: if one worked out how many ships there were with how many guns and their calibres, and the relative speeds of the opposing sides, then the result of battle was easy to calculate. In this case, the superiority of the more powerful ships over the weaker-armed and -armoured left no room for surprises.

One of the few factors which could not be calculated exactly was the weather. That morning in the Falklands was cloudless with full sun. The sea was calm and – important for the gun crews – visibility extended to the horizon. For Sturdee, with faster ships, bigger guns and greater range, this meant that the German squadron was virtually served up to him on a plate. It was he alone who decided when battle would commence. Since each of his 12in shells weighed 850lbs (385kg) and had a range of 17,500yds (16km) while the not even half as heavy German 8.2in shells had a range of only 14,200yds (13km) he need not ever be in danger.

The British admiral took his time. For several hours his ships pursued Spee's squadron without firing. Aboard the German cruisers they had no illusions as to their fate. Everybody knew that there was no escape. 'That was a bitter, a very bitter thing to know,' wrote Korvettenkapitän Pochhammer, first officer of *Gneisenau* and another of the survivors later. 'There was a choking feeling, one swallowed hard and tensed oneself, for this was going to be a struggle for life or death, or better put a struggle for an honourable death ... the old law of naval warfare that the weaker and slower ships on the open sea and in broad daylight went down was our destiny today.'[33] The officers shook hands in farewell.

Kaiser Wilhelm II.

Grossadmiral Alfred von Tirpitz. (*ullstein bild*)

Mobilisation of the Imperial Navy, at beginning of August 1914. (*ullstein bild*)

Admiral Sir John Fisher, RN.

Vizeadmiral Maximilian Reichsgraf von Spee.

The German battlecruiser *Goeben*.

German U-boats with their depot ships, Kiel harbour, 1914. (*Süddeutscher Zeitung Photo*)

Hermann Graf von Schweinitz (photograph taken after World War II).

The Imperial East Asia squadron rounding Cape Horn.

Rear-Admiral Sir Christopher Cradock,
Commander RN squadron at the battle
of Coronel.

Vice-Admiral Sir John Jellicoe.

Admiral Sir David Beatty.

(*Left to right*) Commodore Roger Keyes,
Admiral John de Robeck,
General Ian Hamilton.

Survivors of the armoured cruiser *Gneisenau* in the sea after the battle of the Falklands; in the background the battlecruiser HMS *Inflexible*.

HMS *Good Hope*, flagship of Rear-Admiral Cradock, sunk in action at Coronel.

Vizeadmiral Wilhelm Souchon (*fourth from left*), commander of the Turkish fleet, and Enver Bei, Minister for War, Ottoman Empire (*third from left*), 15 January 1915. (*ullstein bild*)

Konteradmiral Albert Hopman. (*With the kind permission of the WGAZ archive of the Naval School, Mürwik*)

Vizeadmiral Adolf von Trotha.

The armoured cruiser *Blücher* capsized during the battle of the Dogger Bank, 24 January 1915.

HMS *Invincible*, flagship of Vice-Admiral Sir Frederick Doveton Sturdee (here seen at the Falkland Islands) was sunk at Jutland, 31 May 1916.

Aerial photograph of the Imperial High Seas Fleet.

Admiral Reinhard Scheer.

Vizeadmiral Franz (Ritter von) Hipper, elevated to the nobility 1916.

The poop of the battlecruiser *Derfflinger* at high speed.

A German battleship firing off a salvo.

Spouts thrown up by heavy shells.

Battle damage on the battlecruiser *Derfflinger*.

Postcard of 'Our heroic German fleet', commemorating the battle of Jutland.

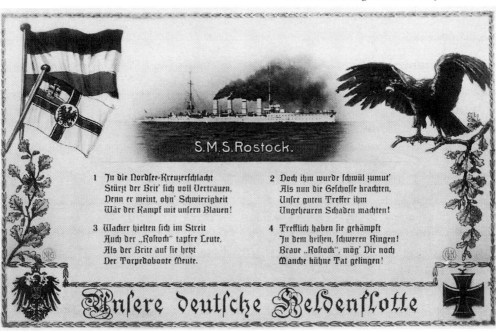

S.M.S. Rostock.

1 In die Nordsee-Kreuzerschlacht
   Stürzt der Brit' sich voll Vertrauen,
   Denn er meint, ohn' Schwierigkeit
   Wär der Kampf mit unsern Blauen!

2 Doch ihm wurde schwül zumut'
   Als nun die Geschosse krachten,
   Unsre guten Treffer ihm
   Ungeheuren Schaden machten!

3 Wacker hielten sich im Streit
   Auch der „Rostock" tapfre Leute,
   Als der Brite auf sie hetzt
   Der Torpedoboote Meute.

4 Trefflich haben sie gekämpft
   In dem heißen, schweren Ringen!
   Brave „Rostock", mög' Dir noch
   Manche kühne Tat gelingen!

Unsere deutsche Heldenflotte

Battle damage on the battleship *König*.

Laundry day
onboard *Moltke*

Sporting activities on deck,
1916. *Süddeutsche
Zeitung Photo*

Control position in the engine room of a German warship, spring 1916. (*ullstein bild*)

Interior of a German U-boat, 1917.

Iced-over foredeck of a German warship in harbour, January 1917. (*ullstein bild*)

On deck of a German torpedo-boat interned at Scapa Flow. Seated with guitar is the commander, the later Vizeadmiral Friedrich Ruge.

The small cruiser *Frankfurt* grounded at Scapa Flow.

A German torpedo boat capsized and sinking at moorings.

Unloading ammunition from German capital ships before internment.

British soldiers guarding a German ship run aground.

After the British had dined at midday, Sturdee finally gave the order to attack and at 1250 hrs the battlecruiser *Inflexible* opened fire at her maximum range of over 17,000 yards on the small cruiser *Leipzig*. Shortly after, gigantic columns of water arose from the sea, frighteningly close to the German ship. The next salvo was even closer. Spee could see that it was only a matter of minutes before *Leipzig* was hit, and so he did the only reasonable thing, signalling his three small cruisers *Leipzig*, *Nürnberg* and *Dresden* to attempt to escape while he would hold off the British force for as long as possible with *Scharnhorst* and *Gneisenau*.

Sturdee had anticipated this move and split his force likewise. While *Invincible* and *Inflexible* engaged *Scharnhorst* and *Gneisenau*, the other British ships gave chase to the German small cruisers running for it at full speed. Spee now found himself in the same situation as had Cradock thirty-eight days previously at Coronel. In order to bring his guns to bear, he had to reduce the distance between him and Sturdee. The latter did all he could to keep the German armoured cruisers within range of his own guns, as well as maintaining his own beyond the range of the German guns. That was not always possible so, despite the unfavourable circumstances, the German gunnery, for which the British subsequently had the highest praise, scored a large number of hits.

For several hours the four ships cruised on parallel courses, firing without a break, until at last the superior firepower of the British became decisive. *Scharnhorst*, hit many times, reduced to a burning wreck, barely afloat but still shooting, sank first. At 1617 hrs she disappeared below the water at approximately 52° 35' S 55° 45' W, taking with her Admiral von Spee and all eight hundred of her crew, 'but the Admiral's flag still flew proudly at the foremast and the war flag at mainmast and gaff.'[34] One of Spee's last signals, to Kapitän zur See Julius Maerker, commander of *Gneisenau*, who had argued against the attack on Port Stanley read: 'Admiral to Commander: You were right.'[35]

The two British battlecruisers concentrated their fire on Maerker's ship, which was now exposed for ninety minutes to the murderous torrent of AP shells without hope of escape. The scenes aboard the cruiser were, in the words of Korvettenkapitän Pochhammer, 'too horrific to repeat.'[36] On a note found later an officer had written: '1710 hrs hit, 1712 hrs hit, 1714 hrs hit, hit, hit again. 1720 hrs rear turret blown off, 1740 hrs hit, hit. Fire everywhere. 1741 hrs hit, hit, on fire everywhere and sinking. 1745 hrs hit. People dying everywhere. 1746 hrs hit, hit.'[37] To give in was no more an option for Maerker than it had been for Graf Spee. Not until half his crew were dead or wounded did he give the order to scuttle his wreck. At 1800 hrs *Gneisenau* sank at approximately 53° 40' S 56° W.

Before the survivors took to the water at Maerker's command (no ship's boat was left intact), they gave three hurrahs for the Kaiser and sang 'Deutschland über alles'. A British sailor aboard *Invincible* watched the cruiser sink:

> Then she sank, and one watched the unfortunates one after another being sucked into the vortex and swallowed up. As we came nearer, we saw that where she had gone down the water was all yellow and there was a ghastly smell of lyddite in the air. It was really terrible seeing all the unfortunate Germans, how they drowned and made pitiful cries for help which we were not able to give because most of our boats were in pieces. I hope I never have to go through anything like it. A crowd of men were swimming when we saw the ship go down, but when we reached the spot half of them had drowned. It was terrible to see them alongside our ship, how they tried to hold on to the slippery sides, and then glided away and went down, how hard they fought for their lives, but how they kept sinking down until they could be seen no longer. It made one sick to see these people in their death struggle: some of them with arms and legs shot away, and it was a terrible thing to see them sink behind a trail of blood.[38]

Of her crew of 850 men, the British rescued 187 from the cold waters, the temperature of which was only 4°C. Amongst the fallen were Kapitän Maerker and Leutnant Heinrich von Spee, the younger of the admiral's two sons who had served at their father's side in the East Asia squadron.

While the survivors of *Gneisenau* were fighting for their lives in the water, sixty miles away two British cruisers pursuing the small cruiser *Leipzig* poured so many shells into her that only eighteen of her crew of 333 survived the inferno. The *Leipzig* had no ammunition left, but because she refused to strike her flag, the British continued shooting.

> The projectiles impacted amongst the thickly grouped crew members and inflicted fearful butchery ... shells hit all areas of the ship, the worse devastation being around the portside cutter. This was swung inboard, and a relatively large number of men were attempting to set

it out loaded with wounded. This caused such a bloodbath that any further attempts to get the boat into the water had to be abandoned. This powerlessness to act and the relative proximity of the British cruisers made it appear to some of the officers and men a suitable time to leave the ship and swim over to the enemy ... but the low water temperature, about 3°C, chilled them to death shortly after they entered the water. From aboard ship we could see a heap of rigid bodies drifting towards the enemy. None of them was saved ... Around 2100 hrs, when it was already dark, a searchlight was suddenly turned on astern. It was *Glasgow* ... about the same time a boat could be seen about 200 metres from the ship making for the *Leipzig*. When the boat got to about 100 metres, the commander ordered 'So, now all jump off.' He answered the most insistent pleas that he should also abandon the ship, since she was going to capsize and sink at any moment and could not be captured by the enemy, with the words: 'You know that the Kaiser made me commander of this ship, and therefore I am not going to leave her until she is under water.' The commander took his leave of the survivors, and smoking a cigar, returned to the bridge. Shortly after, the remainder jumped overboard, and almost at the same time *Leipzig* heeled to port, sinking quickly by the bow so that the starboard propeller jutted high out of the water, and then went down by the head portside with a loud hissing as the flames were extinguished, her flag still flying, and taking with her the commander, Fregattenkapitän Haun.[39]

The *Nürnberg* was also overhauled by her pursuer and destroyed. Only seven of her crew of 334 survived. Leutnant Otto von Spee shared the fate of his father and brother. The German losses at the battle of the Falklands were more than two thousand men; the British suffered ten dead and nineteen wounded. The only warship of the squadron to escape was the small cruiser *Dresden*. She was not discovered until March 1915, close inshore at Juan Fernandez Island off the coast of Chile, where she was scuttled after British warships opened fire on her.

At Kiel and Wilhelmshaven, the loss of Spee's squadron barely six weeks after his great triumph caused deep dismay. For Konteradmiral Hipper the loss of the ships was a 'dreadfully sad report' and a 'fearful blow to us'.[40] Kapitänleutnant Rudolph Firle wrote: 'The brave Spee, this old Prussian, outstanding sailor. That is how the best are lost in the navy, and who knows what we are left with.'[41]

Something else was more important: despite his defeat, it was Spee, as Cradock before him, who had succeeded in the eyes of his contemporaries in preserving the honour of the navy. No German ship had struck her flag. The 'refusal to capitulate', as the historian Holger Afflerbach calls going down with the flag flying, belongs as much to the code of honour of the German naval officer as the Royal Navy officer. The deaths of the crewmen subordinated to him is 'collateral damage for something more important'.[42] Surrender, even in a hopeless situation, was never to be considered. Kaiser Wilhelm II at the outbreak of war had made that unmistakeably clear. He reminded the navy of an edict of his grandfather, Wilhelm I, on 17 March 1885 in which the latter stated: 'The more difficult his situation, the more hopeless it may seem, all the more should the commander hold firm to the rules of military honour ... I will take action with severity against those commanders who compromise the honour of the flag ... I hope that even in misfortune my ships will go down honourably without striking the flag.'[43] The fleet regulations prescribed: 'If all means of fighting are spent, an honourable sinking of the ship will prevent the flag being struck ... The commander who strikes his flag in the face of the enemy will forfeit court-martial and stand before a court of honour.'[44] 'Never strike the flag!' was a service rule in the German Federal Navy until 1969.

Against this background, Admiral Spee would have thought it absurd to consider acting in the Falklands in similar fashion to the Russian Admiral Nebogatov. The Chief of the Imperial Admiral Staff, Admiral Hugo von Pohl, wrote explaining this to his wife in a letter:

> Then you ask, why it might not have been suggested to Graf Spee to run to a neutral port? But then he would have been no better off. He could go wherever it suited him, but he could only stay 24 hours in a neutral port ... if he remained there longer he would have to disarm, and if I had required that of him and his ships, then he would not have understood the order ... Disarmament would have been a humiliation for him and the whole navy.[45]

Wilhelm Souchon saw it the same way: 'It was fate whether or not the swine found him. If he had met them the once, there would have been nothing else for it but to fight and to go down with honour.'[46]

Ironically, it was the ship bearing Spee's name which, twenty-five years after the end of the East Asia squadron, became the first, and until

1945 the only, German warship to refuse to go down with flag flying. On 17 December 1939, Kapitän zur See Hans Langsdorff scuttled the ship he commanded, the armoured ship more popularly known as the pocket battleship *Admiral Graf Spee*, just outside Uruguayan territorial waters as a result of considering himself to be in a hopeless situation. Langsdorff justified his decision, which attracted the wrath of Hitler, by stating that 'a thousand young men were worth more than a thousand dead heroes.'[47] In order to restore the tarnished honour of the Kriegsmarine, two days later Langsdorff shot himself in a Buenos Aires hotel room.

In order to prevent this from happening again, on 22 December 1939 Grossadmiral Erich Raeder, Hipper's former chief of staff and now Commander-in-Chief of the Kriegsmarine, issued the instruction: 'The German warship fights with the full engagement of all her crew to the last shell either until she is victorious or goes down with her flag flying.'[48] With this 'now official and binding edict for suicide', as Holger Afflerbach writes, 'the path was laid down for German warships for the entire future course of the Second World War.'[49]

Thus it was in the case of the *Bismarck*. Her sinking is probably the most spectacular in German naval history. On 27 May 1941 the biggest warship in the world at that time lay unmanoeuvrable and surrounded by a large British force in the North Atlantic. Catastrophe could now only be avoided by striking the flag. Her commander, Kapitän zur See Ernst Lindemann, and the fleet commander, Admiral Günther Lütjens, who was also aboard, had promised Hitler in a wireless signal 'to fight to the last shell'.[50] When the *Bismarck*, hit over fifteen hundred times by shells and a large number of torpedoes, finally went down, Lindemann was seen standing at the bow, his hand in salute at the peak of his white-crowned cap. Only 115 men survived from her crew of 2221. The British officers who had to look on were full of admiration in their reports for the way in which the ship had fought: '*Bismarck* fought extremely bravely against a hugely superior force and went down with her flag flying.'[51]

On 8 December 1914 the British also paid tribute to the German crews for their fearless battle right up to the final minute. After the defeat of Spee's squadron, Vice Admiral Sturdee conveyed to Korvettenkapitän Pochhammer, senior surviving German officer, his best wishes in a hand-written telegram:

The C-in-C is very gratified that your life has been spared and we all feel that the *Gneisenau* fought in a most plucky manner to the end. He much admires the good gunnery of both ships, we sympathise with you on the loss of your admiral and so many officers and men. Unfortunately our two countries are at war. The officers of both navies who can count friends in the other have to carry out their country's duty, which your Admiral, Captain and Officers worthily maintained to the end.[52]

Later Sturdee, elevated to the peerage for his victory, even invited Pochhammer to dine in the wardroom of his flagship where the German was treated not as a prisoner of war, but like a gentleman in a prestigious London club.

For the Royal Navy, the sinking of the East Asia squadron eliminated the most dangerous opponent beyond the North Sea. The handful of German cruisers which had succeeded in eluding the British blood-hounds were tracked down during the course of the next few months and destroyed. The fate of *Dresden* and *Emden* has already been mentioned. At the beginning of November 1914 in the Central Atlantic the small cruiser *Karlsruhe* sank after a mysterious explosion in the forecastle. The small cruiser *Königsberg* held out the longest. Intended to conduct commerce warfare in the Indian Ocean, she was blockaded by British warships for almost ten months in the Rufiji Delta on the East African coast, then the colony of German East Africa, today Tanzania. Finally, in July 1915 she was blown up by her own crew.

At German naval command the conviction grew that, following the defeat at the Falklands, a quick counter-strike was necessary. This counter-strike should ideally be made before the two battlecruisers sent to South America to hunt for *Graf Spee* returned to the North Sea. After various plans had been gone over, Ingenohl, the fleet commander, decided on an attack against the English coastal towns of Scarborough, Whitby and Hartlepool. The navy had tried something similar at the beginning of November 1914 when Hipper's battlecruisers had attacked Yarmouth. Nothing had been achieved by it. The only outcome of the action – the first major sortie of the German fleet into British waters – was the loss of the cruiser *Yorck*, which sank whilst returning to Wilhelmshaven after hitting a German-laid mine.

This time things were to go better. The attack was set for 16 December 1914 and again Hipper was put in charge. The admiral, who would have preferred to engage the Grand Fleet, was sceptical whether the venture made any sense. In any case, he wrote in his diary, whatever losses might occur should not be 'fobbed off onto himself'; the fleet commander, whose plan this was, had to take full responsibility. True, the success of the operation would presumably 'cause a loud outcry in England', but a 'success' of that nature was 'not in harmony with the use of the ships'. If valuable warships were going to be risked, then it was better in battle against other dreadnoughts. 'Therefore,' Hipper demanded, 'if I do not come back and have lost valuable ships, do not throw stones at me, for I am only carrying out a mission I have been given.'[53]

As much as he hated the thought of losing one of his battlecruisers, he equally disliked the possibility that on such a sortie as this, which promised no particular gain, but which in his eyes was the result of pure reaction, he might run into a British minefield. 'To go down without a fight or glory would be a sad end to my career'.[54] He thought it much better if 'I fell commanding my cruisers in battle'.[55]

In the fleet, on the other hand, the planned action was received with great enthusiasm. Kapitänleutnant Reinhold Knobloch, who would be sailing aboard *Rostock* wrote: 'Today there was a happy mood everywhere ... all reconnaissance groups came out, the First Squadron and five flotillas anchored nearby. The place had come to life again ... Everywhere great rejoicing that finally we were going to do something. The ship was cleaned quickly and preparations made for battle, the guns were gone over again and the ammunition looked at.'[56] After four months of waiting around, like many others Knobloch could hardly wait to get out of harbour.

What the German battlecruiser fleet were not aware of when they weighed anchor on the night of 15 December was that the British knew that the Germans were coming to bombard the coast. At the end of August the Russians had salvaged the signal log of the small cruiser *Magdeburg* which had gone aground in the Baltic. The log was now in London. With the help of this register, a team of cryptanalysts, many of them mathematicians and physicists from the universities of Oxford and Cambridge, were able to decipher the encoded German radio traffic from then until the end of the war. This decryption team, known as 'Room 40' after the room in which they worked at the Admiralty building in London, later went on to found the Naval Signals Service at Bletchley Park, which in the Second World War succeeded in cracking the Enigma encoding machine.

When the German ships received their orders by radio for the 16
December sortie, the British code-breakers listened in. German Fleet
Command omitted the precise details, and so the British did not know
where the blows would fall. The Admiralty decided therefore to let the
German attack go ahead, since it could not be prevented, in the hope
that they could bring the perpetrators to book afterwards. Admiral
Jellicoe was ordered to position a strong force consisting of Vice Admiral
Beatty's battlecruisers, Commodore Goodenough's light cruisers and a
dreadnought squadron at a strategically favourable spot in the open
North Sea, in order to cut off the German ships on their return to
Wilhelmshaven. Commodore Tyrwhitt's Harwich Force and Com-
modore Keyes's submarines were also included.

It escaped the notice of Room 40 that not only Hipper with the
battlecruisers, but also the whole German High Seas Fleet would sail
under the command of Admiral Ingenohl. The latter was to cover
Hipper's back – and at almost the same place (180 miles northwest of
Heligoland and 100 miles southeast of Scarborough), there the British
would be waiting for the German battlecruisers. By a very slim margin
on that early morning of 16 December a clash of the two fleets was
missed, the Germans having a clear superiority. As soon as Ingenohl's
vanguard reported the presence of enemy ships, Ingenohl turned away
and headed for Wilhelmshaven. He did not want to risk battle without
the approval of the Kaiser.

There would never again be such a favourable opportunity for
the Germans to inflict at least very heavy damage and adjust the
balance of forces between the two fleets. Soon the scales tipped in
favour of the British, building ship after ship so as to concentrate
their forces wholly on the North Sea after eliminating the German
cruisers overseas.

Hipper, who knew nothing of Ingenohl's volte-face, had meanwhile
reached the English east coast and split up his forces there. The battlecruisers *Von der Tann* and *Derfflinger*, and the small cruiser *Kolberg*
bombarded Scarborough and Whitby; the battlecruisers *Seydlitz* and
Moltke, and the older armoured cruiser *Blücher*, all commanded by
Hipper, shelled Hartlepool. No military success of any significance was
achieved at any of the locations, since the destruction was confined
almost exclusively to dwelling houses. In the hail of German shells 122
men, women and children died and 443 were wounded. Almost worse
than the killing of civilians from the British point of view was the fact

that Hipper's ships escaped undetected to the German Bight. The Royal Navy trap failed to function.

'The dear Lord helped us,' wrote Hipper in his diary the same day.[57] In fact, it was a series of unforeseeable coincidences and misfortunes which prevented the British force, waiting in ambush, from bringing the German cruisers to battle. The most important of these was the sudden deterioration in the weather which hid Hipper's ships in mist, but there were also major misunderstandings in British communications from which tactical mistakes arose. Shortly before he would have intercepted Hipper's force steaming back to Wilhelmshaven, Beatty himself changed the course of his battlecruisers on the basis of wrongly interpreted radio reports and thus allowed the quarry to slip through the British line.

The damage to the image of the Royal Navy was considerable. The British public, which in previous weeks and months had already had to accept the sinking of the three old cruisers by *U-9* and Cradock's defeat at Coronel, was shocked: the Navy was apparently not in a position to protect the English coast against German attacks. 'Where was the Navy?' the headlines of the major newspapers asked reproachfully. That enraged British naval personnel. People simply would not see that the fleet could not be everywhere, perhaps fumed Roger Keyes, whose submarines had let Hipper's ship slip past. They should be glad to have its protection. 'Where would we be without it.'[58]

Beatty too was deeply depressed. He had rejoiced only recently over Sturdee's great victory at the Falklands and hoped that it would silence the press, according to which the Navy 'has been an expensive luxury and is not doing its job'.[59] And it was also he who argued persistently with Jellicoe that if he could not deploy the entire fleet more offensively, then at least he could the battlecruisers. Holding back the fleet, Beatty told him, was not only damaging for the prestige of the Navy, but would also cause a 'considerable loss of morale, which at this juncture is of the highest importance if an enemy force bombarded our coasts and arsenals' ordnance and we did not engage them at once'.[60]

Now, as Beatty had anticipated, exactly that eventuality had come to pass. Hipper's cruisers had got back to the German Bight without a scratch and the Royal Navy had 'missed a good chance of much honour and glory'.[61] No wonder therefore that he had sunk into a mood of deep gloom. 'Truly the past has been the blackest week of my life and I trust earnestly to have the opportunity in the very near future to obliterate it'.[62]

On the German side opinion was divided. While some were pleased that Hipper had outwitted the British and 'killed off around a thousand civilians', others saw in the action nothing more than 'weak revenge for our cruiser squadron'.[63] When he read the newspaper reports of the damage inflicted, the initially sceptical Hipper opined, 'In short, we can be satisfied'.[64] The fact that one year later he received, from the commander of the fleet, 'a very warmly expressed good luck telegram to the cruisers on today's first anniversary', underlines how much naval command set great store in interpreting 16 December 1914 as a success.[65]

By its strategically senseless action the German navy had achieved one thing at least: all England burned with hate and ire against the 'baby murderers' (Winston Churchill). The British newspapers saw in the bombardment of undefended coastal towns a breach of the Hague Convention and 'an infamous crime against humanity and against international law'.[66] In the eyes of many British people, the Imperial Navy had confirmed the rumours circulating for some time about alleged atrocities by German soldiers in Belgium and France.

For 22-year-old Lieutenant James Colvill, the raid by the battlecruisers stood on a par with the barbaric butchery inflicted by the Kaiser's troops in taking the Belgian town of Louvain which he had read about in the English newspapers: 'May we have a chance of paying them back their own coin to the last pfennig, but not by slaughtering non-combatants, when we get into Germany. I would like to see a dozen German towns – beginning with Essen and finishing with Berlin – burned to the ground and utterly sacked, in one word – "Louvained".'[67]

Even if most of the atrocity stories appearing in the English tabloid press were fabrications, historians have established beyond doubt since then that some excesses were committed by German troops against the civilian population in the occupied parts of Belgium and France. These incidents were seized upon by British propaganda and repeated, often as grotesque exaggerations. Thus Kapitän zur See Adolf von Trotha, commander of the battleship *Kaiser*, could hardly credit what he read in British newspapers about the alleged crimes of German soldiers, represented therein as 'the most vulgar, deceitful, underhand and cruel beasts':

Officers and soldiers who slaughtered children, drank and gorged themselves like pigs on the food stocks of the families upon whom they were billeted and then, whip in hand, forced them to burn down their houses; troops who knelt before the British cavalry in surrender and then when the magnanimous British rode past them, shot them down from behind; trenches, in which our people raised their rifles en masse as a token of surrender, and then men in other trenches shot down the British as they approached to accept it, etc, etc. What lengths these people have to go to in order to make the war popular and what a dreadful harvest must follow from it.[68]

More than anything else, these horrific reports of German soldiers as rapists, arsonists and child murderers contributed to the Germans being pictured in the British mind as 'evil Huns' far beyond the parameters of war. Lieutenant Colvill's antipathy for the Germans even extended to something he caught: 'I've got Hun measles – damn 'em.'[69]

On the other side of the North Sea, German propaganda threw everything into the effort to hammer home that Great Britain, 'perfidious Albion', was the principal instigator of the war and 'the root of all evil'. The slogan 'Gott strafe England' (God punish England) decorated postcards, cigarette packs, coffee cups and handkerchiefs. Ernst Lissauer's 'Song of Hate against England' became the most popular lyric of the First World War, German professors churned out anti-British pamphlets, and the war press office never tired of pointing out in countless brochures that 'the war is a battle of Anglo-Saxon capital against the German people'.[70]

This economic argument proved especially successful. Kapitänleutnant Knobloch, as did many of his compatriots, took the view that the British above all 'had gigantic prestige and weight in the world ... thanks to their money bags', while Germany on the other hand 'was only applauded unwillingly', and had to 'fight laboriously with blood and iron' for its own prestige.[71] For Kapitän zur See Walter von Keyserlingk, commander of the battleship Lothringen, it was therefore 'a marvellous feeling for us Germans that our airships and U-boats are weapons to which the enemy has no answer. In their boundless arrogance over the decades, the British have lost the yardstick by which other nations create and put their findings into effect. It benefits us, may it ever be so!'[72]

Those who believed in the atrocities accepted the reproach of brutality with a shrug, so great was the urge to inflict hurt on the British, and at the same time improve the balance of successes. There was little room for scruples, and probably only a few had a bad conscience when, two weeks or so after the attacks on Scarborough and Whitby, *U-24* torpedoed the old battleship *Formidable* and sent her to the bottom with five hundred of her crew.

With this 'strike', 1914 drew to its close without the British fleet having had the opportunity to wipe out the ignominy to which Hipper's battlecruisers had subjected it. The British did not have too long to wait for revenge, however; in the first month of 1915 there occurred the first 'pure' clash of the respective belligerents, so narrowly avoided twice before. In August 1914 it had been low tide in the Jade which had prevented Hipper from joining in the battle of Heligoland Bight, and in December Beatty's unfortunate change of heading allowed Hipper to elude him. This time it all went differently.

For some time German naval command, unaware of the activities of Room 40, had suspected that their operational plans were being betrayed to the British. There were tips about spies and traitors, but the shadow of suspicion also fell on some of the numerous fishing vessels which flew a neutral flag in the Dogger Bank area. In order to establish whether some of these trawlers were also spying for Britain, and incidentally to attack the light British forces which had been sighted there, on 23 January 1915 Konteradmiral Hipper sortied towards the Dogger Bank with the battlecruisers *Seydlitz*, *Moltke*, *Derfflinger* and the older armoured *Scharnhorst*-class cruiser *Blücher*. In support were the small cruisers *Stralsund*, *Graudenz*, *Kolberg* and *Rostock* and twenty torpedo boats.

The British had decrypted the German wireless traffic and were therefore informed of all details pertaining to the planned action. This gave the Royal Navy the unique opportunity to knock out the most modern, and for them the most dangerous, sector of the German fleet at a stroke, so to speak.

The trap into which Hipper would sail was almost perfect: the combined forces of Beatty's battlecruisers and Tyrwhitt's Harwich Force awaited the Germans on the Dogger Bank. Keyes's submarines and a force of older battleships would cut off their retreat. In the background was Jellicoe with the Grand Fleet ready to intervene should the High Seas Fleet sail, contrary to the decrypted German wireless signals (and which did not occur).

When Hipper arrived at the Dogger Bank on the early morning of 24 January 1915, his small cruisers reconnoitring ahead reported the presence of enemy warships. The admiral, realising immediately that this could be no coincidence, turned his force about immediately and headed for home. But this time it was too late and the trap snapped shut.

The battlecruisers *Lion*, *Tiger*, *Princess Royal*, *New Zealand* and *Indomitable* were soon hot on the heels of the battlecruiser squadron, which was held back at the top speed of the slower *Blücher*. Slowly but surely, the British began to catch up and as soon as the range between Beatty's flagship *Lion* and the *Blücher* was down to about twelve miles (20km), she opened fire at about 0900 hrs that morning. Because the range of her 13.4in (34cm) guns exceeded that of the *Blücher*'s main armament of 8.2in, *Lion* needed fear no hits from return fire. Accuracy at such a great range was poor, however, and in order to reduce the range, Beatty urged his stokers to ever greater efforts. An observer aboard *Indomitable* described the dramatic scenes in the battlecruiser's engine room:

Anyone brought up in the oil fuel age can have no idea of the physical effort required of the stokers of a coal-fired ship steaming at high speed. With the fans supplying air to the boilers whirring at full speed the furnaces devoured coal just about as fast as a man could feed them. Black, begrimed and sweating men working in the bunkers in the ship's side dug the coal out and loaded it into skids which were then dragged along the steel deck and emptied on to the floorplates in front of each boiler in turn. No hygienic or sterilised suits for these men. If the ship rolled or pitched there was always a risk that a loaded skid might take charge with resultant danger to life and limb. Looking down from the iron catwalk above, the scene had all the appearance of one from Dante's inferno. 'For flames I saw and wailings smote my ears'. Watching the pressure gauges for any fall in the steam pressure, the Chief Stoker walked to and fro encouraging his men. Now and then the telegraph from the engine room would clang and the finger on the dial move around to the section marked 'MORE STEAM'. The Chief would then press the reply gong with an oath. 'What do the bastards think we're doing,' he would exclaim, 'Come on boys, shake it up, get going', and the sweating men would redouble their efforts, throw open the furnace doors and shovel still more coal into the blazing inferno.[73]

Shortly after nine o'clock *Blücher* was hit for the first time. The Germans now returned fire. As per the battle plan, each ship selected its own opposite number. The closer the two lines approached, the more shells found their target. A British shell which hit the rear turret of Hipper's flagship *Seydlitz* killed 165 men in a fraction of a second. The British battlecruisers were also not spared: Beatty's *Lion* in particular being hit repeatedly and seriously damaged.

Nevertheless, the pursuers were in the more favourable position. It was just a question of time until *Blücher*, which had taken hit after hit and had fallen astern of the battlecruisers, would be overwhelmed. Then there would be five British battlecruisers and three German, and only a miracle would save Hipper. Before it came to that, however, Beatty committed a fatal error. Suddenly fearing that he was about to be attacked by U-boats (which was not the case), he hoisted a signal ordering his ships to turn away and leave the danger area. When he recognised his mistake a few minutes later and hoisted another signal to renew the attack, a confusing combination of flags was misinterpreted by his ships as meaning that all should concentrate their attack on *Blücher* instead of chasing the German battlecruisers.

That saved Hipper. He thought briefly about turning back to aid *Blücher*, but then decided to keep going. The luckless armoured cruiser was overwhelmed by the British battlecruisers. Over a period of three hours in which she received enemy fire, she was hit by seventy shells and seven torpedoes. 'It is a terrible thing to be forced to look on as a ship like that was knocked out by such a huge enemy force',[74] wrote Kapitänleutnant Knobloch, who watched part of the action from the bridge of *Rostock*. It is hardly necessary to add that *Blücher* returned fire to the last and never struck her flag.

When she finally heeled over and sank keel upwards, the survivors tried desperately to save themselves. The photo of the capsizing *Blücher* with her sailors scrambling over her slippery hull became one of the best-known of the First World War. For most of them there was no hope: of her crew of about 1030 men, only around 250 lived to tell the tale. Three other German ships – *Seydlitz*, *Derfflinger* and *Kolberg* – were seriously damaged. The British casualties were comparatively moderate: two battlecruisers, *Tiger* and *Lion* were damaged, fifteen men fell in action and eighty were wounded.

The battle of the Dogger Bank left both sides with mixed feelings. Even if it had not ended with the total destruction of the enemy force, which so many Britons yearned for, the British public was satisfied. The newspapers published the photograph of the sinking *Blücher* and wrote:

'It will be some time before they go baby-killing again!'[75] Even in the
Royal Navy opinion was divided. Vice Admiral Beatty would have given
anything for a complete annihilation of the enemy force, and the fact
that he failed filled him with despair: 'The disappointment of that day
is more than I can bear to think of. Everybody thinks it was a great
success when in reality it was a terrible failure. I had made up my mind
that we were going to get four, the lot, and four we ought to have got.'[76]

The thoroughly favourable press reaction after the battle failed to
console him or others. Stephen King-Hall, a 22-year-old lieutenant
aboard the light cruiser *Southampton*, hoped all the same that the
criticism, in his eyes unjustified, of the fleet would now stop. 'Perhaps
we shan't hear quite so much of this beastly "Where's the Navy?" after
the 24th. It makes me so wild, we might be having the time of our lives
on the Riviera from what some people say and write.'[77]

On the other side of the North Sea there was another picture. The
reaction of the German press was less positive on account of the high
death toll. In the fleet, however, there was rejoicing that despite their
superiority in numbers the British had been given a hiding (it was at first
reported erroneously that the heavily damaged *Tiger* had sunk). Thus,
although he was not happy with Hipper's handling of the battle, since
he thought that it would have been better if the admiral had simply 'gone
for them', Kapitänleutnant Schweinitz wrote: 'Nevertheless everybody is
pleased with the sortie and that finally we returned fire with great
vigour! Self-confidence and optimism have been won back.'[78]
Oberleutnant Heinrich Stenzler, on board Hipper's flagship for the
battle, wrote to his mother: 'It is a great encouragement. The men come
back from ashore beaming. In the streets they are saying, "Look, there's
one from the *Seydlitz*!" Then the boy naturally snaps to attention.'[79]

Hipper, whose decision to take along the slow *Blücher* attracted much
criticism later, was annoyed at the bad press. He had, so he believed,
'done the best I could, acted to the best of my ability and knowledge, and
from the evil situation into which I was thrust through the fault of the
fleet (which failed to put to sea in support of me), did all I possibly
could.'[80] The admiral could console himself that from all sides he
received confirmation that his leadership in battle had been 'not only
sound, but ... splendid.' His Bavarian home town of Weilheim even
decided to name a street after him.[81]

Eventually 24 January 1915 became a very special day in the calendar
of the German navy, celebrated annually from then on. This is not as

surprising as it might at first seem. For although it was not a naval victory, it occurred against the background of a history not rich in glorious feats of arms and belonged quite obviously within a tradition under construction – always under the condition that men had died with honour. The crew of *Blücher* had done just that. Kaiser Wilhelm II saw it in that light. Ten days after the battle, for the first time in the war, he travelled to Wilhelmshaven in order to express personally his recognition for what had been achieved to date.

In his speech to the officers and men, the Kaiser left no doubt that the crew of *Blücher* had acted correctly and honourably by not striking the flag and by defending the totally stricken wreck to the last second.

> It is not important that we have victory every time: it is important that your deeds show your *spirit*. And this spirit, this death-defying, joyful attitude at the moment when the ship goes down, it is that which has won the greatest respect from the enemy and all nations of the world. For that I express my thanks to you. Our task now as before remains, when and where possible, to do harm to the enemy. And if your own ship goes down, he must go down *with it*.

For the Kaiser, the battle of the Dogger Bank stood on a par with Coronel and the Falklands. All this evidence of German heroism, the Kaiser promised, 'will remain on the roll of honour of my people for ever'.[82]

Despite that, his same rule applied – all the more so after the sinking of the *Blücher* – 'that the High Seas Fleet remains an intact political instrument in the hand of the supreme commander'.[83] Risky operations would therefore continue to be avoided. It took about three years to replace a lost ship with a new one. Therefore at the beginning of February 1915 when Admiral Hugo von Pohl replaced the luckless Admiral Ingenohl as commander of the fleet, the German strategy of holding the fleet back in reserve was maintained. In 1915 the High Seas Fleet made seven short sorties, none of them further than 120 nautical miles from Heligoland: 'These sorties had neither strategic effects nor contact with the enemy'.[84] The Germans now placed their expectations for the first time in the U-boat war instead of the capital ships.

For the Royal Navy, as before, it was still more important to avoid a defeat than gain a victory, and it withdrew for the first time into the North Sea. This now became rather like the area between the respective front line trenches on the western front, a kind of no-man's-land into which it was better not to venture. Admiral Jellicoe, Paul Halpern wrote, had not the least desire 'to put his head in the German noose'.[85] In the search for other fields of activity, the Royal Navy now turned its attentions to the eastern Mediterranean. In February 1915 a major offensive began there to conquer the Dardanelles. After an unsuccessful Anglo-French naval attack, Allied troops landed at Gallipoli, but in bitter fighting failed to breach the Turkish defensive front. After heavy losses, the operation, which cost Winston Churchill his post as First Lord of the Admiralty, was finally abandoned at the end of 1915.

The battle of the Dogger Bank brought to a close the comparatively active first phase of the naval war between Germany and Great Britain, after almost six months. The next encounter between the two fleets would not occur for another sixteen months. Until then, the officers and men aboard the 'fat' ships could do only one thing: 'And we keep waiting, waiting, waiting until our hour also comes.'[86]

4

'I feel guilty that our people are having it so good'
Life on Board and Ashore

PERHAPS THE GREATEST SURPRISE for naval people on both sides of the
North Sea was that, despite the war, daily life aboard ship hardly
changed. While soldiers at the front had to accustom themselves to
completely new and often awful and life-threatening conditions, in the
fleet everything carried on as normal. What may seem initially to have
been a great advantage presented commanders and officers, responsible
for maintaining their ships in a constant state of operational readiness,
with quite new challenges. In the long run, the all-too peaceful
atmosphere, as Kapitänleutnant Reinhold Knobloch observed, 'spread a
general insouciance' throughout the fleet.[1] Hermann von Schweinitz
confirmed this impression: 'A total indifference seized hold of the crews
regarding the war situation'.[2]

From the point of view of the officers it thus became all the more
important to keep under daily scrutiny the complex procedures of ship
and weapons handling. In battle, in order to shoot faster and manoeuvre
better than the enemy there had to be perfect interplay between man
and technology. That could only be achieved with drill and discipline.
The service schedule aboard was regulated down to the finest detail and
ran with clockwork precision. The first officer handled the daily
business. The commander had supreme power of command aboard and
his position was not unlike that of a reigning sovereign, remaining
mostly above routine events.

For the execution of his numerous duties, the first officer relied on the
support of the other officers, each with his own sphere of responsibility.
The most important of these were the navigation officer, the watch and
divisions officers, the radio officer and the signals officer. On a battleship
such as *Helgoland*, twenty naval officers commanded a crew of around
1100 men. The officer corps also included the naval engineers responsible for the running, maintenance and care of the ship's machinery.
As was the case with all other leadership groups aboard, they were
subordinate to seaman branch naval officers in the hierarchy. These

other groups included the officers of the naval infantry, medical, ordnance, quartermaster (QM) and torpedo branch, then the deck officers and petty officers. Deck officers (chief petty officers) were ranked between seaman branch officers and NCOs and were frequently men who had risen through the ranks, and covered important functions such as coxswain, boatswain, armourer or worked in the engine rooms.

The crew was divided into seaman branch, whose duties were to assist in the general running of the ship and serve the guns, and engine-room personnel, the stokers. Seamen and stokers were split up into several divisions, each headed by an officer, the number of divisions depending on the size of the ship. Generally, there would be four seaman branch divisions, since in battle the divisions would man the gun turrets, and three engine-room divisions.

The service schedule aboard German ships closely followed the British example and consisted basically of two areas: division service, to which belonged, amongst other things, instruction in seamanship, battle duties, running the ship, the duties of the coxswain, and sport in the form of swimming and gymnastics; and housekeeping and labour, which included all cleaning work and ship maintenance. The Saturday roster was *Großes Reinschiff* (All hands clean ship) instead of the daily cleaning, and on Sundays the ship's company fell in for inspection by the commander followed by divine service. Sunday afternoon was free.

There were few differences from the pre-war routine. 'Service is the same as in peacetime,' Matrose Richard Stumpf of the *Helgoland* thought. 'Mornings, clean ship, parade, battle drill. Afternoons clean guns, labour or make and mend.'[3] Additionally, there were the so-called 'Rollen exercises'. A *Rolle* was a kind of detailed contingency plan for a specific scenario. Most important was the 'Clear ship for action' *Rolle*, in which every man learned his battle position. Service regulations prescribed that each *Rolle* had to be practised regularly by the entire ship's company.

During the war, what was thoroughly sensible and necessary frequently deteriorated into an end in itself, as Stumpf reports:

The previous Friday the *Rolle* officer simply had no idea how he could keep the men occupied all day. Clean the ship? Not possible, we are out of soap. Clean the guns? That has been reduced to only twice a week because we have to go very sparingly with cotton waste, emery, oil and the like. So this time it was the stopgap again, devised for such cases, *Rolle* exercises. The trick of the whole thing is very simple. For example, the firefighting or 'Shut hatches' ordinance is given a minor change and then a big thing made of it and then we do the new exercise for three to eight afternoons one after another, then something else will be changed and so on. This is how they kill time here.[4]

Another important element of everyday routine was watch duty. Comprehensive security precautions and unfailing watchfulness were essential aboard a warship. The crew would be divided into several groups (as a rule usually identical with the divisions) which relieved each other regularly. At sea, the watches usually changed every four hours; in port it was possible to stand twelve- or even twenty-four-hour watches. This system could be suspended at any time if danger threatened and then 'war watch' would be ordered, in which the crew would be divided into two halves, rotating every four hours. One half would remain at battle stations ready to defend against enemy attack, while the other half 'rested', still having to hold themselves at constant readiness. Under these circumstances it would be almost impossible to get any sleep.

Especially trying was watch-keeping in the early phases of the war, when on either side of the North Sea an enemy attack had to be reckoned with every day and the ships' anchorages were not yet fully proof against submarine attacks. A British officer wrote that he would walk up and down constantly while on watch in order to avoid falling asleep – without success: 'I would never have thought it possible to fall asleep walking, but it really is.'[5] Others roped themselves to the railings so as not to fall down in exhaustion. Kapitänleutnant Reinhold Knobloch considered it 'unspeakable stupidity to spend eight hours every day dozing in the grey waters of the Jade', and complained: 'From this eternal watch-keeping day and night one notices how nerves and health gradually suffer.'[6]

A welcome change from the daily monotony were the fleet navigation and gunnery exercises which took place regularly 'to perfect battle readiness' (as the chief of the fleet stated in his order of the day for 14 August 1914). Additionally, this offered the opportunity to get out into the relatively well-protected German Bight and turn one's back for a few days on unloved *Schlicktown* (Wilhemshaven-on-Mud). The Royal Navy carried out its exercises mostly in the Pentland Firth, the narrows between the Scottish mainland and the Orkneys.

Rapidity and precision in loading, aiming and firing the guns were practised intensively, as was steaming in formation and in changing formations, the so-called 'evolutioning'. Exercises of this kind had belonged to the standard repertoire of the fleets for many years. Despite that, even the hundredth repetition of a specific turning manoeuvre seemed more sensible than the unavoidable alternative: lying inactive in harbour. Admiral Hipper thought the same, to his own surprise. 'Remarkable, this evolutioning, of which in peacetime one got sick and tired, but was now great fun. One's pretensions had become rather modest.'[7]

So rare were the occasions when the fleet left the protected sea area in order to sortie into the open North Sea that they were greeted with nothing short of rejoicing. Even if one knew that in most cases, as Kapitän zur See Adolf von Trotha said smugly, it was only being done 'just to bring the nags out of the stable.'[8] Despite that, Kapitänleutnant Schweinitz, who at the beginning of 1915 had received his longed-for posting aboard ship as navigation officer of the small cruiser *Rostock*, showed great enthusiasm upon returning with his new ship from a anti-contraband patrol of merchant shipping in the Skagen. 'Even if we have nothing to report, it was a glorious voyage, and with the navigation I enjoyed myself immensely. The feeling of being set free is so satisfying that there is a quite different mood aboard. We have a mission to carry out, we have a good ship beneath our feet, and we know that we are holding the fort. What more could one want?'[9]

All the same, danger always threatened at sea, whether from mines, submarines or the sudden appearance of enemy warships, and watchfulness could never be relaxed for a second. Additionally, there was often heavy weather, for which the North Sea is notorious. Even smaller ships and boats, which found the forces of nature less challenging than did the powerful dreadnoughts, suffered considerably in conditions of rain, storm, and seas as high as a house. The British destroyer commander, Lennon Goldsmith, described in a letter to his father the dour struggle endured by his unit at sea:

We are having a terrific time and of course the commanders stand most of the anxiety and strain – and the frequent changes in command in this flotilla must just show how men do crumple up before Nature in her sterner moods! Yesterday was typical. I was on the bridge practically all the time from 3am till 10pm being blown, rained and sprayed upon by one of these almost perpetual hurricanes: arrived in stiff and aching, and utterly worn out.[10]

No thought could be given to eating, washing or sleeping when a ship or boat was heeling to forty degrees either side and one had to block up one's ears because the howling of the wind was so intolerably loud. Not to mention that all rooms would be awash with water, and the men would often go for days with not a stitch of dry clothing.

As soon as a ship got back into port, the first task was to re-coal in order to be operational again as soon as possible. This was uncommonly hard and filthy work, for although at least the newest British battleships were oil-fired, during the First World War the German fleet heated its boilers almost exclusively with coal. A battleship such as *Helgoland* consumed several hundred tons daily at normal speed, and she had bunkers for 3200 tons. Enormous quantities had to be moved to fill these bunkers. The men often worked until they were completely exhausted. In order to make the drudgery more tolerable, many commanders arranged for the shipboard band to play to them and ensured that seamen and stokers had an especially good meal after finishing their work.

Aboard *Gneisenau* they even had fancy dress. 'Clothing no longer serviceable would then appear and one would dress up theatrically. We had great fun. An old frock coat would be produced or a gala uniform from the last launch of a battleship. A cap without a peak, and an artistically fashioned stand-up collar or medal ribbon at the breast completed the costume. The comedians would usually doll themselves up causing great frivolity until the time came to quickly strip off their outfits and join in the general toil.'[11]

The longer the war went on, the more sparing the navy had to be with the expensive combustible. In addition, the ships had constant problems with their engines, which had to be overhauled regularly. Therefore it became rarer for the ships to leave port for navigation and gunnery exercises or to make sorties into the open North Sea. In July 1915 Admiral Pohl, commander of the fleet, wrote about this predicament to his wife:

I wanted to make a sortie today to get the ships moving again and if possible attack the enemy: four ships were reported non-operational for engine defects ... it makes one despair that so many ships always require repair and I am prevented from carrying out my intentions. I simply have to get out as soon as I can. It is a quite appalling situation, I would really like to achieve something and cannot. All the officers on land have successes, now Hindenburg and Gallwitz again, while here I sit and can do nothing, and moreover have to console my people by saying that our time will come soon.[12]

Only a few naval men were as busy during the frequent lay-ups of their ships as Vizeadmiral Souchon, who complained to his wife: 'We must always have war, war, war. But I would also like a bit more time for myself in order to do other things.'[13] For most officers and men there was plenty of time 'to do other things'. To use this time sensibly was not always easy, and not everybody could enjoy it. Reading was undoubtedly one of the main ways to occupy oneself onboard ship. Hipper's Chief of Staff Erich Raeder used his leisure hours 'reading systematically through Schiller's works'.[14] Many ships even had their own libraries, while records and films were available to entertain crew members. The *Helgoland*, for example, had a cinematograph aboard from late 1915. Whereas the films came initially from abroad, France, Italy, Denmark or the United States, the new official photo and film office (Bufa) soon obtained suitable local productions. Rather more focused than the Germans, who learned quickly in this respect, however, the British used the medium of film as an instrument of propaganda and showed the ships' companies relevant productions such as *Britain Prepared* or *The Battle of the Somme*. The pictures of cruel static warfare in the trenches of Flanders or France impressed many naval men much more deeply than their own very limited war experiences.

The centre of the officers' social life aboard was the wardroom. There they ate and drank, celebrated, discussed and played. Besides billiards and table-tennis, chess, bridge, halma and backgammon enjoyed great popularity; on the German side, draughts, backgammon and the popular card game, skat. 'The dreadful card game ombre has happily died out.'[15] While the German officers were happier to remain in their own wardroom community, the British liked to have their counterparts visit from other ships. That might involve a round of visits lasting all day, as Commander Edward Roynon-Jones, 35-year-old navigation officer of the battlecruiser *Tiger*, conceded: 'First I visited *Princess Royal*, then had lunch in *Lion*, & afterwards tea in *New Zealand*. Bridge after dinner.'[16]

The atmosphere in the British wardrooms – larger ships even had separate smoking rooms – was more like that of an exclusive London club than a warship. 'We sat comfortably around the fireplace with coffee and cigars and talked about our experiences and questions of the day'. At dinner the shipboard orchestra would usually play.[17] Konter-admiral Hipper's flagship *Seydlitz* also had this pleasant custom. For Hipper, the music of the staff orchestra was the 'best thing I can find aboard for relaxation'. His favourite composer was Wagner. If he had to leave the ship for a while, it was his main worry that his deputy (who in Hipper's opinion had no feel for music) would 'louse up' the orchestra.[18]

A rather remarkable feeling stole over Lieutenant Stephen King-Hall from time to time in the face of so much comfort.

> I could not help thinking this evening of the extraordinary contrast in modern war, and perhaps more particularly in modern naval war. What made me do so were the thoughts which entered my head as I looked round the mess half an hour ago. We had just finished dinner and we were at sea. Without boasting of anything luxurious, I could not help thinking how comfortable it all looked. Tulips on the table, nice white table cloth, a dozen or more officers smoking, drinking their port and coffee, the whole well lit up with electric lights shaded in yellow silk. And yet with all this comfort we were out on business, thank goodness.[19]

Neither in the British or German navies did petty officers and NCOs have access to the comforts of the seaman branch officers. The ratings had canteens.

Anyone who preferred to spend time away from his peers would struggle to find a quiet refuge onboard, and this was even more the case the lower he was in the military hierarchy. While the commander of a capital ship had about a quarter of the living space set aside for himself – aboard *Derfflinger*, apart from a spacious suite with bathroom, he had a large study and a saloon 'large enough to seat about forty persons at table in comfort',[20] the rest of the thousand-man crew had to make do with something much more modest. NCOs and men ate and slept in large rooms in the forecastle. At night the hammocks were slung so close together that it was not possible to speak of one's private space. The air was unventilated and unhealthy, and in summer the heat and humidity below deck were almost intolerable. Tuberculosis was widespread amongst naval personnel. It was even worse on minesweepers, destroyers and U-boats than capital ships. An almost claustrophobic narrowness prevailed in U-boats. Kapitänleutnant Weddigen's *U-9*, for example, had a diameter of 3.65m (12ft). Hundreds of regulating arms, valves, levers and switches reduced freedom of movement considerably. The general consensus, however, was that the worst thing of all was the smell: mist from the diesels mixed with the smell of battery acid and mouldy seawater which splashed in every time the access hatch opened inwards. Added to this was the vomit of the seasick, and the remains of food and faecal matter, which often enough was sprayed into the interior of the boat during attempts to pump it out of the makeshift toilets by means of a complicated mechanism – 'getting your own back' as British submariners called it. When Weddigen's first watch-keeping officer Kapitänleutnant Johannes Spiess, saw the WC on *U-9* for the first time he understood immediately 'why my predecessor recommended taking opium on longer voyages'.[21]

For air purification, potash cartridges had only a limited effect. If the boat remained submerged for some time, oxygen would deplete to the extent that a burning match would go out. 'After fifteen hours it began to get uncomfortable. Breathing became difficult and fatigue would set in. One would become careless and have to call upon all one's reserves of energy to remain awake and alert.'[22]

Because fresh water was very limited the men often washed once a week or less – a change of clothing was out of the question. It was therefore no wonder that a British submarine officer returning to port after a fourteen-day patrol described a hot bath as the 'greatest pleasure of my life'. 'To lie in a hot bath black from exhaust gases, covered in grease, ill at ease and exhausted and fill the tub again and again with fresh hot water until all the muck and tiredness had streamed out of one – that was only one step away from heaven.'[23]

On many boats only the commander had his own bunk: everyone else shared one sleeping place in rotation with two or three others. Because condensation dripped incessantly from the naked steel hull of the boat, the hands would cover themselves with rainwear or rubber-coated sea charts while they slept. The bunk for the *U-9* watch-keeping officers was so small that Spiess had to adopt the foetal position. While the officers aboard capital ships had an orchestra play to them at dinner, on a U-boat dirt-smeared ratings would pass constantly through the 'wardroom', which was no more than a folding table in the middle of the pressure hull.

On a U-boat there was simply no place or time for many formalities, and there was not a rigid hierarchy comparable to that on a large ship. The stress endured in common welded officers and men closer together as they never could aboard a dreadnought. 'On *U-62* we were like a family and the boat was our mother,' wrote the boat's commander Kapitänleutnant Ernst Hashagen after the war. 'When I looked into the faces of my men, I felt strong and secure. They fought for me and I for them.'[24]

Such ideas were remote from the thinking of most battleship officers. They saw seamen and stokers as subordinates and the recipients of orders, existing so far beneath them in the military and social pecking order that there was practically no point of contact. Particularly in the German fleet this chasm between 'above' and 'below' would become a serious problem. In the Royal Navy, on the other hand, it was recognised better and earlier how important a common bond between the ranks was for morale and a readiness to pull one's weight, even though the bond might only be loosely tied. It was an advantage that however great the differences otherwise, officers and men in Britain shared at least one passion in common, namely for games and sport.

Sport was an integral component of British education and culture, the motto 'Play the Game' almost characterising the Victorian era. It had been absorbed so deeply into the British character that some of them saw war as a continuation of the sporting game by other means. 'For war by any other name is just another British game' was a line from a popular patriotic song.[25] It was not by coincidence that whole football teams volunteered for the front en masse. 'In Britain,' a Russian officer seconded to the Grand Fleet considered, 'they take the turf, theatre, football and boxing as seriously as they do war.' The fleet, he wrote later, was in this respect 'a typical representative of the country'.[26]

At Scapa Flow there were regular rowing regattas, boxing tournaments and other competitive sporting events. The officers liked deck-hockey, table tennis and badminton best; Admiral Jellicoe trained with a medicine ball: 'I've already sprained a finger and a knee, but it keeps you as fit as possible'.[27] On the small island of Flotta there was even an eighteen-hole golf course, which soon became a major attraction. 'Every afternoon, weather and circumstances permitting, crowds of officers, from Sir John Jellicoe to the latest joined snotty lined up in the queue at the first tee'.[28]

Ratings also spent a great deal of their free time on Flotta, boxing, playing rugby or football. 'The government,' the Russian officer went on, 'had leased a section of the island of Flotta and laid out football fields for the men and a tea house, later replaced by a canteen set up by the YMCA. If the weather was fine, football teams from various ships would play each other, in bad weather they would work to improve the facility.'[29] Just like at home, there were leagues and an annual championship in which the winners received prizes in money and gifts. The attraction of these sporting events was enormous. The final of the Grand Fleet boxing championship had no less than ten thousand spectators.

While the British fleet used every free minute for sporting activities, the German effort in this respect was fairly modest. Not until the late summer of 1915 did they begin to organise similar competitions on German warships, and apparently rather reluctantly. 'Now we're going to have sporting events, I have to arrange them. There is damned little interest in such puerile rubbish,' Kapitänleutnant Knobloch noted in his diary.[30] Matrose (Ordinary Seaman) Richard Stumpf summarised a sports day aboard the *Helgoland* in autumn 1916: 'There were many prizes on offer, despite that the interest and participation was pitiful.'[31]

The reason can be found in the *Compendium of the Duties Suitable to the Station and Calling of the German Officer*. It says there that the primary purpose of sport is to 'accustom the body to tolerate great effort', in order that it should be 'capable of harsh and enduring mental and physical strain.'[32] In other words, the Germans had simply not come so far that they could see how sport could provide games for fun and pleasure. For them sport was, as propagated by the nineteenth-century gymnastics movement, primarily a means for bodily training and hardening. Their approach to the subject was therefore dull and unimaginative. Drill and discipline was constantly in the foreground, also ashore, where physical hardening was mainly down to cross-country runs and on the parade ground. 'Then for a break,' Stumpf thundered, 'they offer us a diversion by getting us to run up and down for a bit in closed ranks on the pier. Or make us lie down on the mud on the parade ground. I am certainly not against corporal training, it may even be very healthy if done for some reasonable purpose. Our comrades over there also probably lie down in the mud in hail and storm but at least they know why. We do not!!'[33]

The love of games and staging events, in which the British were streets ahead of the Germans, and particularly in dreary Scapa Flow where there was little else to entertain the mind, led to officers and men meeting for concert parties. With much attention to detail they worked on sketches, pantomimes, revues, theatrical pieces and concerts. The ship's company of HMS *Warspite* once even staged a complete opera, of which it was said: 'It was the best show that has ever been given by any ship'.[34] The style and tone of the presentations leaned heavily on the very popular music-hall culture of the time, in which, through a mixture of cabaret and music, all possible political themes of politics and society were covered and social grievances given a satirical airing.

Initially, performances were held exclusively on board individual ships, sometimes on stages built expressly for the purpose, but in the autumn of 1915, in response to great demand, the supply ship *Gourkho* was converted into a floating theatre with several hundred seats. All ships based at Scapa Flow could book dates for their performances there. Also held on the *Gourkho* were church services, cinema releases and boxing tournaments. The steamer had not only a large stage and curtain, but also a substantial collection of backdrops, costumes and musical instruments. Often visitors were given a printed programme of the various presentations. Interest was extraordinary and the ship was often booked up for weeks ahead. Admiral Jellicoe had his own seat in the front row. An officer reported on a pantomime attended by no less than eight hundred officers, including many commanders and admirals. This was then followed up by a special performance for other ranks: 'This was even a better audience to play the ass to, as their laughter is spontaneous and unrestrained. Of course they laughed where the officers didn't and vice versa.'[35]

How important this form of occupational therapy was considered to be for the crews of the Grand Fleet stationed in the remoteness of the Orkney Islands was highlighted in the spring of 1916 when it was decided to transfer the theatre-ship from Scapa Flow to the Mediterranean. Admiral Jellicoe protested vehemently against this plan. In a long letter to the Second Sea Lord, Admiral Sir Frederick Hamilton, the commander of the British fleet recounted all the advantages which the floating stage offered his men. He argued:

It may seem a small thing but I assure you that I have had much anxiety on the subject of keeping the men contented and in good spirits and the *Gourkho* is a valuable asset in this direction. Take her away and I prophesy many evils: gambling, immorality, cases of striking, etc, etc. You know better than most people how easy it is to go from a happy fleet to a bored and discontented fleet.[36]

Jellicoe understood that it was necessary to give officers and men the opportunity to create for themselves in their free time a kind of alternative world away from the dreariness of war routine. Perhaps he was even aware of what historians since then have established by numerous examples: that it was also important in setting up this alternative world that men should be reminded of the normal life from which war had separated them. With its institutions of sport, music and theatre, the Grand Fleet had introduced a piece of home into the monotony of Scapa Flow.

The German fleet, on the other hand, had no football tournaments, boxing championships or theatre groups. Since the ships had hardly ever left their home harbours, officers and men had no need to rebuild a familiar environment. In Wilhelmshaven and Kiel there were abundant offers of ways to kill time. All they had to do was accept. The officers, with more money and free time than the ordinary Jack Tar, clearly had the advantage. They could fence, play golf, tennis or hockey, go horse-riding or visit the officers' mess. Restaurants, wine bars, dance halls, concerts, theatres and cinemas were also available to them.

For the seamen and stokers there were sailors' homes which now and again provided entertainment and music, but the men rather viewed these establishments as service institutions and therefore avoided them. They had a higher opinion of naval hostels (*Marineheime*) associated with the sailors' homes. The one at Kiel had five rooms 'in which were to be found piano, harmonium, a good library and many magazines and newspapers. There was also available, free of charge, a writing room. The hostel was combined with the YMCA, which arranged social and educational groups. The hostel had good, cheap food. Alcohol was forbidden'.[37]

Wandering around town, the contrast with shipboard life was so great that, as Kapitänleutnant Knobloch confided to his diary, 'At first the life of the street quite takes one's breath away' and 'can make one quite dizzy'.[38] Occasionally he would have a guilty conscience. On a rainy Sunday afternoon in November 1915 Knobloch attended a classical concert in the auditorium at Kiel University with one of his comrades ('I found it very stimulating') and afterwards they dined out. 'Everywhere filled to bursting with naval officers, some feasting with their wives. I feel guilty that our people are having it so good while over there our comrades are dying and suffering. One notices very little of war here. Even the Café Uhlmann was packed with people enjoying themselves, eating candy, reading comics and making eyes at people'.[39]

What Knobloch experienced in Kiel that day was nothing unusual. Those in Germany who could do so blocked out the war from their lives, since it was not happening on home soil. Even in July 1918 a report from the I Representative General Command in Berlin stated: 'Places of entertainment of all kinds are overflowing, the best places fully booked for days ahead. Often long queues at the bank counters. The trains to the Baltic resorts are full despite the high price of travel'.[40] Even high-ranking naval officers such as Konteradmiral Hipper and Vizeadmiral Scheer took the cure regularly, perhaps at Bad Ems or Bad Kissingen, to recover from the strain of command at war. Adolf von Trotha, who visited Scheer and his wife in June 1918 on vacation at Bad Kissingen could tell his own wife: 'The people there are not doing badly. Many cabs drawn by well-fed nags. They also seem to have hoarded church bells. But ghastly elegant people and many Jews'.[41]

In view of the narrowness and limited freedom of movement aboard ship, it is not surprising that many naval personnel went ashore to take long walks. Kapitänleutnant Schweinitz, for example, regularly took extensive nature rambles as a welcome opportunity to escape the perpetual contact with other people for a few hours.

> Wandered through the lonely countryside – this is my convalescence, my source of energy. All companionship disturbs me, I shake it off, I want nobody to accompany me. These few hours I wish to be free and alone. To be solitary and in immediate contact with nature, no need to speak, to go on where I want – that is the last bit of freedom I have left. I cling to it, nobody will take it from me. After returning, perfectly happy.[42]

Often these walks would turn into a day's excursion into the nearer outskirts of Wilhelmshaven or Kiel. To go farther afield one would cycle, take the train or go by car. Generally, one would be in the company of persons of one's own rank: even off-duty the differences of rank in the German navy played an important role. A scene described by Vizeadmiral Souchon in a letter to his wife could only be imagined in the special circumstances of German naval personnel in Turkey. One glorious summer's afternoon, Souchon had gone with a group of officers and midshipmen on an excursion to a very beautiful bathing beach on the Turkish coast. Once there, they began to have real fun. 'We chased each other through water and sand, had piggy-back fights, built pyramids, took breakfast in the sand in our bathing suits (all sandy). I have never seen the younger officers in my company so exuberant with the joy of living.'[43]

Souchon enjoyed his free time best when he went shooting. He shared this pastime with Hipper of the same crew intake, also an 'enthusiastic hunter' according to his official assessment. Hipper kept a precise record of his successes. 'In the afternoon went to Westerloy shooting with von Krosigk and Schultz. Glorious day. I shot one hare, 1 hen pheasant and 1 cock-pheasant, Krosigk 1 hare, Schultz 1 hare and 1 cock. It was capital and gave me a work-out. It was high time. Otherwise I'm getting very stiff'.[44]

Because the German fleet kept to its accustomed bases during the war, the private lives of those officers whose domicile was in Wilhelmshaven and Kiel changed little. Thus Kapitänleutnant Ernst von Weizsäcker, who lived with his wife and children in Wilhelmshaven's Holtermann-strasse, could look forward almost every day of the war to 'going home and clambering about with the boy [his son Carl-Friedrich, the later physicist and philosopher] and play with the family'.[45] One of the few restrictions to which the family was subjected was that now and again his wife Marianne 'had to eat the Sunday roast alone', if the ships were at heightened readiness and Weizsäcker could not go ashore.[46]

Like most other officers of the High Seas Fleet he was spared the experience of being torn away from his accustomed world or long separation from family and friends, typical for soldiers at war. Even on the Bosphorus officers eventually had the opportunity to send for their wives to come to Constantinople by the overland route. 'Since the situation for us here has now become favourable,' Vizeadmiral Souchon declared, 'I do not see any objection to officers who are doing their duty almost as if in peacetime, having their wives join them here'.[47]

An unmarried officer such as Hermann von Schweinitz, who had 'found a fine apartment in Roon-Strasse (Wilhelmshaven)' and 'put up my old one in the Niemannsweg (Kiel) on the market', knew what a boon it was to be able to escape shipboard life regularly in this way. 'A glorious feeling to be in one's own flat again. To have a good book to read, a glass of wine and a good cigar – I need nothing else this evening.'[48] Another bachelor, Schweinitz's shipmate Reinhold Knobloch, also found a very comfortable flat in Wilhelmshaven, near the Weizsäckers, after a long search. He hoped, he noted in his diary, 'to enjoy better rest and recuperation there during the days in port.'[49]

Whenever the opportunity arose, Knobloch went ashore: only in the bitterly cold winter of 1916/17 did he spend more time aboard, because his land quarters were not properly heated due to the shortage of coal in Germany.

He usually spent his time at the flat drafting letters, writing up his diary, smoking, reading and sleeping. When the Imperial Fleet put back into Wilhelmshaven after the battle of Jutland, the completely exhausted gunnery officer of the sunken cruiser *Rostock* hurried off immediately to his apartment for a long, hot bath. Next, he would stretch out on the sofa just as though he had just knocked off after a hard day at work. On another occasion after returning from a sortie with the fleet, Knobloch spent the evening doing his tax return and sorting through his bills.

Whereas officers could remain ashore as long as they liked (although they had always to bear in mind the possibility of urgent recall aboard), off-duty seamen and stokers had to report back aboard by 2100 hrs. They were strictly forbidden to sleep ashore unless they had a leave pass. Each crewman received ten days' leave annually, but these days could only be taken when his ship was in the yard for repair or overhaul, and even then not always.

For officers it was less strict. They received leave twice yearly, each time for one to two weeks, but often considerably longer. In 1915 Konteradmiral Hipper, who liked to spend his free days deer-stalking, had no less than five periods of leave, each between four and eight days in length. In November 1916 he sent off his battlecruisers to exercise in the Baltic under the command of a deputy since he wanted to go shooting. He came back a week later. In the following spring he was annoyed that because of a planned sortie by the fleet his hunt for wood grouse in Austria had 'sadly not come off'.[50] As he had bad sciatica and gout, he often went to a spa to 'take the cure', and in the autumns of 1916 and 1917 went to the Harz and Bad Kissingen for a month and a half each time. In September 1918, shortly before the Armistice, when the general scarcity of coal almost immobilised the fleet, Hipper, who had now been made fleet commander, went off for several weeks to Bad Kissingen in his own train: 'My predecessor arranged it very nicely, I do not see why I should give it up'.[51]

Vizeadmiral Souchon never took time off ('Naturally there can be no talk of my taking leave during the war since I am as healthy as a fish in water'),[52] but in the summer of 1915 he sent an officer 'whose energy had fallen off markedly' from the Bosphorus to Germany so that he could 'spend 14 days on his estate in the Uckermark to look after things'.[53] To another he approved no less than forty-five days' convalescent leave in Germany. That was in keeping with the regulations: officers who were sick received supplementary special leave beyond their standard allowance of up to six months per year. Too much, as Matrose Stumpf criticised: 'The second gunnery officer, in charge of all the medium calibre guns in battle, received 16 weeks' leave, allegedly to recover his health. During this time a leutnant [sub lieutenant] took over his "work" and nobody ever noticed he was gone. I believe that many had already forgotten that there had once been another second gunnery officer.'[54]

This gunnery officer mentioned by Stumpf was most probably Kapitänleutnant Walter Zaeschmar. In his diary, Zaeschmar states, without any beating around the bush, that he feigned illness as a means of 'revenge' for having been passed over for promotion so often: 'First I am going to Pyrmont for four weeks for the neurosis cure, then we shall see.'[55] He spent another two weeks at home in Burg near Magdeburg. His plan to get himself declared unfit for duty in order to avoid having to return to the *Helgoland* was unsuccessful. 'For that I have to blame the doctor, who wrote me a stupid certificate. Now I am back onboard the battleship as watch-keeping officer.'[56] Nevertheless, until the end of the war he enjoyed many weeks of leave here and there, most of which he spent in Munich: 'That's the best place to live.'[57]

Zaeschmar was not the only one who thought about putting a premature end to his personal war in this way. Kapitän zur See Adolf von Trotha informed his family that there were 'many officers who got themselves pensioned off without being all that ill. In general one does not require special circumstances. All you really need is a medical certificate and a declaration by one's superior officer that the person concerned is unfit for duty.'[58] Not everyone was as conscientious about their duty as Konteradmiral Albert Hopman, Commander-in-Chief of the Reconnaissance Forces in the Baltic. When his superior told him in October 1915 to take a few weeks' leave, he wrote in his diary: 'I find it remarkable to be sent on leave without being sick. I shall have to think about it.'[59]

Obviously, leave for naval officers, especially when awarded so generously, cannot have had the same value as would have been the case for a soldier at the front in Flanders or France. What the latter could only find in home leave – sleeping in a proper bed again, having a decent meal and seeing wife and children – were practically everyday events in Wilhelmshaven and Kiel. How privileged German naval officers were in this respect is clear from a glance at how things were done on the other side of the North Sea.

The officers of the Grand Fleet eked out a rather bare existence. At Scapa Flow the shore offered so few attractions that many crewmen seldom left their ships. Those who went ashore did little more than fill their leisure time with walks, fishing or hunting after hares and seagulls. 'Apparently if one cannot kill Huns one must kill birds,' observed Lieutenant Commander John McLeod, commander of a destroyer attached to the Grand Fleet.[60] A number of officers kept allotments and grew potatoes and vegetables on the small island of Fara. Others went to Kirkwall (population 4000), capital of the Orkneys. Rather closer to the fleet base was Stromness, a favourite destination because of its golf course.

As a rule anyone who went ashore, officer or rating, had to venture no farther than a four-hour return journey to the ship. It was strictly forbidden to be ashore after dark. In autumn and winter, when dusk fell in the early afternoon and the storms regularly reached hurricane-force, there would be no contact with the shore at all for several days. From the military point of view, all this had the great advantage that ships and units stationed in the far north of Scotland could concentrate fully on their war duties, while the Germans – as was pointed out after the war – 'lived too close to family, friends and the civilian population: as time went on there arose from this situation a serious emotional burden which was not possible at Scapa Flow.'[61]

For those stuck there, the years spent in the barren and inhospitable surroundings of Scapa Flow were difficult to bear, or as Sub Lieutenant Oswald Frewen of HMS *Comus* expressed it: 'The fact is that I am "weary, in the uttermost part of the sea" – war-weary, Scapa-weary, weary of seeing the same old damned agony of grey, grey, grey, grey sky, grey sea, grey ship. I could do with a drop of Mediterranean; and a thousand times more, with a month's leave.'[62]

From the beginning of 1915 a rota was introduced, so that the various individual squadrons of the Grand Fleet based on Scapa Flow could each spend a set period of a few weeks at Cromarty on the Scottish coast farther south. Sailing for Cromarty was, as the previously mentioned Russian officer reported, 'always a cause for celebration for the crew and the wardroom'.[63] Invergordon with its cinemas and golf courses was by no means a city, but was by far more attractive than Kirkwall, more or less cut off from all civilisation. Even the presence of wives was allowed: occasionally they were invited aboard to dine.

Many officers brought all their family to Cromarty. By reason of the great demand, however, 'even a quite modest room was so expensive that only a few favoured by fortune could afford such a luxury.'[64] Amongst these few was Roger Keyes, former head of the British submarine arm, who in the summer of 1916 took command of the battleship HMS *Centurion* stationed at Scapa. Keyes rented a house near Cromarty, into which he moved 'three children, seven servants, two dozen chickens, two prams and about two tons of luggage'.[65] Whenever *Centurion* lay at Cromarty, Keyes could now live with his family. Even Admiral Jellicoe rented a house at Cromarty.

The closest comparable situation to that of the German officers and men is provided by the RN battlecruiser fleet commanded by Vice Admiral Beatty. In December 1914 the battlecruisers were detached from the Grand Fleet and stationed in the Firth of Forth at Rosyth. The remoteness from civilisation which prevailed at Scapa, and to some extent at Cromarty, was absent here in the south of Scotland. Edinburgh, cultural and business centre of the country, was only a few miles away and since the afternoons were usually free at Rosyth, the officers at least had the chance almost daily to go downtown. Whether restaurants, cinemas, theatres or a stroll along Princes Street, there was an equal range of possibilities to pass the time, as enjoyed by many at Wilhelmshaven and Kiel. Commander Edward Roynon-Jones visited museums, the zoo, a whisky distillery, took lunch and tea in the Caledonian Hotel and saw *Madame Butterfly* at the King's Theatre. Sub Lieutenant Stephen King-Hall signed up for piano lessons at the college of music.

Seamen and stokers on the other hand spent their free time on land, just as at Scapa Flow, mainly on sport: football, rugby, boxing and running competitions were available, also occasional theatrical presentations and concerts. While the men could only leave their ships under supervision and for limited periods, all the officers had to do was call in regularly at the North British Hotel to check whether they were required on board. If they were, a taxi would return them swiftly to Rosyth.

Not only Edinburgh, but also the outskirts of Rosyth had its attractions. Very popular, for example, was the golf course at Dunfermline, a little north of Rosyth but easily reachable by train. It also had a park, a Turkish bath, a library and a cinema. Others preferred sunbathing, went swimming or took extended rambles – for Vice Admiral Beatty, 'the best thing for me when I get the blues, which I fear I do rather too often now.'[66]

The less privileged at Scapa Flow observed these goings-on around Rosyth with annoyance. 'This is a different world from Scapa,' Oswald Frewen discovered. 'Officers go to Edinburgh every afternoon. The shores of the Firth of Forth are lined for miles with officers' wives and midshipmen's mothers. They all go "home" and they grouse because here the mail takes a day and a half!'[67] Many officers rented flats for their wives and children around Rosyth and Edinburgh. Beatty's country seat, Aberdour House, six miles from Rosyth and situated on a green ridge, had its own tennis court. The admiral regretted all the more, as he himself roughly calculated, that his extensive duties allowed him to spend no more than fourteen hours per week with his wife there.[68]

Even the married officers were not allowed to spend the night ashore, unless on home leave. From the point of view of those who saw their family only once yearly, presumably that would be a restriction easily borne. Frewen called the attractions in and around Edinburgh 'the fleshpots of Egypt', and he had no patience with those officers who apparently had nothing better to do with their time and succumbed regularly to temptation: 'I hate the battlecruisers, they are Pharisees'.[69]

Stephen King-Hall, who was himself at Rosyth with HMS *Southampton*, also considered the proximity of this base to the Scottish metropolis as 'in many ways a bad thing'. He disapproved especially of the behaviour of battlecruiser officers, who spent a great deal of their time at leisure in the city. 'There is amongst them a natural tendency to live rather for the afternoons, when one can go ashore, instead of the forenoons when the turrets go round. After all, human nature is human nature, even when it is in a battlecruiser in wartime.'[70] The antagonism which very gradually developed between the battle fleet at Scapa and the battlecruiser fleet at Rosyth was not overcome until both units were combined again and both operated out of Rosyth.

Until then, for the men stationed at Rosyth it was relatively easy to disengage themselves from the war for a few hours or days, while their comrades-in-arms at Scapa Flow had only Cromarty or leave. The granting of leave was regulated in similar manner to the German side. Ratings had one or two weeks annually; in case of doubt the ship's commander or squadron commander decided. There was no special ruling for officers: they received fourteen days once or twice per year, in many cases considerably more. As with the German navy, advantage was taken of yard lay-ups to hand out leave. As many ships were sent down to the home yards at Liverpool, Newcastle, Southampton, Portsmouth or Devonport for repairs or overhaul, in this way men were at least spared a long and tiring journey overland: the train journey from Scapa Flow to London included crossing the feared Pentland Firth, with its powerful tides, by ferry, and took a good thirty-six hours.

While others could hardly wait to take their leave in England and 'get back to civilisation', Edward Roynon-Jones stationed at Rosyth was not disappointed when his ship, the battlecruiser *Tiger* was ordered to Cromarty for overhaul in the spring of 1915. From the little town of Dingwall, to where the *Tiger's* officers were brought by car, Roynon-Jones continued directly to his real destination, which he had selected beforehand.

I went on to Strathpeffer another five miles and took a room at the Highland Hotel. This is a pretty little place situated in a valley below Ben Wyvis, nearly 4000 feet high, there are other hotels and many lodging houses and they are only full up in the months July to September. There is a spa where people drink various kinds of waters and have baths. Golf links and tennis courts are other attractions and a band plays in the gardens in the season. I slept in the afternoon.[71]

There, in the Scottish Highlands for a week, Roynon-Jones played golf, billiards and tennis, went bathing, rambled the countryside, read books and solved puzzles. How that fitted his self-image as a professional officer in a war spanning half the world can only be guessed at. The commander was not amongst those who, in their letters and diaries, concerned themselves with questions of this nature. He reconciled himself to whatever was. For others, on the other hand, it was precisely such situations like that of Roynon-Jones with his quiet days in the Highlands which seemed incompatible with wartime and therefore provoked a critical assessment of their own role and that of the Navy. The result was, often enough, depression, or even espair.

5

'I wish I were a soldier'
Self-doubt and Mental Crises

EVERY WAR MAKES ITS MARK on those who experience it and changes them forever, whether they be soldiers at the front or civilians in the homeland. The First World War, unparalleled in its extent and its destructiveness, also had this effect, and in a way that its participants could never have imagined. The conditions which the war created, the destruction which it inflicted, the suffering it caused, were of a completely new order and far removed from existing frameworks of knowledge and policy. The last military conflict involving the German Reich had been against France in 1870/71, more than forty years before, and soldiers who had fought in earlier wars had no concept of what awaited their sons and grandsons in the trenches of Flanders and France. The young men who boarded the trains to the front in August 1914, often in high spirits, promising 'It'll all be over by Christmas,' but mindful of the possibility of 'an inspiring death in the Great War for the Fatherland', never imagined that death would come in a 'confrontation with a mortar bomb'.[1]

The fact that wartime experience would differ from what had been expected, not conforming to previous images and ideas about the nature of war and the role of the individual in that conflict, applied also to the navy, but in another way. At first glance, naval seafaring personnel had an enviable situation: they were not required to leave their home and family in order to take part in the war. They did not have to risk their necks again and again to gain or defend a few yards of worthless terrain, they did not have to live under the most primitive conditions in a filthy trench, and they did not have to watch their comrades-in-arms suffering and dying every day. Yet this did not engender a feeling of relief: quite the contrary. While the soldier in the field was accustomed to experiencing immediate peril to his life, or if he survived, unimaginably severe injury, in the navy it was the 'not participating in the war', the 'not being able to fight', which was so difficult to grasp and filled many naval seafarers, particularly the officers, with deep discontent.

The great decisive sea battle which all had hoped for never took place, and what filled the days instead was not sufficient to satisfy the thirst for action in the fleet. If the first half-year of the war was comparatively rich in events, with two battles in the North Sea and various sorties by the fleet in which, theoretically at least, the chance existed of meeting the enemy, after the battle of the Dogger Bank in January 1915 the valuable capital ships hardly ever ventured out again. Instead of fighting, the High Seas Fleet, bottled up in the German Bight, waited patiently and ensured that the fighting power and battle-readiness of ships and crews never fell off, just as did its superior opponent, the Grand Fleet, waiting for the great day. The usual long-accustomed shipboard routine, practising for contingencies, navigation and gunnery exercises, battle drill and general work, determined everyday life on board. Under these circumstances it was hardly possible for the seaman to feel as if he were playing an active role in the war.

'Apparently no naval war is being conducted any more,' Kapitän-leutnant Walter Zaeschmar complained in October 1914.[2] Weeks later he wrote, 'Nothing is going on in the North Sea any more. Only the U-boats are constantly on the move.'[3] In February 1915, not long after the battle of the Dogger Bank, he saw the navy as a 'Sleeping Beauty', 'sinking ever deeper into sleep. All quiet in the Baltic and North Sea.'[4] Kapitänleutnant Reinhold Knobloch, who found the general tranquillity 'intolerable' began to ask himself, 'Why do we actually have these big ships?'[5] He thought it strange when he looked at the German dreadnoughts in the autumn of 1915: 'All nicely set out in the Schillig Roads at Wilhelmshaven in the beam of the full moon ... nobody can have thought that after fourteen months of war the German fleet would still look like that.'[6]

For the officers, members of a military elite raised for warfare, the transition into this unexpected and literally 'unnatural' situation was anything but simple. All the worse was the fact that the inactivity of the fleet *in* war stood in stark contrast to the exaggerated political and military role which it had played *before* the war. The social ranking and great prestige of the officer corps had been basically nothing else but a kind of investment in confidence about achievements to come, a promissory note for future change. This change had not come about, no advances had been achieved. Many officers sensed this.

'My morale is less good, because we still have had no opportunity to achieve anything,' wrote Oberleutnant Heinrich Stenzler to his mother in October 1914 from aboard Hipper's flagship. '*Seydlitz* seems to me like a life assurance institution.'[7] When he was awarded the Iron Cross two months later for taking in part in the bombardment of Hartlepool, Stenzler gladly accepted the decoration, but could not quite understand why he had received it. 'Dear Mother, at least I can now come home after the war. I was awarded the Iron Cross today and am naturally very pleased about it. I still do not know what I am supposed to have achieved at Hartlepool.'[8] Kapitänleutnant Schweinitz, who at the beginning of the war had been desperate to serve aboard a warship, now saw himself 'locked in and enslaved. We loaf around, creep about the ship. How can one endure this monotony? ... I believe I can do good, perhaps outstanding things, because I feel the dynamism inside me. But I am helpless in the face of it ... the fleet cannot do anything, blockaded inside all the minefields ... and so I sit here doing nothing.'[9]

Kapitänleutnant Reinhold Knobloch described most strikingly the morale in the seaman branch of the Imperial Navy officer corps:

I am a soldier, I want to fight the enemy and must not. Why not? The British have sown practically all the North Sea with mines at their leisure. For that reason we have this lazy and tranquil existence. We receive invitations, eat and drink and sleep yet have no other thought in our heads than 'Let us get at the enemy.' What is the point of pinning Iron Crosses on us and making stirring speeches? We want to fight. Victory or death ... we lie in harbour powerful and well-fed. Well protected. For God's sake, we want out of these holes, we want to fight and shoot. To destroy the enemy![10]

It would not have come as much consolation to Knobloch to know that the commander of the British battlecruiser squadron on the other side of the North Sea had similar thoughts. Vice Admiral David Beatty wrote to his wife:

At times our inactivity frets me to such an extent that I can hardly bear it. The greatest war of all time is proceeding, the finest deeds of heroism are being performed daily, the dreams of the past, of glory and achievement are being uprooted and proved impossible of accomplishment. The country is in such need, the spirit is so willing, and yet we are doomed to do nothing, achieve nothing and sit day after day working out schemes that will never be carried out, endeavouring by pen and paper to impress the Admiralty with the possibility of our doing something.[11]

Against this backdrop, the fact that, despite the war, life onboard and ashore followed to a great extent its accustomed age-old routine was not seen as a relief, but reinforced the discontent. The daily routine was 'monotony', the stationing of ships as sentry vessels ready to engage an enemy 'a period on the treadmill and deadly dull – one cannot leave the ordered position, shoot, take a walk. It is like being a beast of prey in a cage.'[12] Even the regular navigation and gunnery exercises were no substitute for the purpose for which the steel colossi, bursting with strength, had been built, and in the long run it was no consolation that the real aim of all this exercising and keeping ready to fight – the sea battle – would probably never be achieved. 'It makes me despair. We exercise, shoot and practice but never see the enemy. And that in the gigantic world war which has now lasted a year.'[13]

The many hours of liberty which officers spent in the wardroom, at home or in the theatres and restaurants of the ports seemed distasteful in their failure to conform to the image of the soldier at war. 'One has no lust for aesthetic enjoyment, no lust for pleasure and diversion. We have war fever in the blood. We want to take part in the great deeds of this era. To be condemned to lie at anchor and wait is right now dreadfully difficult and depressing. My only wish, my only desire, is for a fight, for action.'[14]

While Knobloch frequently used his diary as a vehicle for expressing his heartfelt discontent at his own inactivity, many others were simply no longer able to tolerate the tense expectation and endless waiting while being at constant readiness. 'Complaints of neurosis amongst officers of the fleet are becoming ever more frequent,' Knobloch reported in February 1915. 'Numerous cases of crying fits, and delusions of grandeur.'[15] Even the most senior officers were not exempt. Konteradmiral Hipper, who admitted in December 1914 that his own nerves were 'dreadfully down', was appalled to see Vizeadmiral Wilhelm von Lans, commander of No 1 Squadron, relieved of duty after a nervous breakdown a little later. 'Various other officers have already left after a nervous breakdown. I am simply amazed that I of all people who up to now had great things to achieve, am still holding out.'[16]

A similar fate to that of Lans overtook Kapitän zu See Paul Kettner, commander of the small cruiser *Breslau* which had accompanied

Goeben into Turkish service. Although – or perhaps because – Kettner on the Bosphorus was so far from the gloom of the North Sea, his health deteriorated to the extent that Vizeadmiral Souchon saw fit to send him home. 'The poor man is no longer sleeping and is increasingly making his men nervous. Naturally he cannot go on like this although I am releasing him very unwillingly. He is a capital person and until now had fought against his nervous affliction admirably.'[17]

Because he himself also had problems sleeping and was disturbed by 'every flapping flag-line, every footstep on deck above the cabin', Hipper also finally consulted a specialist in nervous disorders. For a German navy officer who had learned never to show weakness, this was certainly no easy step. Hipper awaited the diagnosis with apprehension – but to his great relief it turned out negative.[18]

The ongoing preoccupation with 'nerves' and 'nervousness' was not merely the caprice of frustrated German navy officers. Neurasthenia, which embraced a multitude of symptoms such as exhaustion, tiredness, anxiety or irritability was a fashionable complaint at the turn of the nineteenth century. Equally in vogue, particularly in the higher social circles, was the spa or health resort to combat it. The phenomenon was no stranger to the Imperial Navy. Not without due cause had Kaiser Wilhelm II thought it fit several years before the war to remind his naval officers to care about their nerves. 'The next war and the next naval battle,' the monarch had warned, 'demand of you healthy nerves. Nerves will decide it.'[19] Nervousness, the historian Joachim Radkau writes, arises principally 'when an accustomed tempo is changed, or several speeds are superimposed on one another.'[20]

Whereas before 1914 it had been the case that certain developments such as the building up of the fleet under the Tirpitz Plan or technological advances in warship construction had advanced too rapidly and therefore had asked too much of those involved, the opposite was now the case. Now it was the halting, agonisingly slow and generally uneventful course of the naval war which burdened the soul. The official *War Medical Report on the German Navy* recorded a total of 2278 cases of hysteria and 5296 cases of neurasthenia, while more than 120 seagoing naval personnel had attempted to commit suicide.[21]

There are no similar data for the British fleet, although probably it would have had to face a similar problem. When Sub Lieutenant James Colvill took over a ship from an officer who had been written off 'unfit for duty' long term, he wrote, 'We all know what that means.'[22]

Lieutenant Commander John McLeod complained: 'This shadow fighting is getting on my nerves. Here is the finest war the world has ever seen and I am out of it.' Later he suffered for months from deafness and hair loss, according to medical diagnosis a sign that he had only narrowly avoided a nervous breakdown.[23]

To have no appropriate task, not to be able to fight, not to be able to show what the fleet which cost millions could do – for those involved this was difficult to bear and in the true sense of the words 'got on their nerves'. Nevertheless, it would probably have been a little easier to come to terms with this fate if there had not been at the same time so many others who represented the performance of the fleet as being more paltry than it ought to have been.

In this respect it was particularly difficult for the British. They had not only to compare themselves to the heroes of the present, the troops in the trenches, but also the heroes of times long past. Whereas the German navy had no tradition to look back upon, the Royal Navy rested on the laurels of a long line of historical figures obliging it to follow suit.

To the present day, at the head of the British naval pantheon stands Admiral Lord Horatio Nelson, victor at the battle of Trafalgar on 21 October 1805 against the combined fleets of France and Spain. This success destroyed at a stroke Napoleon's hopes of successfully invading the British Isles and secured British mastery of the oceans for many decades. Nelson paid for his victory with his life, and the legend which surrounds him is based, not unreasonably, on his death in the battle. Often overlooked by many of his later admirers, however, is the fact that it was only after years of waiting and watching that finally the chance arrived for the decisive blow.

For generations of British naval officers, Trafalgar became a kind of fixed star in the firmament of a naval tradition stretching back to the Middle Ages, and certainly there were some who fantasised about being the next Nelson. At the outbreak of the First World War, just at that very moment when for many the hour had arrived to show themselves as Nelson's worthy successors, the Royal Navy appeared incapable of adding another glorious chapter to its glittering tradition. As in 1805, the non-negotiable precondition for such an aim was not to bottle up the enemy at a safe distance, but to sink his fleet. Would the statue of Nelson, standing so proudly on its 170ft-high column for more than one hundred years, have lasted so long if all the admiral had done was hold the enemy in check until Napoleon's defeat was decided elsewhere? Assuredly not.

'Nothing less than complete annihilation can or must be allowed to satisfy us,'[24] wrote Vice Admiral David Beatty to Winston Churchill, expressing what everybody thought. Later Beatty repeated his views to the Prime Minister, Asquith. 'They [naval officers] desire, as the whole nation desires, that when we fight the result should be decisive and overwhelming.'[25] Beatty was certainly not the only one who asked himself more than once what the victor of Trafalgar would have made of the passivity of the Grand Fleet. 'I often wonder what Nelson would have thought of it. His high spirit would have chafed him to death by this time.'[26] There was no doubt, as the American naval historian Arthur Marder put it, that the Royal Navy was 'hypnotised by its past'.[27]

Yet it was not necessary to look back into the past to see 'the right way' to fight a war: the soldiers of the British Expeditionary Force (BEF) demonstrated it every day on the battlefields in France and Flanders. Compared with what they achieved, people in the fleet were obliged to admit that naval warfare was child's play. 'The Navy goes to war in a luxurious way compared to our gallant Army. Contrast their hours in the trenches, rain, lying on the ground, marches, etc. with us. We have long hours at sea, but we have to come in for coal and that usually means 24 hrs rest and clean up. Our food is as good as in peace, we have a piano, a comfortable and well lit and warmed mess, with books, magazines, papers, a cabin slightly denuded true, but a cabin with a bunk.'[28]

Despite all that, or perhaps because of it, many officers wanted to exchange an existence in the Navy far too peaceable for their taste for a post in the army. 'I wish I was a soldier in these days. It is most boring on board,' John McLeod wrote to his mother in August 1914. He was actually hoping that the German fleet would soon be wiped out, bringing the naval war to an end so that he could volunteer for the army. He found it almost intolerable that while his brothers were fighting on the western front, he was the only member of the family 'who has not been in the thick of it'.[29] In the opening stages of the war, even David Beatty repeatedly uttered his wish to be a soldier on the continent. 'I'd give anything to be there and would give up my battlecruisers if I could command one regiment of cavalry'.[30] He dismissed his wife's objection that he should be happy not to have to lie in a muddy trench somewhere in France: 'It is foolish no doubt, but can't you understand the feeling of hopeless inutility which comes over me from time to time when we spend days doing nothing, when so many are doing so much?'[31] Beatty wrote to his friend Roger Keyes: 'But when one reads of the gallant deeds done by our army I feel I would give up the battlecruiser squadron like a shot to command a cavalry regiment or even a squadron. That is heresy but it's there deep down.'[32]

Keyes, as Commander-in-Chief of the RN submarine arm, one of the most active of all naval officers, was almost more unhappy than Beatty that he was not able to pull his weight in comparison with the army. After he had told his wife in October 1914, 'I would give anything to be a soldier until the fleet comes out,'[33] two months later in a fit of despair he cursed himself for having chosen the wrong career, or at least the wrong branch of service. He should have recognised in advance, he said, that in war the main burden falls on the army and the Navy is only called upon occasionally.

> I am very sick of this inaction! I think next time I come into the world I shall be a soldier – it was stupid of me not to have thought of it before making up one's mind to go into the Navy. History is plain enough on the subject. Soldiers fight almost every day of a war. Sailors about once a year at the most if they are lucky. The worst of it is one has to make up one's mind for the Navy so young, one probably doesn't know enough about history and those six volumes of James' *Naval History* – (in my room) – which I lived on about that time were misleading, they are crowded with fights big and small but spread over 30 or 40 years.[34]

Shortly after the battle of the Dogger Bank, Keyes's feelings of futility were nullified when to his great surprise he was appointed chief of staff for the combined operation to conquer the Dardanelles. 'I never felt so buoyant and confident about anything in my life before. We are going to have a splendid affair,'[35] he told his wife. As it turned out, however, even the supposedly best job in the Royal Navy was no guarantee of satisfaction: a good half-year later the Dardanelles operation had come to a sorry end, and Keyes was now looking at an uncertain future. He toyed with the idea of quitting the Service and seeking a commission in the army, but then he put in for command of a battleship in the North Sea which he finally obtained, this being HMS *Centurion*.

By having himself transplanted to another post which he considered more attractive, Keyes killed two birds with one stone: he was finally in a position to make his own contribution to the war effort without having to take too much of a back seat behind the army, and he remained in the branch of service he had chosen originally. That was, despite all their admiration for the BEF, the strategy for which many of the discontented settled in the end: hardly anybody actually transferred to the army. Especially sought after instead were the so-called 'maids of all work', the monitors, used for operations in coastal shallows and rivers; destroyers, or the light and manoeuvrable small cruisers which often put to sea to reconnoitre, and in battle had their place in the front line with the battlecruisers.

Behind most applications for transfer was simply the wish to escape the present tedium, rather than some carefully thought-out career move. Those who had had their fill of waiting in northern Scotland for the long hoped for battle tried to get transferred to where 'more was up', perhaps in the Mediterranean. Others, who had been on overseas stations at the outbreak of war wanted to get back to the North Sea, the hub of the naval war, as soon as possible, where the final decision must eventually come. These great hopes were far from being realised, and the new command, if one was achieved, generally brought only temporary relief. The battle everyone wanted to fight and which British naval tradition and the heroic British army seemed to demand of the Grand Fleet was nowhere to be found, and scarcely anybody made any bones about their disappointment at this bitter fact.

Therefore, although its success in the long run legitimised the British defensive strategy, the way in which the Royal Navy had set about winning the naval war left an aftertaste, for the yardstick by which, consciously or subconsciously, its achievements were measured was not the result actually obtained (the neutralisation of the German fleet), but the result which it was possible and necessary to achieve based on the history of the Royal Navy and its numerical superiority (the wiping out of the German fleet).

In Germany, on the other hand, there was no heroic history against which the performance of their navy could be measured. That the German fleet, which had not even existed in this form twenty years ago, lacked a victorious and glorious tradition, might now even prove to be an advantage, for as the British historian Andrew Gordon writes, it was 'in some ways easier to start with a clean slate than to modify long-held attitudes, platitudes, structures and strategies.'[36] The Kaiser's ships, however, were encumbered with a heavy mortgage: the Tirpitz Plan. Tirpitz had devised the fleet to fit the concept of a naval battle between Heligoland and the Thames, and this was its *raison d'être*. Earlier this had been a theoretical option, because the fleet was to be primarily a means of exerting political pressure. Once the calculations to keep Britain out of the war by the use of German dreadnoughts, or even to co-opt Britain as Germany's ally had failed, the navy had then been left with no alternative but to use the ships for their intended purpose. Otherwise, as Ernst von Weizsäcker analysed it:

> the whole fleet policy collapses from its inner falsehood. It is ridiculous to spend billions (of marks) on building a fleet in order to discourage a future enemy from war while lacking the intention of risking it later when the time comes for action. I do not believe that smart-alec Tirpitz had such a gamble in mind ... Therefore if we do not have the courage and conviction to use the fleet to advantage, then it would have been better if it had not been built and we had limited ourselves to cheap guerrilla vessels and fast overseas cruisers.[37]

Weizsäcker knew that it was practically impossible for the Germans to inflict a devastating defeat on the Royal Navy and to assume naval supremacy themselves. Even in the most favourable case, the use of the fleet 'with advantage' in a sea battle fought to its conclusion would in all probability have resulted in the loss of all its ships. This prospect held back neither Weizsäcker nor anybody else from desiring such a decisive battle. So long as this final battle of attrition was still awaited, according to operational orders the main aim of the High Seas Fleet was 'not to lose patience but to be ready at any time to use the favourable moment.'[38]

For German naval men it was almost impossible to envisage a satisfactory opportunity, all the less so since they lacked the comfort of operating from a superior position in numbers enjoyed by their British counterparts. Although it is going too far to say that the Royal Navy achieved its strategic goals by doing nothing, the inactivity of the High Seas Fleet brought with it no advantages other than being spared the 'disadvantage' of being hacked down to size or annihilated. Compared with the efforts made all around them to 'defend' the German Reich against a 'world of enemies', that taken in itself does not seem a great achievement. 'What we are doing makes no sense and is indefensible,' Weizsäcker observed.[39] Or as Kapitänleutnant Reinhold Knobloch put it: 'There are no laurels to be won by naval warfare.'[40]

Compared to what the soldiers on the battlefields on the two fronts, west and east, were going through, naval warfare was 'a wretched occupation', as Adolf von Trotha observed critically, spending his days 'reading, taking walks on deck, eating and sleeping'.[41] Particularly in the opening weeks and months of the war, naval personnel at Wilhelms-haven and Kiel found themselves overshadowed by the violent battles and fast successes of the land forces. On the battleship *Helgoland*, the latest reports from the theatres of war were posted every day, and a large map with colourful little flags pinned on it marked out the positions of the various forces. 'The men crowded in front of it and then discussed enthusiastically the recent changes and reports.'[42]

They sounded very promising. In the east, Generals Paul von Hindenburg and Erich Ludendorff had inflicted heavy defeats on the Russians in the battles of Tannenberg and the Masurian Lakes and driven them from East Prussia. In the west, after rolling through Belgium, German troops had made deep inroads into France within a few weeks. At the beginning of September 1914 the German advance was brought to a halt at the Marne and all attempts to restart it were frustrated by bitter French and British resistance. It was here that trench warfare began. 'From the Belgian coast to the Swiss border the armies of the Kaiser Reich and the troops of the Western Allied Powers faced each other along a closed front over 700 kilometres in length'.[43]

By the end of 1914 the Germans had already lost more than a million men. Because Supreme Army Command made every effort to dissemi-nate only reports of successes and if possible to draw a veil over defeats, or at least play them down, many naval personnel remained as much in ignorance of the true extent of the German losses as did the rest of Germany. Not until the autumn of 1918 did the shocked public learn of the actual fighting strength of their troops.

Above all for the officers it was a torment to have to watch what their comrades in the army had to undergo while they were themselves condemned to inactivity. 'They are fighting for King and Fatherland, to be or not to be, and here we sit drinking frothy beer', raged Hermann von Schweinitz.[44] He found it especially depressing that his four brothers were all at the front, while he was himself 'somewhere to the rear sitting around in an office'. 'All four have the Iron Cross. How that fills me with courage! Siegfried is a company commander who will shine. I was so pleased when I was told. I am proud of my brothers but I envy them.'[45] Later Schweinitz even briefly gave some thought to volunteering for the Flanders Naval Corps, a fighting unit of naval infantry which protected the Belgian coast and covered the right flank of the German army. Those who served in this 'elite corps' were literally at the foremost front and were frequently required to fight.[46]

The mixture of admiration and jealousy which Schweinitz writes about made its mark during the course of the war on the way in which the navy looked at the army. To the last, naval officers could not come to terms with being mere onlookers while others risked their lives day by day for Kaiser and fatherland. 'Oh, if we could only do like them,'[47] wished Konteradmiral Hipper in August 1914. When Warsaw fell a year later, Kapitänleutnant Knobloch commented: 'I have to force myself to rejoice for the general welfare and the general greatness because I, who have now been a soldier for almost 14 years, am not granted (the chance) to take an active part in these great deeds.'[48] The battle of the Somme prompted him to write in September 1916: 'The effort and stress being demanded of our soldiers there must be enormous. Here we see ourselves as idle drones. You brave, good lads, keep on holding out stoutly, we thank you for it!'[49] During the great Allied offensives at the Aisne and in Champagne six months later, thoughts of this kind moved the same officer to note: 'A great battle is raging in the West, the greatest known in world history ... meanwhile we just keep on taking it easy in the Schillig roads and while away the time as best we can.'[50]

During the German spring offensive of 1918 Hermann von Schweinitz had similar thoughts: 'Our great offensive in the West has begun. It is going well. And ourselves? At three hours' notice for steam! Lying around while over there the decisive battle of the war is being fought.'[51] Self-critically and with a look at the great political connections, Ernst von Weizsäcker also compared the achievements of the army with the scanty activities of the navy – and came to a devastating conclusion. 'When I read about the battles which the army is fighting it reminds me again and again of the uselessness of the navy. Apart from U-boats and airships, it sits around inactive. Its usefulness in war bears no relationship to the sacrifices in money, political animosity and the concessions in internal policy.'[52]

The officers were very well aware that the army often lived and fought under the most inhuman conditions. 'In places it must be quite dreadful. The day-long artillery barrages make some men go mad and raving.'[53] When in the spring of 1917 Knobloch together with many other officers watched a propaganda film about the battle of the Somme at the cinema, he found himself 'deeply shocked at the ghastly effect of mine explosions and artillery barrages.'[54]

The Somme was without doubt one of the most horrific battles of the whole war. Before the Anglo-French troops began their offensive against the German lines on 1 July 1916, they subjected them to an artillery barrage lasting seven days without pause in which more than 1.5 million HE, gas and shrapnel shells fell on the German trenches. The Germans, dug in thirty feet underground, waited helplessly for this inferno beyond all imagining to pass. 'Nerves tensed to breaking point they sat there listening to the diabolical noise, waited for the dull impact of the next aerial torpedo to burrow into the earth and then the devastating explosion. The vibrations extinguished candles and acetylene lamps even in the deepest bunkers. The walls shook like the sides of a ship and the darkness was filled with smoke and swathes of gas.'[55]

When after seven days the guns finally fell silent, the Germans, of whom far more had survived the barrage than the British and French had hoped, watched the enemy troops through scissor-telescopes as they assembled behind their parapets. Now began a race of life and death – 'a race in which the British had to get from their own most advanced trenches to the other side of No-Man's-Land, and the Germans from their subterranean lodgings to the uppermost step of the entrances. Whoever reached the German parapets first would survive. The side which failed would die, either by hand grenade in the hills of earth, or shot down in front of the trenches.'[56]

As so often in this war the attackers failed to capture the practically indestructible positions of the defenders. The advancing British infantry had first to cross a strip of open terrain one hundred yards broad (No-Man's-Land), unprotected against German machine-gun and mortar fire. Those who achieved this then saw to their horror that the seven-day long artillery barrage had left the strong barbed wire fortifications ahead of the German trenches undamaged. One after another they were gunned down during the search for a gap. Others got entangled in the wire and bled to death. On the first day of the battle of the Somme alone, the British lost 60,000 men, of whom one-third lost their lives in the opening minutes of the attack. The German defenders had 6000 dead and wounded. During the overall battle more than one million soldiers were killed, wounded or taken prisoner.

In November 1917 Reinhold Knobloch had the opportunity to see for himself how unenviable life really was in the army. For several weeks he toured the front in Flanders and also visited the trenches.

The men in the only weakly defended forward front line were in their quarters. Because the hollows for sleeping were under water, they had to crouch down in the narrow passageway. That is how they live for six days and nights in the most forward trenches ... Hard, very hard! They have lived here for three years and a half, brooding and dozing in their dark mud holes. They have rheumatic aches in all their limbs because they have no chance of getting dry. It is the same story for the British over there.[57]

Knobloch described the hours-long artillery 'destructive fire' as 'grandiose theatre'.[58]

After his visit to the front, Knobloch would probably have agreed at once with what Kapitän zur See Adolf von Trotha wrote to his wife: 'Compared to the poor army, aboard ship we have a life of idleness and luxury.'[59] As on the British side, within the officer corps it was common to wish oneself to be where, as an officer of the Kaiser, one felt one ought to be. That is, not only in a more meaningful role, fitting the image of a soldier at war, but also, as Wilhelm Souchon saw it, the desire 'to fight one's way through all those adventures which happen there in gripping sequence and diversity.'[60] The officer's code of honour, by which each swore to serve the Kaiser loyally unto death, made the dangers and hardships of being in action at the front seem worth aiming for. The greater the danger into which he put himself in the fulfilment of his duty, the less he thought about his own life – as shown by the decision to go down with the flag still flying – the more 'honourably' he acted. In this connection 37-year-old Korvettenkapitän Bogislav von Selchow, first officer of the obsolete cruiser *Victoria Luise*, wrote: 'All naval officers want to cross over to the army: there one can have glory and honour and show that one can do anything. But the navy, is that a chivalrous calling, chivalrous in its whole activity, chivalrous now in the way it is being used?'[61]

This sheds light on what Albert Hopman meant when he enthused to his wife how 'glorious' it was for the army in the east. 'One might almost curse one's luck that one is not an army officer now.'[62] Or how Reinhold Knobloch in all seriousness could write about an officer from the *Rostock*, who had been despatched with a special unit to the battlefront in France: 'What fabulous luck some people have.'[63]

Naturally other avenues were open for German naval officers within their own service. The alternatives were, as on the British side, small, active naval units – primarily the U-boats. In September 1914 after the celebrated return of Kapitänleutnant Weddigen and his crew, who had singlehandedly in *U-9* sunk three obsolete British cruisers, Knobloch wrote: 'It must be an uplifting feeling to run into port after such an achievement.'[64] Thanks to the U-boats, the arm of the Imperial Navy reached to Madeira and the Irish Sea, almost as though there were no British blockade. 'A quite incredible achievement,' wrote Hipper, 'we can be really proud of our U-boats.'[65] Proud and also a little envious. 'What luck! And us? We keep on with the bulletins,' Knobloch observed when one of his friends was drafted aboard a U-boat.[66] A U-boat commander who told him of his adventures was in Knobloch's eyes 'a fresh, dashing type who lives and lets live.' He noticed from this encounter for the first time how ponderous in thought and action he had become.[67] 'The variety of problems which confront a U-boat commander is scarcely imaginable,' Wilhelm Souchon, deeply impressed, wrote to his wife, 'They are real men who can overcome anything.'[68]

U-boats were not only constantly in action and close to the enemy, they were also the guarantor for the few successes which the navy achieved in the war. Amongst these, in contemporary opinion, was the sinking of the British passenger ship *Lusitania* by Kapitänleutnant Walther Schwieger commanding *U-20* on 7 May 1915, in which 1200 people perished. 'That is probably the greatest U-boat success achieved to date which in my opinion in its effect will put the feat of even *U-9* in the shade,' rejoiced Konteradmiral Hipper,[69] and even the circumspect Ernst von Weizsäcker derived from it a certain satisfaction: 'For me, the great loss of life is as significant as the material damage. The important thing about the U-boat war is deterrence.'[70] Seaman Richard Stumpf wrote: '1500 [*sic*] people were killed, amongst them 100 Americans. We are glad!'[71]

Even if the ruthless approach of the U-boats did not quite fall in with the concept of honourable warfare between two enemies of equal rank, as symbolised by going down with flag flying, the initial reservations against 'underhand weapons of modern technology' began to dissolve as the big ships were forced into the background.[72] When in March 1916 Hermann von Schweinitz was recommended with three other officers of the *Rostock* for transfer to a U-boat he could hardly believe his luck. Proudly he accepted the congratulations of his comrades-in-arms. All probably thought the same: 'Nowadays our sort make more progress under water than above it.'[73] After the battle of Jutland, which showed the fleet that the war could not be won in that manner, more and more officers, particularly the younger ones 'who finally wanted to do something and not rot in inactivity', volunteered for the U-boat arm. Even Vizeadmiral Wilhelm Souchon flirted with the idea before deciding in the end that he had 'too many gold rings' for it.[74]

Next to U-boats, German naval officers who had had all they could take of a fleet doomed to inactivity chose the airships. The prospect of dropping bombs on London made the Zeppelins highly desirable. Their need for personnel was less than for U-boats, however. Kapitänleutnant Walter Zaeschmar was one of the few supposedly favoured by fortune. After he had spent three years aboard SMS *Helgoland* as a gunnery officer, at the beginning of 1917 he was awarded his yearned-for command of an airship. The longer he had to wait for his first combat mission the more his doubts grew. 'Even if finally independent, still without any action. All the same, as against my position aboard *Helgoland* a great step forward.'[75] By the time the war ended, Zaeschmar had flown less than half a dozen missions, amongst these being involvement in Operation Albion against the Baltic islands, for which he was decorated. At least from now on he could say: 'In any case I have achieved an ambition to be involved personally in the war and received the Iron Cross first class for it.'[76]

For the great majority of naval officers, meanwhile, this kind of fulfilment was nowhere to be found: the war was too unheroic, too unpredictable in all its attendant phenomena, was going on too long, and was too uncertain in its outcome. And too many officers, both German and British, were fixated on a great naval battle, the goal of all their dreams of glory and honour, and which in their eyes would bring the only opportunity of equalling the achievements of the respective armies. When at last, after endless months of waiting and restraint on both sides, the longed-for duel of the fleets came, almost everybody had already given up hope of it.

6

'The day has come! The enemy is in sight!'
The Battle of Jutland

In January 1916, Kaiser Wilhelm II appointed the former Commander-in-Chief, III Battleship Squadron, Vizeadmiral Reinhard Scheer to be the new fleet commander. His predecessor, Admiral Hugo von Pohl, had been obliged to vacate his post owing to his having cancer and died a short while afterwards in Berlin. In the fleet the Kaiser's personal choice was greeted with applause. 'Without any doubt he has the best grasp of the three men tried so far, and the most spirit. As a leutnant once he pulled out part of a policeman's beard during a disagreement one night,' wrote Ernst von Weizsäcker of the new Commander-in-Chief of the High Seas Fleet.[1]

In contrast to the hesitant Pohl, the 53-year-old Scheer, son of a Hanau schoolmaster, was seen by many as a man of action. Just like Hipper, during the course of a 38-year naval career Scheer had worked his way up from humble origins. At the beginning of the war he had commanded II Squadron, consisting of the last series of German pre-dreadnoughts, before taking command of the newest and most powerful steel colossi of III Squadron in December 1914. So far none of his ships had fired at the enemy. The admiral and the men at his side – Kapitän zur See Adolf von Trotha, who had abandoned command of the battleship *Kaiser* to be Scheer's chief of staff, and Kapitän zur See Magnus von Levetzow who headed the operational section – were determined to change that.

Scheer considered it a matter of urgency to make the battle fleet, which since the battle of the Dogger Bank had spent most of its time in harbour or on outpost duty, more active. It was true that he had no desire to clash with the entire British fleet, but as he saw it there could not be much harm in making more frequent, if riskier, sorties farther afield in the hope of engaging small British formations and thus achieving at least a partial success. The Kaiser agreed. Scheer had a free hand.

The first operation under Scheer's leadership was a fresh bombardment of the English coast. On 24 April 1916 the battlecruisers under the command of Konteradmiral Friedrich Boedicker (Hipper was away taking the cure for his nerves) fired on Lowestoft and Yarmouth. They did not inflict much damage and when they met Commodore Tyrwhitt's Harwich Force on the way back they rejected the chance of battle, even though Boedicker's squadron was clearly superior. As equally annoyed as Scheer at this lost opportunity was Reich Chancellor Theobald von Bethmann Hollweg, who at the end of April withdrew permission from the navy for partial unlimited U-boat warfare after the United States threatened to break off diplomatic relations.

Scheer decided to make a virtue of necessity and link the released U-boats into a combined action of the entire fleet. His plan was that Vizeadmiral Hipper's battlecruisers should bombard the English coast once more, but this time near Sunderland farther north and thus closer to the base of the British battlecruiser fleet in the Firth of Forth. As soon as Vice Admiral Beatty put to sea with his battlecruisers to hunt for Hipper, he would run into an ambush by U-boats. Scheer would be lurking nearby with the High Seas Fleet to intercept and destroy those British ships which escaped the ambush. It was the optimistic assumption that before Admiral Jellicoe had arrived from Scapa Flow with the Grand Fleet, depending on the breaks, the Germans would have put the greater part of the British battlecruiser fleet out of the equation.

In order to protect against unpleasant surprises, Scheer laid down that the operation should only take place when the weather conditions permitted aerial reconnaissance. Zeppelin airships would accompany Hipper's ships and report the sighting of the enemy early enough for the Germans to turn back if necessary. In this way Scheer considered that he would keep the risk to his own force within reasonable bounds.

The X factor intervened. Because of a technical defect caused by a mine explosion aboard the battlecruiser *Seydlitz*, the operation initially scheduled for mid May had to be postponed several times. The U-boats, which played an important role in Scheer's planning, had already taken up their positions in the Firth of Forth, but their fuel was limited. This put Scheer under pressure, and now he calculated that he had either to order his costly operation to go ahead by 1 June at the latest, or call it off. Another difficulty was the weather over the North Sea. It was deteriorating daily, calling into question whether the Zeppelins could take part.

Scheer changed the plan. Instead of bombarding Sunderland, Hipper was to show himself ostentatiously off the Norwegian coast as a threat to British merchant shipping in the Skagerrak, a sea area on the coast of North Jutland. The effect on the British fleet, Scheer hoped, would be the same: Beatty would come out to pursue Hipper and run into the U-boat trap. Scheer, following in Hipper's wake, would finish off the ships that escaped. Should Jellicoe appear with the Grand Fleet, the Germans would retire to the safety of the Heligoland Bight. Under this variant of the plan, aerial reconnaissance was no longer necessary because of the protection to the flanks which the coast of Denmark offered.

Shortly after midnight on Wednesday, 31 May 1916, the German fleet weighed anchor. The battlecruisers left first under the command of Vizeadmiral Hipper aboard his new flagship *Lützow*. They steamed one behind the other in line, a reconnaissance shield of small cruisers and torpedo boats keeping station some sea miles ahead to watch for enemy ships and mines. A little later Vizeadmiral Scheer set out aboard *Friedrich der Grosse* with the rest of the High Seas Fleet. His force of three squadrons followed about fifty nautical miles astern of Hipper, in a single file thirteen nautical miles long led by III Squadron, and protected by a semi-circular formation of small cruisers and torpedo boats. In all the German force was composed of ninety-nine warships with 45,000 men aboard: five battlecruisers, sixteen other capital ships, eleven small cruisers, sixty-one destroyers and six old battleships of II Squadron. These latter were the slowest ships of the German force and kept its top speed down to 18 knots.

What Hipper and Scheer never suspected was that the British were aware of all the German preparations transmitted by radio. The codebreakers in Room 40 did not know in detail what the Germans intended, but a rough picture sufficed for the Royal Navy to be put on alert. Even before the German fleet had weighed anchor, on the late evening of 30 May 1916 a total of 150 British warships with 60,000 men aboard had sailed from Scapa Flow, Cromarty, Rosyth and Harwich for the Skagerrak: twenty-eight modern capital ships, nine battlecruisers, twenty-six light cruisers, eight old armoured cruisers, seventy-eight destroyers and one minelayer.

From aboard his flagship *Iron Duke*, Admiral Jellicoe led the main British force of twenty-four dreadnoughts, which steamed through the darkness in six parallel division lines, four ships per division. The destroyers were close by for protection against U-boats, the old armoured cruisers and light cruisers forming a broad reconnaissance shield some miles ahead. Vice Admiral Beatty's fleet consisted of two squadrons, each with three battlecruisers – *Lion*, *Princess Royal*, *Queen Mary*, *Tiger*, *New Zealand* and *Indefatigable* – in a single line and also protected by a screen of light cruisers.

Because three of Beatty's force of nine battlecruisers had been despatched a few days before to Scapa Flow for gunnery exercises, these ships had been replaced by the four ships of 5 Battleship Squadron under Rear Admiral Hugh Evan-Thomas. Super-dreadnoughts *Barham*, *Valiant*, *Warspite* and *Malaya* were the most modern and powerful capital ships in the world and trailed about five nautical miles astern of Beatty. Each of them could make 25 knots, about 5 knots more than the fastest German battleships and were armed with eight 15in (38.1cm) guns, the greatest calibre at that time.

The British force was therefore superior in every respect to the German one. It not only had a greater number of ships and guns, but also guns of greater calibre, and a higher average speed. The British had no doubt that a battle with the German fleet under these circumstances would turn out well. What they did not know, however, was what the Germans intended. Beatty was therefore ordered to make for a point about a hundred nautical miles northwest of Horns Riff. This was an extensive bank of sand stretching out to seaward from well down the Danish coast. Jellicoe would position the Grand Fleet in a position about seventy nautical miles northwest of it. If neither fleet had sighted the Germans by 1400 hrs the next day, Beatty had orders to steam north and meet up with Jellicoe.

At first it seemed to the British force that they had steamed out for nothing, as no German ship had been sighted. Moreover, Jellicoe received false information from London that only Hipper and the battlecruisers had come out; Scheer and the remainder of the fleet were allegedly still at Wilhelmshaven. This reduced further the prospect of a great naval battle. Meanwhile, Hipper had already reached the Skagerrak from the south and was quite near Beatty but not in sight of him. Scheer was also approaching with the battle fleet but still two and a half hours' steaming distant.

Once the deadline of 1400 hrs agreed with Jellicoe had been reached, and he had still seen no sign of the enemy, Beatty turned north as ordered. Just at that moment, literally at the last second, one of his light cruisers saw smoke on the horizon. It came from a Danish freighter which had been compelled to stop by German destroyers. Beatty, assuming that this would be part of Hipper's battlecruiser force, gave orders at once for a change of course. Because of a misunderstood signal, Rear Admiral Evan-Thomas did not turn the four super-dreadnoughts for another ten minutes so that Beatty was heading for the enemy initially with six instead of ten ships.

Hipper also turned his ships back in the direction from whence he had come as soon as he saw Beatty approaching from the west. For Beatty this looked as if Hipper was taking flight. In reality it was Hipper's intention, also believing that he only had the enemy battlecruisers before him, to lead Beatty's squadron directly into the path of the High Seas Fleet hurrying up from the south. This opening phase of the battle off the Skagerrak is known in the histories as the 'run to the south'.

Whilst the two squadrons were now running on parallel courses to the southeast, the distance between them was closing because of the higher speed of the British ships. When it had dropped to eight miles (13km), at 1548 hrs the Germans opened fire, and the British replied at once. After a few minutes Hipper's gunners scored their first hits, while the British gunnery officers were having difficulty in estimating the range. For that purpose they had to observe if their salvoes were too short or too long – not an easy task at full speed with the pitch and roll of the ship. The Germans optics were generally more sophisticated than the British, for which reason the British ships had a central fire-control position which enabled all guns to be laid and fired at the same time. As the result of a misunderstanding as to the distribution of fire, several British ships all concentrated their fire on one German battlecruiser, so that from the outset the other, *Derfflinger*, benefited from being exempt from their attentions.

When the first rounds fell, the order 'Clear ship for battle' had been given long before. At that, the scenario which had been practised a thousand times was played out. Within a few minutes all requisite preparations for battle had been taken, gas masks and lifejackets distributed, floors watered, watertight doors shut and operational positions readied. Whoever had time changed into clean underwear, this being a measure to reduce the chances of infection in the case of a wound. The decks were now clear of personnel; officers, seamen and stokers were at their battle stations in the gun turrets, casemates, magazines, coal bunkers and boiler rooms. Only the admirals and ship commanders in the armoured control positions on the bridge, the gunnery officers, and lookout posts could follow what was happening outside the ship through viewing slits and periscopes – what information filtered through 'from above' was passed on to everybody else.

While many were frustrated at not being able to form a picture of what was happening outside with their own eyes, Matrose Richard Stumpf thought it better 'if one stands behind the thick armour and neither sees nor hears what is going on outside. It may be all right for those with strong nerves, for them that's all part of the game.'[2]

The possibility that there would probably soon be dead and wounded did nothing to diminish the anticipated joy of battle. Most of all, the officers and men of the battleships which had not taken part in the naval battles off Heligoland and on the Dogger Bank could hardly wait to have their 'baptism of fire'. 'The day has come! The enemy is in sight! And we are there! ... only a handful were white in the face, talked a lot or kept quiet and were frightened to die. By far the most of them were gleeful and in good heart,' wrote Korvettenkapitän Bogislav von Selchow, now first officer of the battleship *Hannover*.[3] On the *Helgoland*, Kapitänleutnant Walter Zaeschmar reported much the same: 'There was heartfelt joy on our ship when the first enemy mastheads appeared above the horizon'.[4] Richard Stumpf confirmed his gunnery officer's impression: 'Finally, finally, finally the great event has come which for twenty-two months has monopolised our yearnings, feeling and thinking, which has been so passionately desired, the event for which we have been working and exercising for years'.[5] Stumpf said that he felt no anxiety. 'I would be lying if I said I was anxious. No, it was an undefinable mixture of joy, anguish, sheer curiosity, nonchalance and something else which the phrase "thirst for action" does not quite cover.'[6]

What they all really felt during the next few minutes and hours can only be imagined. While one dreamed of glory and honour, the first thoughts of others were perhaps for their wives, families, or simply themselves and their own survival. Some saw in the impending battle a kind of game or sporting contest. The commander of the *Helgoland* believed that a naval battle was 'more a kind of sporting festival' and the ships 'so well constructed that nothing at all can happen to them.'[7] Much closer to the reality was the image which Hermann von Schweinitz had formulated long before Jutland. 'At sea the decision of victory or defeat falls within a couple of hours. First weeks or months of waiting, then suddenly enormous tension – and it's over, fought to a finish, like a duel. Victory or defeat, there's not much else.'[8]

The proof of what he said came that afternoon for the first time at just after 1600 hrs. The British battlecruiser *Indefatigable* exploded in a glowing fireball after *Von der Tann* had poured salvo after salvo into the last ship of the British line. A British seaman wrote later: 'It was like a whirlwind flattening a wood.'[9] Of the thousand-man strong ship's company, there were only two survivors, rescued by a German torpedo boat.

Although Hipper's ships had only had to deal with Beatty's six battlecruisers in the opening phase of the battle, the British firepower was increased substantially when Rear Admiral Evan-Thomas's dreadnought squadron caught up and got within range. The rearmost two ships of the German line, *Moltke* and *Von der Tann* soon came under fire, received serious damage and then attempted to zigzag out of the hail of heavy British shells. Despite the British superiority, it was the Germans who scored the next deadly blow: at 1626 hrs the *Queen Mary* blew up under the joint attack of *Derfflinger* and *Seydlitz*. Georg von Hase, gunnery officer of *Derfflinger*, watched the last moments of the British battlecruiser.

> First a dazzling red flame flashed at the forecastle. Then there was an explosion in the forecastle followed by a much more powerful one amidships, black components of the ship flew into the air and at once the whole ship was rocked by an enormous explosion. A gigantic cloud of smoke developed. The masts collapsed inwards, the cloud of smoke covered everything and rose ever higher. Finally there was only a thick black cloud of smoke where the ship had been before. At its base it was not very thick but it expanded upwards, looking rather like a giant black stone-pine.[10]

Of the ship's company of 1274 men, only nine survived.

Beatty was shocked. When the (false) report reached him that the battlecruiser *Princess Royal* had also exploded, he made the famous exclamation which has been quoted on innumerable occasions ever since: 'There seems to be something wrong with our bloody ships today!'[11] One of the reasons why the British ships blew up, while the equally seriously damaged German ships remained afloat, was later established to be the British practice of leaving the fire doors between the gun turrets and the magazines open to enable a faster reload. It would also appear that the German shells had greater penetrative power.

A few minutes after *Queen Mary* went down, Beatty was dismayed to receive the information from Commodore William Goodenough aboard the light cruiser *Southampton* that he had just sighted the German battle fleet. Up until that moment, Beatty and Jellicoe, also in receipt of the news, had not realised that Scheer had sailed. On the spot, Beatty decided to turn the tables and now lead the Germans into the arms of Jellicoe, whose presence fifty nautical miles beyond the horizon was not suspected by Scheer and Hipper. Beatty turned about and 'fled' to the north. The 'run to the south' was over: now began the 'run to the north'.

Half an hour later Admiral Jellicoe was faced with perhaps the most difficult decision of his life. Undoubtedly he was aware that he would soon face the entire German battle fleet, but he had no knowledge of when and where exactly the clash would occur. The reports as to the positions and courses of the Germans received aboard his flagship were incomplete and contradictory. The British historian Correlli Barnett has compared Jellicoe and Scheer with two blind men 'each steering a car based on the instructions of the other, but blind men who could regain their sight at any moment and then had to pronounce the most favourable battle formation for twenty and more battleships and distribute clear orders – and all that with the rapidity with which a car driver swerves to miss a dog.'[12]

In order to take full advantage of his superiority in numbers, Jellicoe had to form up his ships in a long battle line from the six columns of four in which they were presently arranged. He could either build this line based on a turn to the right or left. If he made the wrong choice, he would shorten unintentionally the distance from the enemy and risk the clash while his fleet was still engaged in the difficult manoeuvre. At 1815 hrs Jellicoe had his twenty-four dreadnoughts make a synchronised turn to port and was smiled upon by fortune. 'The Grand Fleet was now on an easterly course diagonally ahead of the leading ships of the High Seas Fleet approaching from the southwest and found himself for the first time in the advantageous tactical position of "crossing the enemy's T" which exposed the enemy to his heaviest fire'.[13]

In 'crossing the T' Jellicoe had succeeded in doing that of which every admiral leading an armada of floating fortresses into battle dreamed: he had crossed the path of the enemy fleet at a right angle and created a decisive tactical advantage for himself. His ships were now in a position literally to fire from all barrels, while in the long German line only the foremost ships could use their guns.

While Jellicoe's dreadnoughts were still taking up their new stations (the whole manoeuvre took about twenty minutes), the Germans achieved two more spectacular successes to add to the two British battlecruisers they had already sunk. At 1820 hrs, after receiving heavy fire from Hipper's battlecruisers and Scheer's battleships, the old British armoured cruiser *Defence* exploded. 'The ship was pulverised into atoms, everybody aboard killed by the explosion ... I shall never forget this event in all its horror,' wrote Georg von Hase, once again an eyewitness to the appalling scene.[14] Only ten minutes later the battlecruiser *Invincible* was overtaken by the same fate. Georg von Hase looked on:

> Similarly as with the other ships several violent explosions followed one after another, masts collapsed, fragments of the ship whirled through the air, a tremendous black cloud rose to the skies, coal dust sprayed in all directions. Flames flickered over the ship, more explosions followed and then the enemy disappeared from our sight behind a black wall of smoke. I shouted into the telephone, 'Our enemy has blown up!' and in the midst of the roar of battle a 'Hurrah!' resounded through the ship like thunder, repeated through all telephones of the fire control centre and spread from battle station to battle station.[15]

The *Invincible* was literally torn apart and her crew of more than a thousand men with her. Because of the shallow depth where she went down, the bow and stern of the wreck remained jutting above the surface. There were only six survivors. Amongst these was gunnery officer Hubert Dannreuter, son of the German pianist Edward Dannreuter and godchild of the composer Richard Wagner. After his rescue Dannreuter lived another sixty years and died at Hastings in 1977, nearing his hundredth birthday.

Rear Admiral Horace Hood, descendant of an old British dynasty of naval officers, also died aboard *Invincible*. His family history apparently impressed Georg von Hase.

> The commander of the Third Battleship Squadron, Admiral Hood, who went down with *Invincible*, is a descendant of the famous British Admiral Hood who distinguished himself laudably in the American War of Independence under Graves and Rodney and then both

strategically and tactically as commander-in-chief in the Battle of St Christopher (1782). During the Anglo-French war between 1793 and 1802 he commanded the Mediterranean Fleet in 1793/94 and in 1793 occupied Toulon.[16]

Hase could probably hardly believe that he and his comrades had succeeded in snuffing out the life of such a man, to a certain extent the embodiment of British naval power. Was that not, he may have thought, the best proof that the former pupil had become the equal of his master?

The Germans had not lost a ship so far, although Hipper's flagship *Seydlitz* had been so badly damaged that the admiral was obliged to transfer his flag to *Moltke*. The small cruiser *Wiesbaden* had received a direct hit in the engine room and was unmanoeuvrable, drifting helplessly between the two battle lines, hit again and again by British shells. The German fleet, though it had escaped lightly so far, was now in a very dangerous situation. Jellicoe had 'crossed its T' and Scheer knew that he had to act quickly or his ships would be overwhelmed.

He decided on a manoeuvre which had never been tried before in a naval battle because it contained within it the danger of unholy confusion: the so-called 'battle about-face'. At 1837 hrs Scheer gave the order and within a few minutes the entire High Seas Fleet had made a 180-degree turn to starboard to turn their backs on the dreadnoughts. The last ship in the line, *Westfalen*, began to turn first and all others followed like puppets on an invisible string. The British looked on in total perplexity as the German fleet, which they thought they had in their grasp, simply steamed away and disappeared into a fogbank.

Although he had saved his ships from an apparently hopeless situation, Scheer did not intend to use his newly-won freedom of manoeuvre to run for safety. Instead, he made a decision which has puzzled experts to the present day. Twenty minutes after he had escaped the deadly embrace of the Grand Fleet, Scheer ordered another about-face. He explained later that he wanted to help the unmanoeuvrable *Wiesbaden* and not risk the British cutting off his route back to Wilhelmshaven. Whatever his motive, his decision returned him within range of the British guns, and Jellicoe accepted this gift only too willingly.

Viewed from the German decks, after the second 180-degree turn the horizon turned into an inferno. Thick billows of smoke and powder, steam belched out incessantly, and from a hundred different places simultaneously the red-green muzzle-fire of the British guns erupted in the gathering dusk, the sound of guns firing rolling like thunder over the waters. One British broadside after another crashed down amongst the German ships, sharply outlined against the setting sun. Georg von Hase watched the enemy shells coming towards him through the air. 'They looked like longish black points. They got gradually bigger and suddenly they arrived. They hit the water or the ship with an enormous explosion. I could judge exactly whether they were going to fall long or short or if they were going to do us the honour.'[17] Again and again around the ship gigantic columns of water up to 300ft (100m) in height rose up, coloured greenish-yellow from the picric acid in the British shells: many of them stood for ten seconds before collapsing. 'We found ourselves literally in a sausage mincer,'[18] he wrote.

After ten minutes of this Scheer realised his mistake and broke off the battle. For him it was now a matter of survival, and of saving as many valuable ships as possible. To this end, at 1918 hrs he ordered the third about-face, but only for the battleships. The battlecruisers and torpedo boats received the almost suicidal order, 'Battle turn towards the enemy! Go for them!'[19] They were to cover the retreat of the big ships and draw the enemy fire on themselves. Although all of Hipper's battlecruisers were already seriously damaged, were flooding, and had numerous dead and wounded, they attacked – and were battered dreadfully by the British guns. 'Particularly on *Derfflinger*, the leading ship, all hell was let loose. We were receiving fire from several ships at once ... salvo after salvo came down in our immediate vicinity, and our ship was hit time after time. Those were very exciting minutes,'[20] Georg von Hase reported. Then one of the heavy British shells bored through the thick armour-plating of one of the battlecruiser's four twin turrets, converting the interior into a hell glowing white-hot:

> Oberleutnant zur See von Boltenstern, the brave turret commander, had both legs torn off, and along with him almost every member of the gun crew was killed. Shrapnel set fire to cartridges in the turret ... they burned with great stabs of flame licking as high as a house outside the turret, but they only burned, and did not explode as they had done aboard our enemy's ships. That was salvation for our ship! But all the same the effect of the deflagration of the cartridges was catastrophic! The enormous stabs of flame killed everybody within their reach. Of the 78 men manning the turret only five managed to

get out, some seriously wounded, through the flap for disposing of the cartridge casings. The other 73 died a hero's death at the same time, in the midst of feverish battle activity, carrying out with the most faithful devotion to duty the orders of their turret commander.[21]

A few seconds after this first catastrophe a second followed:

A 15in shell hit the turret roof of Dora turret, went through it and exploded inside. The same horrific result: apart from one man, thrown clear through the access hatch to the turret by the air pressure of the explosion, the entire turret crew including all those in the ammunition magazine, eighty men in all, died simultaneously ... now flames as high as a house stabbed out from the two after turrets mixed with yellow billows of smoke, two gruesome torches marking the graves within.[22]

Although von Hase's gunnery post was hit repeatedly and 'tossed high as if thrown up by giant fists', he explained that:

I kept the two forward turrets firing salvo after salvo. I sensed that our shooting calmed the nerves of our ship's company. If we had not kept firing, in those moments the ship's company might have been seized by hopelessness and despair, then everybody would have thought: only a few minutes more and we are lost. As long as we kept shooting, however, we could not be that badly off.[23]

The conditions were worse aboard the battlecruiser *Lützow*. A total of twenty-four heavy hits had turned the ship into a charnel-house. Geschütz-Führer (Gunner) Johannes Karl Groth searched for survivors after a direct hit destroyed his turret. At first he found only bodies, most mutilated and with horrific wounds. Then he heard somebody call out. 'Matrose Werner of the reserve crew was buried under the debris. When he heard my voice he said he could not get free by himself, I had to do what I could. After a long struggle I cleared the debris enough to drag him free. A sad sight. Both his legs had been torn off at the knee, and the left arm at the elbow.'[24]

Other men who survived this nightmare experience were for the most part uninjured, but had suffered serious psychic hurt. 'It was noticeable that all had suffered serious memory loss and were unbalanced mentally requiring their demobilisation later. Getting these wounded men out caused great difficulties, since all were more or less raving and the exit was very narrow. Several had to have their hands and feet bound to make transport for them possible. All were shouting out incessantly for water.'[25]

Lützow was so badly damaged that in the early hours of 1 June 1916 her commander ordered her to be sunk by a torpedo boat. All crew men still surviving at that time were saved, with the exception of seventeen men shut in a dynamo room in the bowels of the ship. 'We had to leave them behind, since it was impossible to save them,' Groth reported.[26]

The involvement of the battlecruisers, and particularly the torpedo boats, which fired more than thirty torpedoes at the Grand Fleet (none of which hit), nevertheless had the desired effect: the British ships turned away abruptly to avoid the torpedoes and for the second time on the day the Germans took flight. For pulling back, Jellicoe was later heavily criticised. Had he fought on, the argument went, he might have lost a couple of ships to torpedo hits, but provided himself with a unique opportunity to destroy the entire German fleet. That was not the mission of the British fleet commander as Jellicoe understood it. For him it was more important to preserve his own fleet than destroy that of the Germans. The admiral could not and would not show consideration for the wishes of those who dreamt of a second Trafalgar.

After the British had reorganised their lines, they commenced pursuit of the fleeing Germans. Before night fell at 2020 hrs there was a brief exchange between Beatty's ships and the heavily damaged German battlecruisers. Then darkness fell and the action was broken off.

Jellicoe was anxious to avoid a night battle, since in his opinion the Germans were better equipped and trained for it. Instead he decided to re-engage Hipper and Scheer at dawn. As a result of the way in which the respective courses and positions of the two fleets had changed during the fighting, Jellicoe now found himself with his ships between the German fleet and their route of retreat to their North Sea bases. Because first light came towards 0200 hrs in those northern latitudes, Jellicoe had about five hours to work out the interception point and steer for it. Vizeadmiral Scheer, on the other hand, had decided to escape through the channel which began at Horns Riff, the sandbank projecting into the North Sea from the Danish coast, and led through the minefields in the German Bight to Wilhelmshaven.

Over the next few hours, both fleets steamed through the darkness a mere ten nautical miles apart, the British heading south, the Germans southeast, so that their converging courses looked like the legs of a long-drawn out 'V'. 'Neither side was certain what was really going on.'[27]

During the course of the night there were repeated skirmishes. First there occurred a violent clash of small cruisers, in which the German *Frauenlob* was sunk by a torpedo. Of her crew of 329 men, only nine survived. Then British destroyers joined in, four being sunk for the loss of *Rostock* and *Elbing*. These latter two were rendered unmanoeuvrable and scuttled. Hermann von Schweinitz, navigation officer of the *Rostock*, had abandoned ship with extreme reluctance, and together with gunnery officer Kapitänleutnant Reinhold Knobloch watched his ship go down from the deck of a torpedo boat. 'I stayed on the bridge. Alone on the ship in stoic frame of mind. They noticed that I was missing, came back to fetch me. I should at least have taken my cigars along. *V-71* and *V-73* fired torpedoes at our good old *Rostock* and almost hit her! Finally they succeeded and she sank before our eyes. Painful sight. Was that really necessary?'[28]

Later that night the German dreadnoughts found the British armoured cruiser *Black Prince* straggling. She blew up, taking 857 men with her. In a last encounter, the British destroyers torpedoed the old pre-dreadnought battleship *Pommern*, which went down with all 844 hands. Shortly after dawn, the drifting wreck of the *Wiesbaden* found a watery grave, taking 589 men of her crew down with her, amongst them the author Johann Kinau, alias Gorch Fock. There was only one survivor, Senior Stoker Hugo Zenne, found adrift two days later by a Norwegian steamer.

During all these events Admiral Jellicoe maintained his course to the south. Because the British ships were a few knots faster than the Germans, they were first to reach the apex of the 'V'. The Germans arrived a few minutes later and crossed the British wake unnoticed by Jellicoe's lookouts. Scheer and Hipper were safe. Without any further encounters with the enemy the German fleet reached the Horns Riff light-vessel towards 0230 hrs and steamed through the minefields for Wilhelmshaven.

If the battle was finally over for the officers and men who had escaped injury, many others fought desperately for their lives inside their ships and elsewhere. In the hopelessly overburdened operating theatres aboard ship, terrible scenes were played out. Many wounded only received first aid, initially others had to wait to be seen by medical staff. Chaplain Thomas Bradley wrote down his impression of what he saw on the battlecruiser *Tiger*:

The cries of the wounded and burned men were very terrible to listen to. They were brought in sometimes with feet or hands hanging off. Very soon the deck of the distributing station was packed with wounded and dying men, and when fresh cases were brought in one had some difficulty in avoiding stepping on the others. Very little operating, save of an urgent kind, was done during the action, though we had an operating table ready. The doctors occupied themselves chiefly in first aid work. Morphia was given to a lot of the wounded. After a time they all settled down and we were able to sort them out, putting the slightly wounded in one place and the more serious in the other. A certain number of men were gassed and it was a sad sight to see them die. They began by coughing insistently and then gradually went off in a stupor. The greater number of injuries were caused by burns – some men had all their head, hands and arms burned, but there were not many burned about the body. Those that died were taken out and put in the messdeck portside abreast of the distributing station. When there was no longer room for the wounded in the distributing station they were placed in the corresponding messdeck, starboard side.[29]

In accordance with the traditions of the Royal Navy, the dead were consigned to the deep, sewn into their hammocks weighted down with a practice shell.

Far more men died in the cold waters of the North Sea than found their way into shipboard sick bays. Many hundreds drifted until they died, never having had hope of rescue. Ships searching next day for survivors found a picture of devastation. 'The sea was strewn with wreckage for miles and we steamed for half an hour through large numbers of dead bodies, mostly German, floating in a mass of blood, oil, dead fish, seagulls, cartridge cases, etc.'[30]

Few were still alive at this juncture to be discovered amongst wreckage. Lieutenant Commander Arthur Marsden, whose destroyer *Ardent* was sunk during the night engagement, wrote:

As the smoke and steam cleared off I could see many heads in the water – about 40 to 50 I should think. There was no support beyond lifebelts, lifebuoys and floating waistcoats so I was afraid few of us could possibly survive, especially as I realised that all the destroyers had gone on and no big ship would dare stop, even if they saw us in the water.

I spoke to many men and saw them die one by one ... I was nearly done in once or twice in the first hour by men hanging on to me in the last stages of exhaustion, and I was separated from my lifebuoy and was pulled right over in the water, but managed to recover myself and the buoy. None of the men appeared to have suffered at all; they just seemed to lie back and go to sleep ... I began to feel drowsy and dropped off into a sort of sleep several times, only to be awakened again by waves slapping into my face ... I woke again after what I felt to be a long time to hear a shout and could see ships a long way off. I took a sort of detached interest in them and gave an answering shout to 'Stick it Ardents!' to someone in the water nearby whom I could not see. I watched the ships disappear again without much interest and dozed off again. Once again I awoke to find a flotilla leader – the *Marksman* – close alongside me. I sang out for help and in reply got a welcoming and reassuring shout, 'You're all right, Sir, we're coming!' and once again relapsed into unconsciousness.[31]

When the German fleet ran into Wilhelmshaven on the afternoon of 1 June 1916, the champagne corks popped on the ships' bridges.[32] People were of the opinion that a great victory had been won. Many were still totally overcome by the events of the past twenty-four hours. Adolf von Trotha, who had experienced the battle aboard Scheer's undamaged flagship *Friedrich der Grosse*, felt one thing above all else: gratitude to have been present. He wrote to his wife:

It was a great day in world history and Our Lord God held his hand, wonderfully gracious, above us. I have received impressions that will never leave me. During the night, after a salvo from *Friedrich der Grosse*, the *Black Prince* 800 metres distant blew up in one single enormous explosion, the wall of flame was probably 100 metres high. You will sense how deeply grateful I am. I cannot put it into words.[33]

Hermann von Schweinitz too, after he got the first pains out of his system about the loss of the *Rostock*, enthused: 'A powerful panorama of battle, I feel quite lifted, feel detached from myself.'[34] And even weeks later he still had the same feelings: 'It was powerful theatrical drama, the event still resounds within me.'[35]

In reading the foregoing sentences, the reader must constantly bear in mind what an unusual and extraordinary event this 'panorama of battle' represented for sailors. Despite all the ghastliness which many of them had been forced to watch, the fact remained that naval warfare was a type of warfare 'in which battle and death, rather than survival, were the exception'.[36] Thus in the navy the experience of combat, being wounded and dying horribly, did not have the same determining force for the seaman as it did for the soldier in the trenches of the 'death zone' (Ernst Jünger). Such thinking could only arise there, the historian Michael Salewski wrote, 'as Remarque expressed it so imperishably in his book *All Quiet on the Western Front*. The war at sea including Jutland never produced anything similar.'[37]

On the other hand, that does not mean that there were not many survivors who saw the battle as a traumatic experience. Who would not, like Geschütz-Führer Groth of *Lützow* after seeing the men of his gun turret literally ripped to shreds, have a problem in considering this event 'an enviable heroic death', as Konteradmiral Wilhelm Souchon put it.[38] The British telegraphist J J R Croad, whose destroyer *Broke* was hit repeatedly by the German battleship *Westfalen* in the night action, felt no envy when he came up on deck next morning.

> When we could see and I had time to think it dawned on me what a terrible scene had been enacted. We thought of the 'Honour' and 'Glory', which so many people in their ignorance say is attached to warfare. You should have seen the decks of HMS *Broke* at 4am on 1 June 1916. There you would have seen an exhibition of the 'Honour' and 'Glory' in reality. Forty-eight of our crew lay dead and most of them shattered beyond recognition, another forty were wounded very badly. We were about five hours finding all our dead chums, dragging them out of the wrecked messdeck and throwing their bodies over the side to be buried in the deep ocean. That was the 'Honour' and 'Glory' we had. It strikes you as being one gigantic murder. You wonder how men can have the audacity, for if we stopped to think what we were going to do we should never fight at all.[39]

The statistics of the battle of Jutland are these. The Royal Navy lost fourteen ships: three battlecruisers, three obsolete armoured cruisers and eight destroyers. The Imperial German Navy lost one battlecruiser, one old pre-dreadnought battleship, four small cruisers and five torpedo boats. The British had 6768 dead or wounded, the Germans 3058.

Although when looking at the figures many may talk about a tactical German victory, there can be no doubt that the outcome of the battle changed neither the ratio of strength between the two battle fleets nor the overall strategic situation in the least. A New York newspaper summed it up a few days later: 'The German fleet has assaulted its jailor, but is still in jail.'[40]

Nevertheless, for the British this was not a cause for rejoicing. Everybody, naval personnel as well as the British public, had expected that when the great clash of the two fleets finally came, the Royal Navy would win a great victory. This it had not achieved. As if that were not depressing enough, the Germans had made it worse by getting their version of events to the press as soon as the battle was over. On the evening of 1 June 1916 the naval staff in Berlin released a communiqué claiming a great German victory and speaking of a partial destruction of the British fleet. Their own losses were deliberately understated. Before the Grand Fleet put into Scapa Flow on 2 June, all the world's newspapers carried the German claim.

In Britain these reports came as a bombshell. The authorities in London rushed to state their own position, relating only the facts which Admiral Jellicoe had signalled in his initial report to the Admiralty. Factual and soberly put, the unvarnished list of the British losses served almost as a confirmation of the German sensational bulletin and did nothing to pour oil on these troubled waters.

Even if many British officers were dissatisfied with the outcome of the battle, they reacted with consternation and indignation at what they saw as the unreasonable degradation of their achievement by the press.

It was a great victory, the enemy being driven back into harbour with considerably heavier losses in both men and materials than our own. This did not prevent the press losing its head and starting an unqualified panic. Without waiting for results, abuse and idiocy were powered out ... A more disgusting exhibition can hardly be imagined ... One paper only (the *Morning Post*) had the headline 'Admiral Jellicoe's Victory'. The battle fleet naturally hardly received a mark of recognition from a public which judges results by one's ability for being rapidly sunk. But then one should know better than to expect thanks from a public so obtuse and dull as the British masses.[41]

In the course of the next few days, as more details about the battle became known, the press revised their initial judgement, but it left a bitter aftertaste. Whichever way one looked at it: 'The unpalatable truths remained, however, that British ships and 6000 lives had been traded cheaply in the exchange of battle, and that the RN had failed to obtain a result accordant with its heritage – and immune to the mendacious constructions of journalists.'[42] A year after the battle of Jutland, when Vice Admiral David Beatty was asked by senior officers if he intended to celebrate the first anniversary in some form, he was shocked by the question. 'My answer is that that was one of the saddest days of my life, in which I lost many old and valued friends and trusted comrades, and the Navy missed one of the greatest opportunities of achieving the greatest and most glorious victory, and therefore it could not in any sense be considered a day for celebration.'[43]

For many years in Britain there was bitter controversy about who bore the responsibility for the lost opportunity, David Beatty or John Jellicoe. The two fleet commanders became deeply involved themselves in what came to be known as the 'Jutland controversy'. Beatty, particularly, left no stone unturned in his efforts to deflect blame away from himself and his decisions and pass it on to Jellicoe. This did not damage his career: some months after the battle he was appointed Commander-in-Chief of the Grand Fleet while Jellicoe became First Sea Lord. Beatty followed him into this post after the war. In 1919 both were promoted to be Admirals of the Fleet, the highest naval rank in Britain.

On the other side of the North Sea a completely different picture emerged. In Germany there was unrestrained jubilation, flags waved everywhere in the Reich, children were let off school. On the way home from the port, the *Rostock* officers Knobloch and Schweinitz got a taste of what it meant to be heroes: 'They were standing everywhere, the women and girls, some of them crying, awaiting anxiously the return of their menfolk. Nobody laughed at our attire (their uniforms had suffered considerable damage under the stresses of battle), rather shyly and respectfully they made space for us.'[44] Vizeadmiral Hipper, who had sunk three of Beatty's battlecruisers, was at once the darling of the nation. 'I am receiving letters, telegrams, cards from everywhere: it is almost impossible to cope although two officers of my staff are working at it.'[45]

Kaiser Wilhelm II awarded Hipper and Scheer the highest Prussian decoration, '*Pour le Mérite*', and finally the King of Bavaria elevated him to the nobility as Ritter von Hipper. Scheer was also offered a 'von' but declined it. He was promoted to admiral.

The Kaiser came personally to Wilhelmshaven to congratulate 'his' navy on its great success. In his speech he accentuated the 'heroic spirit' of the fleet which, as it had not previously had the opportunity to prove what it could do, had led to an 'ever greater discord and strain within the fleet taking hold.' But now, after the enemy had been brought to battle, the spell had been broken, 'the nimbus of British world mastery exposed, the tradition of Trafalgar ripped to shreds'. The Kaiser even envisaged 'a new chapter in world history' emerging, and did not forget to thank the men for their loyal service and point out that the 'glorious great deed' they had accomplished was absolutely equal to the achievements of the army:

> Today I stand here before you as your supreme commander in order to express to you my thanks from the bottom of my heart. I stand here as the representative of the Fatherland, on a mission in the name of my army in order to bring to you the greetings and thanks of the sister branch of service, alongside which you are aligned as of equal rank. Looked at from the personal viewpoint, each one of you has done his duty at his gun, in the boiler room, in the signals room.

The Kaiser ended by expressing to the officer corps his 'fullest recognition and thanks'.[46]

This was balm for the spirits of the officers, who in the months before the battle had gradually begun to lose faith in the value of their ships. Hermann von Schweinitz had long considered himself to be a 'Drückeberger' (a shirker or dodger): 'one shuns company, doesn't like to be seen on the street amongst soldiers wearing the Iron Cross, and the wounded.'[47] Now for the first time he no longer had the feeling that he should hide himself away. 'Am going out and about again,' he noted in his diary.[48] Kapitän zur See Walter von Keyserlingk, who had 'always cherished the dream of experiencing the downfall of the anxiously guarded Trafalgar legend, of the Trafalgar spell', was immoderately proud 'of having been involved in bringing it about'. In a letter to his uncle he wrote, 'The honest joy at this success of the fleet reported from all over Germany fills us all with heartfelt gratitude.'[49] From distant Varna, where he had been liaison officer to the staff of the Bulgarian fleet commander since October 1915, Kapitänleutnant Rudolph Firle also rejoiced over the 'shining success' in the North Sea and the associated 'gigantic gain' in prestige for the German fleet. 'What enthusiasm there must be in Germany for our navy. We always knew that our loyal work would prove itself at the decisive hour, but now kind fortune has put us and our navy-blue cloth to such a world-historical proof. Now we stand beside and within our glorious army.'[50]

Others, however, amongst them Admiral Scheer, were sober enough not to allow the joy of the moment to cloud the overall unchanged situation. British mastery of the sea was unbroken, and the lesson which the German fleet commander drew from the battle of Jutland was that another encounter with the High Seas Fleet would not break it. The Royal Navy, after another near-miss of a clash by the Grand Fleet with Scheer's ships on 19 August 1916, decided in future that capital ships would no longer patrol the southern North Sea 'infested' with mines and U-boats.

Thus did the dream of German sea power come to its end. For the Imperial Navy it meant that it had to find another means of proving a reason for its existence and usefulness. The solution upon which Scheer and his comrades finally settled seemed at first to contain great opportunities for the fleet. But in reality it sealed its fate.

7

'And as if the world were full of the devil'
The U-boat War

FOUR WEEKS AFTER THE BATTLE of Jutland, when all the dead had been counted, the damage assessed and the course of the battle set out in numerous sketches and charts, Admiral Reinhard Scheer sent a comprehensive report on the event to Kaiser Wilhelm II. The report was sixty-two typed sheets in extent. Scheer explained what tactical considerations there had been, how he took the fleet out, when and where he met the enemy ships, and the individual phases of the battle. Its most explosive passages are to be found at its end in a section headed 'Future Naval War Policy', in which the admiral stated how the naval war should be prosecuted after the Jutland experience for, despite the undoubted German successes, 'even the happiest outcome of a battle on the high seas will not force Britain to sue for peace in this war.'[1] At this point the Kaiser wrote 'right' in the margin. Because of the disadvantages of Germany's geographical situation against that of Great Britain, and the great material superiority of the enemy, in Scheer's opinion the fleet would not be capable of adjusting the situation to the extent that 'we could overcome the blockade against us or the island kingdom itself, not even if the U-boats are fully available for military purposes.' The admiral therefore recommended an alternative:

> A victorious end to the war in the foreseeable future can only be achieved by wearing down the British economy, therefore by setting the U-boats against the British trade routes. Concerning this matter, now as before I am duty-bound to strongly advise Your Majesty not to opt for any milder form of U-boat warfare, not only because that would contradict the purpose for which the U-boat was conceived, and the expected gains would not be in proportion to the deployment of the boats: but because it would not be possible, despite the greatest conscientiousness on the part of the commanders, to avoid incidents in British waters in which American interests are present and which would force us into humiliating loss of face if we could not act with total ruthlessness.[2]

Scheer's well-chosen words were remarkable in two respects. For the first time, and practically openly, the fleet commander had admitted that the capital ships built with such great hopes were more or less useless for military purposes, since all they could do was scratch the naval mastery of the Royal Navy. Secondly, Scheer now placed all his hopes in the U-boats and asked the Kaiser – this was decisive – for their use 'with total ruthlessness' (*mit voller Schärfe*) and not in some 'milder form' so as to avoid 'humiliating loss of face': in other words, unrestricted U-boat warfare. It was perfectly clear to the admiral that this probably meant the end of the High Seas Fleet operationally, for it could only sail supported by U-boats and would not have much more to do than stand by in the background for emergencies.

Scheer's petition was radical but not new. Almost two years previously there had been discussions between politicians and the military as to how the U-boats could be used most effectively. At the beginning of the war they were overshadowed by the big ships and no great achievements were thought likely to be expected of them. Many naval men considered submarines unfair and cowardly because they did not offer the enemy battle openly, but ambushed him. Neither side had many of them in 1914. Germany had twenty-eight U-boats, the Royal Navy more than double that number of submarines, but the German vessels were much more advanced technologically. They were built on the two-hull principle of the French engineer Maxime Laubeuf, so the fuel and dive-tanks were fitted into a separate outer hull, while the crew, engines and weapons system were located in the tubular inner pressure hull. This made them safe for oceanic voyages. Two MAN diesels provided a range of around eight thousand nautical miles; two electrical motors gave propulsion while submerged. Six torpedoes were carried and were fired through one or other of the torpedo tubes fitted at the bow or stern respectively. Safe diving depth was 50m (160ft).

The initial reservations quickly disappeared, particularly after Kapitänleutnant Otto Weddigen had demonstrated what the supposedly weak dive-boats were capable of. German U-boats sank nine British warships in the first five months of the war, while the surface fleet in the North Sea sank none. It was therefore fairly soon that the first considerations were given to using U-boats not only against warships, but also against the many hundreds of merchant vessels, flying the enemy or a neutral flag, which ran into British ports daily to supply the island with food, weapons, ammunition and other merchandise important for the war effort.

There was only one problem: when the 'Devil's weapon' (Kapitän-leutnant Rudolph Firle) was used against merchant ships as if they were warships, then the proceeding was contrary to the international law of the sea, which forbade the sinking without warning of any unarmed merchant vessel. Furthermore, all warships and U-boats had to adhere to the prize rules set out by the naval powers at the Hague peace conferences of 1899 and 1907 and in the London Declaration of 1909. Steamers suspected of carrying contraband had first to be required to stop, so that their papers and cargoes could be examined. Only when it had been established beyond doubt that the ship in question was enemy or a neutral carrying contraband could she be sunk. Neutral-flag ships even had to be sent undamaged into a port. Before any merchant ship could be sunk, the crew had first to be put in a place of safety, which did not include the ship's lifeboats. Different rules applied, however, if the merchant vessel was equipped with armament. Then she could be sunk without warning.

From the viewpoint of the German naval planners, the prize rules were totally unsuitable for U-boats, these being vessels very vulnerable to damage on the surface. They had been built precisely for the purpose of making a surprise strike from hiding. From the end of 1914 many leading German naval commanders were advocating unrestricted submarine warfare in which all merchant ships – enemy and also neutrals bringing supplies to Germany's enemies – would be sunk without prior warning or inspection.

The political leadership of the Reich around Chancellor Theobald von Bethmann Hollweg saw things differently. The political damage which unrestricted submarine warfare might cause seemed to the chancellor far greater than the military usefulness. For Bethmann Hollweg, there was no doubt that to sink merchant ships from neutral states without warning, which would inevitably involve neutrals being killed and wounded, would seriously prejudice Germany's relationship with those states. Above all, he feared the entry of the United States of America into the war on the side of the Entente. Thus at the end of 1914 there began a struggle between politicians and military about the 'right' form of U-boat warfare, in which at different times either side had the upper hand, and which as time went on became ever more bitter.

One of the arguments forwarded by the advocates of the U-boat war was both attractive and difficult to reject. This argument stated that unrestricted U-boat warfare represented a retributive measure in response to the British blockade. Their blockade was a breach of international law whose declared aim was the 'economic throttling' (Winston Churchill) of Germany. The illegal blockade of the North Sea set up by the Royal Navy at the outbreak of war infringed maritime law, namely the still-valid Paris Declaration of 1856. The British went one step further, however, by declaring the entire North Sea to be a prohibited zone on 2 November 1914.

From then on, without regard to the safety of neutral maritime traffic, Great Britain controlled all merchant ships of all nations found in the North Sea, and confiscated all merchandise and goods which might be used even remotely in the service of the German war economy. The British government had previously avoided ratifying the London Declaration of 1909, which laid down the merchandise not to be considered contraband in war, and so all foodstuffs, whatever their nature, clothing, and important raw materials, which were actually on the 'free list' and exempt from seizure, were declared contraband by the British and confiscated. 'Because Great Britain also expanded the regulations so as to arrogate to itself the right to presume that goods aboard neutral ships were intended to aid its enemy, trade between the neutral states and the Central Powers was finally paralysed.'[3] The Germans were only able to import goods and raw materials across the Baltic from Scandinavia. Particularly in the second half of the war, the consequences of the British blockade for the Reich made themselves drastically obvious.

These illegal British ploys did not escape the attentions of the hard-liners amongst the German military leadership. In response, on 4 February 1915 Germany declared the waters around Britain and Ireland, then a British possession, to be a war zone in which all enemy shipping would be sunk without warning. Thus began the first phase of the U-boat war against Great Britain. The fears of the Reich chancellor that neutral ships might become involved were brushed aside by the Chief of the Admiralty Staff, and later fleet commander, Admiral Hugo von Pohl, in the mistaken belief that U-boat commanders would be able to tell neutral ships from British ships without stopping them.

At the request of the chancellor, a rider was added to the declaration on 4 February that the safety of neutral shipping could not be guaranteed. 'In view of the abuse of neutral flags by the British government, and misunderstandings which occur in naval warfare, it is always possible that attacks being made against what are thought to be enemy ships may actually involve neutral ones.'[4] At this a hail of protest notes arrived from the neutral states, one particularly from the United States, which threatened diplomatic consequences should the Germans mean what they said. U-boat commanders were now instructed to spare ships flying a neutral flag. This made it very difficult to make attacks on enemy-flag ships, for they tried all imaginable ruses to conceal their true identity.

Nevertheless, U-boat commanders did all they could to follow the guidelines of the naval staff. Many voluntarily followed the prize rules, even when they knew the ship they were stopping was enemy – not least because the U-boat's deck gun, which could only be used when the boat was surfaced, was often more effective than the technically still imperfect torpedoes.

> Normally at a known distance apart they would call upon the merchant ship to stop by flag signal or a warning shot, have the ship's papers brought over and before sinking the ship give the crew time to get into the boats and then often tow them some of the way towards the coast. Because the very limited space aboard the U-boat permitted only a couple of the victim's crew members to be taken aboard, this towing procedure was the only way to provide the crews of ships sunk with at least a degree of safety.[5]

This form of naval warfare failed to cause the British serious problems at any stage. The number of British ports and the daily tally of freighters unloading in them was too large, and the number of German U-boats available to stop it all too small. All the same, the U-boat war was uncommonly popular in Germany in this first phase of the war, because it helped soften the feelings of helplessness against Great Britain. 'Our good German people,' the then fleet commander Admiral Pohl wrote to his wife, 'want to read every morning in their newspapers that once more X enemy ships have been sunk'.[6]

In the end it was one ship too many: on 7 May 1915, as already mentioned, *U-20*, commanded by Kapitänleutnant Walther Schwieger, sank the British passenger ship *Lusitania* near the Old Head of Kinsale, south of Ireland. The ship was on the way from New York to Liverpool and, as was later discovered, was carrying munitions for the British Army. Amongst the approximately 1200 fatal casualties were seventy-nine children and 127 American citizens. The argument continues to this day as to whether Schwieger acted correctly in pursuance of his orders, of which he was personally in no doubt, or as the Allies thought, he was guilty of a war crime. He watched the liner sink through the periscope of *U-20*:

> The ship went down incredibly fast. There was total panic on her decks. Lifeboats, filled to overflowing, were lowered uselessly by untrained persons from the height of the boat deck into the water where they capsized. People ran up and down the length of the decks in desperation. Men and women jumped into the water and tried to hang on to the keel of the capsized lifeboats. It was the most terrible thing I ever saw in my life. It was impossible for me to render assistance, I would only have been able to save a handful ... I left the place of the horror, the sight of which I could no longer bear ...[7]

Schwieger's act unleashed worldwide revulsion, the most violent being the reaction of the United States. US President Woodrow Wilson condemned the German U-boat war out of hand and insisted in unmistakeable terms on the implementation of the prize rules in each and every case. Against this background Reich Chancellor Bethmann Hollweg managed to extract from the Kaiser the provisional undertaking that at least large passenger ships should be spared until further notice. The chancellor received unexpected support from the Supreme Army Command under General Erich von Falkenhayn, who was less interested in saving the lives of innocent civilians than the overall strategic situation. For the campaign being planned against Serbia, it was necessary to recruit Bulgaria as Germany's ally. If America entered the war on the side of the Entente beforehand, Falkenhayn feared that Bulgaria's readiness to make common cause with Germany might come to nought.

Naval command considered the partial lifting of the measures to be extremely dangerous and bitterly opposed the chancellor's request. There followed a month-long tug-of-war behind the scenes, ending on 19 August 1915 when *U-24* torpedoed and sank the freighter *Arabic* with three Americans aboard, all of whom lost their lives. This enabled Bethmann Hollweg, still supported by von Falkenhayn, to obtain the undertaking that not only large passenger ships should remain unmolested. In mid September the new chief of the naval staff, Admiral Henning von Holtzendorff, even ordered U-boats to desist from all attacks west of the British Isles. 'Believe me, gentlemen, your U-boat war will not skin the whale,' von Holtzendorff told the officers of his staff.[8]

He was right: the sixty-nine German U-boats deployed in 1915 sank only 640 enemy and neutral merchant ships, about a sixth without warning. This represented only some 5 per cent of the British freight volume, an amount comparatively easy to make good.

In the fleet the premature end to the U-boat war was not received kindly. The officers suspected that the Kaiser, who in these matters usually had the last word, had been forced into a bad decision by incompetent advisers. It had come to the ears of Vizeadmiral Hipper that Wilhelm II was surrounded by 'a ring of scaremongers' attempting to manipulate the monarch for their own purposes.[9] Also counted amongst their numbers was Bethmann Hollweg the Reich Chancellor, General von Falkenhayn and Admiral Holtzendorff, and especially the equally influential and unloved chief of the Imperial Navy Cabinet, Admiral Georg Alexander von Müller. At least in the early years of the war, Müller had been a convinced opponent of U-boat warfare. Hipper accused him of influencing the Kaiser 'in the most unfavourable manner' and forcing the removal from office of all advocates of unrestricted submarine warfare.[10] Kapitänleutnant Ernst von Weizsäcker fumed: 'He kills our honour and reputation, and the successes of the Reich at sea'.[11]

German restraint did not last all that long. This was due to Falkenhayn. After his plans had succeeded and Serbia had been conquered by the Central Powers with Bulgaria's help, the general changed tactics. Now he could not have enough U-boat warfare, which he hoped would shift some of the burden away from the planned offensive at Verdun. With his support, the navy now succeeded in getting its way despite the misgivings of the government, and in February 1916 the U-boat war commenced for the second time. This time, however, U-boat commanders did not have unlimited authority to act, but only permission to sink without warning enemy merchant shipping in British waters. 'Out of regard for the interests of neutral states, especially the United States of America, not only neutral ships, but also enemy passenger ships, even if armed, were expressly excluded from the regulation permitting sinkings without warning,' the historian Joachim Schröder wrote.[12]

Only a few weeks later, however, there was a rethink. On 24 March 1916, *UB-29* torpedoed the French cross-channel ferry *Sussex*, mistaking her for a troop transporter. The attack cost at least fifty passengers their lives, and several American citizens were injured. In its protest, the United States issued an ultimatum that it would break off diplomatic relations unless Germany agreed immediately to return to the prize rules. To the horror of the admirals, the Bethmann Hollweg government acceded to American demands. Vizeadmiral Scheer, who had just been made fleet commander, acted on his own initiative to withdraw all German U-boats from the seas around Britain, since he considered submarine warfare conducted according to the prize rules to be quite impossible. From that point forward, the weight of the U-boat war fell on the Mediterranean, where U-boats achieved some sensational results. By the end of the war Kapitänleutnant Lothar von Arnauld de la Perière alone as commander of *U-35* and *U-139* sank a total of 194 merchant ships and two warships, to become the most successful U-boat commander of all time.

The Reich Chancellor, apparently bending over backwards to accommodate the Americans, now became the leading figure of hate for the navy. Hipper accused Bethmann Hollweg of 'deceiving the German people' by damaging the German chances of victory through his constant interventions. 'If we do not get rid of this Reich Chancellor soon, he will lose the war for us,' the Admiral prophesied.[13] Kapitänleutnant Rudolph Firle turned to prayer: 'Lord God, give us a Bismarck who doesn't give a damn for anyone and will sink all merchant ships inside the war zone.'[14]

The officers would have preferred it if Grossadmiral Alfred von Tirpitz, the creator of the German fleet, were Reich Chancellor. After he began to lose his earlier influence at the beginning of the war, and finally the confidence of Wilhelm II, in March 1916 the Kaiser released him. Konteradmiral Albert Hopman led the field, arguing that not attempting to improve the situation with the aid of Tirpitz was a wasted opportunity. 'It is more than a misfortune that His Majesty has not seen fit to install this tremendous man in a post where he is the only man right for it, namely as Reich Chancellor, or given him at least plenary powers for this war. Then everything would have come out differently.'[15]

As chief of the Reich Navy Office, Tirpitz had masterminded the German naval building programme, and when all was said and done he was the man whom the navy now had to thank that all their hopes must rest with the U-boat arm, while the capital ships which he had said would provide their 'greatest effectiveness between Heligoland and the Thames' were practically powerless against the distant British blockade. It was a bitter realisation and many officers suffered for years in consequence, many to their end of their lives.

Others were more pragmatic. It had assuredly not been an easy task for Admiral Scheer in his report to the Kaiser about the battle of Jutland to admit the unsuitability of the proud German dreadnoughts. He was probably also aware, of course, that there were more important things than such findings. How the war was to terminate in a German victory, for instance. In August 1916 that was something which people were not so sure of as they had been in August 1914. On the battlefields of the western front, as at Verdun and on the Somme, the respective armies butchered each other to gain a few feet of terrain without obtaining any decisive advantage by doing so.

There was little doubt in naval circles that in the event of defeat, Germany would inevitably be relegated into the second rank of the great powers, while Britain would further expand her hegemony. From the point of view of the officers at least, that could not be allowed to happen. Only a 'victorious peace', a peace in which the Kaiser Reich dictated the conditions to its enemies, would make it possible, as the historian Holger Herwig wrote, 'to retain the specific Prussian-German authoritarian state and the elements by which it is constituted.' Only in Kaiser Wilhelm II's class-structured state,' Herwig continued, 'could the naval officers hope to preserve their privileged status in the "highest state caste" since only a victorious Germany would be able to direct world politics in the grand style, for which it required its gigantic battle fleet.'[16] Therefore the officers had to fight on with all means at their disposal, and for so long as need be, until a satisfactory conclusion for the navy was possible. This attitude brought them, just as it did the other conservative bourgeois forces in Germany who hoped for a military triumph and opulent gains in territory, up against the ever increasing antagonism of all those who preferred a conciliatory negotiated peace.

'Peace with honour, worth the enormous sacrifice,' was what the navy wished for.[17] In two memoranda of November and December 1916, the naval staff set out in precise terms what that actually meant. After peace came, a string of naval bases would be set up, circling the globe. These would assist the launching of a future naval war against Great Britain: the Azores, Tahiti and Dakar would become German outposts, the existing possessions of the Reich would obviously remain German. In order to improve the situation for the navy, it was deemed necessary to annex the coast of Belgian Flanders, Kurland in the Baltic, the Faroes and the Albanian port of Valona.[18]

The personal desires of individual officers went much further. Kapitän zur See Walter von Keyserlingk wished for Reich 'predominance in Europe to the exclusion of Britain and Russia.'[19] Vizeadmiral Wilhelm Souchon liked the idea of 'weakening our neighbours to our military advantage', especially 'by means of this war bringing down France as a great power'.[20] Kapitänleutnant Reinhold Knobloch wanted 120 billion marks in reparations from the Entente powers and for Egypt to become a Turkish province.[21] Rudolph Firle wanted to subjugate Russia and to 'think of it as our future colony'.[22] The expansion in the east belonged amongst the most important war aims of the nationalist Right and Supreme Army Command. For the navy, on the other hand, considerations of this kind played a rather subordinate role. Its main enemy was, and remained, Britain and if anything was a priority for the navy it was the 'incorporation' of Flanders into the Reich and free access to the Channel coast.

Whereas the Royal Navy would be anxious for a peace treaty maintaining the status quo, the continuation of the British Empire and with it the existence of the Royal Navy, what mattered for the German navy was to create for Germany a place in the world comparable to that of the British. That was precisely the original task planned for the fleet. Yet neither before the war, by its fear-inducing effect to move the British to make 'world-political' concessions, nor by this stage into the war, had it been able to make a contribution of any great note. As a consequence, many officers now looked upon unrestricted U-boat warfare as 'the last, most powerful means ... which might leave us starving, or bring us reliable and honest success. This is now war to the knife. An eye for an eye, a tooth for a tooth! And as if the world were full of the devil! We must break through.'[23]

The important thing was that the home front should hold out until the U-boats had 'done it'. With great anxiety the officers watched the British naval blockade increasingly making its mark. Before the war, Germany had imported about a quarter of its requirements in food and important fertilisers from overseas. As these imports had for the most part been halted after the outbreak of war, in the spring of 1915 food rationing had been introduced, finally down to a fraction of the average consumption of the pre-war period. Long queues outside shops were commonplace in the towns. Often riots and looting occurred. The setting up of a state authority to control and regulate food distribution, the war food office in May 1916, made little difference: as Thomas Nipperdey wrote, 'Hunger became the central special experience of the home front.'[24] Reinhold Knobloch commented on it in November 1916 thus: 'The entire German people is now actually malnourished to some extent. Fat stomachs are dwindling more and more, which is no bad thing.'[25] His observation was basically correct: during the war the German population lost 20 per cent of its body weight on average, but his cynical conclusion was false: the overall consequences were dangerous to health, particularly for women.[26]

In parallel with the worsening food situation, real wages sank well below the levels of the pre-war years, working hours were lengthened and protective regulations lifted. This all resulted in a clear fall in the standard of living for a large section of the population, be they workers, clerks or officials. In 1916 the first 'wildcat' strikes occurred. As the war went on, the 'discord regarding material shortages and weariness of war' combined with 'resentment against the privileged and ruling classes, social criticism and political protest'.[27] As we shall see, even the navy was not excluded from this development.

It seemed, therefore, all the more important to mobilise all forces in order to emerge victorious in the end. The new, third Supreme Army Command (OHL) under the 'victor of Tannenberg', Generalfeld-marschall Paul von Hindenburg, and his deputy, General Erich Ludendorff, saw this. Scarcely had they required General Falkenhayn to vacate his post at the end of August 1916 after the failure of the Verdun offensive, than they announced the total mobilisation of the German economy for war. In the course of the so-called Hindenburg programme, German armaments production was to more than double – a final Utopian aim to which all other economic targets were subordinated until the end of the war. Under the influence of the OHL, at the beginning of December 1916 the government enacted a law regarding auxiliary service to the fatherland, which introduced labour service for all males aged between seventeen and sixty years of age.

The navy endorsed this measure. 'The people are being saddled with a heavy burden,' Kapitänleutnant Knobloch considered, 'but it has to be.'[28] Korvettenkapitän Bogislav von Selchow expected that 'every German, the artist and academic, the cripple and the typist will focus on nothing else but belief in victory.' It was clear to him that, 'The war can only be won by those who face the reality and nothing else ... thus a people can only be victorious if every muscle and every thought are harnessed to the one great cause ... In war, it is force against force. To make this force as strong as possible, that is the single task of a people at war and its leaders.'[29]

The most important contribution of the navy to this collective strengthening of the force was to argue full out for unrestricted U-boat warfare. In order to break down the resistance from the political leadership of Chancellor Bethmann Hollweg, now, as ever, hesitant (Konteradmiral Albert Hopman thought that 'the man and his clique belong in the madhouse or on the gallows'),[30] some highly-placed officers, amongst them the ousted Tirpitz, did not hold back from political agitation. A target of this influence was Ernst von Weizsäcker, who was urged to convince his father, the prime minister of Württemberg, to speak out in favour of unrestricted U-boat warfare as the Württemberg representative on the Federal Council's committee for foreign affairs. Weizsäcker, who was not inclined to allow himself to be used in this way, noted in his diary, not without a certain scorn, what he thought of the efforts of his comrades: 'The naval officer corps sits around, eats, drinks, discusses politics, intrigues, feels itself to be patriotic while going about obtaining support for the U-boat war in an underhand way. The U-boat war is intended to cover up the stupidities in fleet building and in the uses of the fleet during the war. The fact that they cannot make propaganda openly speaks for a guilty conscience.'[31]

The activities of the navy were nevertheless successful even so. In October 1916 commerce warfare governed by the prize rules, which Admiral Scheer had rejected so vehemently in the spring, was reinstated, but because in the meantime the total of operational U-boats had increased considerably, German U-boats were now sinking over 300,000 tons of enemy shipping monthly. Although these results were better than ever before, the German Admiralty was adamant that the prize rules had to be dropped. In support of this demand, in December 1916 the naval staff prepared a carefully worked out appraisal according to which Britain could be starved into submission if the U-boats sank an average of 600,000 tons of merchant shipping monthly. The source for this figure can no longer be determined. 'This almost spooky certainty,' the political academic Peter Graf Kielmansegg wrote, 'was nevertheless the reason for preferring unrestricted U-boat warfare, which would lead inevitably to conflict with the USA, to a successful U-boat campaign under the prize rules which, if not decisive for the war, avoided the danger of conflict with the USA.'[32]

The military side swept off the table the objection persistently raised by Chancellor Bethmann Hollweg that America must not be drawn into the war under any circumstances, observing that the United States was not a serious opponent for Germany and her allies. The navy even guaranteed that no American troopship would ever reach the shores of France, while Admiral Eduard von Capelle, Tirpitz's successor as secretary of state at the Reich Navy Office, informed the Reichstag: 'In the military respect I consider the effect of the United States strengthening our enemies by entering the war on their side to be nil.'[33]

With the benefit of hindsight, this was a grotesque miscalculation of the actual situation. But at that time, nobody challenged the over-optimistic prophecies of the military. One of the few doubters was Ernst von Weizsäcker. In his diary he noted that experts had assured him it would be two years before the effects of the U-boat war showed themselves. Weizsäcker described the assertions of the naval staff, in his opinion made against their better knowledge, as 'the greatest stupidity and the worst crime committed by the navy in this war'. For the 'incomprehensible optimism' which reigned at fleet staff, comprehension failed him.[34]

In this opinion Wezisäcker was not only almost alone within the navy: many people in Germany believed, influenced by years of propaganda, that U-boat war was the urgently needed wonder-weapon by which Britain could be 'overwhelmed' in the short term, and the war brought to a victorious end. Therefore why should anyone want to delay in finally launching it? Even former opponents such as the Admirals Müller and Holtzendorff changed their minds and now advocated unrestricted U-boat warfare. The new OHL under Hindenburg and Ludendorff supported it. When the Entente powers turned down with unusual brusqueness a peace offer by the German government, which Bethmann Hollweg had announced to the Reichstag in mid December 1916 in his desperate search for a way out, there was no more holding back. On 9 January 1917 at the Kaiser's HQ at Pless, the opening of the unrestricted U-boat warfare campaign was set for 1 February 1917.

The German public greeted the decision with great enthusiasm. The *Münchener Neuesten Nachrichten* summed up the general feeling thus: 'On land we have our affairs in good hands: Feldmarschall von

Hindenburg will continue to lead our armies in the struggle and to victory as the true Eckart, which he is to us. Now at sea too we have raised the decisive weapon ... with proud, determined confidence we now accompany our brave U-boats into the great struggle: after a stiff fight they will bring us victory and peace.'[35]

The navy also rejoiced. 'Finally the ardently desired decree for unrestricted U-boat warfare has come,' Hipper exulted. 'Hooray!'[36] The admiral had the 'rock-solid belief that we will win', and had already noted six months earlier in his diary after a meeting with Graf Zeppelin: 'An old dare-devil. Is obviously all in favour of unrestricted U-boat warfare. In his opinion it is the only way we can win the war. Mine too.'[37] Over the next few months Hipper followed the course of the U-boat war very closely, meticulously noting down which commander with which boat sank how much tonnage. Kapitän-leutnant Reinhold Knobloch did the same, collecting all information he could lay hands on, reading bulletins and memoranda from the naval staff, evaluating newspaper reports, questioning homecoming U-boat men about their experiences and keeping his own statistics about successes and U-boat losses. 'The entire public is watching with confidence and wild expectation. Through them we await the outcome of the war in the final battle.'[38]

The U-boatmen themselves found special satisfaction in all this. Kapitänleutnant Heinrich Stenzler, who had begun the war as an Oberleutnant aboard Hipper's flagship *Seydlitz* and had been transferred at the end of 1915 to the U-boat arm at his own request, wrote to his mother on 2 February 1917: 'We are naturally all very pleased. To help share in deciding the outcome in the front line is something which makes one proud and calm. I hope that finally I shall be able to achieve something. There is still time.'[39] At the end of March Stenzler took his boat *UC-30* to the west coast of England on his first patrol. 'For the next four weeks do not expect to hear from me. There is no cause for disquiet,'[40] he assured his mother. On his return to Germany on 21 April 1917 when north of Heligoland, *UC-30* hit a mine and sank. Heinrich Stenzler's body was recovered on the Danish coast two months later and brought to Germany to be interred in his home town of Stralsund. The Kaiser awarded him a posthumous Iron Cross, first class.

Examples such as that of Stenzler led to U-boatmen being hailed as heroes by the German public as never before. As we know, this encouraged many others to emulate them. In March 1917 Reinhold

Knobloch recorded that 'all officers I meet wish they had a U-boat to command.'[41] He had himself applied after the loss of *Rostock* at Jutland, together with Hermann von Schweinitz, both now transferred aboard the old *Danzig*, but neither was successful. In disappointment he wrote: 'What is the point of this? Why do they want us to rot on the *Danzig*? I shall attempt to find out. If they cannot use us here, we might as well be in the trenches. But our lives now are intolerable.'[42] Finally, in May 1918 Knobloch was transferred to the U-boat school at Glücksburg, but he never got to serve on an operational U-boat.

That was the other side of the coin for those in the U-boat arm, about which the public never heard: just as it had been desperately longed for, how equally difficult was it now to bear for those who were not chosen to sail for the front. The uselessness of war service aboard one of the big ships, immobile on their anchorages since Jutland, was also more obvious than ever before. From 1 February 1917 onwards, the main purpose of the fleet was to protect the channels by which U-boats left and entered port and to guard their bases against attack. In reality it should have been the other way around: the U-boats should have been giving invisible support to the fleet in its forays into the open sea. Now the roles were reversed. This made some mariners happy, namely those who had been able to secure one of the coveted places on a forward U-boat. Meanwhile, the much larger majority remained deeply discontented and frustrated on board the capital ships. Korvettenkapitän Bogislav von Selchow described the mood aboard the battleship *Hannover*:

And ourselves! Here on the *Hannover*. Laid up in port, go to sea a little bit to help in training the U-boats or our own men, do many duties, many more perhaps than those really at sea on the light cruisers and merchant raiders, and yet we feel like people given a cruel fate hammering at a rocky ridge while out there a god is dividing up the world. The lieutenants, the petty officers, the seamen and stokers, all excellent men, all want to take part. Away from this battleship, into the world, into life, into glory. The applications are piling up on my desk. And I, who cannot tolerate it here any longer on this floating base, every day I have to placate them, tell them over and over that we have to have people even here, not every man can be on a U-boat or the *Möwe* (a well-known merchant raider), this nucleus of able men must not be torn apart. That is all well and good and even correct, but nobody believes me and worst of all, I do not believe it myself ...The crew of the *Hannover* is first-class, I have to say it myself, work for each other and are loyal to each other, that is a pure joy. Only, we are at war! And they want to fight and have responsibility ... The German Reich is fighting for its future and I am not a part of it. I go through shipboard procedures, give orders and go to bed each evening. I envy the soldiers in the field their bunker and the lowest ranking stoker on a front-U-boat his hammock.[43]

Selchow was also convinced that the U-boat war could achieve the goal of bringing Britain to her knees. In fact, this fourth and last phase began very promisingly. The initial force of one hundred operational U-boats grew over the coming months to 129, and received the order 'to attack all shipping with all means and without further enquiry'[44] in the blockade zone declared in the waters around the British Isles, in most of the Mediterranean, and in the Arctic. No distinction was to be made from now on between enemy and neutral, armed and unarmed merchant ships, or between freighters and passenger ships. Joachim Schröder has shown nevertheless that even in this last phase of the U-boat war there was a whole series of exclusions provided for, so that even now it was still not true to speak of totally unrestricted U-boat warfare.

All the same, at once the sinkings by U-boats increased significantly, due to the unsparing involvement of men, boats and weapons. Yet although in this way the critical figure demanded by the naval staff of five times 600,000 tons register was sunk within a few months and much more by the end of 1917, London did not come round according to the predictions. Despite all their efforts, even under these circumstances, the Germans could not shut down the imports of goods and raw materials essential to the war effort into Great Britain effectively enough over the long term. The stream of merchandise which came daily from all parts of the world bound for British ports was too great. Moreover, the British did all they could to increase home production, used gardens, parks and even schoolyards for the cultivation of potatoes and vegetables and, just as the Germans had been doing for much longer, turned to cheaper or sub-standard substitutes. The food ministry in London took measures to ensure that the average price of individual foodstuffs remained constant throughout the entire war, and that there was enough food available in all regions of the country.

Accordingly, in contrast to Germany, in Great Britain nobody starved. On the contrary: all in all, state intervention and higher wages in the important war industries even raised the living standards of the lower classes – for the American historian Jay Winter a 'paradox of the Great War'.[45] It is equally paradoxical that unrestricted U-boat warfare also led indirectly to this improvement, by forcing the British to subject their system of provisions supply to scrutiny, and to modify it where necessary. A fair indication of the effectiveness of these changes was, amongst others, the female mortality rate. In Great Britain it remained largely uninfluenced by military events whereas in the German Reich in 1917 it was one-third higher than before the war.[46]

Not only the imminence of the British collapse, but also the airy dismissal of the American danger turned out to be a gross false estimation on the part of the German military. The reluctant exception made by the navy, to spare American passenger ships if possible, served no purpose. On 3 February 1917, just two days after the inception of unrestricted U-boat warfare, the United States broke off diplomatic relations with Germany. On 4 April 1917, as predicted by Chancellor Bethmann Hollweg, they declared war on the German Reich. 'So now we have war with America too! What does it get us? Our motto: Many enemies, much honour!' was the sarcastic comment of Kapitänleutnant Hermann von Schweinitz.[47]

From this point on, the United States not only placed its merchant fleet at the service of the hard-pressed British, it also supplied the Entente powers with ships, weapons, munitions and servicemen. In December 1917 they even placed at the disposal of the Royal Navy a series of modern dreadnoughts, integrated into the Grand Fleet as 6 Battleship Squadron – much to the regret of some British officers, who took the view that such support from overseas was not only superfluous but undesirable.

The American declaration of war darkened the horizon for the Germans very substantially. Yet the darker the prospect looked, the more stubbornly did the navy refuse to face up to it. Many officers regarded it almost as an act of sabotage, when on 19 July 1917 the Reichstag in Berlin passed a resolution to seek a peace of understanding and reconciliation without 'coerced acquisitions of territory and political, economic or financial coercion'.[48]

Previously the Centrist deputy Matthias Erzberger had become the first leading bourgeois politician to paint the military and political situation of Germany in the gloomiest colours and demand that the government should launch an immediate peace initiative. Germany had no need of such a thing – at least not in the view of the navy. Adolf von Trotha saw Erzberger's intervention, which also would have meant the end of the U-boat war, as confirming himself in his own opinion: 'The man seems not only to be a traitor, but mad as well'.[49] Kapitänleutnant Walter Zaeschmar was also beside himself: 'Germany, that is to say, those who have stayed at home, have given up and are snivelling, I do not know how many times they have done so already, for peace. This time by means of a peace resolution. What the enemy hordes could not achieve, internal disunity has managed to do. We are rejecting victory.'[50] The navy did at least have cause for rejoicing. Almost at the same time, the Reich Chancellor stepped down, something long yearned for (and engineered). Bethmann Hollweg tendered his resignation from office, to some extent forced out by the Supreme Army Command (OHL), on 13 July 1917. 'Hooray. I only hope it is not too late,' Vizeadmiral Hipper commented.[51]

Under the new Chancellor Georg Michaelis, who lasted only four months before giving way to the Centrist politician Georg von Hertling, the Reichstag peace plans were not pursued. Instead, the U-boat war was continued. After all was said and done, it was still possible that it might succeed. In the autumn and winter of 1917, however, the initially surprisingly good tonnage figures fell off markedly. The reason for this was not only the increasing exhaustion of the German U-boat crews: the British defensive measures had begun to take effect. Hydrophones and depth charges for anti-submarine work had reached a clearly higher technical level compared to that at the outbreak of war. Many access routes into the English Channel and in the German Bight had been made practically impassable for U-boats by complicated net systems and minefields.

Most important was the introduction by the British of the convoy system. Initially, it was a measure adopted by the Royal Navy with the greatest reluctance, since it was feared it would offer U-boats easier targets, the convoys, which shepherded previously independent vessels into large groups of merchantmen protected by warships, but soon it proved the most effective means of anti-submarine defence. The convoys severely reduced the chances of a U-boat sighting a merchant ship, for now the steamers did not set out on different days and on a variety of routes, but all took the same route at the same time. The U-boat commander who was not at the right place at the right time left empty-handed. The successful U-boat commander could attack, at the most, one or two ships of a convoy before he was discovered and forced below with depth charges. The convoy system also enabled the transport of more than a million American fighting troops to the fronts in Europe – a possibility which the German naval staff had denied constantly.

U-boat commander Ernst Hashagen described how difficult the convoy system made it to 'go marauding'. In October 1917, Hashagen dived his boat U-62 below a convoy and observed through the periscope the movements of the enemy ships. At any moment his boat could have been rammed or discovered by one of the destroyer escorts.

> I am not sure I know how to put into words the dreadful stresses which such an attack inflicted on me. My boat was 70 metres long and 6 metres broad! Therefore a fairly large, or better put, an oversized whale. Submerged, as cumbersome as a turtle on dry land. And we not only had to slither our way through the escorts but also put ourselves at the right moment in just the right spot and at precisely the correct angle to allow us to fire a torpedo. As we were now in the middle of the convoy, we had to keep a constant 360° observation. They could pass over us from any direction. The periscope only had a field of vision of 30°. Can one imagine what that meant? All I know is that in such moments sweat would often stream down my body just from the physical tension.[52]

As soon as he thought the right moment had come, Hashagen fired off a torpedo and took his boat down to 160ft (50m). A good thirty seconds later a dull explosion announced the success of the dangerous action, and the commander accepted the congratulations of his men.

Outwardly, the Imperial Navy seemed to hold firm to the U-boat war, even in the last year of hostilities. Behind the scenes, however, the search began for the causes of the ever-increasing lack of success. The fleet commanders blamed the naval staff for not deploying the U-boats correctly; the Reich Navy Office accused them of not having ordered a sufficiently large building programme. The truth of the matter is that during almost the entire war there had been no continuous, long-term building project for U-boats, a circumstance all the more surprising when one remembers what importance the navy had vested in them since 1915. A reason for this neglect lay once more in the splintered command structure of the navy, which worked to the detriment of efficient co-operation between the respective naval authorities.

In order to resolve this problem, in the summer of 1918, following the example of OHL, for the first time a uniform high command was set up for the navy, the so-called Naval War Directorate (SKL). Admiral Reinhard Scheer became head of SKL and also chief of the naval staff, his post as fleet commander being taken over by Vizeadmiral Franz von Hipper. Adolf von Trotha, now promoted to Konteradmiral, remained chief of staff of the High Seas Fleet. The SKL immediately attempted to breathe new life into the stagnating U-boat war with the development of an unrealistic, large-scale concept (called the Scheer Programme in imitation of the Hindenburg Programme) which planned for thirty-six new U-boats per month. By now it was too late. In the west the omens of defeat for the German army had already begun to manifest, and at the end of September 1918 OHL declared that the war was lost. After that it was only a matter of weeks until the Armistice terms forced a termination of the U-boat war on 20 October 1918.

Whereas the U-boat war still continued into the last days of the conflict in forlorn hope, the High Seas Fleet continued to have a subordinate role for the naval planners. Forays by the fleet or small units hardly ever occurred. The absence of U-boats in the campaign against enemy merchant shipping weakened the operational readiness of the capital ships as much as the constant changeovers in personnel.

During the final years of the war, the fleet made only three military forays: between 11 and 19 October 1917 a 20,000-strong force occupied the Baltic islands of Ösel, Moon and Dagö, protected by eleven capital ships, nine small cruisers and six U-boats, plus dozens of torpedo boats and minesweepers. This was the first army–navy combined operation. The purpose of the offensive was to drive the Russian fleet from the Gulf of Riga and secure the northern flank of the German army in the east. It was also important to 'stiffen the fleet' as Vizeadmiral Albert Hopman, then commander of the reconnaissance forces in the eastern Baltic, expressed it to Tirpitz very directly in a letter.[53] Shortly afterwards, on 17 November 1917 a skirmish occurred off Heligoland when British light cruisers attacked the German security units. The sudden appearance of two battleships forced the British to retire and prevented serious casualties. In April 1918 the High Seas Fleet sailed to disrupt commercial traffic between Norway and Scotland. It was the furthest it had ever ventured and was the last such sortie of the war.

8

'These people should simply be put up against a wall and shot'
Unrest in the Fleet, 1917

ALL IN ALL IT WAS NOT a bad life that the naval personnel of *Sonderkommando Kaiserliche Marine Türkei* enjoyed on the Bosphorus. The *esprit de corps* was good, the weather warm, the work mostly tolerable. 'We live here in Constantinople just like in normal times, the prices are a bit high but we do not go short of anything,' Vizeadmiral Wilhelm Souchon wrote to his wife in March 1915.[1] The officers bought Turkish carpets at the bazaar, looked at the Hagia Sophia and the other sights, in the evening went to the cinema or one of the bars 'where the local German elements meet as they would around a beer table at home'.[2] Now and again Souchon would invite local dignitaries resident in the city to a moonlit dinner on the afterdeck of his flagship *Goeben*, strawberry punch would be served 'until late in the starry, cloudless night', and special occasions would be marked with champagne and caviar.[3] Mention has already been made of the occasional excursions along the sands with 'piggy-back' fights and 'pyramids'.

In the summer of 1917 it came to an end. After three years as commander of the Turkish fleet, Souchon was ordered home to take command of IV Battleship Squadron at Wilhelmshaven. The chance to command a section of the High Seas Fleet in the North Sea and to finally have 'a proper flag flying above me'[4] filled the admiral, who made no secret of his poor opinion of the Turkish navy, with great joy. When he went aboard his new flagship *Prinzregent Luitpold* for the first time in September 1917, however, the conditions aboard shocked him. The men's quarters were totally bare and cheerless, the paintwork had peeled off the walls. Even his own rooms were 'dark as a cellar and cold'.[5] Straight away Souchon allowed the crew to 'decorate the walls with pin-ups from illustrated journals, calendars, postcards and the like which otherwise wouldn't have made much of a blaze.' For, as he told his wife, 'To be lodged for years in these iron holes, who knows how far removed from the daylight, is bound to have a depressing effect on morale'.[6]

This was only too true. Not six weeks before Souchon's arrival at Wilhelmshaven, the stokers aboard the same *Prinzregent Luitpold* had set in train the first mutiny in German naval history by leaving the ship without permission. In itself, the motive for this would seem insignificant. After there had been minor protest demonstrations aboard other ships of the fleet in which the seamen and stokers expressed their displeasure at the poor food or shortened leave, the rumour circulated aboard *Prinzregent Luitpold* on 31 July 1917 to the effect that a cinema show scheduled for the following day had been cancelled – instead, the men must do infantry training. When the rumour was confirmed next morning, about fifty stokers left the ship without permission, in order to avoid the training. When they returned aboard several hours later, the commander, Kapitän zur See Karl von Hornhardt, had eleven of them confined.

At that, the remainder of the crew decided on an action in protest. Led by stoker Albin Köbis, on the early morning of 2 August 1917 about six hundred crewmen left the ship without permission and marched over the dyke into the small village of Rüstersiel. This time it was not treated so lightly. On account of the large number of men involved, and because the unrest spilled over to other ships of IV Squadron, Fleet Command ordered disciplinary measures and subsequently courts martial. This concluded with numerous sentences of imprisonment being handed down, together with five death sentences for 'incitement to mutiny in time of war'. The sentences had to be confirmed by the fleet commander, who could elect to commute the death sentences to terms of imprisonment. Admiral Scheer did so in three of the cases, but he confirmed the death sentences passed on the stoker Albin Köbis and seaman Max Reichpietsch of the battleship *Friedrich der Grosse*. Both men were shot by firing squad on 5 September 1917 at the Köln-Wahn rifle range.

For Matrose Richard Stumpf the executions of Köbis and Reichpietsch were a crime, 'whose enormity boggles the imagination ... I would have called any man a fool who stated that in my fatherland a man could be sentenced to the penitentiary or to death without having done anything illegal. Gradually it is becoming highlighted to me why many people oppose the military and its system with such passion.'[7] However, despite his sympathetic utterances, Vizeadmiral Souchon wrote to Admiral Scheer at the end of September, after first boarding the *Prinzregent Luitpold*, 'that the sentences of the court martial have had their effect and returned the fleet to full operational readiness. While it is true that many seamen were led astray by the ringleaders, now the men are again obeying the orders of their officers without argument.'[8]

What transpired at Wilhelmshaven in August 1917 was as much a sign of the times as an expression of the inner strife in the Imperial Navy. The unrest in the fleet was a reflection of general war weariness and existing political and social circumstances which had now reached the seamen and stokers of the High Seas Fleet. In many sectors of the German people, and especially amongst the working classes, the feelings of unity of the first months of the war had long given way to the bitter recognition that this war was not a lofty, sublime or, above all, short adventure, overcoming all class differences – as many had thought at first. Instead, it brought to Germany death, suffering and hunger on a previously unimagined scale, and there was no end in sight.

Against the background of February revolution in Russia and the entry of the United States into the war as a result of unrestricted U-boat warfare, the first great wave of political strikes in the Kaiser Reich began in April 1917. Hundreds of thousands took part in strikes and demonstrations, demanding better food in greater quantities, an early peace without annexation, and democratic reforms. The motivating political force behind it all was the USPD (German Independent Social Democratic Party) which had now broken away officially from the majority SPD (German Social Democratic Party) after a long period of inter-party wrangling. Within the USPD were now gathered 'all those people opposed to a continuation of the war and who were strictly against co-operating with the government. The new party was an anchor of hope for the hungry, war-weary masses'.[9]

Within the USPD was also the radical-left Spartacus group around Karl Liebknecht and Rosa Luxemburg, which became independent in November 1918 as the Spartacus League and merged a little later into the newly founded KPD (German Communist Party). The speed at which the USPD gained in influence can be seen, as in January 1918 more than a million workers all over Germany went on strike, to oppose a continuation of the war and to demand internal reforms.

The crews of the warships lying quietly in harbour played an active part in these events. Boredom and the lack of useful work left the seamen and stokers with plenty of time on their hands for discussion, reading newspapers and exchanges with shipyard workers, many of whom were USPD members. In this way naval personnel began to develop political ideas which were diametrically opposed to those of their officers. Above all, the demand for a quick end to the war and the ever-growing calls for a democratisation of the authoritarian structure of the Kaiser Reich seemed highly suspect to the conservative officer corps, determined to have a 'victorious peace'.

In order to prevent the 'movement' from spreading, NCOs and men were forbidden to take part in political gatherings, to join a political organisation or read socialist newspapers. Nevertheless, ideas of peace and reform could not be suppressed for long. The 'internal revolution' within German society of the Wilhelm era had begun some time before and did not stop short at the navy. 'Amongst our people one notices the vague, dark spirit of refusal and resistance. There is unrest and the matter is pressing towards a fearsome outcome,' Kapitänleutnant Reinhold Knobloch wrote in his diary.[10] In his eyes, it was principally 'malcontents, the faint-hearted and rabble-rousers' who were at the heart of the unrest amongst the people and who, with 'mad, foolish intent', stirred the workers to strike without regard to 'the desperate emergency and the dead seriousness of the times'.[11]

Konteradmiral Albert Hopman took a greatly different view. He wrote in a letter to his wife:

> At the moment a particular feeling is wafting across the world, calling for peace, for protection against the repetition of those circumstances we have lived through over the last few years, for new orders in the world's affairs in which instead of ambitious monarchs or imperialist statesmen, people themselves can determine their own destinies, etc, in harmony and mutual understanding. It seems to me that this movement, which was bound to come as a reaction to the present catastrophe, should not be underestimated. It would be better to take it in hand at the right time and let it run its rational course rather than ignore it with contempt.[12]

Hopman was realistic enough to recognise that it was people like himself, members of the conservative establishment, who would probably benefit least from these 'new world orders'. 'The world will not become a finer place, at least not for us! Before 1914 it was finer!'[13]

When Kaiser Wilhelm II, pressurised by Reich Chancellor Bethmann Hollweg, in his so-called Easter message of 7 April 1917 held out the prospect of a reform of the antiquated Prussian three-class electoral system, which favoured the monied classes and academics and discriminated against the poor, he was doing precisely what Hopman had suggested, namely 'to take the movement in hand and let it run its rational course'. But however reluctantly the Kaiser may have made the statement, suddenly the admiral was very much less sure now that the concrete proposal lay on the table: 'Measure means finis of the old Borussiae. A less sudden evolution would have been more favourable.'[14] Hopman's fears that old Prussia was on its last legs were not to be met yet: the conservative majority in the Prussian parliament continued to vote against electoral reform, until the end of the war and revolution finally made it obsolete.

Hopman, possibly a more far-sighted thinker in this respect than many others, had apparently seen the difficulties which from the modern viewpoint are almost self-evident: that as the historian Sven Müller writes, 'the identification with the existing political and social order could not be decreed', but was dependent to a decisive extent on the belief 'that alongside the nationalist state at war it would protect a form of society worth defending'.[15] The officers believed that without doubt. But how would the anti-democratic and autocratic system of the Kaiser's class-ridden state appear worth defending to those refused political equality, for example, those in Prussia who after the enactment of the legislation remained second- and third-class subjects?

Matrose Richard Stumpf posed the same question. In his view there were two different ways of looking at it: from the nationalist viewpoint, and then the personal one. The first perspective still breathed the 'spirit of 1914'. 'That we may win the war, and win it outright, I wish both as a good German and also a Catholic. From this standpoint it is a quite intolerable idea for me that the effeminate French, the brutal British or even the stupid Russians might defeat our soldiers. I still have so much national pride, God knows, that I believe the Germans to be the leading, most decent and most honest folk on Earth.'[16] His second angle was from the standpoint of a disillusioned 'Christian worker' after three years of war: 'The other side of the coin is different, completely different. I stand my ground not as a German, but as a proletarian. As such I wish for a heavy, but not devastating, defeat. Why? Because experience shows us that the oppressed benefit from a lost war while the rich lose.' The reverse, as Stumpf feared, would mean in the case of 'peace with victory' that the 'social rights and blessings' for the workers would again become controversial. 'The attitude from above us, as expressed in the Kaiser's Easter edict, does not bear thinking about.'

Few officers seem to have been willing or able to change their outlook, as Stumpf did, and put themselves in other men's shoes. Throughout the war most officers held firm to the myth of national unity. Anything which seemed likely to imperil this unity was condemned out of hand and opposed: whether against the 'grumblers and rabble-rousers' causing unrest with strikes, and demands for a quick 'weak' peace, or the 'effeminate' political leadership which could neither put a stop to the activities of the Social Democrats and trade unions, or from a 'military' point of view recognise the advantages of fighting the war ruthlessly. In all this, as in scarcely any other area, can the increasing rupture of the 'class-society in war' (Jürgen Kocka) be studied to better advantage than in the Imperial Navy.

Long before the internal strife within the navy became brutally obvious in the summer of 1917, anybody who wanted to could have recognised what was brewing in the Kaiser's 'shimmering bulwark'. Already in the autumn of 1916 the first thefts of provisions and disobedience of orders had occurred aboard a number of ships of the High Seas Fleet. On 5 September 1916 Kapitänleutnant Reinhold Knobloch noted in his diary: 'The cases are now beginning to accumulate where the mail censor has sent to the commander letters written by crew members complaining about inadequate rations, too much duty, bad treatment, etc. Mostly a very unsatisfactory attitude is coming to light.' It was simply incredible, Knobloch wrote, how people who 'really had it good' could make such unjustified complaints. 'They should all be sent to the Somme where for days the most fearsome battle has been raging with undiminished intensity.'[17]

These few lines contain everything one needs to know about how the later unrest came to a head. For one thing there is the almost total ignorance of the officers regarding the concerns and needs of their subordinates. The indignation with which Knobloch reacts to the complaints in the intercepted letters shows that apparently he did not know very much about the men's situation. Otherwise he would never have thought that they 'really had it good'. This attitude exemplified the officers' tradition of shutting themselves off hermetically from the rest of the ship's company. As a rule, orders were passed through the deck officers and NCOs and engineers, while there was always a direct communication with the crew on the level of the younger divisional officers. Anything else would have been profoundly contrary to the officers' elitist way of seeing themselves. 'The majority of officers were so dominated by their caste spirit that they lacked the ability to put themselves into their men's shoes. Therefore they showed little understanding for their men's needs and problems. From their first day in the navy they had been trained to regard themselves as infinitely superior to their men.'[18]

Knobloch's diary entries are revelatory of a series of grievances which were also more or less present in the German army: lack of food, too much duty, mistreatment by officers and NCOs. These complaints were so numerous and extensive that after the war a parliamentary commission was set up to analyse the 'Causes of the German Collapse'. The statements, expert opinions and conclusions were published in twelve voluminous tomes, two of which were dedicated to the navy. Konteradmiral von Trotha was the representative of the officers, Matrose Richard Stumpf spoke for the men: numerous witnesses were called, primarily from amongst the lower ranks.

The least of the grievances concerned too much duty. We have seen, for example, that 'Ready ship for battle' and similar exercises repeated over and over again seemed to the men vexatious. When Admiral Scheer maintained after the war that shipboard duties made of the officers 'at least the same, but mostly considerably greater demands than on the majority of the other crew members', then that was at best a half-truth.[19] To compensate for their efforts, the officers received not only more free time and leave than the seamen and stokers, but also had much more comprehensive means and opportunities to make this free time as pleasant as possible. These privileges were possibly far more the cause of the crew's displeasure than the duties in themselves. What did a Kapitänleutnant do to earn his pay of 650 marks, asked Richard Stumpf, and delivered the answer: 'He cleans and polishes his fingernails, gives his hair a sharp parting and only does watch-keeping duty at sea ... can there be anything better than a career in the Imperial Navy?'[20] On another occasion he wrote: 'We sweat and slave and the devil rides us while the "gentlemen" are ashore in their apartments. Today they were all here though, because it's pay day.'[21]

Much worse than the obligation of duty were the other two points made in Knobloch's diary: shortage of food and maltreatment. To begin with the latter, as always and not only in the Imperial Navy of the Great War, the military hierarchy consisted of those above who were there to the prejudice of those below. It was naturally essential for the functioning of the military apparatus that those in command were obliged to uphold and enforce discipline. The manner in which many officers treated their subordinates, however, exceeded the necessary requirements of military severity and sometimes bordered on contempt.

In Matrose Stumpf's diary there is a whole series of examples of the spiteful treatment of the crew by officers of the *Helgoland*. Thus Stumpf's divisional officer on parade found fault with 'every tiny crease and blemish' in his uniform, even though there had been no replacements of uniforms available for a considerable time on account of the general shortage of textiles and wool. 'Such disciplinary procedures spoil, God knows, all joy in the service. I could not care less about anything now and I am not the only one,' although Stumpf added, 'It is fortunate that not all officers are like that.'[22] When he learned in the summer of 1915 that the first officer of the battlecruiser *Derfflinger* had been beaten up by some of the crew, he observed, 'It really is no wonder! When you see with what contempt the men are often treated, it makes your blood boil.'[23] The impotent rage of Stumpf and his comrades aboard *Helgoland* culminated finally in the wish that 'the *Helgoland* runs on a mine and tears to shreds all the people in the officer accommodation deck. It is amazing how everybody has suddenly become interested in politics. They are all agreed that after the war the favouritism shown to the officer caste must cease. It is also true they have far too much power. Every one of them controls the life and freedom of those below them.'[24]

That was literally true. The seaman branch naval officer, in Germany as much as in Great Britain, was not only the military and service superior of all other officers of lower rank, NCOs and men, but exercised jurisdiction over them, short of the death penalty. This almost total authority required caution in use, a fact which the German officers in particular failed to grasp during the war. Although shipboard hearings were mainly for minor offences such as drunkenness, disobedience, theft or late return from leave, the penalties were often very harsh. Reinhold Knobloch mentions a case in which four stokers who had gone ashore one night without permission were given several weeks' confinement.[25] A seaman accused of refusing orders on several occasions was awarded fifteen months' imprisonment.[26] There was no appeal against shipboard justice – once confirmed by the ship's commander it had the effect of law.

Whereas the full rigour of the law was applied against the lower deck, the shipboard courts, composed exclusively of officers, went very easy on their own. The historian Daniel Horn has collected some examples, such as the case of Kapitänleutnant Fünfstück who habitually consorted with ladies of doubtful repute in Wilhelmshaven, or Kapitänleutnant Kossack of the *Derfflinger* who formed a number of immoral liaisons with men of the lower deck, but on orders of the Kaiser did not receive a dishonourable discharge and like Fünfstück was only reprimanded.[27]

The standard manual of the time explaining the 'social and professional duties of the German officer' warned against ever handling or mistreating a subordinate in any way, but this instruction appears to have fallen by the wayside along with the hope also expressed 'that he (the officer), the educated, distinguished man, must understand how to exercise restraint and work unceasingly to master whatever passions and emotions to which he may become prey. The man who wants to control others must never lose control of himself.'[28] Thus a seaman aboard the battleship *Rheinland* awarded unjustifiably excessive punishment for indiscipline and who made a complaint was told by the ship's commander: 'Whether or not you kick the bucket is of no interest to us. The main thing is the battle readiness of the ship. People are a secondary consideration, for we can get as many of those as we want.'[29] The commander of the new replacement small cruiser *Nürnberg-II* informed his crew, in response to their request for better rations, that there was nothing left. 'If one of you starves to death I shall be more than happy to bury him with full military honours.'[30]

After the war the parliamentary board of inquiry received a letter from a former *Helgoland* seaman in which a serious complaint was made against Kapitänleutnant Walter Zaeschmar: 'We saw the cadets come aboard, how they became midshipmen, then sub lieutenants, and stood facing the men and said to long-service men, some of them married: "You load of stupid bollocks, you monkey faces!" Or that Kapitän-leutnant Zaeschmar, whose standard response to the men was always: "Off with you, you swine, you beast, you stink!"'[31]

The situation was made more difficult by the frequent changes of personnel as a result of unrestricted U-boat warfare. It was the younger officers, who as divisional officers had had the closest contact to NCOs and men, who were transferred out from the big ships to the U-boats. As a rule they were replaced by young, inexperienced sub lieutenants who lacked the right touch in their contacts with their new subordinates. Matrose Stumpf experienced this:

> How humiliating it is to have to ask a 20-year-old sub lieutenant if one may be excused. And then to have to hear his question 'Is it urgent or just an excuse to slip away?' I itch for a scrap with him ... it is an absolute disgrace that a snotty-nosed kid like that, whom one knew from a cadet, should be given such power. He croaks something cheeky, and then if you don't watch your words in reply he sends you on top of the turret or up the mainmast or puts you on report. I have to say, however, that he is by no means the worst in this respect.[32]

Even Kapitänleutnant Hermann von Schweinitz could not refrain from remarking, 'These war-issue officers lack the strict training of peacetime, even a decent upbringing.'[33]

The situation was better aboard the smaller ships, the minesweepers, destroyers and U-boats. The very much reduced companies and more equal shipboard life naturally created a closer relationship between officers and men than on the giant dreadnoughts with crews of more than a thousand. After the war, U-boat commander Ernst Hashagen wrote in this respect about U-boat life:

> We have unshakeable trust in each other. Where would we commanders be without the men? Obviously, we do the planning, carry it through and attack. Yet the whole proud edifice collapses at the smallest crew error. A valve opened at the wrong moment, an attack of nerves or some lack of attention to detail, relying on the officer in the conning tower to have thought of something, any of these can transform success into disaster.[34]

How did British officers treat their men? At first in the Royal Navy officers and men lived in different worlds, strictly separated by social origins and military rank. There was not the slightest doubt about orders and obedience. 'There was never any camaraderie between us or anything like that. He was there, and you did what you were told.'[35] Various reforms in the years pre-war had definitely changed the situation of the men for the better, however. The disciplinary system was less rigid than at the beginning of the century, and even the military courts did not display the same predictable one-sidedness which seems to have been typical of the German courts.

When, in the summer of 1915, there occurred a number of cases of seamen and stokers refusing orders aboard the light cruiser *Warrior* based at Scapa Flow, the Fleet Command sent aboard the ship a commission of inquiry made up of neutral officers to determine the cause. It transpired that Sir Robert Arbuthnot, Commanding Admiral 1st Cruiser Squadron, to which *Warrior* was attached, had suspended liberty without good cause and during a lay-up in dock at Liverpool had denied leave for seamen and stokers. The commission of inquiry condemned the action of the admiral and found in favour of the men, a result unimaginable in the German navy. Admiral Jellicoe informed the seamen and stokers personally a short time later that in future everything possible would be done to avoid injustices of this kind. 'The C-in-C pointed out how disgraceful such a business was in wartime and said he hoped there would be no more trouble. Everything on board seems to be going much more happily since.'[36]

Nothing is known of a German commander-in-chief setting himself up as an arbiter for the crews beneath him. After the war, Konteradmiral Paul Heinrich, former commander of the battlecruiser *Derfflinger*, was very critical of the leadership culture in the German navy and came to the conclusion: 'It was not really led, but rather governed, and badly governed ... there was an invisible but almost impenetrable wall around Hipper which separated the admiral from his commanders.'[37] And naturally, one might add, from the men. He himself, Heinrich wrote, hardly saw Hipper for months, and all attempts by the officers to have a closer relationship with him came to nought. 'This disregard for the relationship with the crews and officers was a mistake. But it was also observable amongst the other fleet admirals ... For the whole time I commanded the *Derfflinger* no admiral ever came aboard. And that applied with very few exceptions to all ships.'[38]

The British fleet commanders Jellicoe and Beatty manifested a different leadership style from that of their German counterparts. As we have seen, they arranged free-time events such as concert parties or sporting competitions, which tended to bring officers and men closer and loosen the strict military hierarchical structure somewhat, at least in the off-duty periods. Last but not least, it would appear that British officers did not flaunt their privileges, thus avoiding provoking the envy and ill-will of their subordinates.

The Imperial Navy did exactly the opposite. It was made especially clear from the way in which food was shared out, and was perhaps the major reason for the increasing alienation between officers and men, this being also the third point raised by Kapitänleutnant Knobloch in his diary. Even in the time of the worst famine, many officers continued to live off the fat of the land. As we saw, Knobloch had been posted aboard the small cruiser *Danzig* after the *Rostock* was sunk at Jutland. There was no shortage of food on the *Danzig*. 'We always ate outstandingly well aboard her,' he wrote in January 1917. This was in the middle of the catastrophic 'turnip and swede winter', when the consequences of the British blockade made themselves felt particularly. 'We have all we can eat of potatoes, peas, beans and other vegetables, meat, butter and bread.'[39]

An officer who had left the ship for health reasons told Knobloch about the conditions ashore and of the difficulties he was experiencing to feed his family. 'All they have to eat is swedes and turnips: he longs to return to the meat stews of the *Danzig*.'[40] One only needs to peruse the Christmas 1916 menu for the officers' mess of the *Danzig* to understand how deeply felt this longing must have been: 'There was bouillon with marrow, and a fine Swedish side-dish with caviar, etc. Then carp with butter sauce and sea-radish in amazing quantities. Afterwards home-baked cake, Christmas pastries, nuts, etc. First wine, then punch. Nobody begrudged himself the pleasure.'[41]

Every wardroom had its own cook; the meal was served by stewards. Food and drink was paid for out of the officer's own pocket and because of its quality often had to be bought on the black market, 'where practically everything was available for those prepared to pay for it',[42] but at a horrific price. This was no great problem, for the officers, who usually came from moneyed families, were comparatively well off. Thus a Konteradmiral such as Adolf von Trotha received a basic monthly salary of around 900 marks plus a war supplement of several hundred more. That did not compare well against the salary of the Commander-in-Chief of the High Seas Fleet who received 3,200 marks monthly, but all the same Trotha was able to send his wife 700 marks per month to cover running costs.[43] The younger officers were also not required to starve. A Kapitänleutnant earned around 600 marks made up of a basic salary of 283 marks plus 10 marks war supplement per day. Senior and junior Leutnants had a basic 125 marks per month plus 5.15 marks war supplement per day.[44] An ordinary seamen was paid 21.90 marks per month.[45]

The differences in shipboard rations were as wide as the remuneration. The quality of the food for the ratings fell far below that of the officers' mess. It was mass-produced, substandard and poor in nutritive quality, prepared in great kitchens for one thousand men at a time. On the battleship *Posen* the crew received several times weekly an undefinable mixture of dehydrated roots, winter cabbage and strips of tinned meat, the notorious 'barbed wire entanglement'.[46] On account of the general serious food shortage, the rations were reduced from time to time until in December 1916, in the opinion of the naval liaison officer at the war food office, it had sunk to a critical level.[47]

There existed a special tradition in the navy whereby once a year at Christmas the men could express their opinions openly and without fear of disciplinary measures. Under normal circumstances the seamen and stokers would use this rare opportunity to denounce grievances and pillory over-harsh superiors by the use of home-made placards and banners. In the 'swede and turnip winter' of 1916/1917 it would seem that *Helgoland* was not the only ship in which the victualling officer came under universal fire. 'Nearly all the protests were aimed at his marmalade made with carrot substitute. He was depicted everywhere in the preparation of this marmalade. Gigantic turnips, old rope and fire-fighting hose were its ingredients ... One placard showed him throwing up after accidentally tasting his marmalade.'[48]

The fact that the officers continued to 'not begrudge themselves the pleasure' in the matter of rations, as Knobloch described, caused great ill-will amongst the men. In the summer of 1915 Matrose Richard Stumpf of *Helgoland* wrote:

I can say that during all my service the chasm between the wardroom and the mess tables, between officers and men, was never so wide as it was in the war. Contributing not least to this disagreeable relation-ship was the fact that the officers never put restrictions on their own consumption. While we had to make do with half the bread allowance, there would be feasts in the wardroom in which six to seven plates were served. In peacetime one would not bother to mention it, but can that be right in these grave times?[49]

Once again the relationships within the navy corresponded to the general situation, for as historian Jürgen Kocka remarked, amongst the civilian population 'the unequal distribution of the scarce commodities ... was more striking and provocative ... than the scarcity of the commodities themselves.'[50] The deputy command headquarters at Münster reported in the winter of 1916: 'It is a strange symptom that in times of shortage, nobody can bear it if somebody else has a little more than himself. If it were possible to guarantee to everyone that the food inconveniences are being shared out fairly, then the dissatisfaction would disappear immediately.'[51]

A look at the small fleet units confirms this assumption. On board U-boats, torpedo boats and minesweepers there was a single galley for all: officers and men ate the same food and therefore there were no complaints. On the big ships, on the other hand, the officers did not fight shy of flaunting 'the unequal distribution of scarce commodities':

> The officers arranged for the wardroom a great banquet which reached its high point at midnight ... the wardroom resembled a madhouse. Most scandalous was the servile manner in which these boozers were importuned by the men for beer, cigarettes and schnapps. One could weep to see such self-abasement. Some even went so far as to give assurances that they were good sailors and Prussians. For that they received an extra glass of beer. Finally there were three cheers all round for individual generous benefactors. The scandal lasted until four in the morning. Then I fell asleep.[52]

On some ships the officers did not pass on to the crew provisions which had been donated for the 'young boys in blue' by the population, but redirected them to their private households. In July 1917 the secretary of state at the Reich Navy Office, Admiral Capelle, wrote a letter of concern to Admiral Scheer in which he informed the fleet commander that rumours were circulating even in the Reichstag that officers were diverting large quantities of provisions to their families and making the men pay for the 'sailors' comforts' which the population had sent them. Scheer then asked the officers to tone things down or he would be forced to impose a universal prohibition on food being taken ashore.[53] How weak the officers' concept of justice was in this respect was shown when Admiral Capelle announced the introduction of 'messing commissions' for the navy. These commissions, commonplace for some time in the army, were to be composed of representatives from the lower deck who would control the quality and distribution of provisions aboard ship. The officers made violent protests. They considered that these commissions were too much of a concession to seamen and stokers and would impose a restriction on their own power, but ultimately they could not prevent the setting up of the commissions.

A far greater problem was the immoderate consumption of alcohol by the officers. Whereas drink was forbidden aboard ship for the men, beer, wine and schnapps flowed in streams in the officers' messes. As Georg von Hase reported, on board the battlecruiser *Derfflinger* there was 'not a single despiser of wine, women and song' amongst the officers: the fleet messes would only be 'dry' on forays into the North Sea.[54] Similarly, aboard the small cruiser *Danzig* it was the custom to meet for cocktails in the wardroom on Sundays after divine service. 'On the *Danzig* they really went at it,' Kapitänleutnant Knobloch wrote, 'particularly schnapps, the favourite blue-water drink.'[55] When he was transferred to the *Karlsruhe* later, it was not much different there. 'Once again here, major boozing by the lieutenants. Seems to have something to do with the Wilhelmshaven air. Heavy drinking, loud singing, officers bawling their heads off. Racket and din all through the night.'[56]

Knobloch, although himself not abstemious, hated these drinking bouts. They appeared neither appropriate to a generally inactive navy nor were they to his personal taste. 'At midday they celebrated too gushingly and plentifully the departure of Oberassistenzarzt [senior assistant physician] d R[eserve] Dr Barfurth. Afterwards they sang students' songs and bawled. I found it repugnant. I slipped away and went for a three-hour walk with Schweinitz.'[57] While Schweinitz in this case apparently felt the same as Knobloch, the latter reported of his companion on another occasion: 'Schweinitz quite at his ease, drinking his schnapps, this time from a big glass. He had a glass of frothy beer at lunch.'[58]

The problem of alcohol within the imperial naval officer corps had long been recognised. As early as 1910 Wilhelm II had urged the navy to abstinence and said: 'I know very well that the lust for drink is an old heirloom from the ancient Teutons ... the next war and the next naval battle demand of you healthy nerves. Nerves will decide it. These are undermined by alcohol ... and that nation which imbibes the least amount of alcohol will win. That must be you, gentlemen!'[59]

This appeal by the supreme commander apparently fell on deaf ears. All other attempts to influence naval officers to greater restraint, especially those undertaken repeatedly by the chief of the Imperial Navy cabinet, Admiral Müller, ultimately came to nothing. The Navy Anti-

Alcohol League founded in 1903 by officers at Kiel had to disband for lack of members.

The unexpected and, from the point of view of the officers, unsatisfactory course of the war was an impediment to positive change. 'In the navy, as they tell the people at home, in this war the opponents of alcohol have flopped,' Vizeadmiral Souchon told his wife.[60] If only for the sake of a better relationship with the men, a more moderate consumption of alcohol was called for. Not for nothing were the officers instructed after the unrest in the High Seas Fleet at the beginning of August 1917: 'Drinking bouts are to be stopped altogether. The messes are to close at 11 o'clock.'[61] A few weeks later, however, the old regime was back. 'They are celebrating with heavy drinking on the *Königsberg*. I am not happy with it. We should be much more circumspect with these affairs at a time when people are very inclined to criticise it.'[62]

It has often been debated whether the events in the summer of 1917 might have taken a different course if there had been a more skilful crisis management on the part of the officers on the ships affected and at fleet command. The problem lay in the fact that many officers now saw themselves, perhaps for the first time in their careers, being forced to recognise the difficulties and problems experienced by the men placed under them. They were frequently incapable of doing that. They had not been trained to understand seamen and stokers as anything but subordinates who were there to receive orders, and whose duty was unconditional obedience. Friedrich Ruge, who had been, amongst other things, a watch-keeping officer aboard a torpedo boat, stated after the war, 'During all my training and my time as a lieutenant, I cannot remember hearing anything connected with "leadership", being a senior officer to the men and the handling of men.'[63]

The extent to which officers lacked understanding of the concerns and needs of simple seafarers is clear from their reaction to the unrest. That is to say, most of them found it unnecessary to look within themselves for some element of guilt about the events. They believed, not without some justification, that responsibility was attributable to the inactivity of the fleet and the unfavourable course of the war. 'The navy's misfortune is its failure to do anything,' stated Kapitänleutnant von Weizsäcker. 'It is for this reason alone that those circumstances may have arisen, for the haze of revolution was only thinly spread across Germany beforehand. The proximity of the shipyard was also an evil factor.'[64] Kapitänleutnant Schweinitz saw it similarly and was of the opinion:

It is the consequence of subversion and lying around in port: this makes them susceptible, and also the fact that so many capable officers were transferred out to the U-boats to the detriment of discipline in the fleet. No rigorous action was taken there. We of the 'light cruisers' did at least go to sea now and again, but the big ships lay in port for months and they did not get through to the men in sport and their duties.[65]

On the other hand, and much more significant for the global image of the Imperial Navy officer, they believed that their existence was most threatened by two forces which had recognised the weakness of the fleet and had ruthlessly exploited it: Great Britain and German social democracy. In the navy it was actually believed that the mutiny was the result of a conspiracy funded by Britain and organised by the USPD. The aim of it was allegedly to force the German government to bring the war swiftly to an end without the hoped-for gains in territory. A number of officers, therefore, demanded immediate judicial steps to be taken against the USPD Reichstag deputies and the closure of the party HQ in Berlin. Matrose Richard Stumpf saw this as a transparent attempt to shift the blame for their own shortcomings on to others. 'Therefore it's the British who are the guilty party again. Simply laughable, this conclusion! The gentlemen (officers) have no concept how enormous is the burden of guilt they themselves have amassed. It's the enemy!! I have to say, a very convenient explanation.'[66]

After the war the aforementioned parliamentary commission of inquiry attempted to clarify the matter, but was unable to discover any basis for the belief that the USPD were the authors of the mutiny. Although Stoker Köbis and several others had contacted USPD deputies in the summer of 1917, they had not received any support worth mentioning from them.

Officers such as Kapitänleutnant Reinhold Knobloch needed no proof. They knew they were right and pleaded for drastic action to be taken against the parliamentarians of the Left, in their eyes traitors to the fatherland: 'These people should simply be put up against the wall and shot.'[67] Vizeadmiral Hipper, for whom most of the mutinous seamen and stokers were just fellow travellers, nevertheless advocated merciless action against the ringleaders: 'I believe that we can only take the entire movement in hand by ruthlessly putting a number of them up against the wall. If we do not do that, then things will go awry.'[68] Even the moderate

Ernst von Weizsäcker saw in the mutiny a 'motive for weakening the party (USPD),' and hoped that of the ringleaders, 'two to three can be made an example of. I do not believe we have already reached the stage where we have done all we possibly can.'[69] When a few weeks later, after a 'very skilfully managed investigation', death sentences were handed down, Hipper 'very much' hoped that they would be carried out 'in the interests of discipline'.[70]

Yet even after they had been – at least in two of the five cases – and a fair number of 'politically unreliable elements' had been hauled off the ships and transferred to shore bases of the naval infantry in Flanders, peace and quiet still eluded the fleet. At the end of September around eighty men of I Squadron were arrested. According to Kapitänleutnant Walter Zaeschmar these were the 'most substandard crew men, whose poor discipline was known everywhere.'[71] At the beginning of October, 'some rabble-rousers were locked up from the *Rheinland*. Let us hope that energetic action will be taken against this gang. It is a dreadful thing to feel how the ground is being hollowed out beneath one's feet by incitement and dissent, jealousy and stupidity.'[72]

Unaware of these occurrences, Admiral Reinhard Scheer was convinced that the execution of Stoker Köbis and Seaman Reichpietsch had had a curative effect and the crews were now 'firmly back in the hands of their officers'.[73] In any case, that is what he wrote in his final report to the Kaiser about the unrest. He also conceded a series of defects such as the lack of experienced officers, inadequate food and the monotonous duty, and in an order to the fleet of 7 October 1917 the admiral called upon the officers to avoid in future all injustice in the granting of leave or in attending to requests and complaints, and that they should be more moderate in their eating habits.[74]

The hoped-for effects never arrived. Scheer's measures, historian Holger Herwig explains, did at least contribute to restoring an outward picture of tranquillity and normal relationships in the fleet. 'Ashore, however, the men maintained contact with socialist workers and radical political ideas: this created for them closer contact to working-class circles. After the mutiny the officers on the other hand failed to establish a better relationship with NCOs and men: they forged no new bond of trust and mutual loyalty.'[75]

In the short term the climate in the fleet improved somewhat. The successful conquest of the Baltic Islands by the army and navy in October 1917 undoubtedly contributed to this. Chief of the Naval Staff

Henning von Holtzendorff referred to it in an address to Kaiser Wilhelm II on 27 October 1917. 'Without doubt the tasks involved in the operation against Ösel, Moon and Dagö have had a very favourable effect in the ships, thereby strengthening and raising morale. For this reason Your Majesty's order to capture the islands in the Gulf of Riga was doubly joyfully received.'[76] Vizeadmiral Wilhelm Souchon, who had taken part in the operation with *Prinzregent Luitpold* and IV Squadron, confirmed this: 'I am pleased for my crews that they have been able to take part in a military activity. One could see their joy in being there.'[77] The only drop of sorrow for the admiral was the swift ending of the task: 'I watched the end of the operation with mixed feelings. It was so wonderful for us.'[78]

By the beginning of 1918 at the latest, however, the old problems once again came to the fore. Boredom and monotony in duties were the everyday fare, while the differences between officers and men were now even more obvious, the political divide between the two having widened. In this respect, the year 1917 worked like a kind of catalyst to politicise the navy in a way which would have been unthinkable before the war. It had been a ground rule of the Prussian military to keep politics out of the armed forces and the concept of 'citizens in uniform' lay far ahead in the future. But now that the socialist 'poison' had infiltrated the fleet, it had to be rooted out as quickly as possible.

In order to return naval personnel to the right path and make clear to them the need for unconditional devotion to duty, the navy followed the example of the army and began to give seamen and stokers something called 'fatherland instruction'. Chosen officers delivered lectures on subjects such as 'The causes of the war', 'Germany's position in the world', and supplied the men with 'nationalist' newspapers and bulletins. These were not especially successful, as Bogislav von Selchow noted 'with deep sadness'.[79] The former first officer of the *Hannover* had been transferred to the naval staff and given the job of planning and carrying out these patriotic interludes, which were derisively referred to in the fleet as 'Love of the fatherland from four to five o'clock'. Most officers had really no idea what 'fatherland instruction' really meant, Selchow complained. It appeared now that the navy had too few officers who were 'capable of dealing sympathetically with their men, able to investigate their problems large and small, and help them bear the load, unspeakably heavy, which bears down on thousands of our compatriots'. This did seem to be true if one considered, albeit reluctantly, if there would ever have been a need for 'fatherland instruction' if there had been more officers with these qualities in the Imperial Navy.

One may be forgiven for assuming that the British enjoyed a certain pleasure in hearing of the difficulties raging around their principal opponent. The opposite was the case, however. Admiral Beatty, who had meanwhile become Jellicoe's successor as Commander-in-Chief of the Grand Fleet, watched the events unfolding on the other side of the North Sea with deep concern. In a letter to his wife he wrote that it was by no mean impossible that something similar could happen in the British fleet: 'Yes, the mutiny in the enemy fleet is a sign of the times ... I pray also that it will not touch us, but ... one can never be quite sure what will happen.'[80] For even though the Royal Navy had been more or less spared until then the more serious cases of indiscipline, the stresses of three years of war, the miserable pay of naval personnel in comparison with the constantly increasing remuneration of industrial workers, and not least the 'promised land' of the Russian revolution, amounted to a dangerous brew. Above all, the calls for reform of the pay system were becoming ever more strident.

Shouldering some of the responsibility for finding a peaceful solution to this conflict were the lower-deck associations – works councils with very limited jurisdiction which had been present aboard all larger ships of the British fleet for several years, to the displeasure of many officers. They provided seamen and stokers with the opportunity to express their growing dissatisfaction and to make suggestions for improvements without fear of immediate disciplinary action or court martial, in this case successfully: the Admiralty in London met some of the demands of the men and awarded them a moderate increase in pay.

The British authorities were apparently much better able to see the signs of the times and open an escape valve to let off some of the increasing pressure. It did not alter the fact, however, that the pay question would give rise to more tension in the coming years and culminate in several days of mutiny in 1931.

It was also something of a blessing for the fleet commanders of the First World War that under the auspices of John Fisher and Winston Churchill something had been done shortly before the outbreak of war to improve living conditions for the lower deck. In addition to changes in the system of discipline, the men's food was of much better quality. During the war the Admiralty placed great importance on guaranteeing as far as possible the supply of provisions to the Grand Fleet at Scapa

Flow, despite the remoteness of the base, not least thanks to the provisions ship *Borodino*. In the Scottish wilderness there was not much opportunity of buying on the black market as at Wilhelmshaven and Kiel, not even for well-paid officers.

The income of British naval officers at the outbreak of war in 1914 was still at the level of 1870, but as in Germany it far exceeded what was paid to ratings. An admiral earned a basic £1825 annually; a captain, according to his years of service, £400–600 (plus another £328 as commander of a battleship); a lieutenant about £200 per year. Specialists such as gunnery and navigation officers with the corresponding certificate of competence received a yearly bonus of up to £73 per year. The pay of an ordinary seaman was only £20 per year, while a stoker earned £38.[81] At the end of 1917 an average British working-class family spent about £2 per week on food, about 60 per cent more than before the war. The greatly increased remuneration paid to industrial workers in some areas, and state benefits paid out to the families of conscripted men, enabled most to cope with these higher prices.[82]

Not only at Scapa Flow, but also where the greater purchasing power of the officers came into effect, such as at Rosyth and Edinburgh, the differences in the rations were not so seriously apparent as in the German navy. No doubt this was to some extent because the lack of raw materials and consumer goods became perceptible relatively late, but at no time did it attain the same alarming proportions as in Germany. When in the spring of 1917 the British Ministry of Food urged the public to make voluntary savings, even the officers of the fleet were prepared to accept restrictions. Admiral Beatty himself led by example. 'I think there is a real need to cut things down ...we are cutting down in the mess a good deal. Flags is my food dictator & is very arbitrary.'[83]

There were limits to the empathy of the British officers. Thus they made no effort to hide their contempt and anger for those who openly refused to do their patriotic duty, whether it be as soldiers and sailors or workers in the factories or shipyards. Because conscription was not introduced in Great Britain until the beginning of 1916, in the first eighteen months of the war every man fit for the front was appraised according to whether he had volunteered or not. Those not amongst the approximately 2.5 million men who had joined the colours of their own free will were for Lieutenant John McLeod, for example, 'rats who could come forward but won't'.[84]

At least equally suspect for the officers as a healthy man who was not fighting was the worker who would not work. There were strikes in Britain during the war. In the early summer of 1915 it was the Welsh miners on strike for more pay who attracted the attentions of the Royal Navy, because the boilers of British warships were fired for the most part by Welsh coal. 'The Commander-in-Chief ordered us not to go at greater speed as orders have been given to the fleet to economise coal on account of the strike at home. This after a year of war!!!. It seems to me to be the most disgraceful thing which has happened yet and that is saying a good deal,' Sub Lieutenant Francis Pridham wrote from HMS *Weymouth*.[85]

Another strike was that in May 1917 by metalworkers, from whose ranks in the future many men would be conscripted for military service. This strike was the biggest in Britain during the war, with more than 200,000 protesters. Admiral Beatty pleaded that the strikers should be deprived of their 'reserved occupation' status and sent at once to the front – a easy argument for the Royal Navy when we remember that Kapitänleutnant Knobloch of the German navy would have been happy to see malcontents in the High Seas Fleet sent to the Somme. 'And when we turn to the other side and see the engineers striking, it fairly makes one's blood boil, and nothing is done to them. Why not send them to the trenches?' asked Beatty.[86]

One seeks in vain for sympathy or understanding of the workers' demands in the writings of both British officers and their German counterparts. Instead, there are demands for a 'harsh response' and, where the government would not or could not provide it, there were complaints about 'weak-kneed politicians' who went along with everything: 'the old women who rule us', as Sub Lieutenant Oswald Frewen described them.[87] Whoever failed to push back all personal interests soon fell under suspicion of falling out of line with regard to national unity and endangering the success of all military efforts.

The rifts which now divided that national community created by the war were not as deep in Great Britain as in the eventually revolutionary Germany. Nevertheless, as the war dragged on, the tensions between the social classes won popularity for pacifist parties and groupings. London reacted completely differently to this development than did Berlin: at the beginning of 1918 Great Britain introduced general and equal voting rights for men, all restrictions hitherto being dropped. Women over thirty years of age were also granted suffrage.

The conservative establishments in Germany and Prussia had not conceded such a policy of 'inclusion' by the end of the war. Instead they held firm to a policy of 'exclusion' which was alleged to stabilise the system, so that 'a poor worker decorated with the Iron Cross, first class, had lesser voting rights in his own village than a well-off shirker.'[88] The Imperial Navy officer corps which Holger Herwig described as 'reflecting society in Kaiser Wilhelm's Germany in a microcosm' was a firm component of the establishment. It therefore advocated 'the maintenance of the Hohenzollern authoritarian state and its privileges' unchanged, and denounced the internal reforms demanded by the Liberals and Social Democrats.[89] This did nothing to prevent the eventual collapse of the Kaiser Reich and its navy.

9

'Better to go down with honour!'
The Plan for the Last Foray

Anyone attempting to render an account of the German High Seas Fleet's achievements up to the beginning of 1918 would have found it a melancholy task. Although the fleet had to some extent got away lightly with the unrest of the previous year and enjoyed one of its few true successes with the conquest of the Baltic islands in the autumn of 1917, the 'big ships' had otherwise for the main part remained unemployed since Jutland. It was the small units, above all the U-boats, which fought the war at sea. Neutralised by the British strategy of the distant blockade, the mighty dreadnoughts were only effective as a 'fleet in being', whose mere existence tied down strong forces which would have been of better use to the enemy elsewhere. Later, in lectures on naval war theory at the naval academy, it would be considered a reasonable and important concept. From the point of view of nearly everyone involved in the naval war, however, beyond any doubt it was too meagre a project for the gigantic steel colossi, packed with the latest technologies. And a self-evident fact could not be concealed: the Royal Navy continued its centuries-old tradition of mastery of the sea, against which the German fleet had been as powerless to act as if it had lain on the seabed.

Nevertheless, no seaman or officer who spent his long days in port reading, writing letters, taking walks or passing time in the wardroom was serving less honourably than the man aboard a U-boat. Both were doing their duty; both were fulfilling the oath of loyalty which all naval personnel had sworn to the Kaiser. Ultimately, it was not their fault that there were no great naval battles to be fought. 'Every man must do his best where he is put,' Vizeadmiral Wilhelm Souchon wrote.[1] All the same, it was above all the officers aboard the capital ships who longed for the opportunity to prove their mettle, their abilities and their willingness to die for the cause in battle against an equal opponent. As the British Sub Lieutenant Stephen King-Hall so aptly put it: they were 'not easily appeased by a humdrum diet of service duties and drills', while the fact that they were at war 'sharpened their appetite'.[2] Perhaps more than anybody else who fought in this war, German and also British officers saw in it a never to be repeated opportunity 'to prove one's worth, to die an honourable death for the fatherland'[3] or for King and country.

Thus being prepared to go down with the flag still flying, to be victorious or to sink, were the two sides of the coin from the naval officers' point of view. Where one was not possible, then the other had to come into play. Even Hitler was inspired later by this idea of honour. It is certainly no coincidence that in April 1945 he chose a naval officer – Grossadmiral Karl Dönitz – to be his successor. In his testament, Hitler wrote: 'In days to come may it be part of the German officer's concept of honour – as is already the case in our navy – that the surrender of a region or a city is impossible, and that above all officers have to lead by shining example in the most faithful devotion to duty unto death.'[4]

A professional North Sea fisherman conscripted to serve with the fleet might have taken another view of this 'point of honour'. At the latest, after the 'spirit of 1914' was dispelled, Shakespeare's sad knight Falstaff might have spoken to him from the heart. In the drama *Henry IV*, honour is mercilessly exposed for what it really is in his opinion: an empty phrase.

> Good, it may be: honour pricks me on. But how if honour picks me out to die? How then? Can honour set a leg? No. Or an arm? No. Or take away the pain of a wound? No. Honour hath no skill in surgery then? No. What is honour? A word. What does the word honour entail? What is this honour? A fine account! Who hath it? He, who died on Wednesday: does he feel it? No. Does he hear it? No. 'Tis insensible then? Yea, to the dead. But will it not live within the living? No. Why not? Detraction will not suffer it. Therefore I'll have none of it. Honour is nothing but a funeral cortège. And so ends my catechism.[5]

The longer the war went on without anything happening worth the mention, and the greater were the casualties on the other battlefields, the louder became the rumblings in the German naval officer corps. In order to combat the growing discontent and disappointment, and nip in the bud the dangerous self-doubt on the part of officers perceived by naval command, there was only one thing which could be done: the

Kaiser had to appear in person to declare the immobilisation of the fleet as serving a useful purpose, and the sitting around inactive by his men to be nevertheless the fulfilment of the oath of loyalty sworn to him. He did so. In October 1914 he assured officers and men for the first time in a previously mentioned 'Expression of the Will of the Most High' that he was 'satisfied in no small way' by their performance to date.[6]

At about the same time he sent to his son Prince Adalbert, serving aboard the battleship *Kaiser* in the rank of Korvettenkapitän, a telegram which he wished his son to make known to the ship's company. In it he referred to the 'inestimable service(s)' the navy had paid 'to the army and the country by being held immobile until I order its operational deployment'.[7] If that was not enough, shortly afterwards the commanding admirals of the fleet received a secret letter from main headquarters 'in which His Majesty states again that the fleet is to be held immobile until further notice and that His Majesty reserves to himself the time of that operational deployment.' Only minor sorties by the battlecruisers might be undertaken. 'It is to be added that he expresses his full acknowledgement and satisfaction with the activity of the fleet to date. The presence and operational readiness of the fleet is of enormous value to the army and relieves it of the need to have coastal protection forces which would be essential if the destruction of our fleet became a factor.'[8]

It is not possible to judge if the Kaiser's praise had any effect and, if so, how long it lasted. In any case, a year later Wilhelm was motivated to administer to his naval officers 'a very serious edict of censure' instead of praise. In a cabinet order he emphasised how much pleasure the 'outstanding performance of my navy' gave him, admitted at the same time his understanding for the general disappointment, but that the 'spirit of joyous fulfilment of duty' had to be kept alive, even though the fleet 'might never have to fight.'[9] 'The mumblings had to cease, we had to keep the spirit alive, even though what fell to one's lot might be very hard to bear. Anything else would be criminal. Trust in the naval leaders and in himself, the supreme commander, must be maintained come what may, and the knowledge that everybody should know how he lived and suffered with us under the present circumstances and before.'[10] Thus did Knobloch recollect the Kaiser's statement. The Kaiser had finished by saying: 'In closing I, who carry the heavy burden of responsibility for the future of the Reich, and by whom I wish the fleet to be convinced that I would be happy to be able to throw it at the enemy without restraint, demand the dutiful subordination to my will as supreme commander.'[11]

Though these were harsh words, they were apparently called for. In subsequent years, the Kaiser explained to naval personnel many times, in more or less friendly tones, that the fleet was being operated as he wanted it to be, even if instead of fighting it lay in port. He wrote it in edicts, let it be distributed by Prince Adalbert, and announced it every time he visited one of the German naval bases, including in February 1916 at Wilhelmshaven when the Kaiser delivered an address to the commanders of the battleship squadrons and reconnaissance groups. In it he explained that the task which he had given the fleet was the most onerous, 'because it was the most thankless of all those that a German Kaiser had been obliged to bestow upon his officers'. The knowledge that the enemy would achieve a major war aim in a battle fought under favourable circumstances for the enemy made it his duty 'to refuse you the bold offensive for which you are consumed with impatience'. The fleet would only risk battle if the enemy ventured to the German coast. 'The task of my fleet is therefore provisionally defence and preparedness. That means abnegation and self-denial, all the more so since in defending against the enemy – unlike the army – it is not granted to have the enemy at sword-point. What demands I make of officers and men by that, what I ask of you in strain and strength of will, be assured I am fully aware.'[12]

Even if Wilhelm II played no decisive military or political role during the war, he was for many officers then, as before, an important figure of focus. The navy itself had much to thank him for. For this reason the Kaiser's approval of the passive attitude of the fleet was so important. Those who doubted the sense of what they were doing received confirmation in this way that they were doing the right thing, even if they were not doing it willingly. Honour was satisfied.

There were, of course, critical minds such as Kapitänleutnant Ernst von Weizsäcker, who for some time had considered Wilhelm II to be a rather mediocre monarch, equipped with great powers but little expertise. Very many lacked the keen eye of this highly educated officer who in the course of his activities in the fleet staff and in the naval cabinet had already had many opportunities before the war to peer behind the royal curtain. His intensive study of the official files, to which the Kaiser was accustomed to scribbling in the margins his notorious snotty observations, and numerous personal meetings with Wilhelm II led Weizsäcker to his harsh judgement. Nevertheless, Weizsäcker considered the way in which the Kaiser retold stories from his youth on social occasions, 'with a phenomenal memory for names and details' to be 'very charming'.[13]

Everybody else who lacked access to the closest circle of power was probably more easily impressed by the glittering monarchic facade. Kapitänleutnant Reinhold Knobloch noted in his diary his experience of the Kaiser's address to the fleet at Wilhelmshaven a few days after Jutland:

> He looked pale, but vigorous and resilient. His eyes were especially bright and joyful today. He went up a specially built staircase to the fleet flagship, had the officers and men crowd around him and then delivered a powerful speech in loud, terse words from the heart. It was uplifting to see before us, after all the hardships of bygone years and especially the recent hot days of battle, the man to whom we were duty-bound, who as officer and leader and fatherly benefactor had summoned us again to something new and great. Despite wind and rain he stood up there, solid and resolute, and ... with warmth and joy and fatherliness in his voice and movements made us aware as never before of his tangible gratitude for his navy. It raised us all, even the most diffident and blasé, it chained us again to our Kaiser, whom nobody can imitate and for whose mighty personality all our foes envy us. The Kaiser concluded with three loud Hurrahs! for our dear, beautiful German fatherland. The fleet commander responded, expressing our thanks to the Kaiser for his sympathy and attention to the navy which as his own original creation had arrived at a point in such a short time to deliver severe blows to Albion, so strong at sea. He promised, and this moved us all, that so long as we had a drop of blood in our veins, it would be a joy to sacrifice our lives for our fatherland and Kaiser. Scarcely ever before can there have rung out greater and more enthusiastic roars of Hurrah! for the Kaiser than now.[14]

Wilhelm's cousin George Frederick Ernest Albert of Saxe-Coburg and Gotha, his junior by six years, who had sat on the British throne since 1910 as King George V, could only dream of such a reception. He was not by a long chalk the significant leader figure for the Royal Navy as Wilhelm II was for the Imperial Navy (although no British monarch of recent times had demanded so close a relationship to the military as the German Kaiser). George V gave his best, as his biographer Kenneth Rose wrote of him, 'He donned the mantle of King Henry V with diffidence; he would always do his best but he was not a born leader. The cheers outside the palace saluted the symbol rather than the man.'[15]

Once each year George V paid an official visit to the Grand Fleet, and David Beatty dreaded the unpleasantness which these royal flying visits brought in their train. 'The monarch arrives Thursday, he really is a nuisance and adds much to the labours, and is to remain until Monday. He is to be accompanied by pressmen and cinematographers. It appears he is anxious that the world should know that he is doing something. But it does not help the war.'[16]

The British fleet commander had no scruples about turning the royal visit into a small demonstration of who really held power in the Grand Fleet. After George V had handed out orders and decorations aboard Beatty's flagship *Queen Elizabeth*, he had to knight Rear Admiral Hugh Evan-Thomas, commander of 5 Battleship Squadron at Jutland, to conclude the festive ceremony. Before the King could draw his sword, Beatty graciously handed him his own. Under the eyes of so many naval men and journalists he could hardly refuse it and thus touched the shoulders of the kneeling Evan-Thomas with Beatty's sword to elevate him to the nobility.[17]

David Beatty was the man who, like Wilhelm II on the German side, had the thankless task of providing consolation and warning. Repeatedly he assured naval men, looking forward to a great naval battle à la Trafalgar, that they served sensibly and honourably by tying down the German fleet at a great distance. Beatty found it anything but easy to feed his subordinates with hope and self-confidence when he himself secretly suffered most from this unsatisfactory situation. 'One of my duties, and a deuced hard one, is to keep smiling,' he wrote to Eugenie Godfrey-Faussett, the wife of King George V's personal adjutant, with whom Beatty had a passionate affair from the end of 1916.[18] On another occasion he wrote to her complaining: 'I have to keep them up, to carry them along on the top of the wave of hope, cheerfulness, confidence, etc. and cannot indulge in despondency or grumblings so dear to the heart of every Britisher.'[19]

It was not the problem of the British that they were unsuccessful. The Royal Navy carried out all tasks required of it and maintained British mastery of the sea. But they did it without shining. Just as on the German side, there were therefore many naval people, particularly officers who, casting a look back to the heroic deeds of their legendary forebears and the achievement of the British army on the continental battlefields, felt themselves to be second-rate and useless: for example, Oswald Frewen. At the beginning of 1917 as a 30-year-old sub lieutenant he had been transferred to the cruiser *Bacchante* and sent off to patrol the west coast of Africa. There he spent his time catching butterflies and raising exotic plants in his cabin. Instead of relishing this comparatively unstressful existence, he was soon overcome by other feelings. 'The pangs of conscience are cumulative & I feel I ought, at my age, to take my share in the war, & feel it more daily.'[20]

This guilty conscience, which plagued not only Frewen, but many other officers on both sides of the North Sea, might have remained a regrettable but ultimately an internal navy problem with no great consequences. The war would have ended and left a few thousand dissatisfied men around who perhaps liked to consider themselves as failures, despite having no serious bodily or mental injuries to show for it. It turned out otherwise, however.

As one might suspect, honour was responsible. Honour is not simply a private matter but arises, as historian Wilfried Speitkamp believes, 'in communication. It is displayed by speech, gestures, symbols and objects. It is therefore a public matter and is connected with the position of the individual in society'.[21] When we speak of honour, it is therefore two things, 'an inner honour and an outer honour, self image and the image in the eyes of others, self-pride and recognition or prestige, self-esteem and esteem from others'.[22]

That was precisely the problem: no individual had anything to reproach himself for as long as he had knowingly carried out his orders. In this way the 'inner' or personal honour of officers was not harmed by the course of events. That had not been the case for 'outer honour'. The reputation of the navy and its officer corps, its image, its recognition by society, hung very much in the balance in the opinion of many officers. The fact that a number of ships had gone down without striking the flag changed nothing.

In this respect the Imperial Navy was particularly at risk. For just as easily as the Germans before the war had allowed themselves to be convinced that without question they needed a large fleet in order to be successful 'in world politics', their opinion could change when they saw that this fleet was apparently no longer in a position to fulfil the expectations invested in it. With every week that passed without anything to report, it seemed ever more doubtful that Germany's future really lay on the water, as Wilhelm II had propounded so stridently. Naval people saw it no differently. 'Today's High Seas Fleet is going to the breakers,' Ernst von Weizsäcker wrote to his mother,[23] and even Kapitänleutnant Rudolph Firle took the view that 'after the war the good times for the Navy will be gone'.[24]

Konteradmiral Albert Hopman also saw serious problems approaching for the navy. 'What we did and neglected to do (when the British superiority was not so great and the chances for success in battle were supposedly more favourable) we are paying a heavier price day by day,' he noted in November 1915, 'and the officer corps, insofar as it is capable of profound thinking, is gradually beginning to understand that the fleet has been such a failure that what has been achieved by its cruisers, U-boats, etc, is no counterweight to guarantee its future.'[25] Six months later Vizeadmiral Hipper expressed himself in much the same way: 'What I fear is that when peace comes all the blame will be heaped on the navy and nobody will have a good word to say for it, and it will be all the worse if the fleet, the big capital ships, have never been in action.'[26]

Accordingly all that he wanted, Hipper went on, 'is that very soon we clash with the enemy.' Four days later the fleet sailed on a foray into the North Sea which ended in the battle of Jutland, and gloomy thinking about the future was cast aside. Despite the minor strategic benefits of the battle, the serious British losses ensured that the reputation of the German dreadnoughts improved for the time being. 'The value of a High Seas Fleet has been displayed to the eyes of all Germans,' Kapitän-leutnant Walter Zaeschmar wrote with pride. Those who thought we no longer needed big ships and would be better off building U-boats were now 'somewhat crippled in their efforts'.[27]

The enthusiasm did not last too long, however. The people soon realised that although a number of British battlecruisers had been sunk, it had not changed in the least the basic distribution of naval power. At the latest with the beginning of unrestricted U-boat warfare in February 1917, the U-boat finally arrived not only at the centre of operational planning, but also of public interest. Hipper was particularly embittered that people such as Deputy Wilhelm Struve, who sat in the Reichstag for the liberal Fortschrittliche Volkspartei, should question the value of surface ships in themselves, even though the fleet had put 'all resources at its command' to serve the cause of unrestricted U-boat warfare and even, as Hipper admitted, 'far above the permitted aim'.[28] But it was of no help: the battleships, relegated to the role of auxiliary aides to the U-boats, now disappeared to some extent into the shadow of the highly acclaimed tonnage sunk figures. 'Dear fatherland you may rest quiet, the fleet is sleeping in port'[29] was a widely broadcast rewording of a line of the famous battle hymn 'Wacht am Rhein'.

In the same measure that the fleet not only played a subordinate military role, but was perceived by the public to actually have one, the questions which Hopman, Hipper and presumably many others asked themselves gained weight. After the war's end, after Germany had been defeated, what would happen to a fleet which had not succeeded in justifying its existence by its achievements? What view would be taken of it if the giant battleships and battlecruisers, apart from a few scratches, were found undamaged at their anchorages exactly where they had been before the war? And how would people in Germany look upon the men in their smart navy-blue uniforms, who proudly claimed themselves to be men of war, but who over the three years that this murderous battle of nations had already lasted had only fought the enemy for a couple of hours?

The time had still not come when concrete answers were required to these questions. There was still hope that the war could be won and the navy would not need to justify itself. At the end of 1917 the prospects for a 'victorious peace' looked better than ever. Russia had left the Entente in the wake of the October revolution and since September 1917 had been negotiating a separate peace with the Central Powers. The result of these talks was the Treaty of Brest-Litovsk, which in March 1918 brought Poland, Finland, the Baltic States and the Ukraine more or less directly into the sphere of German domination. But then the tide turned.

The victorious end to the war in the east provided OHL with the possibility of concentrating all Germany's military might on the western front. French and British troops would be crushed by a gigantic offensive before the Americans on the way to Europe were fully operational. Operation Michael began on 21 March 1918 with a five-hour long artillery barrage from around 6600 German guns on a forty-five mile (70km) sector of front along the Somme between Cambrai and St Quentin, the interface between the two opposing armies. Three German armies totalling 800,000 men then overran the enemy positions and forced their way fifty miles (80km) behind the enemy lines.

Although it began well, the attack had as little success in causing the collapse of the Allied forces as did three later offensives in the months following. The Allied defensive line, which could call upon larger reserves than the Germans, ultimately proved itself impenetrable. In mid July the attacks by the exhausted German armies came to a standstill. More and more soldiers were refusing to risk their lives for an obviously lost cause. It is estimated that in the last months of the war alone up to a million men went voluntarily into captivity or deserted – a phenomenon described by the historian Wilhelm Deist as 'a cloaked military strike'. Even if the OHL did not openly admit defeat, and continued to deceive government and public as to the true situation at the front, the military defeat of the Kaiser Reich was now only a question of time.

Led by the French Marshal Ferdinand Foch, the Allies went over to the offensive. On 8 August 1918, the 'black day of the German army', they broke through the German front at Amiens. Only two months later, after the collapse of Bulgaria, on 29 September 1918 General Ludendorff finally the declared the war to be lost. At the same time he denied any responsibility and maintained that 'effeminate' politicians and diplomats had 'cooked up this soup', and now they should kindly sup it.[30] This anticipated the legendary 'stab in the back', the later allegation that revolutionary causes had struck down the undefeated army from the rear.

Kaiser Wilhelm II put an end to his generals' disputes and reluctantly approved the setting up of a parliamentary government, the first and last of the Kaiser Reich. By imposing this 'revolution from above', it was hoped to avoid the chaos of a 'revolution from below' such as had befallen Russia. Heading the new government, which also included the Social Democrats, was the Liberal, Prince Max von Baden. His most pressing task was the initiation of armistice negotiations with the Entente, a duty which the OHL was only too willing to let him have.

'With that, we are at our end: I cannot believe that things can be so bad,' Admiral Hipper wrote in his diary on 3 October 1918. Next day he learned that Ludendorff had stated at headquarters that the fleet might possibly have to be delivered to Britain, as 'it will be mainly the fleet which has to pay the piper. Really enjoyable prospect.'[31] Hipper and the newly formed Naval War Directorate SKL watched appalled as over the next few weeks the new men in Berlin attempted to end the war and were apparently prepared to grant the enemy enormous concessions. The fact that Ludendorff and the OHL were in the background, exerting massive pressure on the politicians, was kept from them.

Scarcely were they in office than the government of Prince Max sent US President Woodrow Wilson a note on the night of 3 October 1918 suing for peace on the basis of his notorious 'Fourteen Points', and an immediate armistice.[32] The Fourteen Points was a peace programme first put before US Congress in January 1918 – and which 'the German side had totally ignored, because they believed they could win the war'.[33] It was moderate in tone, more idealistic than vengeful and thus nourished the German hopes for a mild 'just' peace in which there was neither victor nor vanquished. Alongside basic demands such as freedom of the seas or general disarmament, the Fourteen Points contained concrete territorial provisions, later included in the Treaty of Versailles, as to the evacuation of the last occupied Russian territories, the return of Alsace–Lorraine to France (German since the Franco-Prussian War in 1871) and the restoration of Belgium. All this fuels the suspicion that in Germany the text had not been studied all that carefully.

News of the peace offer by the government hit the German people like a bomb. Kapitänleutnant Hermann von Schweinitz, also in the dark as much as anybody else as to the true situation at the front, reacted with shock and incomprehension. 'Offer of an armistice by the German government? Capitulation? A grovelling peace? Was everything in vain??' He and his comrades considered the German offer as 'a humiliation', and now feared, in a reversal of the facts, 'together with this precipitate parliamentarianisation', the collapse of the front and monarchy.[34] Korvettenkapitän Bogislav von Selchow took a much more dramatic view of what in his opinion would now follow for the Kaiser Reich: 'Does nobody see that this note means revolution, the fall of the monarchy, total collapse? What will be left of Germany? They will not only take our colonies, not only rip away all the members from the body, in south and north, in east and west, they will make slaves of us and so chain us up that we cannot move, quite differently from what happened after the Peace of Tilsit.'[35]

In his note of reply which arrived in Berlin on 9 October, Wilson merely enquired if the German government was prepared to accept the Fourteen Points unconditionally. At the same time he insisted that the withdrawal of German troops from the occupied territories in the West was a precondition for all further negotiations. For Schweinitz that was too much. 'An unreasonable demand, in which we are being dictated to beforehand! But they will give in to it all the same. Yet there are still optimists who think the government will have the courage and pride to resist. We will go along the path of ignominy, perhaps as fate wills it.'[36] Although Schweinitz had reckoned on the German government conceding Wilson's conditions, he was nevertheless taken aback when they actually did so on 12 October. 'Our government has given Wilson his answer just as predicted: all demands met. Dear God, such a people, and they give up disgracing us! One will soon be ashamed of being a German.'[37]

Worse was still to come. In his next note of 14 October the US president wrote in much harsher vein. Just previously, a U-boat had sunk the British passenger ship *Leinster*, killing 450 people. Therefore Wilson now condemned not least the 'illegal and inhuman practices' of German warfare, which had to cease forthwith, as must the system of 'despotism' which ruled in Germany. 'Its tone is in the highest degree insulting and demeaning,' Vizeadmiral Hopman noted in indignation after reading the second Wilson note. 'It should make every German colour up.' Germany had no choice but to accept it, however.

> The masses cannot take, and do not want any more; our deplorable Wilhelm II-government has saddled them with too much. Short of a few hundred thousand or so the troops are weary of war and are set on an end to it through this peace offer. Materially we are close to the certain end ... Therefore it is over, our nation will now probably have to swallow the bitter pill and more or less at once. It is too dreadful to write any more about it.[38]

In its reply to Wilson on 20 October, the German government protested against the severe recriminations by the Americans. At the same time it showed readiness to compromise and announced that future governments would be answerable to the Reichstag. On 28 October 1918 the appropriate constitutional changes came into effect introducing ministerial accountability, parliamentary control of foreign and military affairs and the democratic vote in Prussia. This transformed the Kaiser Reich into the parliamentary democracy which so many had been demanding for so long. Another concession to Wilson was the termination of unrestricted U-boat warfare. This had been discussed beforehand with the naval staff, who gave their approval surprisingly quickly – for some time they had had another use in mind for the U-boats.

Adolf von Trotha, 'immeasurably sad' at the way 'we are now killing ourselves', turned in total despair to his wife: 'On the whole I am frightfully depressed! The note to Wilson is the most unworthy I have ever read. It disowns and reviles our own proud past, pours the blame for everything upon ourselves and abandons our future as an independent people. We are making an enormous laughing stock of ourselves.' Occasionally, he caught himself feeling that it was no longer anything to do with him, so foreign did it all seem to him. 'Therefore in my opinion the navy's future is shattered and I am only doing my duty here because I have to. Everything I have lived for, thought and worked for is collapsing! So we do not have a sunny future to look forward to, my poor Bunny!'[39]

Finally, in his third note on 23 October Wilson demanded the de facto unconditional surrender and democratisation of Germany. Hermann von Schweinitz wrote of this: 'Wilson is now demanding capitulation, our subjugation. The mistake was our offer of an armistice. That opened Pandora's box. The people are making a big thing of it. Everybody is asking why we didn't offer it two years ago.'[40] At the time both OHL, the supreme army command and the naval staff, aware of Germany's apparently unbroken military strength, were not inclined to make even the smallest concessions in order to achieve a quick end to the war. OHL now made a last attempt to wrest the reins from the politicians and break off negotiations. Prince Max arranged for the Kaiser to have Ludendorff relieved of his command on 26 October to be replaced by General Wilhelm Groener, former head of the War Office. Feldmarschall Paul von Hindenburg decided to stay on, earning everlasting hate from his ejected partner.

In these gloomy October weeks, in which the politicians in Berlin haggled with Germany's enemies about the price of peace and, as it seemed, lightly gambled the legacy of Bismarck and the future of the nation, the leadership of the Imperial Navy made the independent decision not to walk this 'path of shame'. The people might be 'making a big thing of it', but the navy, as the SKL around Hipper, Scheer and Trotha were convinced, had no need of an armistice. 'Better to go down with honour,' Hipper wrote in his diary.[41]

That was precisely what the SKL now proposed to do. The mixture of an exaggerated concept of honour on the part of the officers and the naked desire of a perhaps soon to be superfluous institution was an extremely dangerous brew. The decisive blow was probably wielded by Konteradmiral Trotha. In March 1915 he had made it unmistakeably clear to Tirpitz how he saw a possible destruction of the fleet. 'Personally

I believe without any reservations that a fleet which disputes an unjust peace by fighting against it, rises again even after the heaviest losses. The fleet is not really deeply rooted in Germany until there has been such a battle. I cannot have faith in a fleet which has merely come through the war safe and sound.'[42]

At the beginning of October 1918, Trotha presented to SKL a memorandum entitled 'Considerations at a grave hour', arguing that it would be preferable to fight now 'even at the risk of a total engagement', rather than to let the fleet proceed to 'an ignominious end'. Under no circumstances should the fleet end the war 'without the national forces embodied in it having shown their full operational impact.' Only 'following an honourable battle by the fleet, even if it turned out to be a fight to the death in this war, can a new future fleet be born provided our people do not fail totally nationally: a fleet fettered to a humiliating peace is one without value for the future.'[43]

The notorious 'Operational Plan No 19' which resulted from these 'Considerations' had been briefly discussed at the beginning of April 1918, but discarded as 'adventurous' by the then chief of the naval staff, Holtzendorff: now it was suggested again that the High Seas Fleet, in order to avoid the stigma of years of inactivity and the looming ignominy of surrender, should undertake a last foray and force the Royal Navy into the long yearned-for decisive encounter.[44] Everybody involved had to be clear on the point that the risk of suffering a devastating defeat at the hands of the far superior Anglo-American naval forces was very great. Some historians, on the other hand, consider that because of the effect of surprise and other incalculable factors such as the weather, possibly it might not have been lacking all chances of success.[45]

However one assesses the military prospects, deciding how it would have turned out is not the point. For the officers involved in the planning, the question of victory or defeat was purely academic. Even unshakeable optimists in the navy could not have seriously expected to decisively weaken the combined British and American naval forces, not to mention inflict defeat on them. The navy might have needed a victory of at least that magnitude if the purpose were to avert the threatened defeat of Germany. It is confirmed by the documents, however, that this was not the motivation of the SKL. 'It is not to be expected,' the SKL War Diary states, that the sortie by the fleet 'will bring about a decisive change in the course of affairs.' The planned action was much more primarily 'a question of the honour and existence of the navy.'[46]

The few utterances which have come down to us from the leading lights also point in this direction. Hipper, who was to have led the operation in his capacity as fleet commander, had to determine where he wished to take his ships. He decided in favour of a foray into the Hoofden because, as he confided to his diary, 'if anywhere, this can be justified from the military point of view'[47] – from the strategic point of view a rather weak foundation for a do-or-die operation. Reinhard Scheer, chief of the naval staff, was not at Wilhelmshaven at the time of the decision, but at the main headquarters at Spa in Belgium. From there he wrote a letter to his wife implying that he expected a primarily symbolic benefit. 'If our plan succeeds, which begins on your birthday and as we hope has no more interruptions, that will be an auspicious sign. I am awaiting the outcome with great excitement.'[48] Trotha too, haunted by the 'fear of ignominy' at the very thought that the fleet might be 'delivered into internal annihilation without ever coming to battle', saw any possible military victory as a side-effect. He wrote to Scheer's chief of staff Magnus von Levetzow about it: 'The operation to go down with honour will pay off, for then we would still be able to inflict a serious wound on Britain.'[49]

In addition to the doubtful military value of the operation, prepared under the strictest secrecy (neither the Kaiser nor the Reich Chancellor knew about the plan, only Ludendorff), it posed an enormous threat to the government's efforts for a quick armistice. SKL took that into account in issuing its approval. It could rely on the ships' officers not hesitating to take part in this suicidal scheme. For the officers, besides the honour and existence of the navy, their own professional careers and social standing were at stake. Furthermore, now as before they considered themselves duty-bound not to allow any ship to fall into enemy hands without a fight, hence the composure of an officer such as the commander of the battlecruiser *Seydlitz*, Kapitän zur See Wilhelm Tägert, when facing an operation which would almost certainly mean his death. Referring to the evening before the departure planned for 30 October 1918 he expressed his feelings thus: 'A really great, perfectly wonderful moment was the evening of 29th. Then in expectation of other things and fully composed I took my leave of you, and then fell fast asleep.'[50]

The officers, however, had failed to take the men into account. Despite the greatest secrecy, it proved impossible to hide from the war-weary stokers and seamen that something 'big' was afoot even though the only real pointer was the assembling of the entire High Seas Fleet off

Wilhelmshaven – no everyday event. As soon as the last doubts about the intention of the officers were dispelled, the crews aboard a number of ships refused orders to prepare for sea. They had not the least desire to risk their lives for a cause which was not their own, when they could see the Armistice on the horizon. 'Under the impression of the military collapse and following the gruelling years of war, the mass of the crews could not be won over for an act of heroism at the final hour,' the military historian Wilhelm Deist confirmed, 'especially not in the form of a simple order, as was tried.'[51]

Admiral Hipper, like Tägert reconciled to his death, had no choice but to call off the operation. Here is his report:

What dreadful days I have behind me. I really never believed that I would come back, and under what circumstances do I now do so. Our people went on strike. I would not have been able to carry through the operation even if the weather conditions permitted it. During the departure on the 29th it was reported to me that 58 men had gone absent from *Von der Tann*, one hundred from the *Derfflinger*. Everything possible was done to get these people back on board. The ships were in the Schillig Roads at the scheduled time and the crews were present. It gave me cause to reflect however ... In the course of the night there were demonstrations on various ships, particularly those of the III Battleship Squadron, *Kronprinz*, *Markgraf* and *König*. When questioned, the crews stated that they knew the fleet would seek battle so as to be sunk in action: because of the Armistice negotiations the fleet did not need to be consigned and they were not going along with it. The ships' engines would remain immobilised, etc. The same utterances were made on individual ships of I Battleship Squadron. There was no doubt that despite the greatest secrecy the men had been told about an operation in preparation and in the belief that they were going to be sacrificed for nothing would apparently refuse orders at the decisive moment, ie when passing west of Heligoland. As an exercise of inter-squadron movements (*Evolutionieren*) had been scheduled for the 30th in order to disguise the battle operation, under the circumstances and after discussing the matter with my staff officers I considered that if I did not wish to expose the fleet to a grand mutiny I should call off the operation and go ahead with the *Evolutionieren*.[52]

That was the death sentence for Operational Plan No 19. As Hipper reported later, in its desperation SKL wanted to send at least the operational U-boats and capital ships with presumed 'reliable' crews on board towards England. This idea came to grief when the crews of the battleships *Thüringen* and *Helgoland*, which had been peaceable previously, now refused orders. The mutineers were ordered to be arrested, and a bloodbath was only avoided by a hair's breadth.

> The men on *Thüringen* had locked themselves in the crew quarters forward and no power on Earth was going to get them out. The hatch above, which had been bound down, had to be broken open. Men with loaded rifles were stationed above near it. The men below were ordered to come up. Nobody appeared, below was in darkness. The mutineers were then told that if they did not come up the ship would be torpedoed. A torpedo boat was waiting nearby ready to fire. The order to fire had already been given when the mutineers finally came up and were taken away without offering resistance. This was lucky, the consequences would otherwise have been unimaginable. The first round or torpedo fired at the revolutionaries would have had incalculable effects. The same procedure was applied against the *Helgoland* where crew members had shut themselves in. On this ship they had even aimed a gun at the torpedo boat. Three hundred men were taken off the *Thüringen*, a hundred off the *Helgoland*. Naturally a great crowd of these people had to be released, a number of the so-called fellow travellers got off with minor disciplinary punishment. The main thing was that we got the ringleaders.[53]

It would seem that at this point Hipper believed it was still possible to bring the situation under control by energetic action as it had been the year before. Admiral Scheer, following events from his distant observation post at Spa, was of the opinion that the worst had been prevented by fleet command rejecting the use of drastic measures:

> Fleet command does not seem to have intervened very energetically and did not have any proper support from the ship commanders. They preferred not to bring the matter to a head and gave up putting to sea. It seems that the question arose whether one or other of the ships on which the crew refused duty should have been sunk by torpedo boats.

This might equally well have given rise to a major revolt which perhaps would have caused harm on a disastrous scale.[54]

The 'major revolt' feared by Scheer may have been put off for the time being, yet as soon as the ships returned to port, as historian Holger Herwig writes, 'a lack of resolve, uncertainty, aimlessness and waiting to see what was going to happen next characterised the situation.'[55] Fleet command now took an important decision which was to have fatal consequences: in order to prevent unrest spreading to other ships, the ships of the particularly affected III Squadron were separated from the rest of the fleet and transferred to Kiel, where several thousand radical shipyard workers were waiting for the ships' ratings. During the transit of the Kaiser-Wilhelm Canal forty-seven seamen and stokers identified as ringleaders aboard the battleship *Markgraf* were arrested, and three days later another fifty-seven.

Once berthed at Kiel the five thousand crewmen still at liberty left their ships and held several meetings in the city. On 3 November they attended a large rally at the Kiel exercise grounds and then headed for the Kiel naval jail in order to free their arrested comrades. On the way they clashed with a military patrol in the inner city, nine people being killed and twenty-nine wounded. This incident was the signal for insurrection. Supported by shipyard and industrial workers and by the naval coastal artillery units stationed at Kiel, the next day sailors and other naval men occupied the most important military and civilian service offices. On 5 November there was a general strike by Kiel workers. Members of the two social democratic parties and delegations from the major industries set up a workers' council, the naval crews in revolt a soldiers' council, the first in Germany. In collaboration they prepared a long list of demands (the fourteen 'Kiel points') involving internal naval affairs, which was therefore a 'medley as an expression of a political programme': lifting of the state of siege, release of the arrested sailors and political prisoners, freedom from disciplinary punishment for seamen and stokers, no belligerent use of the fleet, right of the soldiers' council to be involved in all decision-making, 'correct handling of ratings by their superiors', personal freedom and cessation of obedience to superiors outside duty periods.[56]

Matrose Richard Stumpf viewed these goings-on with mixed feelings. He felt 'sad, very sad, that it could come to this', but on the other hand he experienced:

a certain malicious joy ... which with the best will in the world I cannot repress. Where did the omnipotence of the proud captains and senior engineers go? Stokers and seamen treated like dogs for years finally realise that without themselves nothing, absolutely nothing, can work. Is that credible? Whoever has served for so long conscious of the iron discipline, with blind obedience of the body as I have, must consider such a thing to be impossible ... Every injustice is avenged on Earth, this old saying is now taking tangible form today.[57]

Most officers stood by helplessly in the face of unfolding events and left their ships voluntarily because nobody would obey their orders. The few who opposed the mutineers or, such as the commander of the battleship *König*, attempted to prevent the hoisting of the red flag, soon fluttering at the mastheads of all ships, were wounded or killed.

In order to avoid a further escalation, Admiral Wilhelm Souchon, who had been appointed governor of Kiel, made far-reaching concessions to the insurgents and stated that he was prepared to release the naval men under arrest. In the eyes of Kapitänleutnant Hermann von Schweinitz this was a grave error. 'We are all deeply upset over the disgraceful mutiny in the fleet,' he wrote. 'We are preparing ourselves for self-defence. Naval command is wilting, not daring to intervene any more. It is reported that Souchon has been negotiating with the refractory ratings and has given in to them.'[58]

Schweinitz had had to break off his recently commenced training course as a U-boat commander at Glücksburg and been ordered to Kiel with other officers in order to save what might be saved. He went straight to the *Markgraf* where chaos reigned. Despite that, he and his fellow officers attempted to keep their composure. 'We are maintaining an iron coolness, mastering our feelings at all we see. Calmness is the first duty aboard ship,' he noted in his diary.[59] After a two-day wait in vain for support he gave up: 'Crew tippling. Any impression on men now totally pointless. We are powerless, all we try to no avail, too late. Soldiers' council is running everything from watch-keeping to the magazines.'[60] Finally, he and the other officers slipped away surreptitiously by night from the *Markgraf*. 'Stranded ashore. Quo vadis?'[61]

This semi-organised situation was not restored to order until after Souchon had abandoned his post on 7 November and SPD deputy Gustav Noske, sent by the Reich government, took over with full authority and worked in combination with the soldiers' council. Even Noske could not prevent numerous naval ratings leaving the city for fear of being encircled by the advancing troops, thus spreading the unrest farther afield. Within a few days, these groups of ratings sparked off a revolutionary wave in the military establishments of the north German ports and other towns in the interior which then spread in all directions unstoppably.

The wave also embraced Wilhelmshaven where Fleet Commander Hipper had, like Souchon, decided on a co-operative attitude. When a deputation from his flagship *Baden* requested his assurance that the fleet would only engage in hostilities to defend against an attack by the British and that a large number of officers in disfavour must be put ashore, he agreed to both demands. 'As what they wanted was relatively mild, there was no point in resisting it, and I gave in to prevent it perhaps leading to an enormous bloodbath, also to keep the revolution within certain bounds and not drive those as yet undecided politically, who are in the majority, into the USPD camp. It was not possible to avoid their setting up a so-called soldiers' council.'[62]

For Wilhelm Tägert, commander of *Seydlitz*, the first days of November 1918 were 'probably the worst of our lives'. His only consolation was that most of his crew remained loyal to him. 'The men are standing by me and are showing it to me in touching manner and I definitely believe I can get them through this honourably,' he wrote to his wife. 'But I am not sitting still. I fight with open visor without secretiveness and build only on trust. If they break that, then I shall tell them they should kill me at once, for I cannot leave the ship without honour.'[63] His great concern was that his men would hoist the red flag on *Seydlitz*. He admitted that in imagining this, he had 'almost lost for a moment my poise and self-control'. Tägert was determined to prevent his ship suffering dishonour in this way, if necessary at the cost of his life. 'Throughout these days I have often reflected on this moment and decided to let them kill me in defence of the [ship's] flag. But my people would probably not have done that, for ultimately it would have come to a fight by a minority against the majority.'[64]

Kapitänleutnant Reinhold Knobloch, who like his former shipboard colleague Schweinitz had begun U-boat commander training at Glücksburg, had also been returned to Wilhelmshaven. On board *Kronprinz Wilhelm* of IV Squadron he had to look on as the crew occupied the ship's magazines and chose informants. To his surprise, they expressed their confidence in the ship's captain and promised to maintain order and discipline. After this conciliatory gesture Knobloch believed for a short moment: 'Now everything will be all right, let us hope that Kiel will also soon come to an understanding.'[65]

Next day he thought better of it, however, when a workers' and soldiers' council, the so-called 21st Council, took full command of Wilhelmshaven. Leading Stoker Bernhard Kuhnt, active in the USPD, was nominated chairman of the council. On 10 November 1918 he declared Wilhelmshaven, the surrounding islands and the entire region of Oldenburg to be the socialist 'republic of Oldenburg–Ostfriesland'. In the meantime IV Reconnaissance Group had been ordered to the Baltic. Officers who refused to sail were brought ashore and interned. 'It is like being in a madhouse or a criminal under guard,' Knobloch wrote. 'We no longer have any kind of authority. Intolerable circumstances. If it carries on like this one will go mad.'[66] A day later he ascertained: 'Hooligans and louts have the regiment.'[67] Finally, after Knobloch and the other officers had signed a declaration not to become involved in any action against the 'Movement', with a few exceptions they were discharged by the shipboard soldiers' council and put ashore.

'It is all up with our beautiful fleet, to which I have devoted almost 35 years of my life. It makes one weep, but what can one do about it now,' wrote Albert Hopman in despair.[68] Instead of a last great naval battle to maintain the honour of the navy and to prove to the nation that the mostly useless ships at least knew how to go down with honour, the miscarriage of the planned 'death voyage' provided the motivation for the outbreak of revolution in Germany. It was actually a devastating outcome, as the self-critical Korvettenkapitän Ernst von Weizsäcker inferred: 'This navy! It was spawned by world power arrogance, ruined our foreign policy for twenty years, failed to keep its promises in the war and has now kindled revolution!'[69] Weizsäcker could see clearly that under these circumstances a continuation of the German fleet policy in force hitherto was unthinkable. But the high price that the navy would have to pay for its failure both surprised and horrified him.

10

'We are destroyed for all time':
Armistice and Internment

THE FATE OF THE GERMAN Kaiser Reich was sealed in two railway coaches. The Allied Commander-in-Chief, French Marshal Ferdinand Foch, had arranged for a discarded dining car to be brought to the wood at Compiègne. There, about fifty miles (80km) north of Paris, on 11 November 1918 the German delegation headed by Centrist politician Matthias Erzberger was obliged to sign the unexpectedly harsh Armistice conditions of the Entente powers. The other coach belonged to the Kaiser's magnificent gold- and white-lacquered royal train which had left the German army headquarters at Spa in Belgium on the morning of 10 November. Its destination was the Dutch border. While Reichstag Deputy Erzberger ended by his signature a war which had cost almost fifteen million people their lives, the monarch who had led the nation into this 'opening catastrophe' of the twentieth century sought his salvation in exile.

The question as to whether Wilhelm II should abdicate had been discussed more or less openly in all German political circles since September 1918. The question had received a particularly explosive impetus through the notes of US President Woodrow Wilson, in which the impression had been given in a rather roundabout way that while the Kaiser remained head of state, Germany would not receive reasonable peace terms. In Wilhelm's eyes that had been 'an absolutely frivolous impertinence'.[1] A parliamentary government was all well and good, but to disclaim the throne – for him such a thing was out of the question. 'I am not going; if I do, the Reich will collapse, therefore it is my duty to remain where I stand and, if that is what has to happen, to go down with my people,' he told the circle of his confidential staff on 25 October 1918.[2] Four days later, on the advice of his entourage, he left Berlin and travelled to Spa to rejoin his generals, which many saw as a flight to avoid his responsibility.

Admiral Hipper also felt that the supreme commander had left him in the lurch. 'It is very bad that the Kaiser has left Berlin and has hidden himself away at headquarters. If he at least showed himself at the front where the bullets are whistling – but as it is it makes a very bad impression and does a great deal of harm,' he wrote in his diary on 2 November.[3] Many officers would have liked it even better if Wilhelm had been aboard the German flagship sailing out to fight the last great battle against the Royal Navy, or if he had placed himself at the head of a regiment on the western front and led an offensive there. An heroic death in battle was not for Wilhelm II, however.

For a few days at Spa, the Kaiser indulged himself in the vague hope of perhaps still somehow surviving the crisis, but then events overwhelmed the injudicious monarch. From the armed resurrection by the ratings at Kiel the revolutionary spark spread like wildfire into the interior of the country. On 7 November 1918 the Bavarian USPD leader Kurt Eisner declared the republic at Munich, and on 9 November the revolution reached Berlin. The workers streamed in masses from their places of work into the streets to join the general strike called by the radical left 'Spartacus Group'. The troops at the Berlin garrison joined them and elected soldiers' councils.

In order to avoid bloodshed, Reich Chancellor Max von Baden saw no alternative but to declare on his own initiative the abdication of Wilhelm II and pass the office of Reich Chancellor to the chairman of the majority Social Democrats, Friedrich Ebert. His hope of at least saving the monarchy as an institution by doing this did not pay off: a few hours later the majority SPD politican Philipp Scheidemann declared the republic, shortly afterwards the Spartacist Karl Liebknecht did the same.

The following day the 'Council of the People's Authorised Representatives' (*Rat der Volksbeauftragten*) came into being as head of the provisional new government: it was composed of three members each from the MSPD and USPD. After the elections for the national assembly on 19 January 1919 which provided a new constitution, in which for the first time there came into being general, equal, secret and direct voting rights for men and women aged twenty and over, the majority Social Democrats formed the first Weimar coalition government with the liberal-left DDP (German Democratic Party) and the Catholic centre under Philipp Scheidemann. Friedrich Ebert was elected the first president of the new republic.

For Wilhelm II, who had debated with himself until the last minute whether or not to abdicate as Kaiser (Emperor) but continue as King of Prussia – which was impossible under the constitution – the news from Berlin came as a blow. There now followed immediate hectic discussions at headquarters in Belgium as to what he should do next. The Kaiser's entourage was only too well aware of the fate which had befallen the Russian Tsar Nicholas II, murdered together with his family by revolutionaries at Ekaterinburg. In order that Wilhelm II be spared a similar fate, he had to seek exile abroad as soon as possible. General Wilhelm Groener, Ludendorff's successor in the OHL, saw with what apathy the Kaiser reacted to this suggestion: 'He said nothing, but just looked – looked from one to the other at first with an expression of surprise, then of pleading which awoke one's feeling of sympathy, and finally of peculiarly vague dismay. He said nothing, and we led him away, just as though he were a small child – and sent him off to Holland.'[4]

In the early hours of 10 November 1918 the Kaiser and his escort arrived at the Dutch-Belgian border point at Eijsden. From there he continued to Amerongen in the province of Utrecht, where Wilhelm spent the next eighteen months in the mansion of Count Bentinck. The ex-Kaiser no longer had a throne, but at least he was not poor. After he had agreed a sum in compensation with the German government for the confiscated imperial properties, over the next three years a total approaching 80 million marks flowed from the exchequer into the Hohenzollern bank accounts. Furthermore, a special train of fifty-nine coaches left Berlin for Holland carrying furniture, works and objects of art, carpeting, tableware and kitchen utensils and other 'removable goods' from the ex-Kaiser's estates. With all this cash, Wilhelm was able to obtain Doorn House near Amerongen, a small palace which had once belonged to Audrey Hepburn's great-aunt. He moved in together with his wife in May 1920. He would never leave Doorn again until his death on 4 June 1941.

When Admiral Hipper learned on 9 November 1918 that the Kaiser had fled Berlin and Friedrich Ebert had been nominated Reich Chancellor, he was overcome by despair: 'We can hardly sink any deeper.'[5] The officers' world now lay in total ruin. Korvettenkapitän Bogislav von Selchow wrote: 'This was too much. One cannot take it in any more. Sometimes tears come and it is impossible to prevent it, until they cease of their own accord.'[6] After the last sortie of the fleet had been abandoned, following the ratings' revolts at Wilhelmshaven and Kiel, the disgrace of the red flag at the masthead of their proud ships, the beginning of the revolution – now came the flight of the Kaiser and the proclamation of the republic. 'These are days of the most painful and bitter experience which are destroying me completely inside,' Adolf von Trotha wrote to his wife. 'May God give us finally lighter days and prevent our poor fatherland from total disintegration. When shall we see each other again?' He added, 'It must be spring again one day!'[7]

The officers, bereft of any illusions, now had to decide where their loyalties should lie: to the Kaiser, or more correctly the monarchy, which in theory could continue as an institution without Wilhelm II, or to the fatherland, which was at the end of its strength and had to be protected against internal decay and bolshevisation. The later Grossadmiral Karl Dönitz described the inner conflict with which many officers of the time found themselves confronted:

> For generations by tradition and breeding we were monarchists. Should we, after the German princes had been forced to abdicate in October 1918, transfer to the enemy camp with flags flying? There were many who believed from inner conviction that they could no longer serve. On the other hand the belief weighed heavy that as a soldier one should not abandon the German state whatever form it took. To do so might contravene the Prussian-German principle of selfless service to the cause.[8]

In the assessment of Ernst von Weizsäcker, at least some senior naval commanders such as Admiral Scheer remained a 'royalist to the bones'.[9] On 7 November Scheer wrote to his wife: 'I am determined to stick to the Kaiser so long as he has command of the troops and I have the feeling that he needs me as chief of the naval staff.'[10] Two days later when the republic was proclaimed, he petitioned Wilhelm II for permission to resign. Weizsäcker found this 'bumptious and absurd' and it gave him a certain satisfaction when the request was denied.[11] 'Herr Admiral, the navy has really let me down,'[12] was the only reply Scheer received from the Kaiser. It was the last time that the two of them ever met.

Weizsäcker himself considered that the flight of the Kaiser released him from his oath of allegiance, and most must have thought as he did. Alongside the idealistic motives of honour and loyalty, such a far-reaching decision would certainly also have involved quite pragmatic considerations. In the final analysis, the future was more than uncertain and who wanted to simply give up a well-paid position and gamble his whole existence? The last doubts were swept aside with the official announcement of his abdication signed by the Kaiser on 28 November 1918. In it he absolved all members of the military from their oath and expressed the expectation 'that until the German Reich is newly organised, they will assist those holding actual power in Germany to protect the German people against the dangers of anarchy, famine and foreign domination with which they are threatened.'[13]

The most urgent danger amongst those identified by Wilhelm was the fulfilment of the Allied Armistice conditions accepted by Matthias Erzberger in the other railway coach in the wood at Compiègne. In Weizsäcker's view they were 'so oppressive that my first thought is: they will cause a new war. Our children will have to fight it.'[14] The German delegation had arrived at Compiègne on 8 November to be greeted by Marshal Ferdinand Foch with the words; 'What brings you gentlemen here? What do you want of me?' When Erzberger replied he was hoping to receive proposals for an armistice, Foch told him, 'I have no proposals to make.' Instead he had his Chief of the General Staff Maxime Weygand read out the terms the Allies had agreed in Paris some days before. While Weygand spoke, according to Erzberger, Foch sat 'at the table in stony calm, occasionally plucking at his moustache. During the entire reading no observations were made.'[15]

What the French general announced horrified the German negotiators. Within fourteen days, German troops had to withdraw from all occupied territory in Belgium, France, Luxemburg and the Reich province of Alsace-Lorraine, German since the Franco-Prussian War in 1871. In the event of failure to comply, French troops would occupy German territory on the left (west) bank of the Rhine and establish bridgeheads on the right of the Rhine around Mainz, Koblenz and Cologne. On the right bank of the Rhine a neutral zone of 30–40km (18–25 miles) in breadth had to be set up. The peace treaties of Brest-Litovsk and Bucharest were cancelled, German troops in the east had to vacate Romania, Poland, the Baltic States and the Ukraine, and withdraw behind the German frontier as it existed on 1 August 1914. The German army had to surrender to the Entente 5000 guns, 30,000 machine-guns, 3000 heavy mortars and 2000 aircraft, together with 5000 locomotives, 150,000 railway wagons and 10,000 lorries. The hardest blow fell on the navy. After heated arguments amongst the Western Allies, which will be returned to later, the British had mostly got their way, and Germany had to surrender the major part of the High Seas Fleet to the Allies, although initially it would only be interned. In order to guarantee that the Germans fulfilled their obligations, the Allies maintained the naval blockade (until April 1919) and threatened to occupy Heligoland and the North Sea river estuaries should there be any infringement of the treaty terms.

This was hardly the 'mild' peace for which the Germans had hoped. The conditions appeared so harsh that even the British Foreign Minister Balfour took the view 'that a people with any self-respect would not grovel to sign a document like this Armistice.'[16] All attempts by the German delegation to negotiate individual points were brusquely rejected by Marshal Foch: he was only prepared to grant minor concessions. Thus the number of machine-guns to be surrendered was reduced from 30,000 to 25,000, the aircraft from 2000 to 1700, the lorries from 10,000 to 5000: there were some minor extensions allowed to the time given for evacuations and delivery dates. In the end Erzberger had no choice. After Ebert and Hindenburg had radioed him their agreement, he signed the Instrument of Armistice at 0500 hrs on 11 November 1918. Six hours later the guns fell silent after 1586 days of war. The Armistice was initially in force for thirty-six days and thereafter extended frequently, finally amended on 16 February 1919 to be without limit of time.

While everywhere in Europe the population celebrated the end of the fighting, perhaps the bitterest time of the entire war now began for the Imperial Navy, which allegedly was not in need of an armistice. Nowadays it is hardly possible to imagine what effort it must have cost the officers, in particular, to continue their duties under these circumstances and practically collaborate in organising their own demise, for whether the ships now going into internment would ever return to Germany was more than uncertain.

At the time, many must have considered putting an end to their lives in preference to abasing themselves in that manner. Including Wilhelm Tägert, who then distanced himself from the idea because it was 'too easy a way out'. What made the father of a family change his mind?

> You all, and then also: one can perhaps still help to rebuild our people and country. But when I loaded my pistol this morning, for a moment I had the sensation of a wild triumph, and I might do it if there is nothing more for it and it is certain for me. Dear love, in such moments everything is so immediate and not at all theatrical. Afterwards maybe the cynicism comes, but when one is going through it all, then it is different.[17]

There were several reasons why the officers returned to their ships, most, apart from a few exceptions, having left when the red flags were hoisted. Foremost for many, as for Tägert, was the feeling of being duty-bound as soldiers not to leave the fatherland in the lurch. This attitude is expressed in an appeal by Admiral Hipper on 13 November 1918 to officers and men in which, amongst other things, he stated: 'The entire German people bears the grief and humiliation of the internment of our fleet. Nobody is dishonoured who now does his duty to maintain the ships for the fatherland. On the contrary, in the future the fatherland will thank those men who held firm in this difficult time of trial and stayed at their posts.'[18] A week before in a secret fleet order, Hipper had called upon the officers for 'loyalty to the government and fatherland' and assured them: 'There is no conflict between the officer corps of the fleet and the government.'[19]

Additionally, the demands of the Allies could not be met without the expert knowledge and executive jurisdiction of the officers. Even the Supreme Soldiers' Council 'very quickly arrived at the conclusion that without officers it could not effect the tasks inherent in the looming demobilisation.'[20] Moreover, in order to maintain law and order, the new social democratic government, the Council of the People's Representatives, had decided on an extensive (and extremely controversial) collaboration with the bureaucratic, military and economic elites. At the request of OHL, the government called upon military servicemen to 'obey unconditionally' the orders of their superiors until their discharge; the soldiers' councils were to give support 'without reserve' to the officers in their important assignments.[21] In this way, over the next few weeks and months naval officers succeeded in gradually restoring their shattered position of power, even if this was not so clear-cut as previously and some of their privileges had to be relinquished.

Most pressing initially was the preparation for internment. Amidst chaotic circumstances the ships listed for surrender had to be disarmed, reprovisioned and fuelled up for the voyage and given a skeleton crew at least numerous enough to provide the ships with a reasonable degree of manoeuvrability. The last point presented difficulties. The overwhelming majority of seamen and stokers lacked any desire to take part in this voyage into the unknown, and preferred to go home. A 'transfer premium' of several hundred marks brought about a rethink.[22]

The officers were also not happy at having to present their undefeated ships to the enemy on a silver platter. Whilst Kapitänleutnant Reinhold Knobloch and also Walter Zaeschmar were both hoping that their presence aboard would not be required ('It would be too painful for me'), but would probably have done so if called upon,[23] Ernst von Weizsäcker declined to take part in the transfer of the fleet 'for the most varied reasons'.[24] The U-boat commander and later theologian and pacifist Martin Niemöller even refused an order to sail two U-boats to England since he found this to be in conflict with his 'notions of honour and truthfulness'.[25]

It almost seems as though these officers suspected what awaited them on the other side of the North Sea, for the Royal Navy also made a big thing of its 'outward' honour, reputation and prestige as the heir of Nelson. The Grand Fleet, though victorious, had done nothing to compare with Trafalgar and their success was much less obvious, because it had been achieved without a major battle in which the enemy had been destroyed. When the war ended, many British officers lost much sleep over having to go home empty-handed – 'slinking home with nothing to show for our four and a quarter years of waiting,' as Sub Lieutenant Geoffrey Harper put it.[26] In almost total accord with their German counterparts, they would have preferred to fight on and have one last grand but strategically totally pointless battle. Clearly, not to go down with honour as the Germans had in mind, but for a glorious victory with the Nelson touch.

To the end, Admiral David Beatty held firm to the hope that the Armistice which the Germans had requested would only extend to their troops on land. When it became clear that that was not to be the case, Beatty and other senior British officers insisted on such harsh conditions for the Imperial Navy that the Germans would rather fight on than sign. For Great Britain, wrote Beatty, 'It would be a very bad thing for the country if our Great Fleet never has an opportunity of showing its power in a more demonstrative manner than it has. The Public are very short-sighted and would murmur at the necessity of expending large sums on the maintenance of the Sea Power if they had no <u>ocular</u> demonstration of its power to command the Seas.'[27]

In fact, after the war, armaments contracts in Great Britain fell off heavily: in the case of the Royal Navy sinking considerably below the pre-war level. In the words of the British historian Paul Kennedy, after the Great War there began for Great Britain the real 'years of decay'. The enormous budget for public spending to which the armed forces in general and the navy in particular had laid claim under the conditions of war could no long be justified in a peacetime in which the German threat no longer existed.

Great Britain was deeply in debt as a result of war loans from the United States. At home there was an urgent need for social and industrial reforms. Therefore in the years 1921/1922 British social spending had soared to £234 million from the 1913/1914 figure of £41.5 million.[28]

The Royal Navy was hit by non-negotiable financial cuts, not so hard comparatively as the army but, to the regret of its officers, hard enough. The naval estimates sank from £356 million in 1918/1919 to only £52 million in 1923. Whereas the Royal Navy had a 25 per cent share in the total state budget in 1914, at the time of the economic crisis this had fallen to 6 per cent: 'That was a yardstick for its diminished prestige in the eyes of the politicians.'[29] Although a ratio of strength of 5:5:3 was agreed with the other major sea powers, America and Japan, at the 1922 Washington Conference, with Japan as the junior partner, Great Britain was no longer the world's strongest naval power, but was falling slowly and irremediably behind the United States.

To this extent Beatty's fears were not unjustified. He was wrong, however, if he believed that a demonstration of might by the Royal Navy in the form of a great naval battle would have changed anything. One of the reasons for cutting back the naval estimates was precisely the fact that after the war had ended, British naval power was no longer threatened by the German fleet, and a battle which ended with the annihilation of the German fleet would have had the same outcome.

Notwithstanding later developments, in November 1918 Beatty put forward his views and the War Cabinet in London decided: 'The naval conditions of the Armistice should represent the admission of German defeat by sea in the same degree as the military conditions recognise the corresponding admission of German defeat by land.'[30] In concrete terms this meant that Great Britain would demand the surrender to itself of the greater part of the German High Seas Fleet. The ten newest German battleships, the fleet flagship *Baden*, all battlecruisers, eight modern small cruisers, fifty torpedo boats and 160 (that meant all) U-boats were to be turned over to them as victors.

This demand was discussed first by the Allied Naval Council, a committee founded in December 1917 to co-ordinate the co-operation of the Allied naval forces. The council accepted the British claim almost as submitted (only the delivery of the flagship was turned down since 'inclusion of the fleet flagship might be thought to be unduly humiliating to Germany') and recommended that the leading politicians and generals of the western powers, who had assembled in Paris to advise on the exact terms of the Armistice treaty, should also take it over.[31]

The French, in particular, showed little inclination to impose such drastic conditions on the German navy since the purpose of the conditions was to bolster the prestige of British naval power, but in the worst case scenario – if the Germans declined to sign as Beatty hoped – the war would continue to be fought by French soldiers on French battlefields. The United States also had no desire 'to sacrifice American lives to maintain British mastery of the seas'.[32] They also feared that the European naval powers would share out the German ships amongst themselves, and principally that the Royal Navy would have the opportunity to expand its fleet to the prejudice of that of the Americans.

In the end, a watered-down version of the conditions suggested by the Allied Naval Council was agreed upon. The Imperial Navy would be deprived of all U-boats. In the case of the surface ships, what was now being asked for, instead of the surrender of the ships, was their *internment in neutral ports* until the peace treaty was concluded, to which time the decision as to their future fate would be reserved.[33]

For Admiral Beatty and many other British naval officers this was a heavy blow. 'I had most of my Captains and Admirals on board this morning ... All suffering from a feeling far greater than disappointment, depressed beyond measure. But they responded gallantly and sank their feelings in their attention to duty.'[34] The fleet commander was not only incensed about the fact that what was the Navy's by right of its great victory was being withheld ('That is hell'), but also that the British government had allowed itself to be cheated 'at the negotiating table by those who are strong in the Council Chamber but who have accomplished but a 100th part of our share, ie Americans, French, Italians, Portuguese and others'. When all was said and done, Beatty went on, there was only one way to establish a clear relationship between Great Britain and Germany: 'The only thing is to sail into their poisonous country and wreck it and take what we want and put the fear of God, Truth and Justice into them, as represented by the British Tommy.'

The tension of the situation was only relieved somewhat when at the last moment the possibility was introduced into the treaty wording that the German ships could be 'interned' in Allied ports as well as neutral ones. This made it easier for British naval personalities to accept the compromise formula, for it was clear that these 'Allied ports' would most probably be British. Subsequently, the choice fell on Scapa Flow as the 'most suitable place'.[35] Furthermore, on the quiet, the Royal Navy received the assurance that none of the interned ships would ever be returned to Germany. Eventually Article 184 of the Treaty of Versailles made this clear, by stipulating that when it came into effect the interned ships were to be seen as surrendered.

After the acceptance of the Armistice terms by the signature of Matthias Erzberger, the dream of a last great naval battle finally evaporated for the British naval officers, and there remained for them only a single possibility of showing to the world who ruled the waves. This involved preparing a reception for the Germans much more humiliating than defeat in an action at sea could ever have been.

It was laid down in the Armistice treaty that all ships designated for internment must be ready to sail from German ports seven days after the treaty was signed. After a supreme effort the preparations were concluded on time, and on 19 November 1918 the German High Seas Fleet sailed from Wilhelmshaven for the last time. 'At 1330 hrs the endlessly long funeral procession was set in motion,' one of the officer witnesses reported.[36] In beaming sunshine, the Imperial Navy flag at the ensign staff, the following ships headed for Scotland: the five battle-cruisers *Seydlitz, Moltke, Hindenburg, Derfflinger* and *Von der Tann*; nine battleships, *Friedrich der Grosse, König Albert, Kaiser, Kronprinz Wilhelm, Kaiserin, Bayern, Markgraf, Prinzregent Luitpold* and *Grosser Kurfürst*; seven small cruisers, *Karlsruhe, Frankfurt*, replacement-*Emden, Nürnberg, Bremse, Brummer* and *Cöln*, and fifty torpedo boats. 'Thus did the endless queue over fifty kilometres long wallow slowly northwards'.[37] The tenth battleship *König* and the eighth small cruiser *Dresden* were laid up for repair in the yards and followed a few weeks later. The sixth battlecruiser *Mackensen* was still under construction: in its place, the British demanded the fleet flagship *Baden*. The German U-boats received instructions to proceed to the port of Harwich, where they were later either destroyed or divided up amongst the Allies.

The so-called 'transfer group' was commanded by Konteradmiral Ludwig von Reuter. Born in 1869 at Guben/Niederlausitz, he had occupied various important positions during the war. First as commander of the battlecruiser *Derfflinger*, later as the commanding officer of IV Reconnaissance Group, with which he had served at Jutland. In the summer of 1918 when Hipper was appointed fleet commander, Reuter took over his post as Commander-in-Chief Reconnaissance Forces. It was also Hipper who requested that Reuter take command of the transfer group, in Hipper's eyes 'a ghastly assignment'.[38] Not only because the voyage promised to be a humiliation, but also because the officers had to accept onboard every ship a workers' and sailors' council which had the right to be consulted in all shipboard affairs. 'The officers will run up against enormous difficulties because there the question of honour plays an important role,' Hipper surmised correctly.[39]

Reuter resolved the problem for himself by accepting 'that honour in this case must serve the welfare of the state'. He considered that the consequences with which the Allies had threatened the Germans were so portentous 'that in the face of this damage to the German Reich, if I can prevent it, my person must play no role.'[40]

From Wilhelmshaven, Reuter's ships were to head for Rosyth on the east coast of Scotland. This had been agreed with Beatty some few days before, without it being made clear whether Rosyth was the destination. Reuter did not discover until later that it was Scapa Flow. Wilhelm Tägert led the line with *Seydlitz*, Reuter was aboard his flagship *Friedrich der Grosse*. The Firth of Forth, the longstanding base for British battlecruisers, had replaced Scapa Flow in April 1918 as the main Royal Navy base and now served as the ideal backdrop for a unique piece of theatre in the history of navigation.

On the early morning of 21 November 1918, when the German ships arrived they were received by an assembly consisting of all 370 ships and 90,000 men of the Grand Fleet, the greatest naval presence by far in history. The German ships, led by the slender light cruiser *Cardiff*, were obliged to steam, as if running the gauntlet, between two endlessly long rows of battle-ready battleships, cruisers and destroyers flying the White Ensign. Reuter's hope that fog would descend to hide the humiliating proceedings was not fulfilled. The sun shone; no more than a light mist was present. Surrounded by excursion vessels, yachts and rowing boats, the transfer group finally dropped anchor off Rosyth observed by numerous spectators and to the jubilation of the British crews. Even Admiral Beatty's wife did not wish to miss the spectacle and sailed her small yacht between the German ships. In the process her boat approached dangerously near to the *Seydlitz* and came in for mocking laughter from the German crews.

British prize crews now inspected the German ships to confirm that no weapons or ammunition had been brought along. Beatty then gave the order that all German war flags had to be taken down at sunset and not hoisted against without his express permission. Konteradmiral Reuter entered a strong protest to no avail. Sub Lieutenant James Colvill almost felt sympathy for the commander of the German torpedo boat to whom he passed Beatty's order. 'That annoyed him and he cursed heartily under his breath. It must be a most humiliating position of a man to have his ship searched by a foreign naval officer.'[41] When the sun sank below the horizon at 1557 hrs and all German ships struck their flags as ordered, there was deafening jubilation aboard the British ships. All hands had appeared on deck in order to witness the unique theatre. On board his flagship *Queen Elizabeth*, David Beatty was probably unable to conceal a satisfied smirk. Turning to his men he remarked drily, 'I always told you they would have to come out.'[42]

For the Royal Navy it was of the greatest importance not to have the German ships interned in a neutral port as originally planned but, as Beatty had demanded, to have them seen to be in the custody of the British as 'conspicuous proof' of the superiority of Britain as a sea power. The intention was to stage the interning of their ships so as to be as humiliating as possible for the Germans, this being an equivalent kind of mental consolation as had been intended in the German plan for the 'death voyage'. The British newspapers took the hint and made the point that it was the first time in the history of naval warfare that a fleet had surrendered itself to its enemy voluntarily, and in such a degrading way. 'No really great nation would have tolerated such a degradation to its flag', wrote the *Naval and Military Record*, while the *Globe* was of the opinion: 'The German navy is not only defeated, it is dishonoured for all time, alike by the foulness of its fighting and by its cowardice in the day of its doom.'[43]

Not a few in the British fleet had expected, even hoped, that the German officers would react at the last moment against the shameful surrender of their fleet. 'A lot of us think one or two ships will make a fight for it at the end to save their honour. Handing over such a fleet without a fight for it seems to me to be the depths of humiliation. Despite his defects the German officer is a proud and brave man and he will find it very hard to be humiliated so.'[44]

When nothing of the kind transpired, it was again left to Admiral Beatty to interpret this disappointing fact as best he could as a 'great silent victory'. On board the battleship *Revenge* on 23 November 1918 he said that even without a decisive naval battle, 'the history of the last forty-eight hours will be written in letters of gold in the Naval History of England, and I congratulate you on being present and on taking part'. The fact that the Germans had accepted their fate so easily was proof that there never could have been a naval battle because 'a force which would permit itself to be given up, handed over and led in like a flock of sheep is not worth the life or a drop of blood of a single British Bluejacket.'[45]

Despite, or precisely because of, his admission, the British public could not be blind to the fact that the Royal Navy had not succeeded in its mission and achieved what was generally expected of the Grand Fleet. The very fact that the German ships were still intact and afloat showed what the Royal Navy had failed to do. For many, therefore, it remained a hollow triumph being celebrated at the end of November 1918:

> It was a great event to take part in, but I am sure that I was not alone in a feeling of disappointment when we sighted the German ships coming to meet us, not to fight, but to be escorted as prisoners into the Firth of Forth. It was difficult to analyse one's feelings. It was the first tangible sign of the nation's victory, and so to be rejoiced at, but it was also the blighting of our hopes to substitute a veritable triumph that no one could question, for the unsatisfactory result of the Battle of Jutland.[46]

Even Admiral Beatty himself, no matter how much he strained himself to gild the British victory, could not help admitting that the sight of the undamaged German ships had been a sickening one for him:

> It was a pitiable sight, in fact I should say it was a horrible sight to see these great ships that we have been looking forward so long to seeing, expecting them to have the same courage that we expect from men whose work lies upon great waters – we did expect them to do something for the honour of their country – and I think it was a pitiable sight to see them come in, led by a British light cruiser, with their old antagonists, the battlecruisers, gazing at them. I am sure that the sides of this gallant old ship, which have been well hammered in the past, must have ached – as I ached, as all ached – to give them another dose of what we had intended for them.[47]

The British fleet commander was presumably not the only officer who, if only rhetorically, secretly wanted the war to go on and have the chance of doing everything better the next time. 'I am beginning to wish we were still at war, this peace business makes me tired, all hopes destroyed, all ideas of glorious achievements gone by the board, nothing but an immense drudgery and masses of problems which there seems to be great difficulty in solving.'[48]

If that was how the victors felt, how must it have been for the defeated?

Kapitänleutnant Walter Zaeschmar called 18 November 1918 the 'day of shame for the navy', and there are few grounds for assuming that he was alone in this:

> Today our fleet set out for Britain and internment. If they will ever let us have our ships back is neither here nor there. British lust for vengeance has not even spared us this insult ... We are destroyed for all time ... Childish institutions such as 'Supreme Naval Council of the Elbe' with ratings as its officers, 'Republic of Oldenburg-Ostfriesland' with Senior Stoker Kuhnt as president, that is the end of the German navy. I shall bury myself in solitude.[49]

Zaeschmar saw no possibility of repair. 'It can only be washed away with blood. And the German people will never again be capable of it.'[50]

Zaeschmar made no secret of his disappointment at his own compatriots, who apparently had no interest in what became of the Kaiser Reich and who by their own failure had brought the navy into this predicament. He lashed out: 'Our national backbone has been broken. The masses do not even sense this disgrace.'[51] Zaeschmar's analysis of the causes of the German collapse was very similar to Hitler's crazy logic in the Second World War, that the German people had deserved their defeat because they had not proved strong enough in the struggle against their opponents:

> When I think about it, I tell myself that the German national character does not qualify us to have a world policy. The women who held back their men instead of driving them from the house with a broomstick will look back with anguish at this war. All our enthusiasm for it was nothing but a flash in the pan ... our genetic factors, our self-indulgence, egotism and vanity will prevent us from having a role in history ever again in the future. We have a total lack of national feeling.[52]

In his convulsion of rage he called Germany 'a gluttonous and boozy land of traitors and cowards.'[53]

A month after the transfer group had headed for Britain, Zaeschmar, who had stayed at home, sought diversion in hunting. There he met up with Admiral Hipper indulging his old passion. It was the first time that the two men had met, and Hipper, as Zaeschmar observed in his diary later, 'told me some interesting things. "He could not see any ratings any more." "He no longer has a fatherland." "All that he had achieved in thirty-seven years of service had been for nothing, one must forget it." "What he had done most recently had been bad." Makes sense.'[54]

At any time in the past it would have been unthinkable for an admiral to bare his heart in this way to a small Kapitänleutnant whom he had never even met before. In this case, however, it was only a pensioner and a former Imperial Navy officer with an uncertain future exchanging reminiscences about the war: only a few days before the conversation with Zaeschmar, with effect from 13 December 1918, Hipper had been retired from active naval service. Watching the ships sailing off into internment he had decided, deeply depressed, to submit his resignation: 'It broke my heart to do it … thus my time as fleet commander has come to an obscure end. All that remains is questions of demobilisation and disarmament and negotiations with soldiers' councils. The chief of staff can handle all that, I no longer have the strength. I shall remain nominal head for a short while but otherwise I am sick to death of it.'[55] Shortly afterwards Hipper handed his affairs of office to Konteradmiral Hugo Meurer. 'I took my leave yesterday from the gentlemen of my staff, and with that my career has come to its end, an end which could not have been sadder.'[56]

In 1919 Hipper settled at Othmarschen near Hamburg. The initial period of his retirement was overshadowed by fears that the victorious powers, who in the Treaty of Versailles had required the handing over of alleged German war criminals, might also seek his own head. It did not come to a handing over – instead the German government put a handful of the accused on trial. A total of seventeen cases were brought before the Reich Court at Leipzig, the highest national court of the period. Ten men were convicted and seven acquitted.

They left Hipper alone. When it was clear that he had nothing to fear, it meant for him 'freedom from a millstone around my neck since last July. Now at last I can really enjoy my life and home for the first time.'[57]

Retired Admiral Franz Ritter von Hipper died on 25 May 1932 at the age of sixty-nine years. The funeral orations at his interment at the Ohlsdorf Cemetery in Hamburg were delivered by his former chief of staff Erich Raeder, now chief of the naval staff, and retired Admiral Wilhelm Souchon, who had begun his career in the Imperial Navy together with Hipper fifty-one years before. Later, Hipper's coffin was removed to his Bavarian home town of Weilheim.

'An end which could not have been sadder,' Hipper had called the concluding moments of his professional career, and his laconic comment might serve as a heading for the last chapter in the history of the Imperial Navy. Such a way of looking at it leaves out an important aspect. The old world of the officers lay in ruins: the wishes, hopes and dreams with which they had gone to war with enthusiasm in 1914 were smashed. Yet not a few of them saw in it the opportunity for a new beginning, for the reconstruction of a new, and perhaps better, world. Goethe's thought 'Die and become' had been the principle underlying the plan for the 'death voyage' against Britain, and it was still present in the minds of those men who, during the months of internment at Scapa Flow, reflected upon how they could become reconciled at the end to the fate of the Tirpitz fleet – how they could create an honourable departure for it from the stage of history.

I I

'A painful and grandiose piece of theatre'
The Scuttling of the Fleet at Scapa Flow

IT WAS NO COINCIDENCE that the peace conference of the First World War victorious powers was begun in Paris on 18 January 1919. Forty-eight years before, on 18 January 1871, the Prussian King Wilhelm I had been declared German emperor in the Mirror Room of the palace at Versailles. It was a symbolic act which many Frenchmen had felt to be a national humiliation. In the view of French President Clemenceau it was therefore only fitting that the talks which would seal the fate of the Kaiser Reich should begin on the same day of the year as had marked its birth. When the peace treaty was signed ten months later, the most 'fitting' place for the ceremony to humiliate the defeated was that same Mirror Room at Versailles. A British diplomat reported, after the two German plenipotentiaries, Foreign Minister Hermann Müller of the SPD and Transport Minister Johannes Bell of the Centre Party had appended their signatures to the treaty, that they had been led away 'like convicts at the bar', their eyes focused on some distant point on the horizon.[1]

In the weeks and months after the conference opened, all Germany looked towards Paris with tense expectation. One man in particular followed events in France with particular interest. For Konteradmiral Ludwig von Reuter, the outcome of these negotiations affected the fate of the ships which he had sailed to the Firth of Forth and then onwards into Scapa Flow. It was not that he had any great illusions: Reuter was a sober-thinking Prussian officer who saw clearly that the British had not staged the internment of the German ships at enormous expense as a humbling spectacle just to let them steam back home again scot-free.

In his view and that of the German naval staff, it would therefore be negligent to let them sail off into internment without a plan on the back-burner in the event that the ships were not returned to Germany. Additionally, the 'question of honour and existence' which had almost led at the end of October 1918 to a suicidal battle with the Royal Navy remained unresolved from the perspective of the officers. Therefore much points to the fact that Reuter already had in mind to scuttle the fleet when he left Wilhelmshaven in November 1918.

Soon after the arrival of the German ships at Scapa Flow, the crew total was reduced from twenty thousand to around five thousand men, so that only sufficient remained aboard to maintain readiness to sail. The surplus men were collected by German merchant ships and brought back to Wilhelmshaven. Konteradmiral Reuter seized the opportunity to return to Germany for a few weeks. He gave as the official reason for this unusual service trip the need to deal with important formalities at the Reich navy office. One would not be far wrong in suspecting, however, that it had more to do with the eventual fate of the German fleet.

Meanwhile, the relocation of the ships to Scapa Flow, of which Reuter was first notified at Rosyth, made it seem far less likely that they would be released for return to Germany. This provided a good reason to speak with the naval leaders in the Reich about the next step, most important of all presumably being Adolf von Trotha. When the Reich navy office was shut down in March 1919 and a newly created admiralty set up to replace it, Trotha was appointed its chief. Thus the Konteradmiral, who had drafted the 'Considerations at a grave hour', and was one of the most fervid advocates of the final battle against Britain, was now the most powerful figure in the 'Provisional Reichsmarine' as the former Imperial Navy was now called (the 'Provisional' was dropped in 1921).

What was discussed in detail in Berlin or elsewhere has never been made known. Reuter himself said of it that after his return to Scapa Flow at the end of January 1919 he had immediately discussed with his chief of staff, Fregattenkapitän Iwan Oldekop, the question of scuttling the fleet.[2] If only to update him about what he had learned in Germany? It is not known, and we can only guess that during the months which followed, in which the 'transfer group' became the 'internment group' of German warships guarded by a British dreadnought squadron at Scapa, Reuter exchanged correspondence regularly with Trotha.

All mail going to or coming from Germany was censored by the British, but all the interned ships were reprovisioned in their entirety from Germany by sea, and this provided numerous opportunities for evading British censorship. Every time a German freighter arrived at Scapa Flow and handed over its cargo – most of it rotten by then – to the interned ships, besides meat, potatoes, bread and vegetables there would most probably have been well-concealed letters.

A letter from Trotha was so important that Reuter kept it in the safe aboard his flagship *Emden-II*. It was found there much later and now resides in The National Archives at Kew. In it, Trotha makes it plain that the fate of the internment group 'whatever guise it may assume under the pressure of the political situation, will not be determined without our involvement and handled by ourselves, and that there is no question of their being surrendered to the enemy.'[3]

These lines confirmed for Reuter what he had presumably known all along: that the naval staff approved of scuttling the fleet as a last resort. Simultaneously, Trotha was reinforcing the old maxim that under no circumstances was the fleet to fall into enemy hands. This concept was so essential a part of the traditional code of honour that it required no explanation, not to mention a formal order. Reuter knew what he had to do when the time came. Trotha only needed to communicate an order to him if Reuter were required not to scuttle the ships.

Now there would be a fresh period of waiting to see what the Allied peace talks came up with, these being basically discussions between the 'Big Three': Clemenceau for France, Prime Minister David Lloyd George for Great Britain and President Woodrow Wilson for the United States. As long as these discussions continued, the conditions of the Armistice, whereby Reuter's ships were only interned and remained German property, remained in force.

Their fate and that of the Imperial Navy were the subject of deliberations taking place in Paris between the Allied naval representatives who had previously laid down the Armistice conditions. Their suggestions and recommendations would then serve the politicians responsible as the foundation for the formulation of the corresponding article in the peace treaty.

On most points agreement was reached quickly. Thus by the beginning of March 1919 the victorious powers had concluded that not only the interned ships at Scapa Flow would be confiscated, but that much heavier sacrifices would be demanded of the Germans. On the other hand, the question that remained open until the Treaty of Versailles was signed was what was to be done with the confiscated ships: whether to condemn them for scrap, sink them or share them out amongst the various Allies remained uncertain.

The Germans at Scapa Flow learned what they could of these deliberations and decisions mainly from the British newspapers. The internment group was provided with a wide selection of these, which always arrived on the ships a few days late. As little of a definite nature percolated through from Paris, what the newspapers conveyed was basically rumour and speculation. Thus for those who waited, reading through them all was not a satisfying occupation.

On the whole these were worrying weeks and months for Konter-admiral Reuter, and not only on account of the uncertain future of his ships. Morale aboard was anything but good. Because of the poor food many men complained of toothache and nutritional deficiency diseases. The British had ordered that during the entire period of the internment no German seaman was to set foot ashore. Thus the days passed in monotony and boredom. There was hardly anything to do except keep the ships reasonably clean and manoeuvrable. Officers and men spent their many free hours in sports and games of all kinds: many read books and old newspapers, others learned English, held discussions, worked at hobbies, sewed, sang or danced. On the battlecruiser *Seydlitz* the men even built a carousel and a cable railway.

Many seamen became passionate anglers in order to augment the dreary menu. Fish were cooked, smoked or fried in torpedo oil. Officers and men devised many methods for the detection and hunting down of the increasing rat and cockroach populations aboard. Apart from the restrictions on daily life, the officers in particular were in a difficult situation. Aboard every ship, their authority could be called into question by the sailors' council, and every man of the internment group was in reality confined by the British. Under these circumstances it was almost impossible to maintain discipline. On many ships frequent arguments broke out between officers and men, the situation aboard ship at any particular time varying 'between mutiny, sailors' council dictatorship and obedience to the officers.'[4]

The point made by seamen and stokers was that they were no longer sailors bound by oath, had sailed the ships of their own free will into internment and were now not prepared to submit themselves to the strict rules of military discipline. Instead, they wanted their say in all decisions, and better pay. All attempts by the officers to restore their authority failed. 'Not until the scuttling was it possible to introduce a general reversal of attitude towards state, fatherland and officer,' Konteradmiral Reuter wrote later.[5]

Reuter himself was also affected. Aboard his first flagship *Friedrich der Grosse* he had such a difficult time that at the end of March 1919 he transferred his pennant to the cruiser *Emden-II* where the crew had remained loyal and accepted the role of the officers. An NCO of the cruiser described the circumstances under which Reuter decided to change flagship:

> The people on the flagship were Communists of the worst sort, shouted their garbage through the windows of the officers' cabins, at night hammered with their fists and iron stakes on the officers' doors hurling personal insults, tried to throw the admiral's no 1 staff officer overboard while taking his constitutional on deck and would never shut up until the British gave them a warning. A British destroyer closed up to 200 metres and aimed its torpedo tubes and guns at the battleship, to be greeted by such a rumpus, with ratings yelling and cajoling and mocking them by sticking out their tongues. I never thought it possible that Germans would behave like that in the presence of their arch-enemy. So now we, the *Emden*, are the flagship of the German fleet.[6]

Even Vice Admiral Sir Sydney Fremantle, the last in a line of commanders of the British squadron guarding the German ships, showed sympathy for his German counterpart having regard to the circumstances: 'One cannot help feeling a certain sympathy for Reuter, who found himself in the very unpleasant situation of nominally commanding ships in the hands of mutineers ... He was a reasonable man with whom one could have a good relationship, a man who kept his word and never knowingly infringed the conditions of internment except in the single significant case.'[7]

It must have been a great relief for Reuter on 7 May 1919 when the peace terms were finally published, bringing the end of the internment closer. At the same time he was deeply dismayed. In the view of the Germans, the Allied demands contained so many crushing passages – all founded on the alleged guilt of the Germans as sole connivers in the outbreak of the war: the deprivation of territories in west and east and the colonies, far-reaching disarmament and the imposition of massive reparations – that the Social Democrat head of government, Philipp Scheidemann, felt compelled to make the famous remark: 'What hand would not wither up at having to sign itself and us into such bondage?'[8]

For Reuter, Article 184 was decisive: 'Upon the coming into force of this present treaty, all surface warships not located in German ports shall no longer belong to Germany, which renounces all rights to the same.

Vessels which are presently interned in the harbours of the Allies and associated powers in accordance with the Armistice treaty of 11 November 1918 are considered as definitively surrendered.'[9]

What Admiral Reuter had long feared had come about: none of the ships interned at Scapa Flow would ever return to Germany. If the German government signed the peace treaty, they would belong officially to the Allies. Should they refuse to sign, that amounted to a hostile act and the British would be justified in seizing the ships by force. At first neither happened, for the German government's peace delegation had the right to respond in writing to the Allied conditions. The German representatives had been excluded from the Paris talks – not until the end of April did they travel to Versailles in order to receive the final draft of the documents.

The German delegates then submitted a list of counter-proposals in an attempt to mitigate the harsh conditions, but without much success. On 16 June 1919 the Allies gave the Germans the final text of the peace treaty. It contained a few minor amendments respecting the territories to be vacated; all other German proposals were rejected. There was no avenue for further negotiation. The treaty had to be signed within five days, therefore by 21 June, otherwise the state of war would be resumed. At the German request the Allies extended the deadline by two days to expire on 23 June.

'In the history of Germany there probably never was a week to compare to the drama of events on the days between 16 and 23 June 1919,' historian Eberhard Kolb wrote.[10] In countless hectic scheduled sittings, conferences and conversation, the politicians of all parties sought an answer to the decisive question: accept or decline? When it was clear that no agreement could be reached, the Scheidemann government resigned on 20 June. A new government formed in all haste next day under the leadership of Social Democrat Gustav Bauer announced on 21 June that it would sign the peace treaty. At the request of the National Assembly at Weimar, it would be signed on the condition that Germany did not recognise sole guilt for the outbreak of war. This was brusquely rejected by the victorious powers. After further heated discussions, on 23 June the National Assembly at Weimar authorised the government to accept the Allied terms unconditionally. Around two hours before the expiry of the ultimatum, the corresponding papers were handed over at Versailles. On 28 June Hermann Müller and Johannes Bell signed the Treaty of Versailles. By then the warships which should have been surrendered to the Allies as required by Article 184 no longer existed.

Konteradmiral Reuter maintained later that he did not learn of the Allied five-day deadline until the morning of 21 June when he read of it in the 17 June edition of *The Times*. Apparently he overlooked an article in the same edition reporting the extension of the deadline by two days to 23 June. Since in his opinion time was up, he considered himself obliged to act at once. The necessary preparations had long been in place. At Reuter's request, the ships' crews had been reduced further to 2700 men in mid June, which gave him the opportunity to rid himself of the particularly recalcitrant 'Red' ratings and keep only reliable men on board. Moreover, all ships had received secret instructions on how to prepare for scuttling and the course of action to be followed. A British mail steamer brought the letters along with other mail as required by the internment conditions and so, ironically, it was the British themselves who brought the German commanders their scuttling instructions. In this case the material had eluded censorship.

Today it seems very likely that Reuter knew of the extension of the deadline to 23 June. He must have taken into account that the British would attempt to occupy the German ships at the moment the ultimatum expired, or perhaps even sooner. In his view this had to be prevented at all costs. The British already suspected that the Germans might not be ready to co-operate in the fate of their ships, while many historians consider it impossible that the British had not noticed the preparations for scuttling.

Vice Admiral Fremantle had planned originally to storm the interned ships at midnight on 21 June when the ultimatum expired. After being notified that the German government had been granted two days' grace he suddenly received the order to take his squadron out to sea and carry out some routine exercises. Only three destroyers and a few auxiliary ships remained behind at Scapa. It remains uncertain to the present day why the guardian squadron was sent away at the critical moment. Even at that time, a number of observers guessed that the British knew what was afoot and had closed their eyes to it in the hope that the continuing wrangling about what was to be done with the surrendered ships would resolve itself in this manner. And so it did.

On the morning of Saturday, 21 June 1919, Fremantle's dreadnoughts put to sea. A short while later, towards 1100 hrs, Konteradmiral Reuter aboard *Emden-II* gave orders to hoist the previously agreed, apparently harmless flag signal: 'Paragraph Eleven. Confirm. Chief Internment Group.' Now the scuttling began. For the first time since they had been lowered on Admiral Beatty's order, the imperial war flags were raised, and additionally on the torpedo boats the signal to attack, the red 'pennant Z'. Everywhere, great excitement reigned. The official report of the scuttling is recorded thus by the *Emden*: 'At first hushed silence, then a storm of enthusiasm to stir the emotions, and with eyes alight at such an honourable end for our fleet the men went about the task.'[11]

It is a fairly simple thing to sink a battleship. Provided a person knows what to do, and has unhindered access to the normally well-protected rooms deep in the underbelly of the ship below the waterline, it is possible, without further ado, to make a steel giant such as the battleship *Friedrich der Grosse* disappear from the surface within half an hour. The easiest way is the judicious placement of scuttling charges along the ship's bottom, but the Germans at Scapa Flow had no explosives, since it was forbidden to have weapons and ammunition aboard ship. The officers and men knew what they needed to do to assist, however, by simply opening everything: the valves for flooding individual rooms in the event of a fire, the condenser covers, the torpedo tubes, the cabin doors, ports and water pipes. With heavy hammers they destroyed all locks and bars; some time beforehand, holes had been bored in the watertight doors which separated individual compartments in the interior of the hull. One by one the German ships went down. Within six hours it was all over. In beaming sunshine, the last ship of the internment fleet to sink into the icy waters was the battlecruiser *Hindenburg*, commissioned only two years before. 'It was a theatre never before seen in naval history: approximately 500,000 tons of warship tonnage with an estimated value of 856 million marks disappeared into the sea.'[12]

For young Leutnant Friedrich Ruge, who had just sunk the torpedo boat he commanded, it seemed like a dream. Ruge, later the first inspector of the federal navy after the Second World War, watched spellbound 'this painful and grandiose piece of theatre ... the giant ship bodies as they reared up, the crashing and bursting as they capsized, the great whirlpools and oil patches with eddies and wreckage inside them'.[13]

The men got away in boats or were fished out of the water by the British, who then attempted to force them back aboard ship to reverse the scuttling measures. The British opened fire on unarmed German seamen, nine being killed and sixteen wounded. Vice Admiral Fremantle, who had broken off his manoeuvres and returned to Scapa Flow, attempted to save the ships still afloat. The battleship *Baden*, and the small cruisers *Emden-II* and *Frankfurt* were towed to the shallows and run aground; the small cruiser *Nürnberg-II* beached herself of her own accord. The British also managed to bring a number of torpedo boats to safety. Other ships sank in water so shallow that for years afterwards their funnels and masts continued to jut above the surface. They were later salved and shared out amongst the victorious powers. Those ships sunk in deeper water were sold to breakers and were raised, as far as possible, in the period up to the end of the 1930s. Seven remain today on the seabed at Scapa Flow: the battleships *König*, *Kronprinz Wilhelm* and *Markgraf*, and the small cruisers *Brummer*, *Dresden-II*, *Karslruhe* and *Cöln*.

The German crews were made prisoners of war. At first they were held at the PoW camp at Nigg near Invergordon, and from there were transferred later to the English west coast. Ratings went to the camp at Henlle Park, the officers to Oswestry and later to Donington Hall, an old mansion west of Nottingham. There they remained until the Treaty of Versailles was ratified in January 1920, and then released.

The men returning after fourteen months of internment and captivity were greeted at Wilhelmshaven as war heroes. Vizeadmiral von Trotha received the men personally, Reich President Friedrich Ebert promoted Reuter to Vizeadmiral. Despite that, he retired from active service a few months later at the age of fifty-one years. There was no suitable post for him in the new Reichsmarine. He settled in Potsdam and engaged in community politics. He died in 1943.

After the victorious powers had at first condemned the scuttling as a breach of the Armistice conditions and as an expression 'of enormous ill-will', the British themselves were not too ill-disposed towards it.[14] No solution had yet been found as to what was to be done with the ships once they had been surrendered. Great Britain, fearing for its status of maritime might, favoured the ships being scrapped or sunk rather than going to strengthen the fleets of other states, while the French in particular were in favour of sharing them out. The scuttling put an end to this unpleasant debate; Admiral Rosslyn Wemyss, the First Sea Lord, wrote in relief to Admiral George P Hope: 'I look upon the sinking of the German Fleet as a real blessing. It disposes once for all of the thorny question of the distribution of these ships and eases us of an enormous amount of difficulties.'[15]

There was still some sharing out to be done, however. Article 185 of the Treaty of Versailles stipulated that in addition to the ships interned at Scapa Flow, they also had to hand over the eight remaining battleships *Oldenburg, Thüringen, Ostfriesland, Helgoland, Posen, Westfalen, Rheinland* and *Nassau*; eight small cruisers *Stettin, Danzig, München, Lübeck, Stralsund, Augsburg, Kolberg* and *Stuttgart*; together with forty-two destroyers. In addition came the demand for indemnification corresponding to the value of the scuttled ships: at the beginning of November 1919 the Allies claimed delivery of the last five modern small cruisers in German hands and 400,000 tonnes (later reduced to 300,000 tonnes) of shipyard material and three U-boat engines.

In view of the extremely harsh conditions imposed by the Treaty of Versailles, similar to surrendering the entire former Imperial High Seas Fleet to the victorious powers, this additional price which the scuttling cost the Reich was almost a minor matter. For Ludwig von Reuter, there was never any question but that he had done the right thing. There were voices everywhere in Germany who accused him of having wilfully endangered the Armistice by his independent action. The admiral was constant in maintaining his position, however, that as he had not known of the extension of the ultimatum to 23 June, it had been his duty not to allow the 'undefeated' ships to fall into enemy hands.[16] He made less of another motive in public: his concern for the 'outer' honour of the navy, its damaged image, which he had hoped to restore by means of the scuttling. As Reuter wrote from Scapa Flow to Adolf von Trotha, the fate of the officers and ships was 'of the most extreme gravity and importance for the reconstruction of the navy'.[17]

Trotha was only too willing to accept the opportunity which Reuter had given him by the scuttling. In a decree to the navy dated 3 July 1919, in a breathtaking new interpretation of the events surrounding the sinking of the German fleet, by which the dream of German naval and world-political power had finally ended in the North Sea, the chief of the admiralty lauded it as an honourable sinking with the flag still flying. Though still an extensively useless military branch of service stigmatised by mutiny, revolution and delivery into internment, in Trotha's eyes the fleet had succeeded by means of its honourable exit in having that all forgotten, replaced by a great legacy to which its successor could now take over with a clear conscience.

In the manly act of our crews at Scapa Flow, the proud past of our undefeated fleet found its end honourably. The stronger British did not dare to confront us in honourable battle, and while the guns spoke never once did we see the French flag, nor did another enemy approach us at sea – but as far as the seas break the German flag speaks of the heroism of our crews. In our collapse under his hunger blockade, starving our civilians contrary to the conventions of international law, the enemy thought he could seize our ships without a fight, and steal from us here what remained of our national honour. Now they have gone down to their proud last resting place, the holy sea, with the German war flag still flying, allowing us to forget many bitter hours of the recent past: the sea shrouds our powerful ships which took down with them the honour of a great, unforgettable period. This legacy is now laid in our hands, and with it responsibility of the noblest kind which, watched by our people and all Germans, we shall carry through the confusion of the present into a better future.[18]

Even if the increase in prestige brought about by the scuttling is difficult to measure, certain things seem to confirm that Reuter and von Trotha achieved their aim, at least in the long term. The German fleet now finally had, as Holger Herwig writes, 'its epic song worthy to stand beside the many army legends up to the "sacrifice at Langemarck": the small, specially chosen officer corps set on the path by Trotha to transform the new Reichsmarine into a better, more powerful future now had its martyrs.'[19]

How did this 'better future', of which Trotha had spoken, look? Initially, anything but rosy. Article 181 of the Treaty of Versailles ruled that the total personnel of the new Reichsmarine including the officers must not exceed 15,000 men. The number of warships was also drastically reduced by the victorious powers: bar six old pre-dreadnought battleships, six old small cruisers, twelve destroyers and twelve torpedo boats, all warships, if not already scuttled at Scapa or scheduled to be surrendered, were to be decommissioned or scrapped. The Reichsmarine was forbidden to have any U-boats or aircraft. The permitted naval forces could not be replaced before the lapse of stipulated periods – for battleships twenty years – and the new vessel had to be of the same displacement as the old one, this being a maximum 10,000 tonnes for battleships.

These harsh conditions, which the new, democratically elected politicians had not bothered to oppose, strengthened the officers' antipathy for the Weimar Republic. In their efforts to oppose the government, they did not shrink from using violence, beginning with the Kapp-Lüttwitz attempted coup in March 1920. The two leading personalities were Wolfgang Kapp, a Prussian general regional director and co-founder of the nationalist Deutsche Vaterlandspartei, and Baron Walther von Lüttwitz, commanding general of the Reichswehr Group Command I in Berlin. The would-be coup collapsed miserably after a few days. Another of the protagonists involved was Korvettenkapitän Hermann Ehrhardt.

Highly decorated in the war and the commander of a torpedo-boat flotilla, Ehrhardt had gone to Scapa Flow in November 1918, but returned to Germany fairly quickly. At the beginning of 1919 he took over leadership of II Marine Brigade ('Brigade Ehrhardt') at Wilhelmshaven. This was one of the newly formed *Freikorps*, and became involved in putting down the republic of soldiers' and sailors' councils at Munich, and in border fighting against the Poles in Upper Silesia. Once the Treaty of Versailles came into effect, all paramilitary units were threatened with closure and Ehrhardt put his men, who wore the swastika on their steel helmets, at the disposal of the coup organisers. The Admiralty, under Trotha, made clear their sympathy for Kapp and Lüttwitz. After the failure of the coup, Trotha was removed from office and the navy lost a great deal of prestige. After his honourable discharge from the Reichsmarine, Ehrhardt founded the extreme right-wing 'Organisation Consul', soon responsible for numerous political assassinations, amongst them the killing of Matthias Erzberger and Walther Rathenau, two of the leading representatives of the Weimar Republic.

Undoubtedly, Ehrhardt is an extreme example who does not lend himself to generalisation, but it is a fact that most former Imperial Navy officers viewed the Weimar system only as an interim solution. If it could not be overthrown, then it could at least be used to the best advantage to rebuild the navy. To this end, a much smaller start had to be made than was the case pre-1914. It so happened that at the beginning of the 1920s a problem arose at the centre of strategic planning regarding the Baltic Sea. The Baltic had an important function flanking potential land warfare against Poland and Russia. Because the Treaty of Versailles had forced Germany to cede certain territories to Poland, the Baltic was now the only freely accessible route to East Prussia, which had been cut off from the Reich by the so-called 'Polish corridor'.

Outwardly, the navy went along willingly in its new role justifying its existence over the next few years. Privately, however, its senior commanders were not content with the modest demands made of it. 'For them all, the Baltic navy was just a transitory stage to a North Sea fleet, and then a renewed High Seas Fleet effective worldwide.'[20] It was with this goal in mind that the outlawed attempts of the navy were made to cast off the 'shackles of Versailles' by the clandestine development of U-boats and aircraft alongside the official warship building programme. In 1928 the Reichstag approved plans for 'Panzerschiff A', a completely new type of warship 'faster than the most powerful enemy ships and more powerful than the fastest': the heavy cruiser. Even if nobody cared to mention the fact openly, this new design was totally unsuitable for the Baltic, and was aimed much more at operations in the North Sea and Atlantic – that is, the region where, according to the contemporary line of thought, the starting point must lie for a new position of maritime power for Germany.

During these years of consolidation and reconstruction, moreover, the Kaiser was kept in kind remembrance as in Erich Raeder's letter to Magnus von Levetzow in January 1924: 'Yesterday we remembered the supreme commander at the Skaggerak club,' wrote Raeder, who knew that von Levetzow was planning to visit Wilhelm II in exile in Holland. 'Had a very pleasant conversation with Prince Waldemar. I often go to the annual Hohenzollern evenings with Prince Heinrich and others. We are going to visit Hemmelmark [Prince Heinrich's residence] this spring. I am hoping to have the chance to express to the all-highest gentleman how all of us here remember him with loyal gratitude and veneration.'[21]

Remembering the Kaiser was coupled with the thought of the 'great' time of the German navy, and so it is not surprising that naval officers, as historian Michael Salewski writes, 'were unswerving in their search for a figure similar in outlook to themselves as Wilhelm II had been.'[22] In the end they found this figure in the person of Adolf Hitler. Erich Raeder, head of the Reichsmarine, later Kriegsmarine, from 1928 until 1943, gave himself credit for 'delivering the navy united and without friction to the Führer in the Third Reich in 1933.' That had been 'achieved unconstrained' so that 'the entire education and training of the navy in the time prior ... was aimed at an inner attitude which gave rise of itself to a truly National Socialist mental outlook. For this reason nothing needed to be changed, and from the very start we were loyal and sincere followers of the Führer.'[23]

The Führer himself rewarded them with the promise of building a strong navy. After it had appeared initially that Hitler would be satisfied with the role of junior partner to the Royal Navy – in the naval agreement of 1935 a 'permanent' ratio of strength between the two fleets of 35:100 was laid down – the German fleet concept finally received a decidedly anti-British thrust. The 1938 'Z-plan', later significantly expanded, envisaged the construction of a strong surface force which in Raeder's words would 'finally solve the British question'.[24] Before the Z-plan could come into being, however, the next war began.

For the fleet it came five years too soon, as Raeder admitted with resignation after the British declaration of war on 3 September 1939. Hipper's former chief of staff understood precisely that the navy was still far too weak to have a decisive effect on the war. The surface forces could therefore only show, according to Raeder's grim inference from this knowledge, 'that they knew how to die with honour and had the will to create the foundations for a later reconstruction.'[25] In May 1940 he urged commanders of the German warships to 'maximum engagement with the fullest risk', declaring that he would take 'the historical responsibility before the Führer and Commander-in-Chief of the Wehrmacht' for the enormous losses to be expected, having regard to the enemy superiority in size. Raeder wrote that he expected that 'the higher centres of command and naval commanders at sea would make the Führer's principles their own in all operational planning. With no great endeavour, no great result!'[26]

The basic idea underlying Raeder's edict bore a fatal resemblance to that behind the last intended sortie of the fleet in October 1918: 'A Kriegsmarine, which is led into a bold operation against the enemy and suffers loss thereby will arise again on a larger scale after victory: but if this operation does not take place, its existence will be threatened even after a victorious war.'[27] In contrast to 1914, this time the navy was conscious of the fact from the outset of the war that it was predestined to be sunk.

Many of the officers we have come across in this book personally experienced the fresh rise and renewed fall of the German navy, some from high command positions, such as Grossadmirals Raeder and Dönitz. Others remained in active service after the end of the First World War. Reinhold Knobloch entered the sister organisation to

Brigade Ehrhardt, III Marine-Brigade under Korvettenkapitän Wilfried von Loewenfeld, after these were disbanded being accepted into the Reichsmarine as a naval staff officers. Later, Knobloch commanded a battleship and left the navy in 1936 in the rank of Konteradmiral. That meant that before leaving the service he had reached the highest rank but one without having been active in the role. Hermann Graf von Schweinitz was also taken into the Reichsmarine and left it in 1931 as a Konteradmiral. He returned to active service in 1934, however, and in the Second World War served variously as Naval Commander Crimea and Ukraine and then as head of the German transporter fleet in Norway.

Others sought fresh fields of activity after the lost war. Bogislav von Selchow, for example, studied history at Marburg and Berlin. He was also active as an author and his works *Unsere geistige Ahnen*, *Wächter der Schwelle* and *Der bürgerliche and der heldische Mensch* made him into 'an ideological pioneer of National Socialism' (Michael Epkenhans) and a highly-praised author in Germany after 1933. Rudolph Firle obtained his doctorate in politics in 1921, collaborated on the official presentation of the naval war and rose finally to be chairman of the board of Norddeutscher Lloyd. After his dismissal as head of the Admiralty in the wake of the Kapp attempted coup, Adolf von Trotha devoted himself to work with youth, amongst other roles being chairman of the Grossdeutscher Jugendbund. In 1933 he was called to the Prussian Privy Council, from 1934 to 1940 he led the Reichsbund Deutscher Seegeltung, the successor organisation to the Deutscher Flottenverein (German Fleet Union), and was also honorary leader of the naval Hitler Youth.

The most surprising career was without doubt that of Ernst von Weizsäcker. During the war he had devoted himself intensively to his professional livelihood. Early on he saw that 'in the administration, perhaps at naval staff of this (future) navy another suitable position will be found for me. The combatant career at the higher levels must be given to those who were able to prove themselves in this war.'[28] In view of the threatened defeat he began to think of alternatives to naval service. 'Otherwise there remains for me only the general belief in our future and the motivation, be it as a naval officer, be it in another profession, to take part in the reconstruction. It would be strange to find an individual in Germany who would not have his uses in this respect,' he wrote to Adolf von Trotha at the beginning of October 1918.[29]

One month later he wrote in his diary – the revolution had already broken out – 'If everything goes topsy-turvy I shall become a handyman, perhaps a writer. In better times a secretary and try to work my way up.'[30] Soon after he made his decision to spend no longer than necessary in the navy, which in the future would probably only have a coastal and customs/border protection role. In banking, as a journalist, or even in the merchant navy, he might be successful, even though without professional training he would naturally have to start at the bottom. That was not important to him provided he could feed his family composed of his sons Carl Friedrich (1912–2007) and Heinrich (1917–1939), and daughter Adelheid (1916–2004); the youngest son Richard was born in 1920. He did not even rule out a position as a teacher at a village school or hotel porter.[31]

As it happened, probably to his own surprise, Weizsäcker continued for some while in naval service, first at the personnel office (the former Imperial Navy Cabinet) in Berlin, then as naval attaché at The Hague. In April 1920 he entered the diplomatic service. He had not abandoned his earlier decision to leave the navy and his seagoing career, and he was happy to realise this aim at last. 'The more I picture the future of the Reich, the happier I am to have found something suitable beyond the navy. In the naval officer corps they still have the old aspirations which can only lead to dissatisfaction. I cannot spend the next twenty years discussing that we should have built more ships then and started the U-boat war in 1916 instead of 1917.'[32]

At the beginning of the 1930s Weizsäcker was German ambassador to Norway, later Switzerland; in 1938 he rose to be Secretary of State at the Foreign Office and in 1943 went to the Vatican at his own request as minister. After the Second World War, Weizsäcker stood trial at Nuremberg, together with other senior officials at the Foreign Office, for his controversial role in the deportation of Jews and was sentenced to five years' imprisonment. His son Richard voluntarily interrupted his study of law at Göttingen to assist in his father's defence. Released from prison early, Ernst von Weizsäcker died at Lindau on Lake Constance in 1951 following a stroke.

On the other side of the North Sea there were also unusual career developments. Destroyer commander Lennon Goldsmith reached the rank of admiral and became personal adjutant to King George V. In the 1920s Oswald Frewen went into the legal profession, where he was apparently not very successful, and in the Second World War re-entered active service as HM Harbourmaster at Scapa Flow. After the war, Roger Keyes had a number of important positions within the Royal Navy, amongst them Commander-in-Chief, Mediterranean Forces. He left active service in 1935 in the rank of Admiral of the Fleet and then sat for ten years in the House of Commons as a Conservative MP. He returned to the Royal Navy in the Second World War and in 1943 was awarded a title for his services. Stephen King-Hall, who had used the long wait to publish several books under the pseudonymn 'Etienne' during the Great War, progressed following the end of his naval career in 1929 to become a popular journalist and author in Britain. He also served as an MP at Westminster, and in 1944 founded the Hansard Society, the independent institution for training in politics, and entered the House of Lords in 1954 as Lord King-Hall.

David Beatty had been correct in his expectation that after the war the Royal Navy would meet hard times, although his own career did not suffer. The youngest ever Admiral of the Fleet in the Royal Navy, he received many decorations and awards including honorary citizenship of the City of London and academic titles from various universities, and became Earl Beatty of the North Sea in August 1919. In addition Parliament awarded him a bonus of £100,000 for his role in the war. This was the same sum as Douglas Haig, Commander-in-Chief of the BEF, had received in settlement of his claim for £250,000. John Jellicoe, on the other hand, had to be satisfied with £50,000 and the lesser title of Viscount Jellicoe of Scapa.

In November 1919 Beatty took over from Admiral Rosslyn Wemyss as First Sea Lord and held this office for the next eight years. Jellicoe went to New Zealand as governor-general. After his return to Britain, in 1925 King George V made him an earl. Although the dispute between Jellicoe and Beatty as to who bore the greater responsibility for the 'lost' battle of Jutland had embittered their relationship, Beatty was much affected by the death of his predecessor in the office of Commander-in-Chief of the Grand Fleet at the age of seventy-five on 20 November 1935 in London. Though terminally ill himself, Beatty was present with hundreds of former naval personnel at the funeral service at St Paul's Cathedral. He was also one of the bearers when Jellicoe's coffin, covered with the Union flag, his sabre and admiral's cocked hat, was interred in the crypt of the cathedral. In March 1936 David Beatty was laid to rest at the side of Jellicoe.

A few steps away from the graves of the two admirals, maintained simply for easy viewing, is the place of honour in the centre of the crypt. Surrounded by a richly decorated mosaic marble floor, within eight Roman columns is a magnificent black sarcophagus. Here lies Nelson, the victor of Trafalgar.

Notes

Foreword
1. Salewski, *Selbstverständnis*, p.171.
2. Nicolas Wolz, 'Das lange Warten. Kriegserfahrungen deutscher und britischer Seeoffiziere 1914 bis 1918', Paderborn 2008.

Prologue
1. Massie, *Castles*, p.27: 'A droop-jawed, determined little man in an ill-fitting frock coat, looking more like a parson than an admiral.'
2. Souchon to his wife, BA/MA N156, literary estate Wilhelm Souchon, letter, 2.8.1914.
3. Souchon to his wife, 21.12.1914.
4. Souchon to his wife, 9.9.1914.
5. In September 1917 Souchon left Turkey to become the commander of IV Squadron, High Seas Fleet; Vizeadmiral Hubert von Rebeur-Paschwitz became his successor in the Bosphorus. In January 1918 *Goeben* and *Breslau* ran into a British minefield. Though seriously damaged the *Goeben* was salved, but the *Breslau* sank with heavy loss of life.
6. Quote from Massie, *Castles*, p.54.
7. Admiral Sir John Fisher in a letter to a friend, quoted in Massie, *Castles*, p.54.

Chapter 1
1. Hase, *Skagerrak*, p.33.
2. Chickering, *Reich*, p.117.
3. Tirpitz, *Erinnerungen*, p.10.
4. Duppler, *Juniorpartner*, p.155.
5. Quoted from Fesser, *Traum*, p.25.
6. Hildebrand, *Allianz*, p.306.
7. Hobson, *Maritimer Imperialismus*, p.326.
8. Quoted from Hobson, ibid, p.264.
9. Tirpitz's memorandum of July 1897, 'General Factors in the Establishment in our Fleet of Ship Classes and Types', in Berghahn & Deist, *Rüstung*, pp.122–7, quote from p.122.
10. Hobson, op cit, esp. pp.283–96 and 325ff. Service memorandum Nr IX 'General Experiences from the Manoeuvres of the Fleet on the Autumn Exercise', appears in Besteck, '*First Line of Defence*', pp.125–208, quoted p.126.
11. 'Notes by the State Secretary of the Reich Navy Office on the Bill of 15.6.1897 respecting the Fleet Armament Programme', in Berghahn & Deist, *Rüstung*, pp.134–6, quote from p.135.
12. Text from Tirpitz's introduction to the second naval act, Berghahn & Deist, pp.285–6.
13. Nipperdey, *Machtstaat*, p.539.
14. This intended weakening of parliament was an important side effect of the Tirpitz Plan, in which many historians have also detected an 'inner-political crisis strategy' on the part of the Establishment to stabilise the existing political and social order.
15. Kelly, *Tirpitz*, p.190.
16. Herwig, *Elitekorps*, p.17.
17. Mertens, *Privileg*, p.59.
18. Rohkrämer, *Militarismus*, p.82.
19. Quote from Rüger, *Great Naval Game*, p.41.
20. Berghahn, *Tirpitz-Plan*, pp.271–304.
21. Hartwig, *Dönitz*, p.29.
22. Scheerer, *Die Marineoffiziere der Kaiserlichen Marine*, p.347, appendix 6.2 referring to Jones, *Making*, p.6.

23. Quoted from Herwig, *Elitekorps*, pp.34–5.
24. Hartwig, op cit, p.29.
25. Herwig, op cit, p.78.
26. Spector, *At War*, p.35.
27. Quoted from Lange, *Fahneneid*, p.75, n.252.
28. Metternich to Bülow, 30.6.1908, in *Die grosse Politik der europäischen Kabinette* (im Folgenden: GP) 24, No 8212.
29. Margin note by Wilhelm II on a telegram from Metternich dated 16.3.1909, GP 28, Nr 10271. 'Blech', etc: Bethmann Hollweg to Wilhelm II, 24.11.1911, GP 31 Nr 11322.
30. Quoted from Epkenhans, *Leben*, p.199, footnote 33.
31. Undated note by Tirpitz (May 1914), quoted from Epkenhans, *Flottenrüstung*, p.391.
32. Figures from Halpern, *Naval History*, pp.7–8.
33. Weizsäcker, *Erinnerungen*, p.31.

Chapter 2
1. Dierks, *Einfluss*, p.240.
2. Ibid.
3. Quoted from Dierks, p.259.
4. Diary Franz Hipper, BA-MA, N 162, literary estate Franz Ritter von Hipper, entry 26.7.1914
5. Ibid, 1.8.1914.
6. Heinrich Stenzler to his mother, BA-MA, military collection, MSg 1/3093, letter 4.8.1914.
7. Diary of Hermann Graf von Schweinitz, printed in Schweinitz, *Das Kriegstagebuch eines kaiserlichen Seeoffiziers*, entry 4.8.1914.
8. Souchon to his wife, 12.8.1914.
9. Chickering, *Reich*, p.26.
10. Jünger, *In Stahlgewittern*, p.7.
11. Souchon to his wife, 12.8.1914.
12. Diary Schweinitz, 19.9.1914.
13. Ibid, 22.10.1914 and 12.4.1915, respectively.
14. Ibid, 30.4.1914.
15. Stumpf, Diary, p.12.
16. Rahn, *Strategische Probleme*, p.343.
17. Tirpitz memorandum on 'Our Naval-maritime Further Development', April 1891, in Berghahn & Deist, *Rüstung*, pp.82–7, quote p.86.
18. Stevenson, *1914–1918*, p.117.
19. Barnett, *Anatomie*, p.126.
20. Lennon Goldsmith to his father, Leeds University Library, Liddle Collection, RNMN/GOLDSMITH, letter of 3.8.1914.
21. David Beatty to his wife, published in *The Beatty Papers*, letter, 5.8.1914.
22. Diary Edward Berthon, Leeds University Library, Liddle Collection, RNMN/BERTHON, entries 29.7.1914 and 9.8.1914.
23. Young, *With the Battle-cruisers*, p.49.
24. Quoted from Goldrick, *The King's Ships*, p.66.
25. Diary Rudolph Firle, BA-MA N 155, literary estate Rudolph Firle, entry 6.8.1914.
26. Diary Reinhold Knobloch, Archive der Marine-Offizier-Vereinigung, Bonn, documentary collection, entry 16.8.1914.
27. Diary Hipper, entry 12.8.1914.
28. Quoted from Röhl, *Wilhelm II*, vol 3, p.1185.
29. *Der Krieg zur See, Nordsee*, vol 2, appendix 4, pp.301–2.
30. Diary Hipper, entry 6.8.1914.
31. Ibid, entry 13.8.1914.

Chapter 3
1. Diary Knobloch, 21.8.1914.
2. Halpern, *Naval History*, p.31 ('The track charts of the action are possibly the most difficult to follow of any battle during the war.').
3. Quoted from Waldeyer-Hartz, *Hipper*, pp.111–12.

4. Diary Hipper, 1.9.1914.
5. Beatty to his wife, 29.8.1914.
6. Roger Keyes to William Goodenough, published in *The Keyes Papers*, letter of 5.9.1914.
7. Diary Hipper, 1.9.1914.
8. Ernst von Weizsäcker to his mother, published in Hill, *Die Weizsäcker-Papiere*, letter of 9.8.1914.
9. Weizsäcker to his father, op cit, 20.10.1914.
10. Schilling, *U-boothelden*, p.203.
11. Diary Schweinitz, 24.9.1914.
12. Letter from Weizsäcker of 23.9.1914, published in Hill, op.cit.
13. Diary Walter Zaeschmar, Archive of the Mürwik Naval Academy, reference no 10983/84/85, entry 23.9.1914.
14. Diary of Geoffrey Harper, Churchill Archives Centre, Cambridge, Manuscripts Collection HRPR 1/1-11, entry 22.10.1914.
15. Ibid.
16. Quote from Herwig, *Luxury Fleet*, p.207.
17. Souchon to his wife, 18.8.1916.
18. Quoted from Bennett, *Seeschlachten*, p.136.
19. Ibid, p.37.
20. Ibid, p.45.
21. Weizsäcker to his mother, 8.11.1914.
22. Quoted from Afflerbach, *Mit wehender Fahne*, p.597.
23. Quoted from Massie, *Castles*, p.219.
24. Afflerbach, op cit, p.602.
25. Ibid, p.603.
26. Afflerbach, *Kunst*, p.142.
27. Afflerbach, *Mit wehender Fahne*, pp.599–600.
28. Beatty to his wife, 2.11.1914.
29. Bennett, *Seeschlachten*, p.134.
30. Ibid, p.50.
31. Ibid, p.138.
32. Pochhammer, *Graf Spees letzte Fahrt*, 1939, p.144.
33. Ibid, p.151.
34. Plaschka, *Matrosen*, vol 1, p.328.
35. Pochhammer, op cit, 1939, p.152.
36. Plaschka, op cit, p.329.
37. Letter from Cadet Esmond to his father, published in the *Penny Pictorial* of 13.3.1915, in BA-MA, RM 3/3165.
38. From Bennett, *Seeschlachten*, pp.191–2.
39. Diary Hipper, 11.12.1914.
40. Diary Firle, 12.12.1914.
41. Afflerbach, *Kunst*, p.156.
42. From Afflerbach, *Mit wehender Fahne*, p.600.
43. *Dienst an Bord*, p.190.
44. Afflerbach, *Mit wehender Fahne*, p.611.
45. Pohl, *Aus Aufzeichnungen und Briefen*, p.111 (letter of 14.2.1915).
46. Souchon to his wife, 31.12.1914.
47. Quoted from Afflerbach, op cit, p.607.
48. Quoted from Salewski, *Seekriegsleitung*, p.164, note 140.
49. Afflerbach, *Kunst*, p.150.
50. Quoted from Afflerbach, *Mit wehender Fahne*, p.609.
51. Quoted from Afflerbach, *Mit wehender Fahne*, p.610.
52. From Pochhammer, *Graf Spees letzte Fahrt*, p.161.
53. Diary Hipper, 25.11.1914.
54. Ibid, 29.11.1914.
55. Ibid, 29.3–4.6.1916.
56. Diary Knobloch, 15.12.1914.
57. Diary Hipper, 16.12.1914.
58. Roger Keyes to his wife, *The Keyes Papers*, letter of 21.11.1914.

59. Beatty to his wife, 10.12.1914.
60. Beatty to John Jellicoe, printed in *The Jellicoe Papers*, letter of 13.11.1914.
61. Keyes to his wife, 17.12.1914.
62. Beatty to Jellicoe, *The Jellicoe Papers*, 20.12.1914.
63. Diary Zaeschmar, 22.12.1914 ('1000 civilians'); Diary Firle, 19.12.1914 ('weak revenge').
64. Diary Hipper, 19.12.1914.
65. Diary Hipper, 16.12.1915.
66. Quoted from Massie, *Castles*, p.325.
67. Diary James Colvill, RN Museum Portsmouth, Manuscripts Collection, ref no 1997/43, entry 18.12.1914.
68. Adolf von Trotha to his wife, State Archive Lower Saxony, Bückeburg, Dep Nr 18, literary estate Adolf von Trotha, letter of 28.10.1914.
69. Diary Colvill, 8.5.1917.
70. Jahr, *Krämervolk*, p.124.
71. Diary Knobloch, 2.2.1916.
72. Walter von Keyserlingk to his uncle, BA/MA N161, literary estate Walter Freiherr von Keyserlingk, undated letter, end 1915.
73. From Goldrick, *The King's Ships*, p.261.
74. Diary Knobloch, 24.1.1915.
75. From Massie, *Castles*, pp.413–14.
76. Beatty to Keyes, 10.2.1915, quote from Roskill, *Beatty*, pp.113–14.
77. King-Hall to his parents, printed in Louise King-Hall, *Sea Saga*, undated letter, February 1915.
78. Diary Schweinitz, 25.1.1915.
79. Stenzler to his mother, 31.1.1915.
80. Diary Hipper, 24.1.1915.
81. Ibid, 26.1.1915.
82. Address by Wilhelm II, 4.2.1915 in BA/MA RM 2/1126 (italic denotes underlinings in original).
83. Instruction to the commander of the fleet, 10.1.1915 in *Der Krieg zur See, Nordsee*, vol 3, p.158.
84. Rahn, *Strategische Probleme*, p.351.
85. Halpern, *Naval History*, p.47.
86. Diary Schweinitz, 19.9.1914.

Chapter 4

1. Diary Knobloch, 16.8.1914.
2. Diary Schweinitz, 17.8.1914.
3. Stumpf, diary, p.16.
4. Ibid, pp.117–18.
5. Diary Harper, 7.9.1914.
6. Diary Knobloch, 1.12.1914 and 17.11.1914.
7. Diary Hipper, 9–13.1.1917.
8. Trotha to his wife, 30.3.1915.
9. Diary Schweinitz, 31.12.1915.
10. Goldsmith to his father, 28.10.1916.
11. Pochhammer, *Graf Spees letzte Fahrt*, p.151.
12. Pohl, *Aus Aufzeichnungen und Briefen*, pp.137–8 (letter, 17.7.1915).
13. Souchon to his wife, 4.3.1915.
14. Raeder, *Mein Leben*, p.140.
15. Diary Knobloch, 18.9.1916.
16. Diary Edward Roynon-Jones, Imperial War Museum, London, Manuscripts Collection, ref no 66/29/1, entry 9.4.1915.
17. Schoultz, *Grand Fleet*, p.348.
18. Waldeyer-Hartz, *Hipper*, pp.181–2.
19. Diary Stephen King-Hall, printed in Louise King-Hall, *Sea Saga*, entry 24.3.1916.
20. Paul Heinrich, *Memoirs* in BA/MA MSgl/2396, p.49.
21. Spiess, *Wir jagten Panzerkreuzer*, p.10.
22. Hashagen, *U-Boote Westwärts*, p.45.

23. Carr, *By Guess and by God*, p.193.
24. Hashagen, op cit, pp.71 and 76.
25. Quoted from Adams, *Adventure*, p.45.
26. Schoultz, op cit, pp.93–4.
27. John Jellicoe to Beatty, 12.12.1914, printed in *The Jellicoe Papers*.
28. King-Hall, *North Sea Diary*, p.36.
29. Schoultz, op cit, p.25.
30. Diary Knobloch, 27.8.1915.
31. Stumpf diary, p.110.
32. Schaible, *Standes- und Berufspflichten*, p.92.
33. Stumpf, diary, p.47.
34. Diary Harper, 19.11.1918.
35. Herbert Packer to his father, Churchill Archives Centre Cambridge, Manuscripts Collection, PCKR 2/1-4, letter of 28.2.1916.
36. Jellicoe to Frederick Hamilton, 16.4.1916 in *The Jellicoe Papers*.
37. *Marine-Rundschau*, 24 (1913), p.1124.
38. Diary Knobloch, 30.9.1915 and 30.10.1916.
39. Ibid, 7.11.1915.
40. Kocka, *Klassengesellschaft*, pp.32–3.
41. Trotha to his wife, 30.6.1918.
42. Diary Schweinitz, 30.9.1917.
43. Souchon to his wife, 11.6.1917.
44. Diary Hipper, 15.10.1914.
45. Weizsäcker to his mother, 12.1.1916.
46. Weizsäcker to his father, 10.10.1915.
47. Souchon to his wife, 29.10.1915.
48. Diary Schweinitz, 29.10.1917 and 4.7.1915.
49. Diary Knobloch, 20.9.1915.
50. Diary Hipper, 13.4.1917.
51. Ibid, 10.9.1918.
52. Souchon to his wife, 18.7.1915.
53. Ibid, 20.9.1915.
54. Stumpf, diary, p.124.
55. Diary Zaeschmar, 12.11.1916.
56. Ibid, 16.1.1917.
57. Ibid, 14.12.1917.
58. Trotha to his wife, 22.4.1916.
59. Diary Albert Hopman, published in Hopman, *Das ereignisreiche Leben*, entry 6.10.1915.
60. John McLeod to his mother, Leeds University library, Liddle Collection RNMN/MCLEOD, letter 24.10.1918.
61. *Krieg zur See, Nordsee*, vol 6, pp.131–2.
62. Diary Oswald Frewen, Frewen family archive, The Sheep House, Brede, Sussex, entry 19.1.1917.
63. Schoultz, op cit, p.103.
64. Ibid, p.67.
65. Keyes, *Memoirs*, vol 2, p.73.
66. Beatty to his wife, 29.6.1915.
67. Diary Frewen, 24.10.1915.
68. Beatty to his wife, 2.5.1915.
69. Diary Frewen, 11.5.1916 and 13.9.1916.
70. Diary King-Hall, *Sea Saga*, p.495, entry 20.3.1917.
71. Diary Roynon-Jones, 1.6.1915.

Chapter 5
1. Hüppauf, *Der Tod*, p.71.
2. Diary Zaeschmar, 9.10.1914.
3. Ibid, 19.11.1914.
4. Ibid, 20.2.1915.
5. Diary Knobloch, 30.5.1915.

6. Ibid, 23.9.1915.
7. Stenzler to his mother, 5.10.1914.
8. Ibid, 5.1.1915.
9. Diary Schweinitz, 4.5.1917.
10. Diary Knobloch, 11.7.1915.
11. Beatty to his wife, 29.6.1915.
12. Diary Knobloch, 27.10.1915.
13. Ibid, 2.8.1915.
14. Ibid, 4.8.1915.
15. Ibid, 9.2.1915.
16. Diary Hipper, 15.2.1915 and 10.12.14.
17. Souchon to his wife, 13.1.1915.
18. Waldeyer-Hartz, *Hipper*, p.182.
19. Quote from Herwig, *Elitekorps*, p.74.
20. Radkau, *Zeitalter*, p.415.
21. *Kriegssanitätsbericht*, p.111, 112, 285.
22. Diary Colvill, 23.9.1916.
23. McLeod to his mother, 14.6.1918 and 3.2.1916.
24. Beatty to Churchill (undated draft), November 1914 in *The Beatty Papers*.
25. Beatty to Asquith, 3.2.1916 in *The Beatty Papers*.
26. Beatty to his wife, 7.4.1918.
27. Marder, *Dreadnought*, vol 5, p.305.
28. King-Hall to his parents, March 1915.
29. McLeod to his mother, 20.8.1914.
30. Beatty to his wife, 30.10.1914.
31. Ibid, 21.5.1915.
32. Beatty to Roger Keyes, 18.9.1914 in *The Keyes Papers*.
33. Keyes to his wife, 9.10.1914.
34. Ibid, 11.12.1914.
35. Ibid, 17.2.1915.
36. Gordon, *Rules*, p.395.
37. Weizsäcker to his father, 28.10.1914.
38. 'Order of the Day from Fleet Commander', 14.8.1914, quoted from Scheer, *Hochseeflotte*, pp.73–4.
39. Weizsäcker to his mother, 12.11.1915.
40. Diary Knobloch, 29.8.1915.
41. Trotha to his wife, 14.9.1914.
42. Stumpf, diary, p.13.
43. Chickering, *Reich*, p.41.
44. Diary Schweinitz, 24.8.1914.
45. Ibid, 5.10.1914 and 18.8.1914.
46. Ibid, 4.1.1915.
47. Diary Hipper, 21.8.1914.
48. Diary Knobloch, 5.8.1915.
49. Ibid, 15.9.1916.
50. Ibid, 16.4.1917.
51. Diary Schweinitz, 27.3.1918.
52. Diary Weizsäcker, in Hill, *Die Weizsäcker Papiere*, entry 27.9.1916.
53. Diary Knobloch, 30.9.1915.
54. Ibid, 21.4.1917.
55. Keegan, *Antlitz*, p.276.
56. Ibid, pp.277–8.
57. Diary Knobloch, 28.11.1917.
58. Ibid, 29.11.1917.
59. Trotha to his wife, 18.9.1914.
60. Souchon to his wife, 18.9.1914.
61. Diary Bogislav von Selchow, BA-MA, N428, literary legacy B von Selchow, 21.8.1914.
62. Albert Hopman to his wife, in Hopman, *Das ereignisreiche Leben*, letter 1.19.1915.
63. Diary Knobloch, 5.12.1915.
64. Ibid, 24.9.1914.

65. Diary Hipper, 20.10.1914.
66. Diary Knobloch, 24.7.1916.
67. Ibid, 5.9.1915.
68. Souchon to his wife, 18.8.1915.
69. Diary Hipper, 8.5.1915.
70. Weizsäcker to his mother, 10.5.1915.
71. Stumpf, diary, p.59.
72. Diary Knobloch, 19.12.1915.
73. Ibid, 9.3.1916.
74. Ibid, 21.12.1916.
75. Souchon to his wife, 29.10.1916.
76. Diary Zaeschmar, 1.8.1917.

Chapter 6
1. Ernst von Weizsäcker to his parents, in Hill, *Die Weizsäcker Papiere*, letter 31.1.1916.
2. Stumpf, diary, p.44.
3. Diary Selchow, 31.5.1916.
4. Diary Zaeschmar, 15.6.1916.
5. Stumpf, diary, p.138.
6. Ibid, p.143.
7. Ibid, pp.128, 139.
8. Diary Schweinitz, 24.8.1914.
9. Hase, *Skagerrak*, p.101.
10. Ibid.
11. Quoted from Steel & Hart, *Jutland*, p.113.
12. Barnett, *Anatomie*, p.162.
13. Rahn, *Seeschlacht*, p.171.
14. Hase, *Skagerrak*, p.113.
15. Ibid, p.116.
16. Ibid, pp.120–1.
17. Ibid, p.93.
18. Ibid, p.123.
19. Quoted from Rahn, op cit, p.175.
20. Hase, *Skagerrak*, p.126.
21. Ibid, pp.126–7.
22. Ibid, p.127.
23. Ibid, p.129.
24. Report of Johannes Karl Groth, gunner aboard battlecruiser *Lützow*, in *Skagerrakschlacht*, pp.256–66, here p.263.
25. Ibid, pp.263–4.
26. Ibid, p.265.
27. Rahn, op cit, p.180.
28. Diary Schweinitz, 2.6.1916.
29. Quote from Steel & Hart, *Jutland*, pp.87–8
30. Ibid, p.400.
31. Ibid, pp.327–8.
32. Reported by both Hase, *Skagerrak*, p.139 and Weizsäcker, *Erinnerungen*, p.36.
33. Trotha to his wife, 3.6.1916.
34. Diary Schweinitz, 2.6.1916.
35. Ibid, 29.8.1916.
36. Krause, *Scapa Flow*, p.20.
37. Salewski, *Skagerrak*, p.75.
38. Souchon to his wife, 18.11.1914.
39. Steel & Hart, *Jutland*, p.373.
40. From Massie, *Castles*, p.663.
41. Diary Charles Daniel, Churchill Archives Centre Cambridge, Manuscripts Collection, DANL 241/1-2, entry 3.6.1916.
42. Gordon, *Rules*, p.505.
43. Beatty to his wife, 24.5.1917.
44. Diary Knobloch, undated, June 1916.

45. Diary Hipper, 7.6.1916.
46. From Granier, *Seekriegsleitung*, vol 2, pp.97ff.
47. Diary Schweinitz, 26.2.1915.
48. Ibid, 29.8.1916.
49. Keyserlingk to his uncle, 10.6.1916.
50. Diary Firle, 3.6.1916 and 2.6.1916.

Chapter 7
1   Immediatbericht, Kommando der Hochseestreitkräfte, dated 4 July 1916 re Battle of
    Jutland, in BA/MA, RM 5/4754, published partly in *Skagerrakschlacht*, pp.205–14,
    quoted from p.213.
2. Ibid, p.214.
3. Schröder, *U-boote*, pp.74–5.
4. Ibid, p.101.
5. Assmann, *Seestrategie*, p.80.
6. Pohl, *Aus Aufzeichnungen und Briefen*, p.131 (letter of 5 June 1916).
7. From Schröder, op cit, pp.134–5.
8. From Stegemann, *Marinepolitik*, p.31.
9. Diary Hipper, 24.6.1915
10. Ibid, 1.9.1915, 8.9.1915.
11. Weizsäcker to his mother, 8.8.1915.
12. Schröder, op cit, p.194.
13. Diary Hipper, 19.2.1916.
14. Diary Firle, 29.2.1916.
15. Diary Hopman, 16.3.1916.
16. Herwig, *Elitekorps*, p.153.
17. Diary Firle, 23.7.1915.
18. Both memoranda in BA-MA, RM 2/1983.
19. Keyserlingk to his uncle, 29.2.1914.
20. Souchon to his wife, 17.1.1916.
21. Diary Knobloch, 4.10.1915.
22. Diary Firle, 13.4.1917.
23. Diary Knobloch, 28.8.1916.
24. Nipperdey, *Machtstaat*, p.855.
25. Diary Knobloch, 29.11.1916.
26. Offer, *First World War*, pp.31ff.
27. Ullrich, *Revolution*, p.13.
28. Diary Knobloch, 27.11.1916.
29. Diary Selchow, 23.1.1918, 22.2.1918.
30. Diary Hopman, 14.8.1916.
31. Diary Weizsäcker, 27.9.1916.
32. Kielmannsegg, *Deutschland*, p.386.
33. From Schröder, op cit, p.308.
34. Diary Weizsäcker, 22.7.1917.
35. From Schröder, op cit, p.318.
36. Diary Hipper, 1.2.1917.
37. Ibid, 26–28.8.1916 incl.
38. Diary Knobloch, 2.2.1917.
39. Stenzler to his mother, 2.2.1917.
40. Ibid, 28.3.1917.
41. Diary Knobloch, 8.3.1917.
42. Ibid, 24.3.1917, 13.1.1917.
43. Diary Selchow, undated, June 1917.
44. From Schröder, op cit, p.314.
45. Winter, *Great War*, pp.103–248.
46. Offer, op cit, pp.34ff.
47. Diary Schweinitz, 31.5.1917, 8.4.1917.
48. Diary Knobloch, 14.7.1917.
49. Trotha to his wife, 29.7.1917.
50. Diary Zaeschmar, 1.8.1917.

51. Diary Hipper, 13.7.1917.
52. Hashagen, *U-boote Westwärts*, p.125.
53. From Herwig, op cit, p.175.

Chapter 8
1. Souchon to his wife, 25.3.1915.
2. Ibid, 20.4.1915.
3. Ibid, 12.6.1917.
4. Ibid, 8.9.1917.
5. Ibid, 29.9.1917.
6. Ibid, 26.9.1917.
7. Stumpf, diary, pp.255–6.
8. From Herwig, *Elitekorps*, p.162.
9. Ullrich, *Revolution*, p.20.
10. Diary Knobloch, 7.7.1917.
11. Ibid, 29.4.1917.
12. Hopman to his wife, 1.4.1917.
13. Ibid, 29.3.1917.
14. Diary Hopman, 8.4.1917.
15. Müller, *Nation*, p.289.
16. Stumpf, diary, p.153.
17. Diary Knobloch, 5.9.1916.
18. Horn, *Naval Mutinies*, p.29.
19. Scheer, *Hochseeflotte*, p.414.
20. Stumpf, diary, pp.123–4.
21. Ibid, p.162.
22. Ibid, p.33.
23. Ibid, p.65.
24. Ibid, p.81.
25. Diary Knobloch, 7.4.1915.
26. Diary Stitzinger, 3.9.1915 and 15.9.1915.
27. Horn, *Naval Mutinies*, pp.34–5.
28. Schaible, 'Ratgeber für die Standes- und Berufspflichten des deutschen Offiziers',
    p.141.
29. 'Das Werk des Untersuchungsausschusses' (WUA), vol 9/1, p.12.
30. WUA, vol 9/1, p.424.
31. WUA, vol 9/2, p.168. The choice in both cases of the informal personal pronoun 'du',
    commonly used only when with family and friends, children and to animals, was an
    insult in itself.
32. Stumpf, diary, p.162.
33. Diary, Schweinitz, 26.11.1917.
34. Hashagen, *U-boote Westwärts*, pp.66–7.
35. Quote from McKee, *Sober Men and True*, p.53.
36. Diary, Edward Parry, Imperial War Museum London, Manuscripts Collection, ref no
    71/19/1, entry 13.10.1915.
37. Memoir, Paul Heinrich, in BA-MA, MSg1/2304, p.60.
38. Ibid, p.61.
39. Diary Knobloch, 26.1.1917.
40. Ibid, 11.2.1917.
41. Ibid, 24.12.1916.
42. Chickering, *Reich*, p.60.
43. *Marine-Taschenbuch* 16 (1918), pp.177–235: Trotha to his wife, 19.12.1916. For
    remuneration of the fleet commander: Hugo von Pohl to Alfred von Tirpitz,
    16.2.1915, in BA-MA, RM 2/1546.
44. BA-MA, RM 2/1546.
45. *Marine-Taschenbuch* 16 (1918) pp.177–235.
46. WUA, vol 9/1, pp.411–12.
47. Horn, op cit, p.40.
48. Stumpf, diary, p.199.
49. Ibid, p.63.

50. Kocka, *Klassengesellschaft*, p.34.
51. Quote from ibid, p.34.
52. Stumpf, diary, pp.240–1.
53. Horn, op cit, p.46.
54. Hase, *Skagerrak*, p.79.
55. Diary Knobloch, 30.4.1917.
56. Ibid, 3.5.1918.
57. Ibid, 31.7.1915.
58. Ibid, 12.7.1916.
59. From Herwig, *Elitekorps*, p.74.
60. Souchon to his wife, 12.5.1915.
61. Diary Knobloch, 10.8.1917.
62. Ibid, 6.10.1917.
63. Quote from Scheerer, *Die Marineoffiziere der Kaiserlichen Marine im Ersten Weltkrieg*, p.280.
64. Diary Weizsäcker, 4.8.1917.
65. Diary Schweinitz, 3.8.1917.
66. Stumpf, diary p.251.
67. Diary Knobloch, 25.8.1917.
68. Diary Hipper, 7.8.1917.
69. Diary Weizsäcker, 19.8.1917.
70. Diary Hipper, 28.8.1917 and 13.8.1917.
71. Diary Zaeschmar, 29.9.1917.
72. Diary Knobloch, 6.10.1917.
73. 'Report by the Fleet Commander to the Kaiser regarding the causes of the unrest in the fleet from 6.10.1917', published in Deist, *Militär und Innenpolitik*, vol 2, pp.1068ff.
74. 'Order to the Fleet by the C-in-C, High Seas Fleet', 7.10.1917, published in *Ursachen und Folgen*, vol 1, pp.229ff.
75. Herwig, op cit, p.164.
76. From ibid, pp.175–6.
77. Souchon to his wife, 15.10.1917.
78. Ibid, 17.10.1917.
79. Diary Selchow, 11.12.1917.
80. Beatty to his wife, 13.10.1917.
81. All data from Navy List 1914, 3rd quarter.
82. Winter, *Great War*, p.225.
83. Beatty to his wife, 1.3.1917.
84. McLeod to his mother, 8.4.1915.
85. Diary Francis Pridham, Churchill Archives Centre Cambridge, Manuscripts Collection, PRID 1/1-5, entry 18.7.1915.
86. Beatty to his wife, 16.5.1917.
87. Diary Frewen, 20.5.1916.
88. Bethmann Hollweg, *Betrachtungen*, p.185.
89. Herwig, op cit, p.203.

Chapter 9
1. Souchon to his wife, 20.10.1914.
2. King-Hall to his parents, undated, end February 1915.
3. Speitkamp, *Ohrfeige*, p.157.
4. From Afflerbach, *Mit wehender Fahne*, p.611.
5. William Shakespeare, *Henry IV*, Act 5, Scene 1.
6. *Der Krieg zur See, Nordsee*, vol 2, Appendix 4, pp.301–2.
7. Diary Hipper, 8.10.1914.
8. Ibid, 12.10.1914.
9. Allerhöchste Kabinettsordre, 7.9.1915 in BA-MA, RM2/1129.
10. Diary Knobloch, 14.9.1915.
11. Allerhöchste Kabinettsordre, 7.9.1915 in BA-MA, RM2/1129.
12. From Schröder, *U-Boote*, p.222.
13. Weizsäcker to his father, 10.3.1910.
14. Diary Knobloch, 5.6.1916.

15. Rose, *King George*, p.169.
16. Beatty to his wife, 19.6.1917.
17. Gordon, *Rules*, pp.529–30.
18. David Beatty to Eugenie Godfrey-Faussett, Churchill Archives Centre Cambridge, Manuscripts Collection, SLGF 14/1-2, letter of 31.3.1917.
19. Ibid, 6.9.1918.
20. Diary Frewen, 26.1.1918.
21. Speitkamp, op cit, p.17.
22. Ibid.
23. Weizsäcker to his mother, 19.9.1915.
24. Diary Firle, 3.2.1916.
25. Hopman to his wife, 11.11.1915.
26. Diary Hipper, 27.5.1916.
27. Diary Zaeschmar, 25.7.1916.
28. Diary Hipper, 9.5.1917.
29. Stumpf, diary, p.25.
30. Ludendorff told officers of his staff in words to this effect on 1 October 1918 that he had 'asked His Majesty to include in his government all those circles to whom we owe the greatest thanks that we are where we are. We shall now see these gentlemen moving into the ministries. They will conclude the peace, which now must be concluded. Now they will sup the soup with all the bits they put into it for us!' Quoted from Hildebrand, *Reich*, p.403.
31. Diary Hipper, 3.10.1918, 4.10.1918.
32. The exchange of notes is documented in *Ursachen und Folgen*, vol 2, pp.373–470.
33. Kolb, *Versailles*, p.27.
34. Diary Schweinitz, 6.10.1918.
35. Diary Selchow, 5.10.1918.
36. Diary Schweinitz, 10.10.1918.
37. Ibid, 13.10.1918.
38. Diary Hopman, 17.10.1918.
39. Trotha to his wife, 22.10.1918, 20.10.1918.
40. Diary Schweinitz, 24.10.1918.
41. Diary Hipper, 17.10.1918.
42. Trotha to Alfred von Tirpitz, 31.3.1915, published in Trotha, *Volkstum und Staatsführung*, pp.29–32, quote on p.30.
43. Diary Hipper, 7.10.1918.
44. Herwig, *Elitekorps*, p.187.
45. Gross, *Frage*, p.352, note 16.
46. Quote from Deist, *Politik*, p.198.
47. Diary Hipper, 22.10.1918.
48. Scheer to his wife, quoted in Epkenhans, *Mein lieber Schatz*, letter 27.10.1918.
49. Trotha to Magnus von Leventzow, 8.10.1918, quoted in Deist, *Politik*, p.196.
50. Wilhelm Tägert to his wife, BA-MA, N284, literary estate Wilhelm Tägert, letter 9.11.1918.
51. Deist, *Politik*, p.206.
52. Diary Hipper, 31.10.1918.
53. Ibid.
54. Scheer to his wife, 1.11.1918.
55. Herwig, *Elitekorps*, p.200.
56. Dähnhardt, *Revolution*, p.91.
57. Stumpf diary, p.302.
58. Diary Schweinitz, 2.11.1918.
59. Ibid, 5.11.1918.
60. Ibid, 7.11.1918.
61. Ibid, 8.11.1918.
62. Diary Hipper, 6.11.1918.
63. Tägert to his wife, 5.11.1918.
64. Ibid, 9.11.1918.
65. Diary Knobloch, 6/7.11.1918.
66. Ibid, 8.11.1918.

67. Ibid, 9.11.1918.
68. Hopman to his wife, 7.11.1918.
69. Diary Weizsäcker, 5/6.11.1918.

Chapter 10
1. Quote from Röhl, *Wilhelm II*, vol 3, p.1239.
2. Ibid, p.1241.
3. Diary Hipper, 2.11.1918.
4. Quote from Röhl, op cit, p.1245.
5. Diary Hipper, 9.11.1918.
6. Diary Selchow, 10.11.1918.
7. Trotha to his wife, 7.11.1918.
8. Dönitz, *Mein wechselvolles Leben*, p.132.
9. Diary Weizsäcker, 2.11.1918.
10. Scheer to his wife, 7.11.1918.
11. Diary Weizsäcker, 9.11.1918.
12. Herwig, *Elitekorps*, p.201.
13. 'Announcement of Abdication', Kaiser Wilhelm II, 28.11.1918, quoted in *Ursachen und Folgen*, vol 2, p.579.
14. Diary Weizsäcker, 9.11.1918.
15. Quote from Kolb, *Versailles*, p.34.
16. Ibid, p.35.
17. Ibid, p.35.
18. BA-MA, RM 47/810.
19. WUA, vol 10/1, pp.206ff.
20. Dähnhardt, *Revolution*, p.118.
21. Quote from Ullrich, *Revolution*, p.127.
22. Dähnhardt, op cit, p.118.
23. Diary Knobloch, 14.11.1918.
24. Weizsäcker to his parents, 18.11.1918.
25. Niemöller, *Vom U-boot*, p.148.
26. Diary Harper, 9.11.1918.
27. Beatty to Eugenie Godfrey-Faussett, 31.10.1918.
28. Kennedy, *Aufstieg*, p.298.
29. Ibid.
30. Quote from Marder, *Dreadnought*, vol 5, p.179.
31. Ibid, p.180.
32. Quote from Krause, *Scapa Flow*, p.118.
33. The conditions appear in Corbett & Newbolt, *Naval Operations*, vol 5, pp.413–18.
34. Beatty to Eugenie Godfrey-Faussett, 9.11.1918.
35. Quote from Krause, *Scapa Flow*, p.158.
36. Quote from Herwig, op cit, p.205.
37. Ibid.
38. Diary Hipper, 16.11.1918.
39. Ibid, 12.11.1918.
40. Reuter, *Scapa Flow*, p.13.
41. Diary Colvill, 21.11.1918.
42. Quote from Marder, *Dreadnought*, vol 5, p.191.
43. Ibid, p.194.
44. Diary Colvill, 19.11.1918.
45. Quote from diary, Pridham, 23.11.1918.
46. Cork, *My Naval Life*, p.120.
47. Statement by Beatty, 24.11.1918.
48. Beatty to Eugenie Godfrey-Faussett, 26.11.1918.
49. Diary Zaeschmar, 18.11.1918.
50. Ibid.
51. Ibid.
52. Diary Zaeschmar, 14.11.1918.
53. Diary Zaeschmar, 17.12.1918.
54. Ibid.

55. Diary Hipper, 19.11.1918.
56. Ibid, 29.11.1918.
57. Ibid, 16.2.1920.

Chapter 11
1. Nicolson, *Friedensmacher*, p.353.
2. Reuter, Scapa Flow, p.78.
3. The letter is published in Trotha, *Volkstum und Staatsführung*, pp.182–3, quote p.183.
4. Krause, *Scapa Flow*, p.225.
5. Reuter, *Scapa Flow*, p.64.
6. Quote from Krause, op cit, p.250.
7. Ibid, p.233.
8. Quote from Kolb, *Versailles*, p.76.
9. For text of treaty see *Der Versailler Vertrag*.
10. Kolb, op cit, p.80.
11. Quote from Krause, op cit, p.296.
12. Herwig, *Elitekorps*, p.206.
13. Ruge, *Scapa Flow*, pp.152–3.
14. Quote from Krause, op cit, p.323.
15. Rosslyn Wemyss to George P Hope, 22.6.1919, quote in Marder, *Dreadnought*, vol 5, p.290.
16. Reuter, op cit, p.115.
17. Reuter to Trotha, 10.6.1919, quoted in Herwig, op cit, p.204.
18. Trotha's edict to the navy, 3.7.1919, in Trotha, *Volkstum und Staatsführung*, pp.184–6
19. Herwig, op cit, p.207.
20. Salewski, *England*, p.218.
21. Erich Raeder to Magnus von Levetzow, 28.1.1924, quote from Dülffer, *Weimar*, p.39, note 2.
22. Salewski, *Offizierkorps*, p.109.
23. Quote from Schreiber, *Kontinuität*, p.118.
24. Ibid, p.125.
25. Quote from *Grundzüge der deutschen Militärgeschichte*, vol 2, p.391.
26. Instruction of the C-in-C Kriegsmarine and chief of the SKL, 23.5.1949, in Salewski, *Seekriegsleitung*, pp.522ff.
27. Ibid.
28. Weizsäcker to his mother, 19.9.1915.
29. Weizsäcker to Trotha, 4.10.1918.
30. Diary Weizsäcker, 9.11.1918.
31. Weizsäcker to his parents, 18.11.1918, also diary, 16.11.1198, 20–22.11.1918, 25.11.1918.
32. Weizsäcker to his father, 20.2.1920.

Bibliography

I. Unpublished Sources

1. Bundesarchiv-Militärarchiv, Freiburg i Br (BA-MA)

Nachlässe

N 155 Rudolph Firle

N 156 Wilhelm Souchon

N 161 Walter Freiherr von Keyserlingk

N 162 Franz Ritter von Hipper

N 284 Wilhelm Tägert

N 428 Bogislav von Selchow

Militärgeschichtliche Sammlung

MSg 1 / 2304 Erinnerungen Paul Heinrich

MSg 1 / 2306 ditto

MSg 1 / 3093 Feldpostbriefe Heinrich Stenzler

Marineakten

RM 2 Kaiserliches Marinekabinett

RM 3 Reichsmarineamt

RM 5 Admiralstab der Marine

RM 47 Kommando der Hochseestreitkräfte

RM 51 Geschwader und Gruppen

RM 92 Schwere und mittlere Kampfschiffe

2. Niedersächsisches Staatsarchiv, Bückeburg

Dep 18 Adolf von Trotha

3. Marine-Offizier-Vereinigung, Bonn

o Sign Tagebuch Reinhold Knobloch

4. Wissenschaftliches Institut für Schiffahrts- u Marinegeschichte, Hamburg

Kart 45 Tagebuch Walther Stitzinger

5. Marineschule Mürwik, Flensburg

10983/84/85 Tagebuch Walter Zaeschmar

6. Imperial War Museum, London

66/29/1 Diary Edward Roynon-Jones

71/19/1 Diary Sir Edward Parry

7. Royal Naval Museum, Portsmouth

1997/43 Diary James Colvill

8. Liddle Collection, Leeds

RNMN/BERTHON Diary Edward Berthon
RNMN/GOLDSMITH Letters Sir Lennon Goldsmith
RNMN/MCLEOD Letters John McLeod
9. Churchill Archives Centre, Cambridge
DANL 241/1-2 Diary Sir Charles Daniel
HRPR 1/1-11 Diary Geoffrey Harper
PCKR 2/1-4 Letters Sir Herbert Packer
PRID 1/1-5 Diary Sir Francis Pridham
SLGF 14/1-2 Letters David Beatty and Eugenie Godfrey-Faussett
10. Frewen Family Archive, Brede, Sussex
Diary Oswald Frewen
11. Public Record Office, London (now The National Archives at Kew)
Admiralty Files
ADM 1 Correspondence and Papers
ADM 116 Record Office/Cases
ADM 156 Courts Martial Cases and Files
ADM 178 Naval Courts Martial Cases, Boards of Inquiry Reports and
    Other Papers
ADM 196 Registers of Officers' Services
ADM 242 Naval Casualties. Indexes, War Grave Rolls and Statistics Book

II. Printed Sources and Literature

Adams, Michael, *The Great Adventure. Male Desire and the Coming of World War I*, Bloomington 1990

Afflerbach, Holger, *Die Kunst der Niederlage. Eine Geschichte der Kapitulation*, Munich 2013

——, *Der Dreibund. Europäische Großmacht und Allianzpolitik vor dem Ersten Weltkrieg*, Wien 2002

——, '"Mit wehender Fahne untergehen". Kapitulationsverweigerungen in der deutschen Marine', in *Vierteljahrshefte für Zeitgeschichte*, 49 (2001), 595-612

——, *Falkenhayn. Politisches Denken und Handeln im Kaiserreich*, Munich 1994

Allerhöchste Verordnungen über die Ehrengerichte der Offiziere und Sanitätsoffiziere in der Kaiserlichen Marine, Berlin 1902

Arbuthnot, Robert K, *Details and Station Bill for a Battleship*, Portsmouth 1901

Aspinall-Oglander, Cecil, *Roger Keyes*, London 1951

Assmann, Kurt, *Deutsche Seestrategie in zwei Weltkriegen*, Heidelberg 1957

August 1914. Ein Volk zieht in den Krieg, hg von der Berliner Geschichtswerkstatt, Berlin 1989

Bacon, Reginald, *The Dover Patrol 1915–1917*, 2 vols, London 1919

——, *From 1900 Onward*, London 1939

Bailey, Thomas A & Paul B Ryan, *The Lusitania Disaster. An Episode in Modern Warfare and Diplomacy*, New York 1975

Bald, Detlef, *Der deutsche Offizier. Sozialund Bildungsgeschichte des deutschen Offizierkorps im 20 Jahrhundert*, Munich 1982

——, *Vom Kaiserheer zur Bundeswehr. Sozialstruktur des Militärs: Politik der Rekrutierung von Offizieren und Unteroffizieren*, Frankfurt 1981

——, *Der deutsche Generalstab 1859–1939. Reform und Restauration in Ausbildung und Bildung*, Munich 1977

——, 'Sozialgeschichte der Rekrutierung des deutschen Offizierkorps von der Reichsgründung bis zur Gegenwart', in *Sozialwissenschaftliches Institut der Bundeswehr, Berichte* (3), Munich 1977, 17–47

Balfour, Michael, *Der Kaiser. Wilhelm II und seine Zeit*, 2nd edn, Berlin 1996 (*The Kaiser and his times*, London 2013)

Barnett, Correlli, *Anatomie eines Krieges. Eine Studie über Hintergründe und entscheidende Phasen des Ersten Weltkrieges*, Munich 1963

Barnett, L Margaret, *British Food Policy During the First World War*, Boston 1985

Barth, Boris, *Dolchstoßlegenden und politische Desintegration. Das Trauma der deutschen Niederlage im Ersten Weltkrieg 1914–1933*, Düsseldorf 2003

Bauer, Hermann, *Reichsleitung und U-Bootseinsatz 1914–1918. Zusammenarbeit zwischen politischer und militärischer Führung im Kriege*, Lippoldsberg 1956

——, *Als Führer der U-Boote im Weltkriege. Der Eintritt der U-Boot-Waffe in die Seekriegführung*, Leipzig 1941

Bauerkämper, Arnd, *Die 'radikale Rechte' in Großbritannien. Nationalistische, antisemitische und faschistische Bewegungen vom späten 19 Jahrhundert bis 1945*, Göttingen 1991

Baum, Walter, 'Marine, Nationalsozialismus und Widerstand', in *Vierteljahrshefte für Zeitgeschichte*, 11 (1963), 16–48

Bayly, Lewis, *Pull Together!*, London 1939

Baynham, Henry, *Men from the Dreadnoughts*, London 1976

The Beatty Papers. Selections from the Private and Official Correspondence of Admiral of the Fleet Earl Beatty, vol I: 1902–1918, ed B McL Ranft, Aldershot 1989

Becker, Frank, 'Strammstehen vor der Obrigkeit? Bürgerliche Wahrnehmung der Einigungskriege und Militarismus im Deutschen Kaiserreich', in *Historische Zeitschrift*, 277 (2003), 87–113

Beckett, Ian F W & Keith Simpson, *A Nation in Arms. A Social Study of the British Army in the First World War*, Manchester 1985

Beesly, Patrick, *Room 40. British Naval Intelligence 1914–18*, London 1982

Bell, Christopher M & Bruce A Elleman (eds), *Naval Mutinies of the Twentieth Century. An International Perspective*, London 2003

Bennett, Geoffrey, *Die Seeschlachten von Coronel und Falkland und der Untergang des deutschen Kreuzergeschwaders unter Admiral Graf Spee*, Munich 1980 (*The Battles of Coronel and the Falklands 1914*, Barnsley 2014)

——, *Naval Battles of the First World War*, London 1968

Bercuson, David J & Holger H Herwig, *The Destruction of the Bismarck*, Toronto 2001

Berger, Peter L & Thomas Luckmann, *Die gesellschaftliche Konstruktion der Wirklichkeit. Eine Theorie der Wissenssoziologie*, 5th edn, Frankfurt 1998

Berghahn, Volker R, *Germany and the Approach of War in 1914*, London 1973

——, *Rüstung und Machtpolitik. Zur Anatomie des 'Kalten Krieges' vor 1914*, Düsseldorf 1973

——, *Der Tirpitz-Plan. Genesis und Verfall einer innenpolitischen Krisenstrategie unter Wilhelm II*, Düsseldorf 1971

——, 'Zu den Zielen des deutschen Flottenbaus unter Wilhelm II', *Historische Zeitschrift*, 210 (1970), 34–100

——, 'Flottenrüstung und Machtgefüge' in Stürmer, Michael (ed), *Das kaiserliche Deutschland. Politik und Gesellschaft 1870–1918*, Düsseldorf 1970, 378–96

——, 'Kaiserliche Marine und Kriegsausbruch 1914. Neue Dokumente zur Juli-Krise', *Militärgeschichtliche Mitteilungen*, 7 (1970), 37–58

Berghahn, Volker R & Wilhelm Deist (eds), *Rüstung im Zeichen der wilhelminischen Weltpolitik. Grundlegende Dokumente 1890–1914*, Düsseldorf 1988

Graf Bernstorff, *Deutsches Marineleben. Eine Erzählung aus dem Leben und Treiben an Bord deutscher Kriegsschiffe*, Minden 1908

Besteck, Eva, *Die trügerische 'First Line of Defence'. Zum deutschbritischen Wettrüsten vor dem Ersten Weltkrieg*, Freiburg & Berlin 2006

Bestimmungen für den Dienst an Bord, hg vom Reichs-Marine-Amt, Berlin 1909

Bethmann Hollweg, Theobald von, *Betrachtungen zum Weltkriege*, vol 2, Berlin 1921

Bidlingmaier, Gerhard, *Seegeltung in der deutschen Geschichte. Ein seekriegsgeschichtliches Handbuch*, Darmstadt 1967

Bingham, Barry, *Falklands, Jutland and the Bight*, London 1919

Bird, Keith, *Weimar, the German Naval Officer Corps and the Rise of National Socialism*, Amsterdam 1977

Birley, Derek, *Land of Sport and Glory. Sport and British Society 1887–1910*, Manchester 1995

Bisset, James, *Commodore. War, Peace and Big Ships*, London 1961

Bourne, J M, *Britain and The Great War 1914–1918*, London 1989

Bräckow, Werner, *Die Geschichte des deutschen Marine-Ingenieuroffizierkorps*, Oldenburg 1974

Breyer, Siegfried, *Schlachtschiffe und Schlachtkreuzer 1905–1970*, Munich 1970

The British Navy from Within, by 'Ex-Royal Navy', London 1916

Brodsky, G W Stephen, *Gentlemen of the Blade. A Social and Literary History of the British Army since 1660*, New York 1988

Brown, Malcolm & Patricia Meehan (eds), *Scapa Flow. The Reminiscences of Men and Women who served in Scapa Flow in the Two World Wars*, London 1968

Brownrigg, Douglas, *Indiscretions of the Naval Censor*, London 1920

Bruendel, Steffen, *Volksgemeinschaft oder Volksstaat. Die 'Ideen von 1914' und die Neuordnung Deutschlands im Ersten Weltkrieg*, Berlin 2003

Burchardt, Lothar, 'Die Auswirkungen der Kriegswirtschaft auf die deutsche Zivilbevölkerung im Ersten und im Zweiten Weltkrieg', *Militärgeschichtliche Mitteilungen*, 15 (1974), 65–97

Burgess, Robert & Roland Blackburn, *We joined the Navy. Traditions, Customs and Nomenclature of the Royal Navy*, London 1943

Burt, R A, *British Battleships of World War One*, London 1986

Buschmann, Nikolaus & Horst Carl (eds), *Die Erfahrung des Krieges. Erfahrungsgeschichtliche Perspektiven von der Französischen Revolution bis zum Zweiten Weltkrieg*, Paderborn 2001

Callender, Geoffrey & F H Hinsley, *The Naval Side of British History 1485–1945*, London 1954

Campbell, A B, *Customs and Traditions of the Royal Navy*, Aldershot 1956

Campbell, Gordon, *My Mystery Ships*, London 1928

Campbell, John, *Jutland. An Analysis of the Fighting*, 2nd edn, London 1998

Carew, Anthony, *The Lower Deck of The Royal Navy 1900–39. The Invergordon Mutiny in Perspective*, Manchester 1981

Carr, William Guy, *By Guess and by God. The Story of the British Submarines in the War*, New York 1930

Cecil, Hugh & Peter Liddle (eds), *Facing Armageddon. The First World War Experienced*, London 1996

Chalmers, William S, *The Life and Letters of David Earl Beatty*, London 1951

Chatfield, Lord, *The Navy and Defence*, London & Toronto 1942

Chickering, Roger, *Das Deutsche Reich und der Erste Weltkrieg*, Munich 2002

——, *We Men who feel most German. A Cultural Study of the Pan-German League 1886–1914*, Boston 1984

Churchill, Winston, *The World Crisis 1911–1918*, 6 vols, London 1923–31

Clark, Christopher M, *The Sleepwalkers. How Europe went to War in 1914*, London 2012

——, *Wilhelm II. Die Herrschaft des letzten deutschen Kaisers*, Munich 2008

Coetzee, Frans & Marilyn Shevin-Coetzee (eds), *Authority, Identity and the Social History of the Great War*, Providence & Oxford 1995

Compton-Hall, Richard, *Submarines and the War at Sea*, London 1991

Corbett, Julian S & Henry Newbolt, *Naval Operations. History of the Great War Based on Official Documents*, 5 vols, London 1920–31

Cork & Orrery, Admiral of the Fleet The Earl of, *My Naval Life 1886–1941*, London 1942

Creutz, Martin, *Die Pressepolitik der kaiserlichen Regierung während des Ersten Weltkriegs. Die Exekutive, die Journalisten und der Teufelskreis der Berichterstattung*, Frankfurt 1996

Dade, Peter, *Fahneneid und feierliches Gelöbnis. Zur militärischen Verpflichtungsform in der deutschen Wehrgeschichte. Insbesondere zur geltenden Regelung für die Soldaten der Bundeswehr*, Darmstadt 1971

Dähnhardt, Dirk, *Revolution in Kiel. Der Übergang vom Kaiserreich zur Weimarer Republik 1918/19*, Neumünster 1978

De Chair, Dudley, *The Sea is Strong*, London 1961

DeGroot, Gerard J, *Blighty. British Society in the Era of the Great War*, London & New York 1996

Deist, Wilhelm, *Militär, Staat und Gesellschaft. Studien zur preußisch-*

deutschen Militärgeschichte, Munich 1991

——, *Flottenpolitik und Flottenpropaganda. Das Nachrichtenbureau des Reichsmarineamtes 1897–1914*, Stuttgart 1976

——, 'Die Politik der Seekriegsleitung und die Rebellion der Flotte Ende Oktober 1918', in Deist, *Militär, Staat und Gesellschaft*, 185–210

——, 'Die Unruhen in der Marine 1917/18', in Deist, *Militär, Staat und Gesellschaft*, 165–84

——, 'Kaiser Wilhelm II als Oberster Kriegsherr', in Deist, *Militär, Staat und Gesellschaft*, 1–18

——, 'Verdeckter Militärstreik im Kriegsjahr 1918?', in Wette (ed), *Der Krieg des kleinen Mannes*, 146–67

Demeter, Karl, *Das deutsche Offizierkorps in Gesellschaft und Staat 1650–1945*, Frankfurt 1964

Die deutsche Flotte im Spannungsfeld der Politik 1848–1985. Vorträge und Diskussionen der 25. Historisch-Taktischen Tagung der Flotte 1985, hg vom Deutschen Marine-Institut & vom Militärgeschichtlichen Forschungsamt, Herford 1985

Die deutsche Marine. Historisches Selbstverständnis und Standort-bestimmung, hg vom Deutschen Marine-Institut und der Deutschen Marine-Akademie, Herford 1983

Deutsche Marinen im Wandel. Vom Symbol nationaler Einheit zum Instrument internationaler Sicherheit. Im Auftr des Militär-geschichtlichen Forschungsamtes hg von Werner Rahn, Munich 2005

Dewar, K G B, *The Navy from Within*, London 1939

Diercks, Wulff, 'Der Einfluß der Personalsteuerung auf die deutsche Seekriegführung 1914 bis 1918', in *Deutsche Marinen im Wandel*, 235–67

Dönitz, Karl, *Mein wechselvolles Leben*, Göttingen 1968

Doepgen, Peter, 'Die Washingtoner Konferenz, das Deutsche Reich und die Reichsmarine. Die Auswirkungen der Washingtoner Abrüstungskonferenz 1921/1922 auf das Deutsche Reich und die Reichsmarine 1922–1935', dissertation, Kiel 2000

Drascher, Wahrhold, 'Zur Soziologie des deutschen Seeoffizierkorps', *Wehrwissenschaftliche Rundschau*, 10 (1962), 555–69

Dülffer, Jost, *Regeln gegen den Krieg? Die Haager Friedenskonferenzen von 1899 und 1907 in der internationalen Politik*, Berlin 1981

——, 'Die Reichsund Kriegsmarine 1918–1939', in *Handbuch zur deutschen Militärgeschichte 1648–1939*, hg vom Militärgeschichtlichen Forschungsamt, vol 4 section VIII, Munich 1977, 337–488

——, *Weimar, Hitler und die Marine. Reichspolitik und Flottenbau 1920–1939*, Düsseldorf 1973

Dülffer, Jost & Karl Holl (eds), *Bereit zum Krieg. Kriegsmentalität im wilhelminischen Deutschland 1890–1914*, Göttingen 1986

Duppler, Jörg (ed), *Seemacht und Seestrategie im 19 und 20 Jahrhundert*, Hamburg 1999

——, *Prinz Adalbert von Preußen. Gründer der deutschen Marine*, Herford & Bonn 1986

——, *Der Juniorpartner. England und die Entwicklung der Deutschen Marine 1848–1890*, Herford 1985

Edwards, Kenneth, *We Dive at Dawn*, London 1939

Ehrenrangliste der Kaiserlich Deutschen Marine 1914–18, bearb von Konteradmiral aD Stoelzel, Berlin 1930

Ehrensberger, Konrad, *Hundert Jahre Organisation der deutschen Marine 1890–1990*, Bonn 1993

Eisenberg, Christiane, '*English Sports' und deutsche Bürger. Eine Gesellschaftsgeschichte 1800–1939*, Paderborn 1999

Eley, Geoff, 'The View from the Throne: The Personal Rule of Kaiser Wilhelm II', in *Historical Journal*, 28 (1985), 469–85

Elvert, Jürgen, Jürgen Jensen & Michael Salewski (eds), *Kiel, die Deutschen und die See*, Stuttgart 1992

Elz, Wolfgang& Sönke Neitzel (eds), *Internationale Beziehungen im 19 und 20 Jahrhundert. Festschrift für Winfried Baumgart zum 65 Geburtstag*, Paderborn 2003

Endres, Franz Carl, 'Soziologische Struktur und ihr entsprechende Ideologien des deutschen Offizierkorps vor dem Weltkriege', *Archiv für Sozialwissenschaft und Sozialpolitik*, 58 (1927), 282–319

Epkenhans, Michael (ed), *Mein lieber Schatz! Briefe von Admiral Reinhard Scheer an seine Ehefrau; August bis November 1918*, Bochum 2006

——, *Die wilhelminische Flottenrüstung 1908–1914. Weltmachtstreben, industrieller Fortschritt, soziale Integration*, Munich 1991

——, 'Die kaiserliche Marine im Ersten Weltkrieg: Weltmacht oder Untergang?', in *Der Erste Weltkrieg*, 319–40

——, 'Wilhelm II and "his" Navy 1888–1918', in *The Kaiser*, 12–36

——, '"Wir als deutsches Volk sind doch nicht klein zu kriegen..." Aus den Tagebüchern des Fregattenkapitäns Bogislav von Selchow 1918/19', *Militärgeschichtliche Mitteilungen*, 55 (1996), 165–224

——, '"Der Dreizack gehört in unsere Faust." Die Bedeutung von Seemacht im kaiserlichen Deutschland', in *Liberalismus, Parlamentarismus und*

Demokratie. Festschrift für Manfred Botzenhart zum 60. Geburtstag, Michael Epkenhans, Martin Kottkamp & Lothar Snyders (eds), Göttingen 1994, 191–211

——, 'Großindustrie und Schlachtflottenbau 1897–1914', *Militärgeschichtliche Mitteilungen*, 1 (1988), 65–140

——, '"Red Sailors" and the Demise of the German Empire 1918', in Bell & Elleman (eds), *Naval Mutinies of the Twentieth Century*, 80–105

Der Erste Weltkrieg. Wirkung, Wahrnehmung, Analyse, Im Auftr des Militärgeschichtlichen Forschungsamtes hg von Wolfgang Michalka, Weyarn 1997

Erster Weltkrieg – Zweiter Weltkrieg. Ein Vergleich. Krieg, Kriegserlebnis, Kriegserfahrung in Deutschland, Im Auftr des Militärgeschichtlichen Forschungsamtes hg von Bruno Thoß & Hans-Erich Volkmann, Paderborn 2002

Fälschle, Christian, *Rivalität als Prinzip. Die englische Demokratie im Denken des wilhelminischen Deutschland 1900–1914*, Frankfurt 1991

Fairbairn, Douglas, *The Narrative of a Naval Nobody 1907–1924*, London 1929

Fawcett, H W & G W W Hooper (eds), *The Fighting at Jutland. The Personal Experiences of Sixty Officers and Men of the British Fleet*, London 2001

Feldman, Gerald D, *Army, Industry and Labor in Germany 1914–1918*, Princeton 1966

Ferber, Konstantin, *Organisation und Dienstbetrieb der Kaiserlich deutschen Marine*, 4th edn, Berlin 1903

Ferguson, Niall, *Der falsche Krieg. Der Erste Weltkrieg und das 20 Jahrhundert*, 2nd edn, Stuttgart 1999

Fesser, Gerd, *Reichskanzler Fürst von Bülow. Architekt der deutschen Weltpolitik*, Leipzig 2003

——, *Der Traum vom Platz an der Sonne. Deutsche 'Weltpolitik' 1897–1914*, Bremen 1996

Fischer, Fritz, *Griff nach der Weltmacht. Die Kriegszielpolitik des kaiserlichen Deutschland 1914/18*, 4th edn, Düsseldorf 1971

Fischer, Jörg-Uwe, *Admiral des Kaisers. Georg Alexander von Müller als Chef des Marinekabinetts Wilhelms II*, Frankfurt 1992

Flasch, Kurt, *Die geistige Mobilmachung. Die deutschen Intellektuellen und der Erste Weltkrieg*, Berlin 2000

Förster, Stig, *Der doppelte Militarismus. Die deutsche Heeresrüstungspolitik zwischen Statusquo-Sicherung und Aggression 1890–1913*, Stuttgart 1985

Forstmeier, Friedrich, 'Probleme der Erziehung und Ausbildung in der Kaiserlichen Marine in Abhängigkeit von geistiger Situation und sozialer Struktur,' *Marine-Rundschau*, 63 (1966), 189–98

——, 'Stellung und Disziplinarbefugnisse des Ersten Offiziers an Bord von Kriegsschiffen der deutschen Marinen 1847–1945', *Marine-Rundschau*, 66 (1969), 34–50

Fremantle, Sydney Robert, *My Naval Career 1880–1928*, London 1949

French, David, *British Strategy and War Aims 1914–1916*, London 1986

Frevert, Ute, *Die kasernierte Nation. Militärdienst und Zivilgesellschaft in Deutschland*, Munich 2001

Frevert, Ute (ed), *Militär und Gesellschaft im 19 und 20 Jahrhundert*, Stuttgart 1997

——, *Ehrenmänner. Das Duell in der bürgerlichen Gesellschaft*, Munich 1991

Frewen, Oswald, *Sailor's Soliloquy*, ed G P Griggs, London 1961

Friedman, Norman, *Battleship Design and Development 1905–1945*, London 1978

Fuller, John G, *Troop Morale and Popular Culture in the British and Dominion Armies 1914–1918*, Oxford 1990

Gade, Christel, *Gleichgewichtspolitik oder Bündnispflege? Maximen britischer Außenpolitik (1909–1914)*, Göttingen & Zürich 1997

Geinitz, Christian, *Kriegsfurcht und Kampfbereitschaft. Das Augusterlebnis in Freiburg. Eine Studie zum Kriegsbeginn 1914*, Essen 1998

Gemzell, Carl-Axel, *Organization, Conflict and Innovation. A Study of German Naval Strategic Planning 1888–1940*, Lund 1973

Geyer, Michael, *Deutsche Rüstungspolitik 1860–1980*, Frankfurt 1984

Giessler, Klaus-Volker, *Die Institution des Marineattachés im Kaiserreich*, Boppard 1976

Girouard, Mark, *The Return to Camelot. Chivalry and the English Gentleman*, New Haven & London 1981

Goldrick, James, *The King's Ships Were at Sea. The War in the North Sea August 1914–February 1915*, Annapolis 1984

——, 'The Battleship Fleet: The Test of War 1895–1919', in *The Oxford Illustrated History of the Royal Navy*, 280–318

Goltermann, Svenja, *Körper der Nation. Habitusformierung und die Politik des Turnens 1860–1890*, Göttingen 1998

Gordon, Andrew, *The Rules of the Game. Jutland and British Naval*

Command, London 1996

Graham, Admiral Sir Angus Cunninghame, *Random Naval Recollections 1905–1951*, Gartocharn 1980

Granier, Gerhard, *Die deutsche Seekriegsleitung im Ersten Weltkrieg*, 4 vols, Koblenz 1999–2004

——, *Magnus von Levetzow. Seeoffizier, Monarchist und Wegbereiter Hitlers. Lebensweg und ausgewählte Dokumente*, Boppard 1982

Graubohm, Herbert, *Die Ausbildung in der deutschen Marine. Von ihrer Gründung bis zum Jahre 1914*, Düsseldorf 1977

——, 'Historische Wurzeln der Ausbildung in der Marine', in *Die deutsche Marine*, 131–42

Gretton, Peter, *Former Naval Person. Winston Churchill and the Royal Navy*, London 1968

Groß, Gerhard Paul, *Die Seekriegführung der Kaiserlichen Marine im Jahre 1918*, Frankfurt 1989

——, 'Eine Frage der Ehre? Die Marineführung und der letzte Flottenvorstoß 1918', in *Deutsche Marinen im Wandel*, 287–304

——, 'Unternehmen "Albion". Eine Studie zur Zusammenarbeit von Armee und Marine während des Ersten Weltkrieges', in Elz & Neitzel (eds), *Internationale Beziehungen im 19 und 20 Jahrhundert*, 171–86

Die Große Politik der Europäischen Kabinette von 1871–1914. Sammlung der diplomatischen Akten des Auswärtigen Amtes, hg von Johannes Lepsius, 40 vols, Berlin 1922–27

Grundzüge der deutschen Militärgeschichte, hg von Karl-Volker Neugebauer, 2 vols, Freiburg 1993

Güth, Rolf, *Admiralstabsausbildung in der deutschen Marine*, Bonn 1979

——, 'Die Organisation der deutschen Marine in Krieg und Frieden 1913–1933', in *Handbuch zur deutschen Militärgeschichte 1648–1939*, hg vom Militärgeschichtlichen Forschungsamt, vol 4, section VIII, Munich 1977, 263–336

Guth, Ekkehart P, *Der Loyalitätskonflikt des deutschen Offizierkorps in der Revolution 1918–20*, Frankfurt 1983

Guttandin, Friedhelm, *Das paradoxe Schicksal der Ehre. Zum Wandel der adeligen Ehre und zur Bedeutung von Duell und Ehre für den monarchischen Zentralstaat*, Berlin 1993

Hagenlücke, Heinz, *Deutsche Vaterlandspartei. Die nationale Rechte am Ende des Kaiserreiches*, Düsseldorf 1997

Haggie, Paul, 'The Royal Navy and War Planning in the Fisher Era', in Kennedy (ed), *The War Plans of the Great Powers*, 118–32

Halpern, Paul G, *A Naval History of World War I*, Annapolis 1994

——, *The Naval War in the Mediterranean 1914–1918*, London 1987

Hamilton, W Mark, *The Nation and the Navy. Methods and Organization of British Navalist Propaganda 1889–1914*, New York & London 1986

Hamilton, K A, 'Great Britain and France 1905–1911', in Hinsley (ed), *British Foreign Policy under Sir Edward Grey*, 113–19

Handbuch der Deutschen Marine und der Seestreitkräfte des Auslandes, Kiel 1917

Hankel, Gerd, *Die Leipziger Prozesse. Deutsche Kriegsverbrechen und ihre strafrechtliche Verfolgung nach dem Ersten Weltkrieg*, Hamburg 2003

Hartwig, Dieter, *Großadmiral Karl Dönitz. Legende und Wirklichkeit*, Paderborn 2010

Hase, Georg von, *Skagerrak. Erinnerungen eines deutschen Seeoffiziers*, 8th edn, Leipzig 1934

Hashagen, Ernst, *U-Boote Westwärts! Meine Fahrten um England 1914–1918*, Berlin 1942

Haste, Cate, *Keep the Home Fires Burning. Propaganda in the First World War*, London 1977

Hayes, Paul, 'Britain, Germany and the Admiralty's Plans for Attacking German Territory 1906–1915', in Freedman, Lawrence, Paul Hayes & Robert O'Neill (eds), *War, Strategy and International Politics. Essays in Honour of Sir Michael Howard*, Oxford 1992

Hayward, Victor, *HMS Tiger at Bay. A Sailor's Memoir 1914–18*, London 1977

Heinsius, Paul, 'Die deutsche Marine, eine Schöpfung des Jahres 1848', in *Die deutsche Marine*, 25–34

Heitmann, Jan, *Unter Wasser in die Neue Welt. Handelsunterseeboote und kaiserliche Unterseekreuzer im Spannungsfeld von Politik und Kriegsführung*, Berlin 1999

Hering, Rainer, *Konstruierte Nation. Der Alldeutsche Verband 1890 bis 1939*, Hamburg 2003

Herrmann, David G, *The Arming of Europe and the Making of the First World War*, Princeton 1996

Herrmann, Erich, *Auf dem Panzerkreuzer 'Seydlitz' während der Revolution und bei der Versenkung der Hochseeflotte in Scapa Flow*, Minden 1922

Herwig, Holger, *'Luxury' Fleet. The Imperial German Navy 1888–1918*, London 1980

——, *Das Elitekorps des Kaisers. Die Marineoffiziere im Wilhelminischen*

Deutschland, Hamburg 1977

——, 'Admirals versus Generals: The War Aims of the Imperial German Navy 1914–1918', *Central European History*, 5 (1972), 208–33

——, 'Das Offizierkorps der Kaiserlichen Marine vor 1918', in Hofmann (ed), *Das deutsche Offizierkorps 1860–1960*, 139–62

——, 'Soziale Herkunft und wissenschaftliche Vorbildung des Seeoffiziers der Kaiserlichen Marine vor 1914', *Militärgeschichtliche Mitteilungen*, 2 (1971), 81–111

——, 'Zur Soziologie des kaiserlichen Seeoffizierkorps vor 1914', in Schottelius & Deist (eds), *Marine und Marinepolitik im kaiserlichen Deutschland*, 73–88

Herzog, Bodo, *60 Jahre deutsche U-Boote. 1906–1966*, Munich 1968

Hildebrand, Hans H, *Die organisatorische Entwicklung der Marine nebst Stellenbesetzung 1848–1945*, 3 vols, Osnabrück 2000

Hildebrand, Hans H & Ernest Henriot, *Deutschlands Admirale 1849–1945. Die militärischen Werdegänge der See, Ingenieur-, Sanitäts-, Waffen- und Verwaltungsoffiziere im Admiralsrang*, 4 vols, Osnabrück 1988–96

Hildebrand, Klaus, *Das vergangene Reich. Deutsche Außenpolitik von Bismarck bis Hitler 1871–1945*, 2nd edn, Stuttgart 1996

——, *Deutsche Außenpolitik 1871–1918*, Munich 1989

——, 'Zwischen Allianz und Antagonismus. Das Problem bilateraler Normalität in den britisch deutschen Beziehungen des 19 Jahrhunderts (1870–1914)', in Dollinger, Heinz, Horst Gründer & Alwin Hanschmidt (eds), *Weltpolitik, Europagedanke, Regionalismus. Festschrift für Heinz Gollwitzer*, Münster 1982

——, 'Imperialismus, Wettrüsten und Kriegsausbruch 1914', *Neue Politische Literatur*, 20 (1975), part 1, 160–94

Hill, Leonidas E (ed), *Die Weizsäcker-Papiere 1900–1932*, Berlin 1982

——, 'Signal zur Konterrevolution? Der Plan zum letzten Vorstoß der deutschen Hochseeflotte am 30. Oktober 1918', *Vierteljahrshefte für Zeitgeschichte*, 36 (1988), 113–29

Hillgruber, Andreas, *Die gescheiterte Großmacht. Eine Skizze des Deutschen Reiches 1871–1945*, 4th edn, Düsseldorf 1984

Hinsley, F H (ed), *British Foreign Policy under Sir Edward Grey*, Cambridge 1977

Hirschfeld, Gerhard, Gerd Krumeich & Irina Renz (eds), *Enzyklopädie Erster Weltkrieg*, Paderborn 2003

Hobson, Rolf, *Maritimer Imperialismus. Seemachtideologie,*

seestrategisches Denken und der Tirpitzplan 1875 bis 1914, Munich
    2004 (Imperialism at Sea, Naval Strategic Thought, the Ideology of
    Sea Power and the Tirpitz Plan, 1875–1914, London 2002)

Hofmann, Hanns Hubert (ed), Das deutsche Offizierkorps 1860–1960,
    Boppard 1980

Holt, Richard, Sport and the British. A Modern History, Oxford 1989

Hopman, Albert, Das ereignisreiche Leben eines 'Wilhelminers'. Tage-
    bücher, Briefe, Aufzeichnungen 1901 bis 1920. Im Auftr des Militär-
    geschichtlichen Forschungsamtes hg von Michael Epkenhans, Munich
    2004

Horn, Daniel, The German Naval Mutinies of World War I, New Brunswick
    1969

Horne, John & Alan Kramer, Deutsche Kriegsgreuel 1914. Die umstrittene
    Wahrheit, Hamburg 2004

Hough, Richard, The Great War at Sea 1914–1918, Oxford 1983

Hubatsch, Walther, Kaiserliche Marine. Aufgaben und Leistungen, Munich
    1975

Hubatsch, Walther, Der Admiralstab und die obersten Marinebehörden in
    Deutschland 1848–1945, Frankfurt 1958

Hubatsch, Walther, Die Ära Tirpitz. Studien zur deutschen Marinepolitik
    1890–1918, Göttingen 1955

Hüppauf, Bernd (ed), Ansichten vom Krieg. Vergleichende Studien zum
    Ersten Weltkrieg in Literatur und Gesellschaft, Königstein 1984

——, '"Der Tod ist verschlungen in den Sieg." Todesbilder aus dem Ersten
    Weltkrieg und der Nachkriegszeit', in Hüppauf (ed), Ansichten vom
    Krieg, 55–91

Hughes, Matthew & Matthew Seligmann (eds), Leadership in Conflict
    1914–1918, Barnsley 2000

Humphreys, Roy, The Dover Patrol 1914–18, Stroud 1998

Jahr, Christoph, Uwe Mai & Kathrin Roller (eds), Feindbilder in der
    deutschen Geschichte. Studien zur Vorurteilsgeschichte im 19 und 20
    Jahrhundert, Berlin 1994

——, '"Das Krämervolk der eitlen Briten". Das deutsche Englandfeindbild
    im Ersten Weltkrieg', in Jahr, Mai & Roller (eds), Feindbilder in der
    deutschen Geschichte, 115–42

Jalevich, Peter, 'German Culture in the Great War', in European Culture in
    the Great War. The Arts, Entertainment, and Propaganda 1914–1918,
    ed Aviel Roshwald & Richard Stites, Cambridge 1999, 32–58

James, William, The Sky was Always Blue, London 1951

James, W M, *New Battleship Organisations and Notes for Executive Officers*, Portsmouth 1916

Jansen, Christian (ed), *Der Bürger als Soldat. Die Militarisierung europäischer Gesellschaften im langen 19 Jahrhundert: ein internationaler Vergleich*, Essen 2004

Jarausch, Konrad H, *The Enigmatic Chancellor. Bethmann Hollweg and the Hubris of Imperial Germany*, New Haven & London 1973

Jeismann, Michael, *Das Vaterland der Feinde. Studien zum nationalen Feindbegriff und Selbstverständnis in Deutschland und Frankreich 1792–1918*, Stuttgart 1992

Jellicoe, John, *The Grand Fleet 1914–1916. Its Creation, Development and Work*, London 1919

The Jellicoe Papers. Selections from the Private and Official Correspondence of Admiral of the Fleet Earl Jellicoe of Scapa, vol I, 1893–1916, ed A Temple Patterson, London 1966

John, Hartmut, *Das Reserveoffizierkorps im Deutschen Kaiserreich 1890–1914. Ein sozialgeschichtlicher Beitrag zur Untersuchung der gesellschaftlichen Militarisierung im Wilhelminischen Deutschland*, Frankfurt 1981

Joll, James, *The Origins of the First World War*, London & New York 1984

Jones, Mary, 'The Making of the Royal Naval Officer Corps 1860–1914', dissertation, Exeter 1999

Jones, T M, *Watchdogs of the Deep. Life in a Submarine During the Great War*, Sydney 1935

Jordan, Gerald (ed), *Naval Warfare in the Twentieth Century 1900–1945. Essays in Honour of Arthur Marder*, London & New York 1977

Jünger, Ernst, *In Stahlgewittern*, 43rd edn, Stuttgart 2003

The Kaiser. New Research on Wilhelm II's Role in Imperial Germany, ed Annika Mombauer & Wilhelm Deist, Cambridge 2003

Kaiser Wilhelm II als Oberster Kriegsherr im Ersten Weltkrieg. Quellen aus der militärischen Umgebung des Kaisers 1914–1918, bearbeitet und eingeleitet von Holger Afflerbach, Munich 2005

Keegan, John, *Das Antlitz des Krieges. Die Schlachten von Azincourt 1415, Waterloo 1815 und an der Somme 1916*, Frankfurt & New York 1991 (*The Face of Battle: A Study of Agincourt, Waterloo and the Somme*, London 2014)

Keiner fühlt sich hier mehr als Mensch ... Erlebnis und Wirkung des Ersten Weltkriegs, ed Gerhard Hirschfeld, Gerd Krumeich & Irina Renz, Essen 1993

Kelly, Patrick J, *Tirpitz and the Imperial German Navy*, Bloomington 2011

Kennedy, Paul M (ed), *The War Plans of the Great Powers 1880–1914*, Boston 1985

——, *The Rise of the Anglo-German Antagonism 1860–1914*, London 1980

——, *Aufstieg und Verfall der britischen Seemacht*, Bonn 1978 (*The Rise and Fall of British Naval Mastery*, London 2001)

Kerr, Mark, *The Navy in My Time*, London 1933

Keyes, Roger, *The Naval Memoirs*, 2 vols, London 1934 & 1935

The Keyes Papers. Selections from the Private and Official Correspondence of Admiral of the Fleet Baron Keyes of Zeebrugge, vol I, 1914–1918, ed Paul G Halpern, 2nd edn, London 1979

Kielmansegg, Peter Graf, *Deutschland und der Erste Weltkrieg*, 2nd edn, Stuttgart 1980

Kift, Dagmar, *Arbeiterkultur im gesellschaftlichen Konflikt: Die englische Music Hall im 19 Jahrhundert*, Essen 1991

King-Hall, Louise (ed), *Sea Saga. Being the Naval Diaries of four Generations of the King-Hall Family*, London 1935

King-Hall, Stephen, *A North Sea Diary 1914–1918*, London 1936

——, *My Naval Life 1906–1929*, London 1952

The King's Regulations and Admiralty Instructions, London 1913

Kitchen, Martin, *The German Officer Corps 1890–1914*, Oxford 1968

Kluge, Ulrich, *Soldatenräte und Revolution. Studien zur Militärpolitik in Deutschland 1918/19*, Göttingen 1975

Knoch, Peter (ed), *Kriegsalltag. Die Rekonstruktion des Kriegsalltags als Aufgabe der historischen Forschung und der Friedenserziehung*, Stuttgart 1989

Koch, H W, (ed), *The Origins of the First World War. Great Power Rivalry and German War Aims*, New York 1972

——, 'The Anglo-German Alliance Negotiations: Missed Opportunity or Myth?', *History*, 54 (1969), 378–92

Kocka, Jürgen, *Klassengesellschaft im Krieg. Deutsche Sozialgeschichte 1914–1918*, 2nd edn, Göttingen 1978

Kolb, Eberhard, *Der Frieden von Versailles*, 2nd edn, Munich 2011

Komo, Günter, *'Für Volk und Vaterland'. Die Militärpsychiatrie in den Weltkriegen*, Münster & Hamburg 1992

Koop, Gerhard & Erich Mulitze, *Die Marine in Wilhelmshaven. Eine Bildchronik zur deutschen Marinegeschichte von 1853 bis heute*, 2nd edn, Bonn 1997

Koselleck, Reinhart, 'Der Einfluß der beiden Weltkriege auf das soziale Bewußtsein', in Wette (ed), *Der Krieg des kleinen Mannes*, 324–43

Koszyk, Kurt, *Deutsche Pressepolitik im Ersten Weltkrieg*, Düsseldorf 1968

Krause, Andreas, *Scapa Flow. Die Selbstversenkung der Wilhelminischen Flotte*, Berlin 1999

Kriegsende 1918. Ereignis, Wirkung, Nachwirkung, im Auftr des Militärgeschichtlichen Forschungsamtes hg von Jörg Duppler und Gerhard P Groß, Munich 1999

Kriegserfahrungen. Studien zur Sozial- und Mentalitätsgeschichte des Ersten Weltkriegs, ed Gerhard Hirschfeld, Gerd Krumeich, Dieter Langewiesche & Hans-Peter Ullmann, Essen 1997

Kriegssanitätsbericht über die Deutsche Marine 1914–1918, hg von der Medizinalabteilung der Marineleitung im Reichswehrministerium, II. Band: Statistik über die Erkrankungen, Verwundungen durch Kriegswaffen, Unfälle und ihre Ausgänge im Kriege 1914–1918, Berlin 1934

Der Krieg zur See 1914–1918. Reihe I: Der Krieg in der Nordsee, 7 vols, Berlin 1920–1937, Frankfurt 1965; Reihe II: Der Krieg in der Ostsee, 3 vols, Berlin 1921/1929, Frankfurt 1964; Reihe III: Der Kreuzerkrieg in den ausländischen Gewässern, 3 vols, Berlin 1922–1937; Reihe IV: Der Krieg in den türkischen Gewässern, 2 vols, Berlin 1938; Reihe V: Die Kämpfe der Kaiserlichen Marine in den deutschen Kolonien, 2 vols, Berlin 1935; Reihe VI: Der Handelskrieg mit U-Booten, 5 vols, Berlin 1932–1934, Frankfurt 1964/1966; Reihe VII: Die Überwasserstreitkräfte und ihre Technik, Berlin 1930

Krumeich, Gerd (ed), *Versailles 1919. Ziele, Wirkung, Wahrnehmung*, Essen 2001

Kruse, Wolfgang, 'Krieg und Klassenheer. Zur Revolutionierung der deutschen Armee im Ersten Weltkrieg', *Geschichte und Gesellschaft*, 22 (1996), 530–61

Kühne, Thomas, 'Der Soldat', in Frevert, Ute & Heinz-Gerhard Haupt (eds), *Der Mensch des 20 Jahrhunderts*, Frankfurt & New York 1999, 344–72

Lambert, Nicholas (ed), *The Submarine Service 1900–1918*, Aldershot 2001

——, *Sir John Fisher's Naval Revolution*, Columbia 1999

——, 'British Naval Policy 1913–1914: Financial Limitation and Strategic Revolution', *Journal of Military History*, 67 (1995), 595–626

——, '"Our Bloody Ships" or "Our Bloody System"? Jutland and the Loss of the Battle Cruisers 1916', *Journal of Military History*, 62 (1998), 29–56

Lambi, Ivo Nikolai, *The Navy and German Power Politics 1862–1914*, Boston 1984

Lange, Sven, *Der Fahneneid. Die Geschichte der Schwurverpflichtung im deutschen Militär*, Bremen 2002

Langensiepen, Bernd, Dirk Nottelmann & Jochen Krüsmann, *Halbmond und Kaiseradler. Goeben und Breslau am Bosporus 1914–1918*, Hamburg 1999

Langhorne, Richard, 'Anglo-German Negotiations concerning the Future of the Portuguese Colonies 1911–1914', *Historical Journal*, 16 (1973), 361–87

——, 'The Naval Question in Anglo-German Relations 1912–1914', *Historical Journal*, 14 (1971), 359–70

Laverrenz, Victor, *Deutschlands Kriegsflotte. Eine Darstellung der Entwickelung und des gegenwärtigen Bestandes der gesamten Reichsmarine, ihrer Organisation und ihres Materials*, Erfurt 1906

Leed, Eric J, *No Man's Land. Combat and Identity in World War I*, Cambridge 1979

Legahn, Ernst, *Meuterei in der Kaiserlichen Marine 1917/1918. Ursachen und Folgen*, Herford 1970

Leitfaden für den Dienst-Unterricht in der Hochseeflotte, 17th edn, Oldenburg 1915

Lerner, Paul, '"Ein Sieg deutschen Willens": Wille und Gemeinschaft in der deutschen Kriegspsychiatrie', in Eckart, Wolfgang U & Christoph Gradmann (eds), *Die Medizin und der Erste Weltkrieg*, Pfaffenweiler 1996, 85–107

Lewis, Michael, *England's Sea Officers. The Story of the Naval Profession*, London 1939

Lewis, Wallace Leigh, 'The Survival of the German Navy 1917–1920: Officers, Sailors and Politics', dissertation, Iowa 1969

Lipp, Anne, *Meinungslenkung im Krieg. Kriegserfahrungen deutscher Soldaten und ihre Deutung 1914–1918*, Göttingen 2003

Lochner, Reinhard K, *Die Kaperfahrten des kleinen Kreuzers Emden*, 6th edn, Munich 1990

Mackay, Ruddock F, *Fisher of Kilverstone*, Oxford 1973

Mai, Gunther, *Das Ende des Kaiserreichs. Politik und Kriegführung im Ersten Weltkrieg*, Munich 1987

Marder, Arthur J, *The Anatomy of British Sea Power. A History of British Naval Policy in the Pre-Dreadnought Era 1880–1905*, 3rd edn, London 1974

——, *From The Dardanelles to Oran*, London 1974

——, *From the Dreadnought to Scapa Flow. The Royal Navy in the Fisher Era 1904–1919*, 5 vols, London 1961–70

Marienfeld, Wolfgang, *Wissenschaft und Schlachtflottenbau in Deutschland 1897–1906*, Frankfurt 1957

Marine-Taschenbuch 1914–1918

Marine-Verordnungs-Blatt 1914–1918

Marwick, Arthur, *The Deluge. British Society and the First World War*, London 1973

Massie, Robert K, *Castles of Steel. Britain, Germany and the Winning of the Great War at Sea*, New York 2003

Maurer, John H, 'Churchill's Naval Holiday: Arms Control and the Anglo-German Naval Race 1912–1914', in *Strategic Studies*, 15 (1992), 102–27

McKee, Christopher, *Sober Men and True. Sailor Lives in the Royal Navy 1900–1945*, Cambridge (MA) & London 2002

Mertens, Lothar, 'Das Privileg des Einjährig Freiwilligen Militärdienstes im Kaiserreich und seine gesellschaftliche Bedeutung', in *Militärgeschichtliche Mitteilungen*, 1 (1986), 59–66

Messerschmidt, Manfred, *Militär und Politik in der Bismarckzeit und im Wilhelminischen Deutschland*, Darmstadt 1975

Messinger, Gary S, *British Propaganda and the State in the First World War*, Manchester & New York 1992

Militär und Innenpolitik im Weltkrieg 1914–1918, bearb. von Wilhelm Deist, 2 vols, Düsseldorf 1970

Militärstrafgerichtsordnung vom 1.12.1898, 4th edn, Berlin 1907

Miller, Geoffrey, *Superior Force. The Conspiracy behind the Escape of Goeben and Breslau*, Hull 1996

Miller, Susanne, *Burgfrieden und Klassenkampf. Die deutsche Sozialdemokratie im Ersten Weltkrieg*, Düsseldorf 1974

Mommsen, Wolfgang J, *War der Kaiser an allem schuld? Wilhelm II und die preußischdeutschen Machteliten*, Munich 2002

—— (ed), *Die ungleichen Partner. Deutschbritische Beziehungen im 19 und 20 Jahrhundert*, Stuttgart 1999

——, *Großmachtstellung und Weltpolitik. Die Außenpolitik des Deutschen Reiches 1870 bis 1914*, Frankfurt & Berlin 1993

——, *Der autoritäre Nationalstaat. Verfassung, Gesellschaft und Kultur des deutschen Kaiserreiches*, Frankfurt 1990

——, 'Kaiser Wilhelm II and German Politics', in *Journal of Contemporary History*, 25 (1990), 289–316

—— & Elisabeth Müller-Luckner (eds), *Kultur und Krieg: Die Rolle der Intellektuellen, Künstler und Schriftsteller im Ersten Weltkrieg*, Munich 1996

Monger, George, *The End of Isolation. British Foreign Policy 1900–1907*, London & New York 1963

Moraht, Robert, 'Zehn Jahre neues System der Offizierausbildung in England', in *Marine-Rundschau* 1913, 1293–1302

Moseley, Sydney A, *The Fleet from Within. Being the Impressions of a RNVR Officer*, London & Edinburgh 1919

Mosse, George L, *Gefallen für das Vaterland. Nationales Heldentum und namenloses Sterben*, Stuttgart 1993

Mühlhahn, Klaus, *Herrschaft und Widerstand in der 'Musterkolonie' Kiautschou. Interaktionen zwischen China und Deutschland 1897–1914*, Munich 2000

Müller, Georg Alexander von, *Regierte der Kaiser? Kriegstagebücher, Aufzeichnungen und Briefe 1914–1918*, ed Walter Görlitz, Göttingen 1959

Müller, Georg Alexander von, *Der Kaiser... Aufzeichnungen des Chefs des Marinekabinetts Admiral Georg Alexander v Müller über die Ära Wilhelms II*, ed Walter Görlitz, Göttingen 1965

Müller, Sven Oliver, *Die Nation als Waffe und Vorstellung. Nationalismus in Deutschland und Großbritannien im Ersten Weltkrieg*, Göttingen 2002

Munro, D J, *Scapa Flow. A Naval Retrospect*, London 1932

The Navy List 1914–1918

Neilson, Keith, *Britain and the Last Tsar. British Policy and Russia 1894–1917*, Oxford 1995

Neitzel, Sönke & Harald Welzer, *Soldaten. Protokolle vom Kämpfen, Töten und Sterben*, 5th edn, Frankfurt 2011

Neitzel, Sönke, *Weltmacht oder Untergang. Die Weltreichslehre im Zeitalter des Imperialismus*, Paderborn 2000

Nicolai, Britta, *Die Lebensmittelversorgung in Flensburg 1914–1918. Zur Mangelwirtschaft während des Ersten Weltkrieges*, Flensburg 1988

Nicolson, Harold, *Friedensmacher 1919*, Berlin 1933

Niemöller, Martin, *Vom U-Boot zur Kanzel*, Berlin 1934

Nipperdey, Thomas, *Deutsche Geschichte 1866–1918, vol 2: Machtstaat vor der Demokratie*, 3rd edn, Munich 1995

Offer, Avner, *The First World War. An Agrarian Interpretation*, Oxford 1989

Offiziere im Bild von Dokumenten aus drei Jahrhunderten, hg vom Militärgeschichtlichen Forschungsamt, Stuttgart 1964

Oppelland, Torsten, *Reichstag und Außenpolitik im Ersten Weltkrieg. Die deutschen Parteien und die Politik der USA 1914–1918*, Düsseldorf 1995

Oppelt, Ulrike, *Film und Propaganda im Ersten Weltkrieg. Propaganda als Medienrealität im Aktualitäten und Dokumentarfilm*, Stuttgart 2002

O'Sullivan, Patrick, *Die Lusitania. Mythos und Wirklichkeit*, Hamburg 1999 (*Lusitania: Unravelling the Mysteries*, Staplehurst 2000)

Ostertag, Heiger, *Bildung, Ausbildung und Erziehung des Offizierkorps im deutschen Kaiserreich 1871 bis 1918. Eliteideal, Anspruch und Wirklichkeit*, Frankfurt 1990

The Oxford Illustrated History of the Royal Navy, ed J R Hill and Bryan Ranft, Oxford 2002

Packer, Joy, *Deep as the Sea*, London 1976

Padfield, Peter, *The Great Naval Race. The Anglo-German Naval Rivalry, 1900–1914*, London 1974

Parker, Peter, *The Old Lie. The Great War and the Public School Ethos*, London 1987

Partridge, Michael, *The Royal Naval College Osborne. A History 1903–1921*, Stroud 1999

Patemann, Reinhard, *Der Kampf um die preußische Wahlreform im Ersten Weltkrieg*, Düsseldorf 1964

Patterson, A, Temple, *Jellicoe. A Biography*, London 1969

Pelly, Henry, *300,000 Sea Miles. An Autobiography*, London 1938

Penn, Geoffrey, '*Up Funnel, Down Screw!' The Story of the Naval Engineer*, London 1955

Persius, Lothar, *Menschen und Schiffe in der kaiserlichen Flotte*, Berlin 1925

Petter, Martin, '"Temporary Gentlemen" in the Aftermath of the Great War: Rank, Status and the Ex-Officer Problem', *Historical Journal*, 37 (1994), 127–52

Petter, Wolfgang, 'Deutsche Flottenrüstung von Wallenstein bis Tirpitz', in *Handbuch zur deutschen Militärgeschichte 1648–1939*, hg vom Militärgeschichtlichen Forschungsamt, vol 4, section VIII, Munich 1977, 13–262

Philbin, Tobias R, *Admiral von Hipper. The Inconvenient Hero*, Amsterdam 1982

Plagemann, Volker (ed), *Übersee. Seefahrt und Seemacht im deutschen Kaiserreich*, Munich 1988

Plaschka, Richard Georg, *Matrosen, Offiziere, Rebellen. Krisen-konfrontationen zur See 1900–1918*, 2 vols, Wien 1984

Plunkett-Drax, R, *The Modern Officer of the Watch*, 6th edn, London 1918

Pochhammer, Hans, *Graf Spees letzte Fahrt. Erinnerungen an das Kreuzergeschwader*, 11th edn, Leipzig 1939

Podestá (Marine-Stabsarzt), 'Häufigkeit und Ursachen seelischer Erkrankungen in der deutschen Marine unter Vergleich mit der Statistik der Armee', in *Archiv für Psychiatrie*, 40 (1905), 651–703

Pohl, Hugo von, *Aus Aufzeichnungen und Briefen während der Kriegszeit*, Berlin 1920

Poolman, Kenneth, *Zeppelins over England*, London 1975

Pound, A D, *Man of War Organization*, Portsmouth 1913

Pyta, Wolfram, *Hindenburg. Herrschaft zwischen Hohenzollern und Hitler*, Munich 2007

Radkau, Joachim, *Das Zeitalter der Nervosität. Deutschland zwischen Bismarck und Hitler*, Munich 1998

Raeder, Erich, *Mein Leben, vol 1: Bis zum Flottenabkommen mit England 1935*, Tübingen 1956

Rahn, Werner, *Reichsmarine und Landesverteidigung 1919–1928. Konzeption und Führung der Marine in der Weimarer Republik*, Munich 1976

——, 'Die Seeschlacht vor dem Skagerrak: Verlauf und Analyse aus deutscher Perspektive', in *Skagerrakschlacht*, 139–96

——, 'Strategische Probleme der deutschen Seekriegführung 1914–1918', in *Der Erste Weltkrieg*, 341–65

Raithel, Thomas, *Das 'Wunder' der inneren Einheit. Studien zur deutschen und französischen Öffentlichkeit bei Beginn des Ersten Weltkrieges*, Bonn 1996

Rauh, Manfred, *Die Parlamentarisierung des Deutschen Reiches*, Düsseldorf 1977

Reeve, John & David Stevens (eds), *The Face of Naval Battle. The Human Experience of Modern War at Sea*, Crows Nest 2003

Rehder, Jacob, *Die Verluste der Kriegsflotten 1914–1918*, ed Helmut Sander, Munich 1969

Reinermann, Lothar, *Der Kaiser in England. Wilhelm II und sein Bild in der britischen Öffentlichkeit*, Paderborn 2001

Reuter, Ludwig von, *Scapa Flow. Das Grab der deutschen Flotte*, 4th edn, Leipzig 1921

Reventlow, Graf Ernst zu, *Deutschland zur See. Ein Buch von der deutschen*

Kriegsflotte, Leipzig 1914

Richter, A & O Szczesny, *Ratgeber für den Dienstbetrieb in der Kaiserlichen Marine*, Berlin 1913

Ritter, Gerhard, *Staatskunst und Kriegshandwerk. Das Problem des 'Militarismus' in Deutschland*, 4 vols, Munich 1960–68

Ritter, Gerhard A & Peter Wende (eds), *Rivalität und Partnerschaft. Studien zu den deutschbritischen Beziehungen im 19 und 20 Jahrhundert*, Paderborn 1999

Roberts, John, *The Battleship Dreadnought*, London 1992

Robinson, Douglas H, *The Zeppelin in Combat. A History of the German Naval Airship Division 1912–1918*, 3rd edn, Henley-on-Thames 1971

Rodger, N A M, *The Command of the Ocean 1649–1815*, London 2004

——, *The Admiralty*, Lavenham 1979

Rödel, Christian, *Krieger, Denker, Amateure. Alfred von Tirpitz und das Seekriegsbild vor dem Ersten Weltkrieg*, Stuttgart 2003

Röhl, John C G, *Wilhelm II*, 3 vols, Munich 1993–2008

——, *Kaiser, Hof und Staat. Wilhelm II. und die deutsche Politik*, 4th edn, Munich 1995

—— (ed), *Der Ort Kaiser Wilhelms II. in der deutschen Geschichte*, Munich 1991

—— & Nicolaus Sombart (eds), *Kaiser Wilhelm II. New Interpretations. The Corfu Papers*, Cambridge 1982

Roerkohl, Anne, *Hungerblockade und Heimatfront. Die kommunale Lebensmittelversorgung in Westfalen während des Ersten Weltkrieges*, Stuttgart 1991

Rössler, Eberhard, *Geschichte des deutschen U-Bootbaus*, Munich 1975

Rohkrämer, Thomas, *Der Militarismus der 'kleinen Leute'. Die Kriegervereine im Deutschen Kaiserreich 1871–1914*, Munich 1990

Rose, Kenneth, *King George V*, London 1983

Roskill, Stephen, *Admiral of the Fleet Earl Beatty. The Last Naval Hero. An Intimate Biography*, London 1980

——, *Naval Policy Between the Wars*, 2 vols, London 1968 & 1976

——, *The Naval Air Service*, London 1969

The Royal Navy by a Lieutenant, London 1897

Rüger, Jan, *The Great Naval Game. Britain and Germany in the Age of Empire*, Cambridge 2007

Ruge, Friedrich, *Scapa Flow 1919. Das Ende der deutschen Flotte*, Oldenburg & Hamburg 1969

Russell, Dave, '"We carved our way to glory": The British Soldier in Music

Hall Song and Sketch, 1880–1914', in MacKenzie, John M (ed), *Popular Imperialism and the Military 1850–1950*, Manchester 1992, 50–79

Ryheul, Johan, *Marinekorps Flandern 1914–1918*, Hamburg 1997

Salewski, Michael, *Die Deutschen und die See. Studien zur deutschen Marinegeschichte des 19 und 20 Jahrhunderts*, Stuttgart 1998

——, *Die Deutschen und die See, Studien zur deutschen Marinegeschichte des 19 und 20 Jahrhunderts*, part II, Stuttgart 2002

——, *Tirpitz. Aufstieg-Macht-Scheitern*, Göttingen 1979

——, *Die deutsche Seekriegsleitung 1935–1945*, vol I: *1935–1941*, Frankfurt 1970

——, *Entwaffnung und Militärkontrolle in Deutschland 1919–1927*, Munich 1966

——, 'England, Hitler und die Marine', in Salewski, *Die Deutschen und die See*, I, 215–27

——, 'Skagerrak! Sechzig Jahre Rückblick', in Salewski, *Die Deutschen und die See*, II, 74–8

——, 'Das Offizierkorps der Reichsund Kriegsmarine', in Salewski, *Die Deutschen und die See*, II, 102–14

——, 'Selbstverständnis und historisches Bewußtsein der deutschen Kriegsmarine', in Salewski, *Die Deutschen und die See*, I, 170–90

Sanders, M L & Philip M Taylor, *Britische Propaganda im Ersten Weltkrieg 1914–1918*, Berlin 1990 (*British Propaganda during the First World War, 1914–18*, London & New York 1983)

Schaible, Camell, *Standes- und Berufspflichten des deutschen Offiziers*, 6th edn, Berlin 1908

Scheck, Raffael, *Alfred von Tirpitz and German Right Wing Politics 1914–1930*, New Jersey 1998

Scheck, Raffael, 'Der Kampf des Tirpitz-Kreises für den uneingeschränkten U-Boot-Krieg und einen politischen Kurswechsel im deutschen Kaiserreich 1916–1917', in *Militärgeschichtliche Mitteilungen*, 55 (1996), 69–91

Scheer, Reinhard, *Deutschlands Hochseeflotte im Weltkrieg*, Berlin 1919

——, *Vom Segelschiff zum U-Boot*, Leipzig 1925

Scheerer, Thomas, 'Die Marineoffiziere der Kaiserlichen Marine im Ersten Weltkrieg', in *Deutsche Marinen im Wandel*, 269–85

——, 'Die Marineoffiziere der Kaiserlichen Marine. Sozialisation und Konflikte', dissertation, Hamburg 1993

Schieder, Wolfgang & Volker Sellin (eds), *Sozialgeschichte in Deutschland*,

4 vols, Göttingen 1986 & 1987

Schilling, René, *'Kriegshelden'. Deutungsmuster heroischer Männlichkeit in Deutschland 1813–1945*, Paderborn 2002

——, 'U-Boothelden in Deutschland von 1914 bis in die Gegenwart. Die Beispiele Otto Weddigen und Günter Prien', in Stephan Huck (ed), *100 Jahre U-Boote in deutschen Marinen. Ereignisse – Technik – Mentalitäten – Rezeption*, Bochum 2011, 201–10

Der Schlieffenplan. Analysen und Dokumente. Im Auftr des Militärgeschichtlichen Forschungsamtes und der Otto-von-Bismarck-Stiftung hg von Hans Ehlert, Michael Epkenhans und Gerhard P Groß, 2nd edn, Paderborn 2007

Schneider, Ulrich, *Die Londoner Music Hall und ihre Songs 1850–1920*, Tübingen 1984

Schöllgen, Gregor, *Imperialismus und Gleichgewicht. Deutschland, England und die orientalische Frage 1871–1914*, 2nd edn, Munich 1992

Schöllgen, Gregor (ed), *Flucht in den Krieg? Die Außenpolitik des kaiserlichen Deutschland*, Darmstadt 1991

Schönberger, Christoph, 'Die überholte Parlamentarisierung. Einflußgewinn und fehlende Herrschaftsfähigkeit des Reichstags im sich demokratisierenden Kaiserreich', *Historische Zeitschrift*, 272 (2001), 623–66

Schottelius, Herbert & Wilhelm Deist (eds), *Marine und Marinepolitik im kaiserlichen Deutschland 1871–1914*, Düsseldorf 1972

Schoultz, Gustav von, *Mit der Grand Fleet im Weltkrieg. Erinnerungen eines Teilnehmers*, Leipzig 1925

Schreiber, Gerhard, 'Zur Kontinuität des Groß- und Weltmachtstrebens der deutschen Marineführung', in *Militärgeschichtliche Mitteilungen*, 2 (1979), 101–71

Schröder, Joachim, *Die U-Boote des Kaisers. Die Geschichte des deutschen U-Boot-Krieges gegen Großbritannien im Ersten Weltkrieg*, Lauf ad Pregnitz 2000

Schröder, Karsten, *Parlament und Außenpolitik in England 1911–1914, dargestellt an der englischen Deutschlandpolitik von der Agadirkrise bis zum Beginn des Ersten Weltkrieges*, Göttingen 1974

Schröder, Stephen, *Die englischrussische Marinekonvention. Das Deutsche Reich und die Flottenverhandlungen der Tripleentente am Vorabend des Ersten Weltkriegs*, Göttingen 2006

Schröder, Hans-Jürgen, 'Demokratie und Hegemonie. Woodrow Wilsons Konzept einer neuen Weltordnung', in *Der Erste Weltkrieg*, 159–77

Schubert, Helmuth, 'Admiral Adolf von Trotha (1868–1940). Ein Versuch zur historisch-psychologischen Biographik', dissertation, Freiburg 1976

Schulze, Winfried (ed), *Ego-Dokumente: Annäherung an den Menschen in der Geschichte*, Berlin 1996

Schwabe, Klaus, *Deutsche Revolution und Wilson-Frieden. Die amerikanische und deutsche Friedensstrategie zwischen Ideologie und Machtpolitik 1918/19*, Düsseldorf 1971

Schweinitz, Kurt Graf von (ed), *Das Kriegstagebuch eines kaiserlichen Seeoffiziers (1914–1918). Kapitänleutnant Hermann Graf von Schweinitz*, Bochum 2003

Schwengler, Walter, *Völkerrecht, Versailler Vertrag und Auslieferungsfrage. Die Strafverfolgung als Problem des Friedensschlusses 1919/20*, Stuttgart 1982

Sears, Jason, 'Discipline in the Royal Navy 1913–1946', in *War & Society*, 9 (1991), 39–60

Selchow, Bogislav von, *Hundert Tage aus meinem Leben*, Leipzig 1943

Sheffield, Gary D, *Leadership in the Trenches. Officer–Man Relations, Morale and Discipline in the British Army in the Era of the First World War*, Basingstoke 2000

Sieferle, Rolf Peter, '"Der deutschenglische Gegensatz" und die "Ideen von 1914"', in Niedhart, Gottfried (ed), *Das kontinentale Europa und die britischen Inseln. Wahrnehmungsmuster und Wechselwirkungen seit der Antike*, Mannheim 1993, 139–60

Skagerrakschlacht. Vorgeschichte – Ereignis – Verarbeitung. Im Auftr des Militärgeschichtlichen Forschungsamtes hg von Michael Epkenhans, Jörg Hillmann und Frank Nägler, Munich 2009

Smith, Humphrey Hugh, *A Yellow Admiral Remembers*, London 1932

Spector, Ronald, *At War at Sea. Sailors and Naval Warfare in the Twentieth Century*, London 2001

Speitkamp, Winfried, *Ohrfeige, Duell und Ehrenmord. Eine Geschichte der Ehre*, Stuttgart 2010

Spiers, Edward M, *The Army and Society 1815–1914*, London 1980

Spiess, Johannes, *Wir jagten Panzerkreuzer. Kriegsabenteuer eines U-Boot-Offiziers*, Berlin 1938

Spode, Hasso, *Die Macht der Trunkenheit. Kultur und Sozialgeschichte des Alkohols in Deutschland*, Opladen 1993

Spohn, Klemens, *Ratgeber in Ehrenfragen aller Art für Heer und Marine*, 6th edn, Berlin 1918

Steel, Nigel & Peter Hart, *Jutland 1916. Death in The Grey Wastes*, London 2003

Stegemann, Bernd, *Die deutsche Marinepolitik 1916–1918*, Berlin 1970

Stegmann, Dirk, *Die Erben Bismarcks. Parteien und Verbände in der Spätphase des Wilhelminischen Deutschlands. Sammlungspolitik 1897– 1918*, Cologne & Berlin 1970

Steinberg, Jonathan, *Yesterday's Deterrent. Tirpitz and the Birth of the German Battle Fleet*, London 1965

——, 'The Tirpitz-Plan', in *Historical Journal*, 16 (1973), 196–204

——, 'The Copenhagen Complex', in *Journal of Contemporary History*, 1 (1966), 23–46

Steiner, Zara S & Keith Neilson, *Britain and the Origins of the First World War*, 2nd edn, Basingstoke & New York 2003

Steinmetz, Hans-Otto, *Bismarck und die deutsche Marine*, Herford 1974

Steltzer, Hans Georg, *Die deutsche Flotte. Ein historischer Überblick von 1640 bis 1918*, Frankfurt 1989

Stevenson, David, *1914–1918. Der Erste Weltkrieg*, 3rd edn, Düsseldorf 2006 (*1914–1918: The History of the First World War*, London 2012)

Stibbe, Matthew, *German Anglophobia and the Great War 1914–1918*, Cambridge 2001

Strachan, Hew, *The First World War, vol I: To Arms*, Oxford 2001

Stumpf, Richard, 'Das Tagebuch des Matrosen Richard Stumpf', in *Das Werk des Untersuchungsausschusses*, vol X/2, Berlin 1928

Sumida, Jon Tetsuro, *In Defence of Naval Supremacy. Finance, Technology and British Naval Policy 1889–1914*, 2nd edn, London & New York 1993

——, 'Sir John Fisher and the *Dreadnought*: The Sources of Naval Mythology', in *Journal of Military History*, 59 (1995), 619–38

Tarrant, V E, *Jutland. The German Perspective*, London 2001

Thoß, Bruno, 'Nationale Rechte, militärische Führung und Diktaturfrage in Deutschland 1913–1923', in *Militärgeschichtliche Mitteilungen*, 2 (1987), 27–76

Tirpitz, Alfred von, *Politische Dokumente*, 2 vols, Stuttgart 1924 & Hamburg 1926

——, *Erinnerungen*, Leipzig 1919

Trotha, Adolf von, *Der Organismus der Kaiserlichen Marine und der Weltkrieg*, Berlin 1930

——, *Volkstum und Staatsführung. Briefe und Aufzeichnungen aus den Jahren 1915–1920*, Berlin 1928

Tupper, Reginald, *Reminiscences*, London 1929

Tweedie, Hugh, *The Story of a Naval Life*, London 1939

Ullrich, Volker, *Die Revolution von 1918/19*, Munich 2009

——, *Vom Augusterlebnis zur Novemberrevolution. Beiträge zur Sozialgeschichte Hamburgs und Norddeutschlands im Ersten Weltkrieg*, Bremen 1999

Ulrich, Bernd, *Die Augenzeugen. Deutsche Feldpostbriefe in Kriegs- und Nachkriegszeit 1914–1933*, Essen 1997

——, 'Nerven und Krieg. Skizzierung einer Beziehung', in Loewenstein, Bedrich (ed), *Geschichte und Psychologie. Annäherungsversuche*, Pfaffenweiler 1992, 163–92

—— & Benjamin Ziemann, 'Das soldatische Kriegserlebnis', in Kruse, Wolfgang (ed), *Eine Welt von Feinden. Der Große Krieg 1914–1918*, Frankfurt 1997, 127–58

Untersuchungen zur Geschichte des Offizierkorps. Anciennität und Beförderung nach Leistung, hg vom Militärgeschichtlichen Forschungsamt, Stuttgart 1962

Ursachen und Folgen. Vom deutschen Zusammenbruch 1918 und 1945 bis zur staatlichen Neuordnung Deutschlands in der Gegenwart, hg von Herbert Michaelis & Ernst Schraepler, vol 1: *Die Wende des Ersten Weltkrieges und der Beginn der innerpolitischen Wandlung 1916/1917*, Berlin 1959, vol 2: *Der militärische Zusammenbruch und das Ende des Kaiserreiches*, Berlin 1959

Veitch, Colin, '"Play up! Play up! and Win the War!" Football, the Nation, and the First World War 1914–15', *Journal of Contemporary History*, 20 (1985), 363–78

Verhey, Jeffrey, *Der 'Geist von 1914' und die Erfindung der Volksgemeinschaft*, Hamburg 2000

Der Vertrag von Versailles, Munich 1978

Vietsch, Eberhard von, *Bethmann Hollweg. Staatsmann zwischen Macht und Ethos*, Boppard am Rhein 1969

Vincent, C Paul, *The Politics of Hunger. The Allied Blockade of Germany 1915–1919*, Athens 1985

Vogel, Jakob, *Nationen im Gleichschritt. Der Kult der 'Nation in Waffen' in Deutschland und Frankreich 1871–1914*, Göttingen 1997

Waites, Bernard, *A Class Society At War. England 1914–1918*, Leamington Spa 1987

Waldeyer-Hartz, Hugo von, *Admiral Hipper. Das Lebensbild eines deutschen Flottenführers*, Leipzig 1933

Wall, Richard & Jay Winter (eds), *The Upheaval of War. Family, Work and Welfare in Europe 1914–1918*, Cambridge 1988

Wallach, Jehuda L, *Das Dogma der Vernichtungsschlacht. Die Lehren von Clausewitz und Schlieffen und ihre Wirkungen in zwei Weltkriegen*, Frankfurt 1967

Walton, Oliver, 'Social History of the Royal Navy 1856–1900. Corporation and Community', dissertation, Exeter 2003

Walvin, James, *Leisure and Society 1830–1950*, London 1978

Wegener, Edward, 'Selbstverständnis und historisches Bewußtsein der deutschen Kriegsmarine', in *Marine-Rundschau*, 67 (1970), 321–40

Wehler, Hans-Ulrich, *Deutsche Gesellschaftsgeschichte*, 4 vols, Munich 1996–2003

Weir, Gary E, *Building the Kaiser's Navy. The Imperial Navy Office and German Industry in the von Tirpitz Era 1890–1919*, Annapolis 1992

Weizsäcker, Ernst von, *Erinnerungen*, Munich 1950

Welch, David, *Germany, Propaganda and Total War 1914–1918. The Sins of Omission*, New Brunswick 2000

Wells, John, *The Royal Navy. An Illustrated Social History 1870–1982*, Stroud 2000

Das Werk des Untersuchungsausschusses der Verfassunggebenden Deutschen Nationalversammlung und des Deutschen Reichstages 1919–1928. Vierte Reihe: Die Ursachen des Deutschen Zusammenbruchs im Jahre 1918. Zweite Abteilung: Der Innere Zusammenbruch, vols IX, 1 & 2; X, 1 & 2, Berlin 1928

Wernecke, Klaus, *Der Wille zur Weltgeltung. Außenpolitik und Öffentlichkeit im Kaiserreich am Vorabend des Ersten Weltkrieges*, Düsseldorf 1970

Werner, Reinhold, *Das Buch von der deutschen Flotte*, Bielefeld & Leipzig 1898

Wette, Wolfram (ed), *Der Krieg des kleinen Mannes. Eine Militärgeschichte von unten*, 2nd edn, Munich 1995

—— (ed), *Militarismus in Deutschland 1871–1945. Zeitgenössische Analysen und Kritik*, Münster 1999

Weyer, Bruno (ed), *Taschenbuch der Kriegsflotten*. XVII Jahrgang, Munich 1916

The White Ensign, Notes on Life and Work in Her Majesty's Navy, contributed by Naval Officers, London 1896

Wilson, Keith M, *The Policy of the Entente. Essays on the Determinants of British Foreign Policy 1904–1914*, Cambridge 1985

Wilson, Trevor, *The Myriad Faces of War. Britain and the Great War 1914–1918*, Cambridge 1986

Winter, Denis, *Death's Men. Soldiers of the Great War*, London 1979

Winter, Jay M, *The Experience of World War I*, London 1988

——, *The Great War and the British People*, Basingstoke 1986

——, Geoffrey Parker & Mary R Habeck (eds), *Der Erste Weltkrieg und das 20 Jahrhundert*, Hamburg 2002

Winzen, Peter, *Bülows Weltmachtkonzept. Untersuchungen zur Frühphase seiner Außenpolitik 1897–1901*, Boppard am Rhein 1977

Wipperfürth, Christian, *Von der Souveränität zur Angst. Britische Außenpolitik und Sozialökonomie im Zeitalter des Imperialismus*, Stuttgart 2004

Wippermann, Wolfgang, *Der 'deutsche Drang nach Osten'. Ideologie und Wirklichkeit eines politischen Schlagwortes*, Darmstadt 1981

Witt, Peter-Christian, *Die Finanzpolitik des Deutschen Reiches von 1903–1913. Eine Studie zur Innenpolitik des Wilhelminischen Deutschland*, Lübeck & Hamburg 1970

Wolz, Nicolas, *Das lange Warten. Kriegserfahrungen deutscher und britischer Seeoffiziere 1914 bis 1918*, Paderborn 2008

Woodward, David, *The Collapse of Power. Mutiny in the High Seas Fleet*, London 1973

Woollard, Claude L A, *With the Harwich Naval Forces 1914–1918 or Under Commodore Tyrwhitt in the North Sea*, Privatdruck 1934

Yates, Keith, *Flawed Victory. Jutland 1916*, London 2000

Yexley, Lionel, *The Inner Life of the Navy*, London 1908

Young, Filson, *With the Battle Cruisers*, London 1921

Young, E Hilton, *By Sea and Land*, 2nd edn, London 1924

Zeisler, Kurt, 'Die revolutionäre Matrosenbewegung in Deutschland im Oktober/November 1918', in *Revolutionäre Ereignisse und Probleme in Deutschland während der Periode der Großen Sozialistischen Oktoberrevolution 1917/18*, Berlin 1957

Index